Bringing opera to life

BORIS GOLDOVSKY

Bringing opera to life

Operatic acting and stage direction

Prentice-Hall, Inc., Englewood Cliffs, New Jersey

782.107
G-58 b
119 667
nov.1981

PRENTICE-HALL INTERNATIONAL, INC., *London*
PRENTICE-HALL OF AUSTRALIA, PTY. LTD., *Sydney*
PRENTICE-HALL OF CANADA, LTD., *Toronto*
PRENTICE-HALL OF INDIA PRIVATE LIMITED, *New Delhi*
PRENTICE-HALL OF JAPAN, INC., *Tokyo*

To Maggy

Preface

THE SKILLS of operatic acting and stage direction are based on the interplay of music and drama. They grow and sharpen in the friendly clash of many personalities, now assertive, now self-effacing, but always meshing in the spirit of ensemble performance. To develop successful training methods in this field, therefore, one must have been in a long-term working partnership with a great number of advanced, sensitive, strong minded, and yet willing participants. In this respect I have been unusually fortunate, and this volume is little more than a repository of my teaching and learning experiences ranging over more than a quarter of a century.

Without wishing to belittle the contributions of the hundreds of excellent young people taught by me and my associates at the New England Conservatory of Music in Boston and at the Oglebay Park Opera Workshop in West Virginia, I must give the lion's share of whatever credit this book deserves to the Berkshire Music Center (Tanglewood) in Lenox, Massachusetts, and especially to its founder, Dr. Serge Koussevitzky.

During the summer months of the years between 1940 and 1951, Koussevitzky's magic name attracted to Tanglewood the cream of America's musical youth. What is even more to the point, Koussevitzky's enlightened leadership made it possible for his faculty members to give free rein to their imaginations without having to worry about examinations, grades, academic credits, or any of the many other necessary but distracting aspects of winter pedagogy.

The eagerness and ease with which our opera students learned to blend musical and theatrical values came as a revelation and indicated to what extent we had been underestimating the flexible talents of our singers. In the course of years, I discovered to my delight that the methods evolved here with exceptionally brilliant students were readily applicable outside Tanglewood. Given half a chance, most American singers seem to thrive on educational procedures originally designed for those endowed with superior gifts.

After Dr. Koussevitzky's death in 1951, the development of my operatic ideas was continued under the egis of the Goldovsky Opera Institute, the directors of which underwrote the substantial costs of the Leadership Training Program. Here I was given the rewarding opportunity of working with many outstandingly gifted directors and conductors. The pantomimes presented in Chapter 4 and many of the staging ideas discussed in the second half of this volume were tempered and refined in the intellectual give-and-take of these Leadership seminars.

Gradually, this entire system of operatic training—born in Tangle-wood and nurtured in Boston, New York, and Oglebay Park—spread throughout the country where, via my many Leadership alumni, it is being tested and improved in music departments and opera workshops ranging from California and Colorado to Wisconsin and Minnesota; from Florida and Missouri to Ohio and New Mexico.

It is an axiom in the performing arts that the value of educational methods must be proven in the competitive hurly-burly of the open mar-ket place. Here again I have been fortunate in being able to test my ideas in a series of national tours which, over a period of eighteen years, took me to more than four hundred cities in the United States and Canada. This non-academic outgrowth of my system of training is embodied in the Goldovsky Opera Theater, which is also sponsored by the Opera Insti-tute. It is a completely professional company where, thanks to careful management and the enormous national interest in this form of art, I am able to keep alive a pure strain of the opera theater idea, undiluted by imported "star" singers, sensational publicity gimmicks, performances in foreign languages, or any of the other tempting and glamorous by-products of "grand" opera.

The Goldovsky Opera Institute depends for its existence on hundreds of well-wishers, but here again the main share of the credit belongs to one individual: the organization's chairman of the board, Mrs. Richard H. Thompson. Without her dedication, energy, and business acumen, both the Leadership Training Program and the Opera Theater would have long ago joined the ranks of "erstwhile" operatic organizations with which our country is, alas, so richly provided.

It is of course impossible to name all those who contributed their talents to this volume. Even so, I wish to express my deep and sincere gratitude to my many teaching associates whose critical judgment is re-flected on every page of this volume. Special thanks are due to Ruth and Thomas Martin for permitting me to adapt their translation of Leporello's aria in *Don Giovanni* to my staging, to Peter Elvins for his editorial assis-tance, and to Anthony Addison for his help in the preparation of the music and subtexts of the pantomimes.

B. G.

Contents

Al più le raccomando l'espressione—di rifletter bene al senso ed alla forza delle parole—di mettersi con serietà nello stato e nella situazione d'Andromeda—e di figurarsi d'esser quella stessa persona . . .

Above all, I urge you to concentrate on expressive characterization: consider well the meaning and the energy of the words, put yourself quite seriously into the situation and the emotional state of Andromeda, and imagine yourself to be that very person.

MOZART to ALOISIA WEBER
July 30, 1778

Bringing opera to life

Introduction

HOW DOES ONE STUDY operatic stage direction? How does one learn what the various singers should be doing on stage in *Carmen*, or *Rigoletto*, or *Don Giovanni?*

I do not know how many young people ask themselves this question, but I remember only too vividly my own puzzlement when, in the spring of 1936, I was offered the job of heading the opera department at the Cleveland Institute of Music. I had been brought to Cleveland the preceding fall by Arthur Rodzinski, the conductor of the famed local symphony orchestra. He was putting on several operas at Severance Hall and I was to help him prepare them by training the choruses and teaching the music of the minor roles to local singers. As it turned out, I also played the piano for all stage rehearsals, conducted the offstage music, substituted for Rodzinski when he was ill or unavailable, gave lighting and curtain cues, and made myself generally useful both before and during performances. Reports of my operatic endeavors eventually reached the ears of the brilliant pianist Beryl Rubinstein, who was then the director of the Cleveland Institute of Music, and he asked me to come and see him.

"Mr. Goldovsky," he said to me, "we have a number of fine singing teachers here at the school and quite a few promising voice students. I hear that you have a knack for teaching opera to young people. How would you like to organize an opera department for us?"

"Nothing could please me better," I told him. "I will be glad to handle the singers and orchestral players. Whom do you have in mind to be the dramatics teacher and the stage director for our performances?"

Rubinstein looked up in surprise. "But the Institute couldn't possibly afford two new appointments of this magnitude!" he exclaimed. "We will, of course, expect you to take care of the theatrical as well as the musical side of the job."

This notion took me completely by surprise. "But I have never done anything like that! I have no experience and no background for dramatic instruction and I know mighty little about staging an opera!"

Rubinstein was not swayed by my protestations. "You have worked with stage directors, haven't you?" he asked.

"Yes," I admitted. "As pianist for staging rehearsals I have assisted quite a few of them."

"Well, did you find them so terribly knowledgeable and effective?" I had to confess that most of the stage-direction work I had observed in the past did not impress me as being particularly admirable. "Then you know perfectly well," said Rubinstein, "that you will do no worse and perhaps even better than anyone else we could hire for this position."

I did not know anything of the kind, but the thought of organizing a brand-new opera department was so tantalizing that I asked Rubinstein to let me have a few weeks to think it over. After all, I said to myself, not very long ago I did not know very much about the musical side of opera. But by studying the scores, playing them on the piano, and listening to recordings, I eventually learned enough to hold my own. Certainly, I could do something of the sort to learn opera's theatrical side: staging opera could not be so difficult.

I began by studying the acting and staging directions printed in the librettos and scores. It was soon clear, however, that only a very meager harvest could be gleaned from these sources. German librettists and composers, beginning with Richard Wagner, were quite helpful, although even in their scores long stretches of music were left without any remarks relating to stage movement. Among Italians, only the scores of Puccini and the later Verdi had anything useful to offer. But I was not thinking of Wagner, Richard Strauss, or the later Verdi. In considering the repertoire of my future opera department, I had in mind such works as *The Bartered Bride, La Traviata, Don Pasquale,* and *Così fan tutte. Così fan tutte* seemed particularly appropriate because this opera was virtually unknown in the United States at that time, and it would speak well for my resourcefulness if I could begin in my new position with a neglected masterpiece of such high quality.

But any hope I had for staging this opera on the basis of the information contained in the libretto or the score was quickly scotched. The setting of the opening scene is described in three words: "Bottega di caffè," a coffee house. Nothing more. In the entire first scene, consisting of three lively terzettos separated by two elaborate recitatives, there are only six descriptive remarks. Three of them ("with fire," "placidly," and "jokingly") indicate the type of expression with which certain lines are to be sung; two remarks ("aside," and "to Ferrando") specify to whom the words are to be addressed. The remaining stage direction ("they put their hands on their swords") is the only one that deals with an action, and even here one does not learn anything new because the words that are sung at the time make the need for an illustrative gesture fairly obvious. The next setting is described as "a garden by the seashore," and throughout that scene there are even fewer acting observations than in the opening scene.

Inexperienced as I was in theatrical matters, I realized that a great deal of action in the form of gesturing and movement could be attached to the vocal lines, but from the manner in which most opera scores and librettos were annotated, one received the impression that unless a character was in the process of singing, he might as well not be present on the stage at all. The few directions I found always referred to the personages who were singing at that very moment. The other characters were treated as if they were simply to stand around waiting for their next turn to sing. The very thing that disturbed me so much in most of the operatic performances I had witnessed was that the singers behaved like orchestra musicians who, when they have rests, sit in their chairs quietly counting measures and waiting for their cues. I felt very strongly that a character in a drama should not lead this sort of passive and intermittent existence, coming to life only when he sings. I wanted to show singers how to continue to live and act when they were *not* singing, but I had no idea how to accomplish this.

I looked next for a textbook on the subject, but to my amazement no one had ever heard of one. I finally located a booklet that showed pictures of "standard" positions and gestures, but both the text and the illustrations were even more ludicrous than the operatic modus operandi gracing the conventional stages.

I came to the conclusion that I was confronted with an art form that was transmitted by word of mouth rather than by the printed page. A new singer engaged to perform an operatic role was indoctrinated by those who had participated in earlier productions of the work. These in turn had been taught by their elders, who had learned it from their predecessors. When they became too old to sing, experienced singers who had performed in many different operas would take advantage of their accumulated knowledge of traditional procedures and turn to stage directing. In my predicament I toyed with the idea of learning my new métier by attending a number of performances of the operas that interested me and noting what happened on stage. Unfortunately, I had been seeing such performances for many years and had found most of them hardly worth attending and certainly not worth imitating.

The very idea of traditional acting and staging made me shudder. Almost everyone knows the story of the tenor who would always walk to an upstage window and look outside in the middle of a certain aria. He eventually became so famous for his rendition of this role that all his younger colleagues imitated every detail of his interpretation, and his walk to the window soon became part of the traditional action for the aria. Many years later a young tenor who was studying the role questioned the purpose of this particular stage maneuver. Unable to get an explanation from any of his colleagues, the young man summoned up his courage and approached the world-famous originator of this upstage walk. The old gentleman enlightened him. "You want to know what I was looking for outside that window?" he asked. "It is very simple. For some reason I was always bothered with phlegm right in the middle of this aria and the window was the most convenient place to go and spit it out!"

I am not as a rule fond of stories that make fun of opera, but this particular anecdote, ridiculous as it is, points up the flimsy foundations of many firmly established operatic conventions and affectations. In the performance of opera, which relies heavily on word-of-mouth communication, habitual procedures are apt to appear cloaked with traditional authority. I am quite willing to respect traditions, but it seems to me that the fundamental question is not whether an action or staging is traditional, but whether or not it makes sense. Anything that clearly does not fit in with the plot or is in direct contradiction with the words of the text should be rejected out of hand without regard to its origin. The origins of such entrenched aberrations are seldom particularly respectable. Just as many of the poor procedures which have become "singers' traditions" had their beginnings in some famous person's lack of stamina, poor technique, or desire to show off his vocal prowess at the expense of the music, so is an illogical or erratic theatrical procedure often traceable to laziness or vanity or some other equally disreputable cause.

This was made painfully clear to me many years ago, when I was invited to attend a dress rehearsal of *Rigoletto* in Philadelphia. Unfortunately, I did not get to the theater until the middle of the second scene, just in time to hear the love scene between Gilda and the Duke. At the end of their duet I saw something quite unexpected and puzzling. As the Duke left the stage, he did not go through the door that led to Gilda's house, but used the garden gate which opened on the street. I was quite unprepared for this action, which struck me as rather appalling. In the intermission I saw the stage director of the performance, a good friend of mine. "For pity's sake," I stormed at him, "what is the idea of having the Duke make his exit into the street? Doesn't Gilda specifically urge her nurse to escort him through the door that leads to the bastion?"

"So, you don't think he should leave by the street?" my friend asked, looking at me with a peculiar and rather bitter expression.

"No, I certainly do not!" I went on. "The nurse hears a noise from the direction of the street. Gilda suspects it is her father returning. It would be disastrous for the lovers if he should see the Duke coming out of Gilda's garden gate. Earlier in the scene Rigoletto asked the nurse if she kept the other door safely locked, and he very carefully described this door as the one leading to the bastion. Actually, of course, it is not Rigoletto who is returning, but . . ."

At this point I was interrupted by my friend, whose face was getting redder and redder. "Save your breath," he whispered. "I'm quite familiar with the story of the opera and it certainly was not my idea to send that tenor in the wrong direction. The devil of it is that there is nothing I can do about it."

"What do you mean?" I gasped in amazement. "Why don't you simply tell him to leave through the house on stage right?"

"It's no use! He would agree to do it, but in the performance tomorrow night he will still go the other way and pretend that my request simply slipped his mind."

I was completely baffled. "But what in Heaven's name does that fellow hope to accomplish by this absurd behavior?"

"Just come to the performance tomorrow and see for yourself what will happen," said the stage director. "As soon as the tenor closes the garden gate behind him, he will slow down to a snail's pace. As you know, there are always bravos after the duet. Because the audience instinctively applauds the artist leaving the stage, our tenor will not only milk this applause with his slow exit walk, but he will return and take a bow, thanking the audience. In Washington I actually saw him come back twice to take bows!"

"But I don't understand," I stammered. "If he insists on returning to take bows, couldn't he just as easily do it after leaving through the proper door?"

You *are* naive, aren't you?" smiled my friend. "Returning from the house side he would have to share the applause with the soprano. This way, she remains behind the garden wall and does not even realize that her partner is getting the lion's share of the ovation."

Frankly, I thought all this was being invented just to tease me, so I went to see the performance the next evening. Not only was my friend's prediction accurate in every detail, but there was even an additional touch of showmanship. When the tenor returned to take his bow, he first gestured toward the garden wall as if to say: "Remember, I was not the only one who sang the duet!" The audience thought this was very generous of him and clapped even harder. He smiled and took his time and bowed to the boxes and to the balconies while Gilda sat on her bench and waited for the applause to subside so that she could go on with her "Caro nome." And this was not the only novelty in the staging of the opera. In the opening scene I noticed that Count Ceprano, who, according to the plot as I understood it, is anxious to protect his marital rights, did not find it necessary to follow his wife and the Duke when they left the stage, but remained on the set and participated in the scene with Marullo along with the other courtiers! When I went back-stage after the performance to apologize to my friend for doubting him, I decided to ask him also about Ceprano's lack of concern for his wife's infidelity.

"I should have known that you would notice it!" said the long-suffering stage director. "This, however, is different; this is a matter of professional courtesy."

"Courtesy?" I could scarcely believe my ears. "To whom? To the Duke? To Count Ceprano? Or to the Countess perhaps?"

"Don't be an idiot," said my friend. "The conductor was unhappy about the sound of the courtiers' chorus in the scene with Marullo, and he asked Ceprano to learn the bass part and sing it with them. I couldn't very well deny the conductor's request, especially since he is so very cooperative when it is my turn to ask for favors. It hardly seemed worthwhile to make a fuss over such a minor matter as this." I wanted to ask him how the Duke, after his return on stage, could complain about Ceprano's interference, when Ceprano in fact had so courteously left him alone with his wife, but I decided not to heap coals on the fire.

This episode had an unexpected sequel some twenty-five years later, a sequel with an even more distressing twist. I was visiting the campus of a large Western university to give a few lectures when I was accosted by the man in charge of the student production of *Rigoletto*, which was to take place a few days later. He told me how very much he would appreciate it if I would come to the dress rehearsal and give him the benefit of my advice. Curious to learn what kind of musical and dramatic standards they had in that part of the country, I promised to attend the rehearsal. He begged me not to forget to take notes of everything I thought needed correcting.

There was absolutely no need to take notes: what I heard and saw at that dress rehearsal was consistently dreadful. The orchestra and the singers could not stay together for more than a few measures at a time, in spite of the most intense staring at the conductor. The style of gestur-ing was of the most semaphoric variety, with scenery and costumes to match. And on top of all this, I saw in front of me my old friends: the cooperative husband Ceprano and the danger-seeking Duke of Mantua. It was all just as in Philadelphia, except that Ceprano listened to Marullo and the courtiers, instead of singing with them, and the Duke did not return for a curtain call after his escape through the garden gate.

After the rehearsal I was taken to the office of the producer to be quizzed on my reactions to what I had heard and seen. I tried to fore-stall the inquisition by assuring the director that everything had been just lovely and most satisfactory, but he insisted that there must have been a few details that could bear improvement. Since there was no escaping without comment, I asked him if it would not have been more in keeping with the text and the story to have Ceprano follow his wife and the Duke in the first scene, and also to have the Duke leave Gilda's garden in the opposite direction in the following scene.

"I know exactly what you mean," the director responded. "I realize that it would be much more logical and correct to do as you suggest, but I have a strong conviction that we must honor traditions." I could not believe my ears and, noticing my expression of blank amazement, he proceeded to elaborate his thesis with great warmth. "You know, of course, that this is the way it is now done everywhere," he continued. "Yes sir, I made it my business to see several *Rigolettos* in the East, and I made copious notes of exactly how it was being done there."

"But why do you want to imitate procedures that you yourself consider incorrect and illogical?" I interjected, unable to grasp the gist of his argument. "Your students would certainly be willing to follow whatever instructions you give them."

"But that's just the point," he said. "I believe it is our duty here in the West to prepare our students for a professional career. When they go East, and many of them do," he added proudly, "they must be able to join any professional outfit and be completely familiar with the traditions. There is a new company in Philadelphia, for instance . . ." I interrupted him with the assurance that I knew all about Philadelphia.

I could hardly sleep that night. Something about our conversation made me physically ill. I realized I had not felt that way about my old friend in the ill-starred Philadelphia production. He was in a situation where he could not help himself. He was checkmated by the vanity of the tenor and the dramatic insensibility of the conductor. But the situation at the university was quite different: here was a teacher who purposely taught his charges something that he knew was wrong and illogical. The cause of it all, the conceits and insensibilities, were gone and forgotten, but the results had become habitual and were henceforth accepted as dogma.

Back in that spring of 1936, when I was trying to decide if I could learn enough about operatic stage direction to accept Rubinstein's offer, I did not know much about traditions, but I had an instinctive hostility to conventional routine. I knew even then that the only operatic style I would ever want to be connected with would have to be in the direction of believable theater rather than of grandness and artificiality. Suddenly I realized that on several occasions I had witnessed a form of musical drama that was totally sympathetic to me. This had taken place in the classes of Dr. Ernst Lert, who at that time was teaching operatic acting at the Curtis Institute of Music in Philadelphia, where I had studied conducting with Fritz Reiner. On the few occasions I had been asked to

substitute for Lert's regular accompanist, I had witnessed operatic behavior that was very different from any other I had ever seen. The singers
acted like normal human beings, and there was none of the stiffness and
clumsiness that clings so persistently to the very name of opera. Best of
all, the music itself acquired a humanity and warmth which made it infinitely more expressive and meaningful. Whether the excerpts were from
the *Valkyrie, Hansel and Gretel,* or *La Bohème,* every movement of the
performers was subtly coordinated with the flow of the music, without
ever lapsing into the mincing danciness that I have always found so artificial and offensive. Lert had a magic that made everything he touched
become simple and natural.

Since I had nothing to lose, I decided to telephone Dr. Lert at his
Manhattan home. I told him the whole story of Rubinstein's offer and
of my reluctance to accept it. "How can I attempt to teach opera dramatics," I asked him, "when I know so little about it? Would you consider
taking me on as a pupil this summer, and could I hope to learn enough
to make a go of it next fall?"

Lert's response was not merely encouraging; it was positively enthusiastic. "By all means, accept this position. I'll be happy to teach you,"
he said. "Come to New York for six weeks in July and August. After
twelve sessions—we will have two a week—you will be fully prepared to
handle the task." That was all the prodding I needed. I immediately
telephoned Rubinstein and told him that he could make a public announcement of his new opera department.

Those two telephone calls changed my entire life and initiated a
fundamental break with all my former attitudes to opera and to music
in general. That summer I learned how to hear music with my entire
body and how to convert operatic stories into personal experiences.
Although I did not know it at the time, Lert had long been convinced of
the need to involve musicians, particularly conductors, in the dramatic
guidance of opera. "The great tragedy in our field," he told me later,
"is that opera conductors fail to realize the fundamental interdependence of musical and dramatic nuances. It will be a great day for opera
when all conductors study stage direction and all dramatic directors are
required to master more than the bare essentials of music."

My lessons with Dr. Lert were a revelation to me and established the
basis for all my later operatic endeavors. Although Lert was not a professional musician in the sense of being an instrumentalist, a singer, or
a conductor, he had a remarkably fine ear for the dramatic meaning of
music and made me aware of many musical subtleties of the type discussed in Chapter 2. What was even more startling was his belief in the
common-sense reality of operatic events. In working with him I noticed
to what extent I had been affected by a certain ironic attitude so common
among opera lovers. "It is all very well to talk about dramatic values
in opera," they seem to say, "but everyone knows that opera is not *really*

supposed to make sense." Lert would have none of this. If opera did not make sense, he used to say, it was because the people who produced, designed, conducted, stage-directed, and sang opera did not make sense! He insisted that not only the words that were being sung, but the scenery, costumes, lights, instrumental passages, and everything else in opera had to be integrated into a totality that was as real and true as the things that happen to us in our daily lives. He could put himself in the place of operatic characters to such an extent that he knew all their thoughts and feelings not only when they acted and sang, but even when they were offstage.

When I asked Lert to help me with the staging of the opening scene of *Così fan tutte*, he did not seem particularly enthusiastic. "You don't need me for that," he said. "You should be able to figure this out all by yourself, just on the basis of the indications in the libretto."

"I studied the libretto," I said, "but there wasn't anything there that offered me the slightest clue."

"Very well," he relented, "let me give you a hint. How is the setting described?"

"Described?" I stared at him. "There is no description. It simply says, 'A coffee house.'"

"That's it," said Lert. "Didn't you say that you spent several years in Paris and Budapest? You should know all about coffee houses."

"I've been in lots of coffee houses," I admitted.

"Excellent!" shouted Lert. "Then tell me everything you can remember about a coffee house: what it looks like, what happens there—everything. Take your time; I am not in any hurry!"

"Let me see," I began. "A coffee house is a large room filled with small tables surrounded by chairs. There is a main entrance and at least one other door leading to the kitchen. The place is usually swarming with waiters who dash about and customers who smoke, play checkers or chess, and read newspapers. There is much ordering, serving, and consuming of food and drinks. I guess that's all I can think of."

"Not at all! You know much more," Lert urged me on. "Imagine yourself going into a coffee house and tell me everything you do."

"I would first look to see if there was an empty table. Then I would take off my overcoat and hang it up. After sitting down, I would try to catch the waiter's eye and ask to see the menu; then I would order. Let me see . . . I already mentioned eating and drinking. I might ask for a napkin or decide to order another drink. After getting the bill, I would leave a tip, pick up my coat, pay the cashier, get the change, and put on my coat." I saw that Lert was laughing. "What is wrong?" I asked. "Have I forgotten something?"

"I don't know about that," he said, "but you have just staged the opening scene of *Così!*"

"You mean that Ferrando, Guglielmo, and Don Alfonso can do all these things? But when? They have to sing, don't they?"

"You are very hard to please," said Lert, still laughing. "First you complain that non-singing characters stand still without having anything to do, and now you imply that there is too much to do and no time to do it. Think: who in this scene has the least to sing?"

"It's Don Alfonso. Of course!" I exclaimed. "It is he who should study the menu and order something to eat for all three of them, and then . . ." I was getting quite excited with all the possibilities that suddenly came to mind. "Couldn't he order a leg of lamb or a shank of ham, so that when he sings of fighting duels he could brandish a carving knife; and then, at the end, when they all sing about toasting the God of Love, they could drink champagne and clink their glasses . . ." Lert was having a good time watching me. "But wait," I said. "What about other customers? Why should a coffee house be empty? And if I bring in other customers, wouldn't that be distracting to the audience?"

"You must not expect to solve all your problems in five minutes," said Lert in a more serious mood. "Think about it and you will remember occasions when you visited coffee houses that had only very few guests. And, what is even more crucial, don't try to stage anything without first consulting the score. The mood of the music is all-important and not every staging idea can be squeezed into the time made available by the composer. You will save yourself much grief if you first analyze every aspect of the music and then decide which of your coffee house notions fits within the existing musical framework and how it can be utilized to best advantage."

One of the first assignments Dr. Lert gave me was to decide on the scenic arrangement and actions in the opening scene of Verdi's *La Forza del Destino*. We were in the midst of this session when he suddenly said: "By the way, there is something Leonora wears under her skirt that she is hiding from her father. Do you know what it is?"

This gave me quite a jolt! What would she wear under her skirt except petticoats? But Lert was waiting for an answer, so I said: "I don't know what sort of underclothing Spanish girls wore in those days, but I imagine it was not much different from what they wear today. I don't see why her father should care one way or another."

"Forget her underclothing!" he answered scornfully. "She is wearing her riding boots. She is about to elope. Don Alvaro is coming to fetch her with saddled horses, and during the night they expect to ride for many hours, all the way to Seville and beyond. Riding boots are essential! Her father, of course, imagines that she is about to retire for the night and should he notice that she is wearing riding boots, the jig would be up. This obviously is not the only reason for Leonora's nervousness," Lert added, "but this is one thing that serves to remind her painfully and continually of her tragic conflict of emotions."

I was profoundly impressed. Here was a ridiculously unimportant detail, something that the people in the audience might never even notice. Yet it illuminated an approach to opera that was fundamentally different from anything I had encountered. In thinking of Leonora's participation in this scene, I had been mainly concerned with how well she would interpret her aria and her duet with the tenor, how much expression she would put into her sadness at the prospect of leaving Spain, how sincerely she would portray her fear and guilt at deceiving her father. All this was still of paramount importance, but now these riding boots affected everything Leonora sang and did. I could feel myself being Leonora and experiencing the reality of these riding boots; I could feel the extent to which wearing them represented her actual decision to elope and to abandon her country and her family. She was no longer just thinking about this: now it was happening.

Ever since that memorable afternoon at Dr. Lert's, I have searched for such symbols of believable reality in every opera I have staged. Norina's furniture which is moved into Don Pasquale's library in the last act, Susanna's wedding veil which hounds the Count in the second act of *The Marriage of Figaro*, Elvira's name which is found in Don Giovanni's list of seductees, the ring which Don José puts on Carmen's finger at the end of the second act, Tosca's reading the farewell letter from Cavaradossi in the Castle of Sant'Angelo: all these, and countless more, are the spiritual descendants of Lert's and Leonora's riding boots.

Many years later when staging this opening scene of *La Forza del Destino*, I had Leonora wear an entire masculine riding habit underneath her dress. After she sang her aria, her servant, Curra, helped her out of her dress, so that when Alvaro arrived Leonora was ready to go with him. This transformation not only heightened the element of urgency which pervades the duet of the lovers, but it had a staggering effect on the old Marchese when he came to his daughter's chambers to look for the cause of the disturbance. When the old gentleman saw his daughter, who just a short while ago had bid him a fond good night, dressed in men's clothing, he became instantly aware of her duplicity, deceit, and unworthiness to be the daughter of the Marchese of Calatrava. When Alvaro hurried Leonora away at the end of the scene, it was obvious that the lovers would try to escape on horseback, and when we saw Leonora disguised as a man later in the inn scene and the monastery scene, we accepted it as something quite natural which we had already seen earlier.

At the time I staged these scenes from *Forza*, Lert was long dead, but I think it might have pleased him to know that his riding boots had blossomed into a full-blown garment. My search for theatrical clarity and variety was influenced by many other experiences, but in my pursuit of what I consider to be the very essence of opera, its musical and dramatic believability, the inspiration came fully and directly from the teachings of this wonderful man.

Opera has often been described as a marriage of theater and music. This union, which has given mankind some of its most glorious revelations, has also had its share of detractors, who contend that opera is not so much a marriage as an artistic battleground.

As long as the two partners function exclusively on their own home grounds, their co-existence is quite harmonious. The theater controls everything that is purely visual: scenery, costumes, make-up, and lighting; music has sovereign rights in the domain of instrumental playing and singing. It is only in the areas of dramatic action and verbal communication that we cross into contested territory. The moment we touch upon such matters as the timing of stage movements, the length and distribution of syllables and words, or the theatrical handling of orchestral interludes and vocal ensembles, amicable relations come to an end, and theater and music seem to pull in opposite directions. This tug of war is particularly painful to opera singers, who are most directly involved in the uttering of words and the execution of actions. These singers are like children who receive seemingly contradictory orders from their parents and do not quite know how to interpret them.

This conflict is not the result of a basic incompatibility, but of a failure to understand exactly what each of these arts is trying to communicate. Theater and music are not antagonistic. They merely address us in different languages, and the parallelism of their intentions is revealed only by a careful study of their special forms of imagery.

An actor's gesture and the orchestral passage that is played alongside it may seem to belong to two different artistic worlds, but their essential identity of purpose can and must be revealed in any satisfactory operatic production. The movements of singers on stage and the distribution of phrases in the accompanying music must seem to be generated by a single plan of the composer and the stage director; they must exhibit similar elements of symmetry, unity, and ornamentation. When a single plan is not apparent or is difficult to establish, it is the stage director's duty to find a way to reconcile the seemingly divergent tendencies.

This need to reconcile theater and music in opera helps to explain both the omissions and the preoccupations of this book, which is not concerned with what I have termed the "exclusive home grounds" of the two arts. Matters dealing with the purely visual or auditory aspects of these arts will be touched upon only when they influence each other. Anyone who wishes to learn about strictly theatrical subjects such as make-up, lighting, or the design and execution of scenery and costumes, can find at his disposal an abundance of published material. This is equally true of such subjects as musical theory and harmony, voice development, instrumental playing, and orchestral conducting.

In this book, I shall concentrate on those facets of theater and music that relate specifically to their co-existence in opera. In this area—

the "contested territory"—I shall try to demonstrate that although on the surface the procedures and languages of the two arts may differ, in opera their ultimate aims are not only compatible, but identical. The task of seeing that these aims remain clearly united falls for the most part on the shoulders of singing actors and operatic stage directors. The criteria I find most useful in helping them to accomplish this task, and to evaluate the acting and staging of others, are three: credibility, clarity, and variety.

An operatic performance, like any other artistic endeavor, must possess beauty. But assuming that the opera itself, the voices of the singers, the orchestral sound, the scenery, and the costumes are sufficiently "beautiful," the first requisite of a successful operatic production is that it be *believable*. To the extent that the audience can identify with the characters on stage and accept their appearance, their utterances, the sound of their voices, and the instrumental music that surrounds them as being suitable and compatible, to that extent the performance can be said to be completely believable.

It is unfortunate that believable opera is rarely seen or heard. There are many musically and theatrically sensitive people who have never witnessed a completely convincing operatic performance. Consequently, we are often told that we should not expect opera to make sense, that its situations, by and large, are too artificial, and that we should not pay attention to the dramatic elements in opera. Instead, we should concentrate on the music and find our aesthetic satisfaction in great singing and fine orchestral playing.

My main objection to this attitude is that it flatly contradicts the intentions of the men who created the operas. The great composers of opera certainly expected their creations to be completely believable. We know of Verdi's vigorous search for the *parola scenica* (convincing theatrical utterance); we know that Puccini drove his librettists to despair with his almost neurotic insistence on believable situations and lifelike dialogue; Wagner ridiculed the tenor Tichatchek because this dull gentleman, when singing the praises of the goddess Venus, addressed his remarks to the chaste Elisabeth; Verdi objected to the idea of engaging Mme. Tadolini for the role of Lady Macbeth because Tadolini "has the voice and face of an angel, while Lady Macbeth must be ugly and wicked, and have the voice of a devil." It is clear that Verdi and Wagner had no doubts about the basic credibility of their operas. It was the Tichatcheks and Tadolinis who were ridiculous or unsuitable, not the drama and music of *Tannhäuser* and *Macbeth*.

We have countless reports of how composers identified with the characters in their operas. In connection with *The Queen of Spades*, Tchaikovsky wrote to his friends that he shared the feelings and sufferings of his characters to such an extent that for a while he was actually afraid of the Countess' ghost. Tchaikovsky's friend, Kashkin, tells us that the composer "lived surrounded by the characters of his plots. He suffered and felt everything that was experienced by the heroes of his works. He was angry at some, loved others, and sometimes confused his own life with that of his creations." Obviously, there exist any number of poorly conceived and executed operatic compositions with lame plots, wooden characters, and unsuitable or trite music; but in considering the hundred or so works that one usually calls "great operas," it is certain that if they fall short of being dramatically convincing, the fault lies not so much in the compositions themselves as in the manner in which they are presented on stage.

Those who complain about dramatic deficiencies in opera usually put the blame squarely on the singers. Believable opera, they tell us, does not exist because singers cannot act and, in fact, are not interested in acting. This, however, is no longer true. Today thousands of young singers are anxious to develop into fine actors, and a surprising number of them succeed. In this book I hope to lead them even further in their quest for believable operatic behavior and to show directors how they can help singers achieve a continuous line of characteristic actions, which at all times reflect the timing, mood, and energy of the music and are in absolute conformity with the words of the text.

Clarity is the second important ingredient of artistic productions. Since opera is meant to appeal to both the eye and the ear, clarity requires that what happens on stage be not only audible and visible, but also be highlighted in such a manner that the attention of the audience is concentrated on the characters and events that carry the main dramatic burden. It is important to distinguish between mere audibility or visibility and the proper highlighting of the various elements of a performance.

This distinction is familiar in instrumental music where, as every performer knows, accompanying figures and secondary themes are always subdued so that the melody, or principal theme, will stand out. Unless music is correctly highlighted, it becomes distorted and unintelligible. Until the middle of the nineteenth century, musical textures remained relatively simple, and the necessary adjustments were left to the performers. Composers in those days were content to indicate their wishes in a general way by such markings as *forte, piano, crescendo,* or *diminuendo;* they left matters of more detailed highlighting to the performers, who, they felt, were quite capable of balancing loudness and softness in the correct proportions. As musical complications increased and styles became more esoteric, the notation of dynamics became more and more detailed. One of the most far-reaching and valuable innovations in the history of musical notation was introduced by Arnold Schoenberg and his disciples, who added special signs to indicate which strands of music should predominate. In their scores the letter *H* (an abbreviation of the German word *Hauptstimme*—main voice) is attached to the musical phrases that are to stand out most clearly, and the letter *N* (for *Ne-*

benstimme—secondary voice) to the passages to be played somewhat less prominently. The absence of the letters *H* or *N* indicates that the music in question is to be played very discreetly, purely as an accompaniment to the other voices. Applying a similar division to the activities on stage, we may identify the *leading* actions, the less vigorous *supporting* actions, and the unobtrusive *background* actions.

Problems in the highlighting of stage behavior occur automatically whenever there are two or more characters on stage at the same time. The audience's attention must always be drawn to the leading action. To accomplish this, every singer on stage must understand the degree of importance of his actions at all times and must behave accordingly. The well-trained artist is proud of his ability to handle supporting and background behavior. He enjoys seeing the leading action pass from singer to singer and is content to support, or serve as background, according to the demands of the play. The stage director who knows how to imbue his company with the spirit of ensemble performing will never be faced with that common blight known as scene stealing, mugging, or upstaging, which is so prevalent in many star-studded productions.

Finally, there is the matter of *variety* which belongs entirely in the province of the stage director. As every opera lover knows, action on the lyric stage has a frightening tendency to become rigidly static and monotonous. Many singers, accustomed to the relative immobility of the vocal studio and the concert platform, are quite content to remain in one place, usually downstage center, for an entire scene. To avoid such lifeless and boring presentations, the stage director must arrange for a sufficient number of changes of position and grouping. It is true, of course, that too much activity can be as disturbing as no activity. Continuous running around on the stage produces the same stultifying effect as constant gesturing: it makes all movements equally insignificant. The sensible approach is to change positions and groupings whenever the author and the composer introduce a new dramatic or musical idea. Repetitions of sentences or musical phrases should also be matched by corresponding, but minor, changes in the stage picture. An exact dosage for the amount of stage movement in any given situation cannot be precribed. This is and must remain the expression of every stage director's personal style.

The skills analyzed in this volume are much more than practical. What composers and playwrights actually create is not the work of art itself, but only a symbolic blueprint, a recipe for bringing it to life. The creations of painters and sculptors stand alone; no one else is needed to complete them. But librettists and composers need conductors, instrumentalists, and scenic designers. And most of all they need singing actors and stage directors. In a very real sense these performing artists become the authors' actual partners. It is this feeling of artistic collaboration that gives the professions of the operatic singer and the stage director their intoxicating aura.

~~~ 1

The language of the theater

AN EXPERT ACTOR is a person who is able to communicate a great variety of thoughts, moods, and emotional states to his audience. He accomplishes this by uttering words and by moving the muscles of his face, arms, and body. An expert opera singer is a person who, in addition to these skills, has a well-trained voice and a considerable knowledge of music.

There is nothing intrinsically wrong with these statements except that I have put the cart before the horse. In opera, with very few exceptions, the vocal and musical skills are acquired first and the verbal and visible communication of thoughts and emotional states comes much later, or, sometimes, not at all.

This book is primarily for stage directors and fairly advanced singers, and therefore does not attempt to treat the problems of vocal training and development in any way whatsoever. It also presupposes a certain degree of musicianship, such as the ability to read music and understand common musical terms. For our purposes then, the problem of operatic acting is: given adequate vocal and musical preparation, what are the responsibilities of the singing actor? They consist of developing his person and his body as an expressive acting instrument and of mastering the techniques of the proscenium stage.

The singer as actor

To mold himself into an expressive acting instrument, a singer must first learn to lend his intellectual and emotional resources to the character he is portraying. He must force himself to think the thoughts of that character: not only those thoughts he is required to speak or sing, but also unwritten thoughts which he either verbalizes silently by means of a so-called *subtext** or which he experiences as less clearly-defined images and feelings.

Ideally speaking, the accomplished actor should be aware only of the thoughts and feelings of his stage character. This ideal, however, is not easy to achieve. The student of acting soon discovers that no matter how hard he tries, thoughts and feelings not related to his stage character keep interfering and distracting him. We can distinguish between *technical* and *irrelevant* thoughts. Technical thoughts are those dealing with the mechanics of the performance—vocalization, musical accuracy, or the intricacies of acting and stage movement. Irrelevant thoughts are the disturbing intrusions of the performer's personal environment, stemming from the everyday world of his offstage personality.

Making the mechanics of performing automatic

It may seem wildly improbable to the aspiring opera singer that he will ever be able to sing and act an entire role thinking only the thoughts of his stage character. After all, his vocal teacher has been urging him to concentrate on sensations designed to produce the right kind of singing tone; his repertoire coach has warned him to pay close attention to rests, listen to pitches, and count beats; his stage director expects him to remember complicated stage maneuvers. Doesn't all this concentrating, listening, watching, paying close attention, and remembering involve thinking of the most intense kind—a type of thinking that has little in common with the ideas and emotions presumably circulating in the minds of a Leonora or a Figaro? Doubtless it does, and this is exactly why the opera singer should try to eliminate these technical thoughts. The best way to accomplish this is to practice the various vocal, musical, and theatrical skills until they become automatic and entirely self-propelling.

Consider how many complicated activities we can perform without paying much attention to them. Try to imagine the muscular intricacies connected with walking. We have been walking for so long that we have forgotten how difficult it was to learn in the first place. A woman will walk to the market, push a baby buggy in front of her, brush a fly off her face, greet a friend, notice the prices in a display window, and all the while be thinking of something really important: her sick child or her philandering husband. As a matter of fact, she performs this complicated mental and muscular juggling quite effortlessly. Her attention can be

---

* The term *subtext* as used here, refers to unspoken words reflecting silent, but particularly appropriate, thoughts and inner feelings of the stage character. In Chapter 6 the reader will encounter "self-prompting" subtexts, subtexts that relate to stage movement, and other varieties of this invaluable theatrical and musical device.

diverted to more weighty matters because her muscles, having practiced all these operations for years, are now functioning independently.

The experienced performer achieves something very similar. He practices his vocalizing, his musical rendition, and his stage movement until the mechanics of these acts become second nature and can then be merged with and governed by the thoughts of the character.

To make the mechanics of these acts automatic, not only must the various techniques be subjected to intensive and prolonged drill, but they must at first be treated separately. Musical exactness, for instance, cannot be mastered at the same time as one attempts to learn stage movement, and vice versa. This separateness, which is quite well understood in learning singing and music, is unfortunately not always observed in the acquisition of stage techniques.

The singer "vocalizes" regularly under the supervision of his voice teacher. He has also probably taken a methodical course of solfege, theory, and harmony and then solidified this knowledge in countless hours spent with his repertoire coach; but then, having developed his voice and musicianship, he immediately goes into operatic rehearsals. It is in these rehearsals and *while singing* that he gradually picks up bits of stage know-how on which he then relies for the rest of his career. Furthermore, many directors expect singers to remember complicated stage business and changes of position and grouping after only two or three sessions devoted to sketchy blocking and perfunctory explanations. Because stage directions are usually given by word of mouth and in a hurried manner, the singer can neither digest them on the spot nor review them between rehearsals. Under these conditions, staging arrangements can be made automatic only after a series of public presentations. The early performances suffer most, naturally, and often cause a lasting impression of mediocrity which affects both the opera and its performers.* Automatic performance techniques do not guarantee excellence, of course, but they are necessary prerequisites for artistic accomplishment.

Some singers attempt to supplement their theatrical training by attending regular drama schools, but these have proven of only limited value in opera. The influence of music on operatic stage behavior is so fundamental that it cannot be omitted in the learning process.

The operatic pantomimes which the reader will find in Chapter 4 offer the best method of learning and perfecting the specific stage techniques required in opera. Without having to worry about his vocal apparatus, the singer can concentrate on musically motivated and correctly timed stage movements and actions. What is more, he can repeat these

---

* The well-established classic is not harmed, of course. No one after seeing a poor performance of *Carmen* imagines that Bizet's opera is an inferior work. It is the new and obscure operas that suffer most, and many a charming creation has been relegated to undeserved oblivion because it was premiered or revived in a slipshod manner.

exercises often enough to lay the foundation for technical mastery. The need for such repetitive drill cannot be overemphasized.

The quality of the student's final result will depend upon the care with which he "cuts the initial grooves" when learning the various skills essential to opera. And, he must not expect to make every single technical detail automatic. There are certain muscular operations that will always require intense watchfulness. Because of a personal experience which I had a number of years ago, I like to refer to these special technical difficulties as "razor-blade moments."

Due to a snow storm, I arrived in a certain college town only an hour or so before the start of a morning assembly, where I was scheduled to address the students. Shaving hurriedly in my hotel room, I thought over the remarks I planned to make in my talk. While concentrating on a fine musical point with which I intended to impress my listeners, I noticed that the blade of my safety razor had fallen into the wash basin. Reaching down absent-mindedly to pick up the blade, I made a deep and very painful gash in the index finger of my right hand. This unfortunate experience proved to me that even in such thoroughly rehearsed skills as washing and shaving there are certain moments which require complete concentration on the task at hand. Picking up a double-edged razor blade is definitely one activity that one should not attempt to automatize!

Since that time I have become aware that difficulties of this type occur in most artistic occupations. For instance, no matter how completely a pianist may have mastered Schumann's C-Major Fantasy, the passage at the end of the second movement where both hands have to perform lightning-fast skips in opposite directions will always require the closest possible vigilance. In opera, as in all other arts, one should treat these technical "razor blades" with the greatest respect and, while they last, should allot them complete and undivided attention.

Thinking in character

Having learned how to eliminate technical thoughts, the singer is now ready to deal with his personal, or irrelevant, thoughts. These are the thoughts that are not likely to cross the mind of the operatic character he is portraying. For instance, suppose that a soprano named Jane Smith is entering the stage in the first act of *La Bohème*, prepared to sing the role of Mimi. Some of Mimi's thoughts on that occasion may be: "How stupid of me to forget to buy matches! Now I have to annoy strangers! They have a nice room here. And so warm! What an attractive and polite young man! I feel so dizzy! I shouldn't have run up these steps so fast!"

Jane Smith's thoughts, on the other hand, could easily be: "I hope that high C comes out all right tonight! Maestro will kill me if I make

that stupid mistake again! It's too bad that tenor is so fat! I wonder if
they remembered to put tea into the wine bottle. I couldn't sing two
notes after swallowing that stuff at the rehearsal yesterday!" Quite clearly,
not a single one of Miss Smith's reflections could possibly have entered
Mimi's head. On the other hand, it may be argued that the difference between the two lines of thinking would not be too apparent to the audience
at this point. The role of Mimi, in the first two acts at least, can be quite
adequately impersonated by any comely girl with a sufficiently attractive
voice and normal feminine impulses. It is in the third and fourth acts of
La Bohème that our Jane Smith will give herself away unless she succeeds
in re-educating her thinking processes. And when it comes to more complicated roles, such as Violetta, Tosca, Aida, or Manon, the soprano's
ability to govern what goes on in her mind becomes more and more
essential.

Many singers are not aware that *being* in character also means *thinking* in character. Some of them perhaps have sung opera only in foreign
languages in which they could not possibly begin to think.* But, another
reason why our Jane Smith could not think as Mimi was that she probably
did not know enough about Mimi. She knew a great deal about Jane
Smith, about her experiences at yesterday's rehearsal, about her musical
difficulties for which she had been scolded by the maestro, and her vocal
fears concerning high notes. But she had never imagined herself as the
little seamstress who forgot to buy matches, whose room was probably
unheated, and who got out of breath by running up those steps. To stimulate her imagination, Jane will have to assemble every possible bit of information about Mimi, her occupation, daily habits, likes and dislikes,
mode of life, and sickness. If Jane is to become an actress, she will also
have to train her emotional responses. Judging from her thoughts when
she entered the stage, the Rodolfo she saw there was just a pudgy tenor.
No so with Mimi. Be he fat or thin, *her* Rodolfo is always a handsome,
refined young stranger who has no difficulty sweeping her off her feet with
his poetic and impetuous love-making.

I have taught the role of Mimi to many Jane Smiths who began
as prim young ladies unable to hide their "don't-you-get-any-ideas-my-dear-
fellow" reactions when their Rodolfos embraced them. Like most irrelevant thoughts, such inhibitions arise, I believe, from a confusion about the
nature of the actor's split personality, a confusion which is universal
among beginners and prevalent even among experienced performers.

Every human being has a personal way of reasoning, imagining, planning, calculating, and making decisions. His thinking powers extend from
drowsy lethargy to sharp alertness. He also has his own individual capacity

---

* A strong argument for opera in the vernacular is that it enables operatic actors
to think "in character" when they sing and continue to do so when they are not
singing. Appendix A, "Opera in English," discusses at length the presentation of opera
in foreign languages and opera in translation.

for desiring, loving, and hating, for being tender, generous, and self-sacrificing, or antagonistic, malicious, and murderous. His potential emotional range covers every nuance from angelic kindness to vilest beastliness. These mental and emotional resources are a basic part of a man's personality: his thinking, his feeling. We can call these *primary* characteristics.

In addition, there is also a person's position in time, place, and social environment. He is born in a certain historical period; he has parents, a name, a nationality, an occupation, family friends, an income, a home, an education, a job, a schedule; he has habits and expectations about food, shelter, clothing, transportation, cleanliness, cultural needs, and entertainment. All these characteristics are *secondary*.

On stage the actor splits his personality: he keeps his primary characteristics but exchanges his secondary ones for those of the character in the play. It is a fascinating process: First, we must realize that our own secondary characteristics have a strong influence on our primaries. The usual effect is that of greatly restricting the range of our primaries. Most of us live in an environment that rarely makes us think very hard, even when far-reaching decisions have to be made. Furthermore, most of us use only a small segment of our emotional resources. In the course of our upbringing our extreme feelings have been dulled, sometimes to the point of atrophy, by the "civilizing" process of education. We cannot afford to be either angelic or beastly. We know that people take advantage of angels and that beasts are put behind bars. Expressing our feelings is a precarious business. Even less drastic expressions of feelings, such as tenderness or revulsion, can have unwelcome effects, can make us ridiculous or unpopular. For fear of being laughed at or disliked, many people reduce their emotional responses to the level of tepid pleasantness and impersonal courtesy. In ordinary life few of us can risk the consequences of strong feelings. But the extraordinary thing about theatrical acting is that *there are no consequences.*

As Violetta, Jane Smith can make the most heroic and soul-shattering sacrifice for her Alfredo. As Carmen, she can fight like a wildcat to attract Don José's attention; she can take him as her lover and then discard him in cold blood, and risk death rather than leave her next lover, Escamillo. As Tosca, she can hate Scarpia bitterly enough to kill him, and in fact she must kill him. Having done all this, Jane can return safely to her own comfortable environment with its easy thoughts and gentle feelings. But she can portray her "other selves" fully and truly only if—while acting out Violetta, Carmen, or Tosca—she discards Jane's secondaries. Her ordinary thoughts and feelings, if permitted to survive during her acting, will dilute the vitality and strength of her characterizations. The actress who remains Jane Smith portrays only what she is: a rather tame young girl trying very hard to behave like an operatic heroine!

At this point I want to reassure all young Janes and Joes that no one ever confuses stage secondaries with the singing actor's own personality. This is perhaps the most fundamental of all theatrical conventions. No matter what you think, feel, or do on stage, no one, neither your audiences nor your partners, will ever connect it with your offstage behavior. Your stage lovers will no more think of "getting fresh" with you after rehearsals or performances than the town policeman would dream of arresting you for a murder you committed on stage. In exchanging your own secondaries for those of your stage character, you can even change gender. Startling as it may seem at first glance, gender is not a primary, but a secondary characteristic. This is why such masculine roles as Cherubino, Octavian, or Siebel can be acted so brilliantly by women. When, as director, I am demonstrating the staging of such love episodes as those at the end of the Garden Scene in *Faust*, or in the first act of *La Bohème*, I can act Marguerite and Mimi just as easily as Faust and Rodolfo. Whatever the character in a drama is called upon to imagine, feel, and do, you can throw yourself into it safely. This absence of consequences is the source of a most exhilarating sensation of emotional and intellectual freedom.

A character's thoughts and feelings must be as continuous as possible and visible even when not audible. Moreover, they must be sharply focused on the moment at hand. When a singer onstage thinks of something the character he is portraying does not learn until later in the drama, he is guilty of a seriously "irrelevant" thought.

Words do not necessarily have to correspond with thoughts and actions. A character in a play does not always mean what he says; sometimes he hides his real intentions behind false words and actions. There are countless operatic plots that depend on such deceptions and dissimulations, and the audience should usually not be left in doubt as to whether a character is lying or telling the truth. Behind his partner's back, the face of an accomplished actor must be able to divulge his true feelings. When consoling Aida, Princess Amneris's looks and demeanor must simulate sisterly love; when Aida is turned away, however, the princess's facial expressions must plainly show the hatred and suspicion generated by her jealousy of the slave. In her duet with Figaro, Rosina must behave so as to convince the wily barber that she is too modest to write a letter to Lindoro; when not observed by him, she must just as unmistakably reveal her delight in being able to outsmart Figaro, who imagines himself to be a superior virtuoso in the realm of intrigue. Operatic scenes occasionally contain a fairly rapid alternation of such truth and pretense. Furthermore, thoughts are often expressed long after they occur or perhaps not at all, but shown only by means of facial expressions and bodily movements.

Listening to the singing partner is another art that must be carefully cultivated by singing actors. Out-of-character thoughts and blank minds (including the common "I'm-waiting-for-my-next cue" facial expression—

the most odious of irrelevancies) are much more difficult to overcome when a stage character is silent. In these places careful listening to one's partners and reacting to their thoughts and feelings is an efficient weapon. This is an art that the singer must master as fully as that of dramatically effective vocal expression.

Developing the character

We mentioned earlier that before Jane Smith could think as Mimi, she had to know a great deal about Mimi. This knowledge can come from four sources: the text of the opera, authentic background sources (in this case, Murger's Scènes de la Vie de Bohème), her own personal experiences akin to those of Mimi, and recollections of what she may have read about the historic period.

A careful analysis of an opera's text is, without doubt, the first duty of every self-respecting and conscientious singer. A great deal of indispensable information is contained in the scenic descriptions and stage directions given in the libretto. The singer will also learn much about his own role from what is said about him by other characters in the plot.

The tenor entrusted with the role of Grigory in Boris Godunov must not wait until the day of the dress rehearsal or of the first performance to discover that the official description of his appearance, as deciphered in the tavern scene by Varlaam, reads: "He is twenty years old, of medium height, and red-haired. He has a wart on his nose, another on his forehead, and one of his arms is shorter than the other."

The artist interpreting Don Basilio in The Marriage of Figaro should learn everything that is said about him while he is not on stage. The realization that it is his responsibility to give voice lessons to Susanna, that it is he who sees to it that the Count gets the anonymous note written by Figaro, and that it is part of his duties to prepare the officer's commission for Cherubino, will go a long way to clarify his position as the factotum of the castle.

Concerning the study of background texts and historical documents, the singer's responsibility cannot be defined quite as categorically. When working on La Bohème, for instance, it would probably be useless to ask our Jane Smith to study Murger's novel, since at present this book is available only in the original French.* I suspect that a conscientious stage director would be more likely to have a fluent reading command of that language. It would be ideal, of course, if singers themselves would engage in this kind of thorough literary and psychological research, and

* The English versions of this work have been out of print for some time and are practically unobtainable at this writing.

some particularly conscientious performers do it. However, realistically speaking, a singer rarely has enough time or access to the pertinent sources to indulge in all these complicated investigations, and it is here that the help of the stage director is essential. It is his duty to help the singer clarify the meaning of the dramatic situation, pinpoint the exact timing of the thoughts, feelings, and actions, and arrive at the best manner of visual execution.

The stage director can impart this information to the singer in several ways. I use and recommend a sequence which may be described as: first explain *what* happens, then indicate *when* and *why* it happens, and only after this has been done, help (very sparingly) with *how* it happens.

To determine what a particular character is thinking, feeling, and doing, the stage director must (*a*) study the text and music of the opera, (*b*) consult authentic background texts whenever they exist, (*c*) do a systematic research on the habits and conditions prevalent in the opera's epoch, and (*d*) add his own ideas and interpretations when this seems necessary or appropriate.

The problem of timing really consists of two separate questions: at what moment does a particular thought-feeling-action complex begin, and at what speed does it grow and develop? The singer must be made aware of the instant a new idea strikes him and of the tempo at which it and the actions flowing from it unfold.

In opera all the questions of dramatic meaning and timing are answered and controlled by the creators and producers, that is, by librettists, composers, stage directors, conductors, and scenic designers. All this may be different for every set of producers (conductors, stage directors, and scenic designers), but the singer is not supposed to make original contributions to what he is to think, feel, or do, nor to its timing. This has been organized for him beforehand by the creators and producers. All words, vocal lines, and actions are presented to the singer, so to speak, on a silver platter. His first duty is to learn, digest, memorize, and make automatic the mechanics of all this. Once this technical foundation is built, the singer is free to add his own vocal, musical, intellectual, emotional, and muscular artistry. It is in this interpretative capacity that he becomes a part of the creative team and sometimes its most valuable member.

The artistic contribution of the singer cannot be fully treated until we have discussed the physical aspects of acting and the techniques of the stage. At this point it will be useful to study a sequence of thoughts, feelings, actions, and timing as they are combined and developed in an extended operatic scene.

Within the confines of a book it is impossible to duplicate what occurs in real-life demonstrations, but I will nevertheless try to describe what happens when two singers, having memorized the words and music of an opera, come to me to learn the theatrical interpretation of a particular section. The scene between Violetta and Father Germont from the second act of *La Traviata* will serve as an example.

We start with a discussion of the general outline of the story, and continue with a more and more detailed description until we reach the specific content of their thoughts, feelings, and actions. Finally, we analyze the beginning of these actions and thoughts and the speed at which they unfold.

The story of Violetta Valery (or Marguerite Gautier, as she is called in Dumas' novel and play) is so well known that there is no need to review it. It will be sufficient to remind the reader that Violetta is about twenty-two years old, very beautiful, and very much in love with Alfredo, who is twenty-four. At the beginning of the scene with Father Germont, she is expecting a business agent who has been put in charge of selling her jewelry, carriages, and the other valuables which she obtained from her former rich lovers. Since she has never seen either the business agent or Father Germont, she imagines that the person who has been ushered into her living room is the agent. She stands near the table and is going over the inventory of the things which are to be sold.

The details of Father Germont's background are less well known and therefore worth retelling. He has just arrived at Violetta's suburban villa near Paris, hoping to save his son from the clutches of Violetta, a girl he knows nothing about except that she is a notorious, kept woman. He has been warned of her charm and smooth manners, but he still expects her to be rather coarse and little more than a common streetwalker. The old gentleman (Father Germont is only in his early fifties, but a hundred years ago this was considered a fairly advanced age) is worried about his son Alfredo, his daughter Blanche, and the financial threat brought on by his son's unfortunate involvement with this unsavory and (as he imagines) greedy woman. Alfredo has requested the release of a principal portion of the inheritance left him three years ago by his mother, Marie. The family of Blanche's fiancé is seriously upset about the news of Alfredo's liaison with a notorious Parisian courtesan. Unless something is done right away, the wedding will have to be postponed and perhaps cancelled altogether. Father Germont's own position may be jeopardized as well. Provincial Frenchmen are the most conservative souls imaginable, and his official post as chief collector of county taxes depends on a reputation of unquestioned honesty and strict propriety. The thrifty Germont, who during the last ten years has managed to repay in full the security deposit required by his official position, is distressed at the elegant appearance of this country estate with its gardens and expensive looking furnishings, the cost of which he believes to be defrayed by his son. To his provincial eyes this establishment has the look and flavor of a flashy Parisian house of ill repute. He is stiffly uncomfortable, does not remove his gloves, and refuses to part with his hat, which he keeps under his arm. His intention is to try to buy off Violetta with a single and (he hopes) not too large sum of money. He is, however, a dignified and polite gentleman, and before making any proposals wants to be certain that he is in fact addressing Violetta Valery.

Before turning to the actual staging of a scene, I find it quite essential to give the participants a clear idea of its overall construction. Otherwise, they inevitably get bogged down in small details and lose sight of the main line and the totality of their assignment.

This scene, for instance, is fundamentally a long drawn-out battle between Father Germont and Violetta, with Alfredo's future happiness as the main point at issue. The outcome is in doubt for some time, but eventually Father Germont prevails; his arguments triumph.

We can divide the entire sequence into eight plainly defined episodes:

1. The initial clash, which is won by Violetta when she convinces Germont that he has been accusing her unjustly.
2. The sacrifice suggested by Germont for the sake of Blanche. This episode ends when Violetta's offer of a temporary separation is turned down by Germont.
3. Eloquent, almost hysterical pleading by Violetta, who refuses to agree to a permanent separation.
4. Germont's convincing plea for the protection of Alfredo's future, ending in Violetta's tragic resignation.
5. Violetta's tearful acceptance of her fate and Germont's heartfelt consolations.
6. Discussion of the best method of separation and Violetta's heroic decision to make Alfredo hate her.
7. Germont's gratitude and promise, in time, to reveal the truth to Alfredo.
8. Farewells.

A discussion of the first two episodes will suffice for our purposes.

Since the scene is set in a room, I point out to the singers the location of the doors and the most important furniture props. In this case there are three doors: the main entrance downstage right, the door into Violetta's room upstage left, and the French doors leading into the garden in upstage center. In my staging, the couch is located at the right, and the table with two chairs is at the left.

To facilitate the presentation of the various components, Violetta's and Father Germont's silent thoughts are enclosed in parentheses, the directions concerning their stage movements are italicized, and the timing of their actions is in brackets.

LA TRAVIATA, ACT II: Scene between Violetta and Father Germont

Father Germont	Violetta
Enters [moderately] *and stops not far from door, above couch.* (I wonder if this is she. She doesn't look like a cocotte. I had better make sure!) Miss Valery?	*Stands near table, looking* [slowly] *through papers and barely glances at Germont.* (This must be the man from the auctioneer's.)
	I am she.
Alfredo's father stands before you!	*Points to chair, inviting him to sit down. Looks up* [quickly]. (Alfredo's father! Heavens! He'll probably stay overnight. Thank God the blue guest room has been fixed up! And Alfredo's not home!)
	You!
(What is she doing? I don't want to shake hands with this creature! No!) *Backs away* [quickly] *a couple of steps.*	*Drops papers on table* [quickly] *and runs to Germont.* (Where's Annina? He will want some tea, I'm sure. I must welcome him warmly!)
Yes, father of the foolish boy who is ruining himself, bewitched by you!	*Slows down and stops some distance away from him.* (What's that? Ruined? Bewitched? How dare he . . . I must control myself. After all, he is his father . . .)
(Good! This has stopped her.)	Sir, I am a lady and in my own home! Permit me to leave, more for your sake than for mine!
(She certainly acts like a lady! I guess I was rude. This is unforgivable. And my hat still in my hand! I must get rid of it.) *Turns and goes* [quickly] *to small table near entrance door. Puts down hat.*	*Turns and goes* [moderately] *toward her room.*
(*Aside*) What manners! *Turns* [quickly] (If she leaves now, all is lost!) But. . .	(I must not cry 'til I close the door! I must not cry 'til I close the door! I must not cry 'til I close the door!) *Turns back* [quickly] *at the door and faces Germont.*
(Mistaken? Not at all!) He plans to give you all he owns!	You are mistaken! (That is not true!)
(There is something funny here.)	So far he has not dared. I would refuse.

Father Germont	Violetta

Looks around [slowly]. (What about this house and the gardens? Why, that rug in the hallway must have cost at least a thousand.)

Returns [moderately] *to table.* (I will have to tell him about the money. Let's hope he does not say anything to Alfredo. Yes, this inventory will do!) *Picks up the paper from the table.*

Still, all this elegance . . .

(What's this? A trick of some sort? No, I don't think so. She's not that kind.)

This document is confidential, but you may see it.

Goes [moderately] *to Violetta and takes paper. Then walks to below couch, takes out pince-nez and unfolds paper.*

Goes [moderately] *to Germont with the paper. Then returns to the upstage chair and watches Germont over her shoulder.*

(Let's see. An inventory and order to sell. Yes, that is the official form. Aha! Three diamond rings. One at three thousand, the others at two thousand.)

(This should convince him. After all, it's not his fault he's so provincial and prejudiced. He walks just like Alfredo. How sweet that is!

Glances at Violetta. (I wonder if the tax man here knows about this. Two carriages at . . . well, well. Four horses. I see . . . Cashmere shawls . . . eight hundred . . .) *Turns* [quickly] *toward Violetta.*

Yes, yes. Keep on reading. . . . Imagine thinking that I would let Alfredo pay for the villa! Unfortunately, it's only too understandable!)

Heaven what is this? You are selling everything you own?

Nods her head without turning.

Turns away [moderately], *puts away the pince-nez, and refolds paper.*
What a pity your past is so against you!
Turns [slowly] *toward Violetta.*

(He can see for himself!)

Turns to face Germont and backs up slightly. (The past? It seems years ago.)

(Dead? Is she really so naive? It *is* a pity! I must tell her about Blanche. Strange. She reminds me of Blanche's mother when she was a bride.)

The past is dead. Now that I love Alfredo, the good Lord has erased it . . .

Goes [moderately] *toward Germont.*
With my repentance . . .
Walks [slowly] *slightly away from Germont.*

These are noble feelings . . .

(Oh, thank God, thank God! Now all is well. He understands; he will accept me. We will be friends!)

(What shall I do with this inventory?)
Goes [moderately] *to Violetta.*

Turns and goes [moderately] *to Germont.*

Father Germont

Violetta

And since you have these feelings,
Lets go of the inventory.
I must ask you to make a sacrifice.
(What eyes! Mon Dieu! No wonder
Alfredo's in love with her! Still, she
seems kind and will understand our
position. I had better take off these
gloves.)

Takes off gloves.

Walks [slowly] *toward table.*
(I must tell her about Blanche.)
I'm here as Alfredo's father to ask
you for the future and happiness of
my two children!

(Please let me tell you.)

Sits down [slowly]. *Puts gloves on
table and leans back.*
Heaven has sent me a daughter lovely
and pure as an angel . . . If Alfredo
fails to come back to his home and
family . . .

Leans forward [moderately], *stopping
Violetta from interrupting him.*
(Please, let me finish.)
The young and loving fellow, whose
bride she was to be, now will break
the tie that made them both so
happy.

*Disturbed by Violetta's frown, gets
up.*

Do not turn their blossoming love
into sorrow . . .

How sweet your words sound to me!
(Poor dear. So embarrassed about the
inventory. Here, I'll take it.)
Takes paper unnoticeably.
(Oh, God, I knew it!) *Backs away*
[quickly] *a step or two.*

Oh no! Be silent. You'll ask for
something dreadful!
Turns and walks [quickly] *toward
table.*
I knew it . . . I was expecting you . . .
I was much too happy!
Sits down [slowly] *on downstage
chair with her back to Germont.*

(I must not cry!)
(What does he mean?) *Turns*
[quickly] *toward Germont, and puts
inventory on table.*
Your two children?
Motions Germont to sit down.

(Could it be that Alfredo is married?
No! What's the matter with me? I
am completely confused. Of course,
it's his sister. Alfredo spoke about
her . . . But what's all this got to do
with a sacrifice?)
Gestures [slowly] *as if about to say
something.*

(Very well, but explain yourself.)
Leans back [slowly] *to listen.*
(What business is this of theirs?
Those dreadful provincial hypocrites,
they do want their pound of flesh!
Fine happiness she'll have with that
sort.) *Turns away* [slowly] *frowning.*
(Bigoted vultures! So that's the sacrifice they want! Very well, we will pretend to separate; we will give these
fine provincials their temporary satisfaction!)

Father Germont   Violetta

*Goes slightly to right, talking more
to himself than Violetta.*
Do not turn their blossoming love in-
to sorrow . . .
Backs up, turning to Violetta and   (This solution should take care of
goes [slowly] around chair to above   everything!)
table.
Please, don't let your heart . . .   (We'll separate for a month or so . . .
Don't let it resist my pleading!   why am I so nervous?)
(I think I have convinced her. Let's   *Gets up and turns slightly to left.*
hope so.)   Yes, I understand . . . For a while
(No, *not* "for a while.")   . . . *Turns and goes [moderately]*
Shaking his head, goes [moderately]   *toward couch.*
in a clockwise semicircle to below   Alfredo and I will separate . . . It
table.   will be painful for me . . .
(No, no, that will not do at all!) . . .   *Backs up, turning to Germont.*
That is not what I demand . . .   But . . . Heaven!

                                             Backs away [quickly].
                                             What more do you want? I have
Facing Violetta, shakes his head.   offered much. . . .
And yet, it's not enough!   *Goes [quickly] toward Germont.*
With an emphatic gesture.   You want me to give him up forever?
It's necessary!   *Backs away [quickly].*
(It will hurt, but if she loves Alfredo   Ah, no! Never! . . .
as much as I think she does, she will   *Turns away from Germont and goes*
have to admit that it is the only   *[quickly].*
way!)   No, never!
                                             to upstage right where she stands,
                                             weeping.

Obviously, some of the thought sequences given to Germont and
Violetta cannot be completed within the time allotted to them when this
scene is sung and acted at the correct musical speed. At the very beginning, for instance, when Germont reveals himself as Alfredo's father, Violetta's stream of thoughts cannot possibly be fitted into the short time
(barely two seconds) which elapses before Germont's harsh rejection stops
her dead in her tracks. But it must be remembered that these thoughts are
not to be spoken or sung with the music; they convey Violetta's mental
state, her total feelings at this moment. It may take many words to describe them, but such states explode all at once, in a fraction of a second.
Surprise, confusion, and a desire to welcome her future father-in-law and
to be welcomed by him all crowd together in one composite emotion.

The main purpose of this preparatory exercise is to saturate the performers, to flood them, so to speak, with the concerns of Germont and Violetta, so as to leave no place in their minds for any other technical or personal ideas.

Many singers are afraid of the effect of strong emotions on their vocal production. "Suppose I should get all choked up when I start pleading with Father Germont," a soprano might say to me. "How will I sing? I'll just fall to pieces, vocally!" But strong emotions rarely stop people from speaking. In the play Marguerite Gautier still speaks at this point, and in the opera Violetta still sings. "If you *cannot* sing," I tell the singer, "then your technique is faulty." Verdi knew better than almost anyone what emotions do to people. He was aware that strong feelings affect the breath, and he wrote his vocal lines accordingly. He realized that in the section which worried my soprano, Violetta is so upset that she cannot sing without taking many extra breaths. Notice that her sentences are broken up into short phrases separated by sobs. Instead of:

> If I told you how I love him, you would realize I can't leave him.
> I have no one but Alfredo to protect me and to love me.*

Verdi writes:

> If I told you . . . how I love him . . . you would realize—
> I can't leave him . . . I have no one . . . but Alfredo . . .
> to protect me—and to love me.

The tone of Violetta's voice must also change accordingly. We must feel that she is close to tears. Far from interfering with the soprano's performance, her emotional involvement should help her to arrive at the most suitable vocal sound for this particular moment. This is precisely where her vocal technique should pay off. If she permits her feelings to constrict her throat, they will certainly choke her, just as she feared. But if she sees to it that her emotional excitement does not affect her vocal apparatus, this added energy should help, not hinder her. There is no doubt but that this interplay of emotions and technique varies with every performer. Some singers prefer to remain relatively "cool" while others can "let themselves go" almost to the point of hysteria. But to assume (as some performers do) that feelings have no place in performing is to deprive oneself quite unnecessarily of an immensely valuable artistic force.

Another worry may disturb singers at this point. "If I am to think and feel all this and to follow all these stage directions you are giving me," they ask, "then what about my individual artistic contribution? Won't I behave just like a marionette whose strings are being pulled by the stage director?" The answer to this question is an unequivocal No. The stage director *must* organize all the basic theatrical arrangements just as the author and composer organize the words and music. Singers are not wor-

---

ried over the fact that they are asked to memorize words, notes, durations, dynamics, and tunes which are notated in the score. They know that the better they memorize them, the more of themselves—their own voices, phrasing, and interpretation—they will be able to superimpose on all these words and notes. After all, the Violetta-Germont scene is sung by all sopranos and baritones pretty much as it is notated, and yet the differences in interpretation are much more important than the resemblances in words and notes. In spite of all notational identities, there are singers who make us feel that we are hearing this scene for the first time, perhaps more beautifully than we had ever imagined it to be.

In the same way, gifted singing actors and actresses can contribute infinitely more to a role by their physical appearance and charm, their magnetism, psychological understanding, and believable humanity than a stage director could possibly suggest to them in hundreds of rehearsals. For this reason, in describing Violetta's and Germont's thoughts, feelings, and actions, I have avoided any indications as to how all this should be done. I prefer to omit such words as "joyfully" or "half-ashamed" or "angrily" because an action is executed differently by every singer. I have seen Violettas whose "half-ashamed" reference to their repentance made tears come to my eyes; others left me cold. The specific detail of an action should come from a singer's own highly personal artistry. The operatic stage director can free the singer from the concern of what to think, where to go, when to react, and at what speed to perform an action, just as the author and the composer free him from the necessity of inventing words and tunes, so that he can then devote his energies to making his own unique contribution to a given role. It is this highly individual contribution that constitutes a singer's creativity, and which has identified certain roles with specific singing actors. For example, the words, notes, actions, costumes, and sets of *Boris Godunov* were pretty much as they are today, but Chaliapin *was* Godunov, and to us who have seen him, all those who have performed the role since Chaliapin seem little more than feeble imitators.

In summary, to develop a personal contribution, a singer must first steep himself in the character's words, notes, thoughts, feelings, and stage movements to the point that they become automatic. Far from making him into a marionette, all this preparatory work will free him and give him a chance to become a memorable dramatic personality. Likewise, the stage director, by doing the necessary background research and by telling the singer what to do and when to do it, can free him to apply his personal touch to a role and may even turn an unimaginative singer into an effective dramatic artist.

As necessary as it is for a singer to understand an operatic situation, think the characters' thoughts, and feel their emotions, it takes more

than this to make him an actor. Acting begins only when this understanding, these thoughts and these feelings, are clearly communicated,
when they are visibly projected to the audience. Operatic characters must
come alive so that the audience can read their thoughts and sympathize
with their feelings. In order to accomplish this, singers must develop the
muscular, physical side of their acting and must master the techniques of
the proscenium stage.

The enormous importance of these muscular and stage skills was
made vividly clear to me many years ago at one of my summer workshops. A visiting stage director had expressed the wish to teach a group of
students an entire act of Verdi's *Simon Boccanegra*. He said that he had
studied this opera very carefully and would appreciate the opportunity
to develop its dramatic and psychological subtleties in a new and different
style of presentation. I was greatly impressed with the man's obvious dedication to this unusual project and together we selected suitable vocalists
with whom he then worked for several hours every day. From time to
time I would hear the most enthusiastic reports from the students of his
group and when, after about four weeks of rehearsing, I was told that the
entire act was ready to be shown in one of our public recitals, I was eager
to see just what had been accomplished.

It is sad to report that the performance was unbelievably dull and
meaningless. The music was sung quite accurately, but the faces of the
singers were blank, their bodies passive, and their behavior gave no hint
of the violent conflicts that permeate the turbulent plot of the opera.
To make matters worse, the performers constantly got in each other's
way, and at times it was actually difficult to see them. At one point a
seemingly crucial action remained completely incomprehensible because
the executant's back was turned to the audience. I half guessed that he
was pouring poison into a water pitcher, but I could not really tell what
he was doing. The whole thing looked in many ways like a preliminary
musical run-through of the sort that is often done before any dramatic
or staging ideas are discussed.

Remembering the countless hours of practice and the favorable comments of the students, I was extremely curious to find out just what had
been going on in these daily sessions. Questioning (as diplomatically as I
could) a few of the singers, I discovered to my surprise that they had
obtained an amazing knowledge of the most obscure details of this opera
and an extraordinary understanding of the psychological ramifications of
the plot. A veritable psychoanalytic study had been performed on each of
the personages of the drama, and their most hidden impulses had been
laid bare. Indeed, I was so fascinated with this approach that I regretted
not having attended all those rehearsals myself. The only trouble was that
all this precious information remained solidly locked up in the minds of
the singers, and the audience that witnessed the performance remained
just as solidly unaware of all these compelling dramatic insights.

Making thoughts and emotions visible

This experience was a most convincing proof that thoughts and emotions have no theatrical existence unless they are made visible, and that this visibility can be accomplished *only* by muscular movements which are seen by the audience. The muscles must move, and the actor must be placed in such a manner that the audience can see them move. It is therefore essential that the actor's facial expressions, gestures, and bodily movements be developed to the full.

While the importance of these muscular skills cannot be exaggerated, it is singularly ungraceful and in some ways almost ridiculous, to describe the details of muscular activities in words. To begin with, we are confronted with an overwhelming number of possible expressions of the human body, of the eyes, face, head, shoulders, arms, legs, and the torso; of postural changes involved in standing, bending, sitting, kneeling, crouching, embracing, bowing, curtseying, and lying down; in walking, backing up, turning, walking up and down steps, falling down, getting up, or dancing. In addition there are complex activities such as wrestling, fist-fighting, fencing, tumbling, acrobatics, and riding on horseback. Finally, one should not omit problems connected with costumes: the handling of hoop skirts, swords, long trains, and high turbans. Obviously, all these problems cannot be discussed here. Describing how one tumbles, rides on horseback, fences, or sits down in a hoop skirt is quite out of the question. These things—and to a certain extent this is true of all muscular activities—can be learned only by doing them. Although individual faults and mannerisms are usually the most pressing matters a teacher has to deal with, these will also have to be disregarded. The best we can hope to achieve here is a short discussion of the most important muscular problems and the most common faults encountered in young opera singers.

Dramatic expressiveness

Few people realize how little they normally do with the muscles of their bodies. In the process of growing up, they tend to immobilize their faces, arms, and torsos along with the neutralizing of their feelings. At the beginning of this chapter I defined the expert actor as one who can communicate to his audience a great variety of mental and emotional states. To do this he obviously has to depend upon a correspondingly wide repertoire of muscular possibilities. It is surprising, however, how limited these possibilities are in many adults. In their daily lives they use few changes of facial expression, gesture, and torso movement. For their ordinary needs these may be sufficient, but they are quite inadequate for the purpose of acting.

Operatic acting has become proverbial for its artificiality and stiffness. Deplorable as these qualities are, I find the dreadful monotony of many singers' faces and bodies even more objectionable. It is not their fault, of course. Nobody would dream of letting a person sing opera without first training his voice, but acting opera with untrained muscles is considered perfectly normal. When a stage performer is forced to rely on only one posture, two facial expressions, and three gestures, there is no wonder that he keeps repeating them over and over. In terms of dramatic expressiveness, such an actor can be compared to a singer attempting an important operatic role with a vocal range of only five or six semitones.

The inexpressive facial mask, so common among singers, is the result of long years of enforced inactivity. A little child is fascinated by the rubber-like flexibility of his face. He looks at himself in the mirror and indulges in the most outrageous contortions of his mouth, nose, eyes, forehead, and cheeks. He sticks out his tongue, purses his lips, and almost dislocates his jaw by twisting it in every conceivable direction. One could not wish for a better method of developing potential dramatic expressiveness. But all this stops as soon as his mother happens to catch him. What was begun by the mother is later completed by the cosmetics manufacturers, with their sinister hints of the dire consequences of a single blemish on one's complexion. While this persuasive advertising barrage is aimed mostly at girls, there is evidence that it also has its effects on the masculine population.

The best remedy is to return to childhood and to make faces—and never mind the wrinkles! Young women must be made to realize that there is nothing more beautiful than a mouth wreathed in smiles, a disdainfully curled lip, a brow knitted in concentration, or a nose puckered in amusement. Of course, one does not purposely curl, knit, wreathe, or pucker one's facial muscles to give the impression of disdain, concentration, or amusement. One simply makes certain of the availability of these muscles so that when one is concentrating or feels disdainful or amused, the facial machinery is there to reflect these mental states and make them visible.

One does not practice dramatic effects. Instead, one builds muscles by flexing and contracting them, by lifting and extending them, and it does not matter whether one looks in the mirror or not.

This approach shows the singer the general way to build, train, and, to coin a word, *versatilize* all the muscles of his body, not just the facial ones. To awaken and educate his arms, a singer can imagine any number of useful exercises. He can start, for instance, by keeping his left arm behind his back, and then, holding the back of his neck with his right hand, lift his right elbow high in the air. He can reverse this position and then find dozens of other ways of rotating, bending, and lifting his arms singly, or of interlacing them in various combinations, thus gradually learning to overcome the pitiful monotony of the symmetrical, robot-like gyrations known as operatic gestures.

Muscular movements of the face and arms produce immediate and obvious effects. The audience sees an arched eyebrow, a smile, a raised arm, or a balled fist and responds directly to the thought and the feeling behind it. No less important, however, are the more hidden activities of the muscles that control firmness in the joints or sustained muscular tensions.

Normally, our bodies function so smoothly that we are not aware of the many complicated joint fixations that are needed to keep us standing erect, but should we suddenly relax our knees, hips, waist, and shoulders, the body would at once collapse like an empty sack. Fortunately, for the purposes of dramatic expression, we have complete voluntary control over all our joints; we can relax them as we wish or stiffen them until they are tightly locked. A baritone portraying the lame, hunchbacked Tonio or Rigoletto can learn to keep the joints of his knees, hips, and shoulders permanently locked, while a touch of stiffness in the sacroiliac joint will help considerably toward the "aging" of characters such as Marcellina and Dr. Bartolo in *The Marriage of Figaro* or Benoit in *La Bohème*.

Besides possessing control over our joints, we are able to make the fleshy parts of our body harder or softer at will. The leg, thigh, buttocks, upper and lower arm can all be made to respond to an adjustment of muscle-tone, and this ability helps the actor with some of his most difficult assignments. For instance, complete control of the firmness of the joints and muscle-tone is essential for actresses who are to play such trouser roles as Cherubino, Siebel, and Octavian. In a woman's somewhat more relaxed knee, the gentler fixations of her hip, waist, and shoulder joints, as well as in the comparative softness of her flesh, lie the secret of her shorter steps and pleasant undulating walk. The man's knee is stiffer, causing him to swing his whole leg from a correspondingly firmer hip, and there is a lack of "give" in his waist and shoulder and a general hardness of the flesh. It is the combination of these qualities that we see in his longer stride and his muscular, athletic appearance. While he can purposely make his appearance more feminine by reducing the fixation of his joints and the hardness of his muscle tone, a woman by an opposite process can achieve the appearance of a man. Women who approach male roles "from the outside" rarely succeed; they may put on trousers and prance around in an exaggerated imitation of the masculine stride, but they still give the impression of women wearing trousers. Working "from inside," however, an actress need not worry about her appearance or indulge in foolish exaggerations; to acquire the habit of a more firmly fixated knee, hip, and waist, and the harder muscular tone of the man's body, she must *feel* like a man, and as Cherubino, or Octavian, practice this total sensation until her masculine appearance is independent of the clothes she is wearing.

In order to develop the control of fixations and bodily hardness and softness, I would recommend exercises of a general, muscle-building type, along the same principles as the "making of faces" described earlier. Simple ways of learning to feel looseness or firmness in joints and the flesh include skipping a rope, jumping on one foot, punching the body in playful boxing, swinging arms and legs without flexing the elbow or the knee, weaving the knees, hips, and shoulders in and out, and even attempting artificial wobbliness in order to cultivate versatility in muscular control and a quick recognition of various instantly available muscular sensations.

One should aim at reaching a point at which such mental commands as "I am vigorous," "I am lame," "I am an old woman," "I am a young man," or even "I feel voluptuous," or "I am frozen with horror," would immediately bring about the appropriate changes in limb, torso, and feature.

I pointed out earlier that thoughts and emotions have no theatrical existences unless they are made visible by means of muscular movements. The reverse is equally true: muscular movements are convincing only when they are extensions of thoughts and feelings. Unfortunately, muscular actions can generate from other sources, and much of what passes for acting in opera houses, instead of arising from the mind and the emotions, is rather an accidental outgrowth of the physical effort of singing.

It is easy to make fun of conventional operatic behavior, but what is not sufficiently appreciated is that besides being an actor, the opera singer is also a hard-working athlete. Singing with orchestral accompaniment in large theaters is arduous physical exercise, and it cannot help but interfere with the simultaneous execution of other muscular tasks.

Imagine a person who is visible only from the waist up. Suppose that while indulging in a normal dinner conversation, he would at the same time be asked to move his legs vigorously, performing motions of swimming and occasionally kicking a football. Such a person would have quite a time acting naturally and refraining from sympathetic contortions of his arms and facial muscles. The analogy between our imaginary dinner companion and an opera singer is not too far-fetched. The weird gyrations performed on many opera stages are not arm gestures in the ordinary sense of the word. They are rather visible extensions of the vigorous efforts connected with operatic singing. Over the years some of these sympathetic contortions have become part of the tradition associated with "grand opera," but there is no reason to attach any expressive or artistic value to these awkward outgrowths of a muscular machinery, which, like most machinery in the arts, is only admirable when it is invisible. The recent operatic trend toward a more "natural" behavior has led to a desire to do away with the old-fashioned operatic gesture, but unfortunately the remedy is often hardly less objectionable than the former disease. Today one constantly sees singers who "girdle," that is, stiffen their hands and attach them to their thighs while singing. These rigid fingers pathetically pressing below the hips are unmistakable symptoms of the familiar operatic tensions, and the fact that the energy is now applied toward the body rather than away from it makes these "anti-gestures" neither more expressive nor more attractive.

Most performers are not aware of the existence or the dangers of sympathetic tensions and contortions. They are usually quite surprised when involuntary movements of their arms, wrists, and fingers are brought to their attention. It is a good idea, therefore, to have singers occasionally look at their hands and arms while they sing. This can be done best by asking them to put their hands on top of the piano in musical rehearsals, and it is quite astonishing how much unconscious twitching, cramping, and beating of time can be observed while the hands are in this position. Once these unwelcome contortions are brought to the singer's attention, he develops an awareness of the problem, and this is the first step toward the ultimate goal: the ability to sing and act at the same time.

Besides being an actor and a vocalist, the opera singer is also a musician, and this adds a still further complication to his task of achieving dramatic credibility. Certain technical problems connected with the functions of the eye and the head, which pose only minor difficulties in the spoken drama, acquire a much greater significance in opera.

The task of overcoming these technical problems is greatly facilitated if the singing actor realizes that, from the visual point of view, his contacts with other characters onstage, as well as with inanimate objects, can be pitched to any of these three degrees of intensity: direct rapport, indirect rapport, and disengagement. Direct rapport results from eye contact. Indirect rapport occurs when the actor, standing (or sitting) with his back to a partner (or an object), turns his head toward him without necessarily looking at him or seeing him. Disengagement, as the name implies, occurs when the actor gets rid of an object or disassociates himself from his partner, when he walks away from him, when he does not want to see him, listen to him, address him, or be heard by him.

Disengagement rarely presents problems, but matters relating to rapport are not simple, and, especially in opera, are seldom treated with the attention they deserve. Because direct rapport is largely a matter of eye focus, and indirect rapport is just as closely related to the position of the head, our review of the physical side of acting would be incomplete without discussing the correct use of the eye and the head.

The eye

The eye is the most eloquent of the human body's expressive mech-
anisms. It is also the one that is often the most neglected. Since the average person rarely has a chance to observe his own eyes, he imagines that
no one else is paying much attention to them. The eyes may or may not
be the "window of the soul," but they are the one part of the anatomy
that everyone watches closely both on and off stage.

Who has not been amused by noticing the surreptitious looks that
men give to the legs and figures of pretty women who happen to cross
their paths? The poor innocent lechers imagine that if they peek out
of the corners of their eyes, or look away quickly, or pretend not to look,
they can keep their looking secret. In the same way, many well-meaning
opera singers and conductors mistakenly believe that the audience will
not notice that the baton is watched by means of "peripheral vision." It
is true that when peripheral vision is used we often cannot tell whether
the singer is or is not watching the baton, but we most certainly can
tell that he is *not* watching the girl whom he worships, or the opponent
whom he is fighting, or the picture he supposedly admires, or the letter
he presumably reads.

If I were asked to give just one piece of advice about stage behavior
and to pick the one item I consider the most valuable, I would unhesitatingly say: "Look into the eyes of your partners; not around, or over,
or through your partners, but directly and unashamedly straight into
their eyes!" I use the word "unashamedly" because there is something very
personal, intimate, and at first rather embarrassing about looking straight
into one's partner's eyes, particularly when the partner is a young, attractive, and not too familiar member of the opposite sex. And
by looking I do not mean just giving a quick glance, but keeping one's
eyes locked with those of the girl or the fellow. I suspect that it's this
feeling of unconscious embarrassment that keeps so many opera singers
from looking into the eyes of their colleagues.

Somewhere I read that in the early eighteenth century operatic
actors were not supposed to come into bodily contact with each other
and that when a soprano once accidentally touched her fellow performer,
the startled gentleman fainted dead away from sheer shock! A somewhat
similar convention seems to have persisted to our day in regard to eye
contact. Of course, things have been improving immensely in recent years,
but at one time the situation was so grim that I wondered if there might
not be a secret clause in singers' contracts specifically forbidding them to
look at each other.

Italians quite rightly praise *l'occhio che parla*, the "eloquent" eye; less
well-known, but no less important, is the concept of the "listening" eye.

David Belasco* has this to say about it: "The power to listen well on the part of an actor or actress has a greater effect upon the heart and imagination of an audience than any words written by a poet. I have always found that the men and women who have come under my direction and listened well with their eyes have invariably been the ones who have climbed to the heights of their profession."

Although close eye contact is of paramount importance in relationships demanding direct rapport, there are many situations where it is completely out of place. Generally speaking, characters who share strong emotions—lovers or mortal enemies, for example—should use direct eye contact. But there are many relationships which seem to demand a mixture of the direct and indirect forms of communication. Servants, for example, must watch their master carefully, while he may prefer to communicate with them indirectly. The same situation exists with humble supplicants or admirers and the indifferent or proud objects of their quests.

Quite aside from questions of rapport, I should like to make two other observations on the use and misuse of the eyes.

I do not recommend closing the eyes or making them invisible by looking down on the ground. I know that there are fine actors and drama teachers who advocate this invisible, lowered eye, believing that in certain situations it is very advantageous. On the basis of my own experience as an operatic stage director, I still maintain that in an operatic production the lowered eye is not an effective acting instrument; everything that one can express with closed or lowered eyes can be expressed more tellingly with open eyes. Naturally, I do not include weeping spells or embraces and other situations where the face must be hidden or the head buried in one's arms.

As my last observation on the use and misuse of the eyes, I would like to draw attention to a certain highly concentrated, glassy stare peculiar to opera singers. There are times when their attention and their eyes focus on a spot just a few inches in front of their noses. After puzzling for years over this mysterious ocular phenomenon, I finally figured out what it meant. The thing at which singers are looking intently is the vocal tone itself, which seems to materialize in front of them. Perhaps watching the tone in this manner helps singers to "place" it correctly, but as a vehicle for dramatic communication I do not recommend it.

The head

The position of the head in relation to the shoulders and the rest of the body is of the greatest dramatic significance. Most young singers who come to study opera dramatics with me need corrective exercises be-

* *The Theatre Through Its Stage Door* (New York: Harper & Brothers, 1919).

cause they habitually let their heads hang in front of their bodies, instead of holding them high and above their shoulders. When they walk they look like beachcombers, and when they stand still we call them "droopheads." Of course, this posture is not necessarily wrong or bad. If the script calls for a beachcomber or a droophead—I say script because I cannot think of an opera score specifying these characters—then this is the right attitude. But otherwise the singer looks very much out of character.

The trouble is not in the head, but in the posture, specifically in the sagging chest which in turn is caused by weak or lazy muscles in the region of the abdomen. To straighten the head, lift your chest and draw in your chin. This at first may feel rather uncomfortable, and it may be necessary to un-stiffen the neck (by moving the head gently from side to side) and also to check that the shoulders are not lifted, or hunched, or thrown back unnecessarily. Sympathetic muscular contractions are to be expected and patiently eliminated.

To check if your head is really above your shoulders, do a so-called "chin-chest" test. Put the little finger of your right hand on the top of the middle section of your breast bone and extend your right thumb until it touches your chin, which is now gently drawn in. The distance separating the tips of your thumb and little finger should now equal that between C and G on the piano keyboard. In this position, with heads and chests high, men look much more masculine and girls ten times more beautiful.

The moment I start manipulating (or even talking about) the chin, which is part of the jaw, I am poaching on the preserve of the voice teacher, and here the only sensible precept to the singer is: "Keep your head as high as your voice teacher will allow." In return for my cooperative attitude in connection with the jaw, I request singers to ask their voice teachers to cooperate with us stage directors in another most important matter affecting the singer's head. It is immensely helpful if teachers train their pupils to sing also with their heads turned slightly at an angle over their shoulders. It is not difficult, anyone can do it, but nobody does it because all the vocalizing and all the singing that goes on in vocal studies is always done with the head at a right angle to the shoulders. As a result, every time the singer is asked to turn his head while singing, he turns his shoulders and, with them, his torso and legs. The singer has become so used to this four-square approach to the stage that he turns his shoulders to parallel the footlights not only when he sings, but as soon as he possibly can, after each single stage movement. He will obediently turn and walk in whatever direction he is told to go, but as soon as he gets to his destination his shoulders turn, and he faces the audience again with his chest, shoulders, legs, and all. One would think there was an iron needle in his shoulders which was pulled by some powerful magnet to make him return to this cursed right-left shoulder line. When requested to leave his shoulders as they are, he immediately objects with: "Must I really sing into the wings?" When he is told that it is possible to turn his head and face the audience without necessarily dragging his whole body along with his face, he seems amazed. He is further astonished to discover that singing in this new position is not one iota more difficult than in his accustomed steel-necked stance.

The enormous advantage of a slight head-over-the-shoulder turn is that it permits a singer to maintain an indirect, but highly effective rapport with a partner who is standing behind him. With his body turned somewhat to the left, the singer can, by turning his head slightly to the right, remain in obvious communication with an upstage partner and yet show his entire face to the audience.

I wish that voice teachers would insist that their pupils vocalize and sing in more than one single-angle shoulder-head position. This alone would help them become much more versatile and effective singing actors.

Techniques of the proscenium stage

One would imagine that anyone wishing to become a competent actor would try to become familiar with standard procedures of stage positions, movement, and the highlighting of dramatic actions. The student would analyze examples of stage behavior as practiced by the best artists in order to learn the underlying principles of grouping, regrouping, and theatrical business in general. As in all other fields, he would wish to profit from the accumulated experience of the past. Such a wish, however, is not easily fulfilled.

Mapping the stage

Because the field of directing opera had no literature, very little terminology, and no generally accepted notation, it soon became clear to me that what was needed—first and foremost—was a system of notating stage directions, a method of mapping the acting area of the stage to indicate quickly and precisely the location of every piece of scenery, every prop, and the position of every singer. In the map I finally created, as in all maps, north is "up," toward the top of the page, and south is "down." To conform with theatrical parlance, *downstage* (abbreviated as D) is toward the audience, *upstage* (U) is away from it, and west and east are called *right* and *left* (abbreviated as R and L), but these are *always* from the point of view of the actor facing the audience. In other words, the western half of my stage is permanently its right side and the eastern half is always its left side, no matter whether what is described is scenery, props, or the position and movements of the actors.* The basic outline of my stage in relation to the audience can be seen in Diagram 1–1, where the position of the proscenium opening is shown by appropriate symbols, and the location of the stage wings is indicated by the letters LW (for left wing) and RW (for right wing).

Diagram 1–1

The acting area of this stage is divided, as shown in Diagram 1–2, into eighteen squares. The squares nearest the center of the stage are called Right Center and Left Center (RC and LC); as we move away from the center of the stage, the squares become Right B and Left B (RB and LB), and then Right A and Left A (RA and LA). This A-B-C sequence is easy to remember. The squares on the side of the stage are A's (RA and LA), those closer to the center are B's (RB and LB), and those in the center are the C's (RC and LC). The row of squares nearest the audience is 1, the next one back is 2, and the last one is 3. This conforms to the usual theatrical expression, where playing "in one" means acting in the lane nearest the footlights. By combining the letters of each square with the number of its row, each obtains an individual designation. A stage direction such as "Rosina sits down in an armchair in RB2; Figaro enters through the main door in LA3 and goes to RC2" combines simplicity with great precision.

* There are no standard rules here and I, for one, find it very confusing to read descriptions of scenery as it appears from the auditorium while the acting directions for walking or turning are given from the point of view of the actors. A stage remark such as "The main entrance is on stage right. Rosina enters from the right and runs left to the main entrance" makes one feel uncomfortable, to say the least!

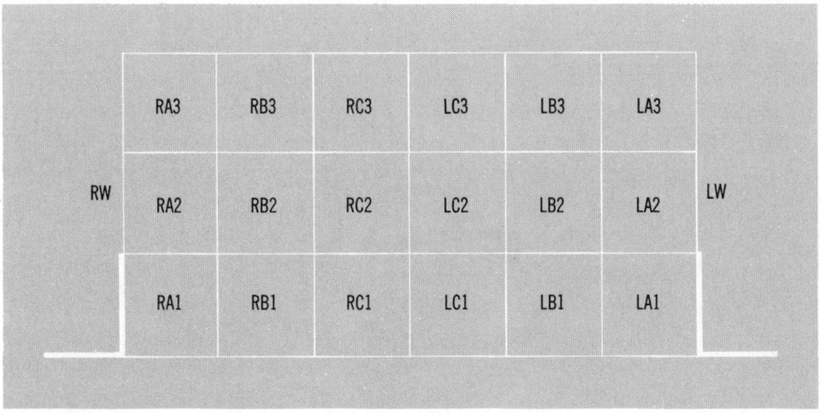

Diagram 1–2

By attaching numbers and letters to the horizontal and vertical lines (Diagram 1–3), we acquire an additional set of coordinates. The line separating row 1 from row 2 becomes line 12; the next line, the one between 2 and 3, is called 23. For the sake of consistency, the line nearest the audience is called 01; the one farthest from it is line 34. The lines that run up and down are labeled on the same principle as the lateral lines (Diagram 1–4). Since the center line separates the RC and LC squares, it now becomes known as CC. The lines on stage right—RBC, RAB, and RWA—are named after the squares that adjoin them: line RBC lies between the B and C columns on the R side of the stage. Lines RAB and RWA get their names the same way. So do the lines LBC, LAB, and LWA, which are located on stage left.

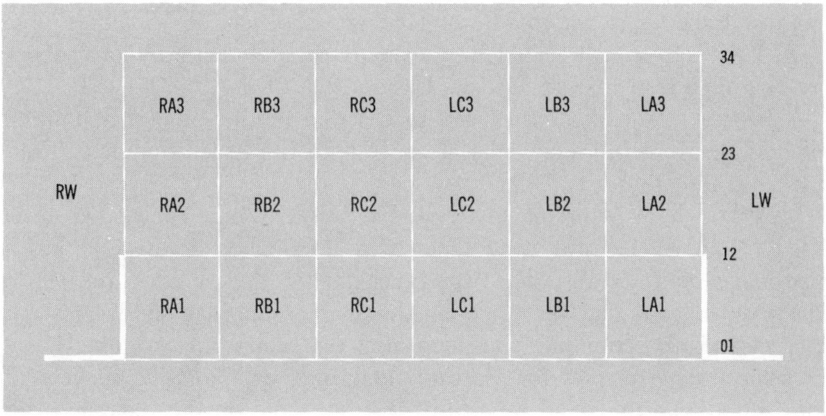

Diagram 1–3

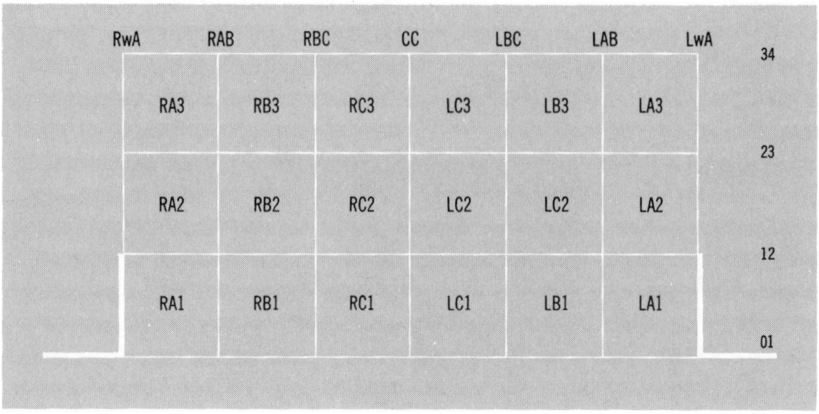

RwA	RAB	RBC	CC	LBC	LAB	LwA	
							34
RA3	RB3	RC3	LC3	LB3	LA3		
							23
RA2	RB2	RC2	LC2	LC2	LA2		
							12
RA1	RB1	RC1	LC1	LB1	LA1		
							01

Diagram 1–4

This network of identifiable lines is particularly valuable in describing the position of scenery. The director need not rely on general and vague terms, but can show the actors the exact location of walls, windows, doors, steps, platforms, and all other items of visible theatrical equipment. On page 27 of this chapter, for example, Violetta's room was described as having "three doors: the main entrance downstage right, the door into Violetta's room upstage left, and the French doors leading into the garden in upstage center. The couch is located at the right, and the table with two chairs is at the left." By using our stage diagram with the names of the squares and lines, we can now substitute a much more precise description: The U stage wall runs along 34 and has French doors that straddle CC; the R wall runs from the intersection of 34 and RBC to the intersection of RWA and 12; the L wall runs from the intersection of 34 and LAB to the intersection of 12 and LWA. The main entrance is in the middle of RA2 and the door to Violetta's room is in LA3. The couch is in RB2; it stands parallel to 12 and just above it. The table is in LB2 with chairs UR and DL of it.

Notice how easily I managed to describe the asymmetrical position of the lateral walls, a detail that I could not even have attempted to explain without these symbols.

Although diagrams of this type have not, to my knowledge, been used in opera, they are not unknown in the spoken drama. No less a personage than Goethe, who was in charge of the Weimar theater in the early 1800's, had his stage lined out in somewhat similar fashion and moved his actors like chessmen from one square to another. Useful as such a stage plan is for plotting, analyzing, and notating movement and actions, I strongly advise against painting lines on the stage floor for rehearsals. The singer must relate his activities and positions to other characters, or to properties; he should not be encouraged to allow his eyes or his mind to be occupied with the floor. When acting out the stage directions given earlier, Rosina need not be concerned with the fact that her chair is located in RB2. She sees the chair and sits down on it, no matter where it is placed. Figaro, who enters through the UL door, does not aim for a rectangle on the floor. He sees Rosina and goes to her left.

Placing and moving the characters

To show the placement of a character, I use a short line that illustrates the position of the actor's shoulders; two dots on one side of the line, representing the actor's eyes, show which way he is facing, and the first three letters of the character's name are added to identify him. Thus, "Figaro is facing DR" becomes:

Diagram 1–5

Indirect rapport, with its typical angle between the head and the shoulder line, can be notated by means of a slight change in the position of the dots that symbolize the eyes. Thus a notation such as:

shows that while Figaro is in direct rapport with Susanna, she is focusing her attention on him indirectly by singing or listening with her head (and her eyes) turned slightly over her right shoulder. Two characters can thus remain in indirect rapport with each other even though they stand back to back:

A forward walk is shown by an arrow pointing to the place where the actor is moving. The stage direction describes this forward movement as "going to" a person, object, or position.

Figaro goes DR to below* chair:

When a movement is to be made by backing,† a square arrow is used on the map and the stage direction describes the movement as "backing to."

Figaro backs UL to above table:

Turns that do not cause the actor to move out of his stage position are described as clockwise (Clw) and counterclockwise (Cclw). When the turn results in a slight change of location, it is described by letters that indicate the necessary movement of the shoulders.

RSF—right shoulder forward:

LSF—left shoulder forward:

---

* The terms "below" and "above" are preferable to "in front of" and "behind," which become confusing when an actor moves toward characters that are facing upstage.

† I find the term "backing" less ambiguous than "backing up." In describing stage movement, "up" always means away from the audience; "backing," however, can also be done toward the audience.

RSB—right shoulder back:

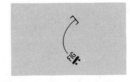

LSB—left shoulder back:

These turns are often extended into "going to" or "backing to" completely new locations.

Figaro turns RSF and goes
DL to below table:

Figaro turns LSF and goes
DR to above chair:

Figaro turns RSB and backs
UL to UL of table:

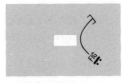

Figaro turns LSB and backs
UR to UL of chair

The last two moves are particularly valuable in situations where the actor must "take the stage" without sacrificing his facial visibility.

It is seldom that an actor is alone on an empty stage. As soon as another person or a piece of furniture is on the stage with him, the actor's position is seen in relation to the second person or object. Every singer should remember this and visualize himself as the spectator sees him, linked at all times to whatever other characters and objects are onstage.

In relation to actor A (or a prop represented by A) actor B can occupy any one of eight stage positions: UR, U, UL, R, L, DR, D, and DL:

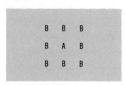

Disregarding for the moment the positions directly above and below, which present special problems, we can speak of three alignments from the R:

We also have three alignments from the L:

Depending upon whether B stands above, on the same level, or below A, we say that he has "taken" the stage, is "sharing" the stage, or has "given" the stage, respectively.

As long as the right-left relationship of A and B remains unaltered, fluctuations in their up-down positions—which occur when they take, share, or give the stage—are called changes in alignment. The moment that B passes above or below A (or vice versa) and reverses their right-left relationship, we speak of *regrouping,* and the act of passing to the other side of the partner (or object) we call a *crossing.* Abbreviating this term, we refer to crossing as "X-ing." The expression "A X's B" is equivalent to "A crosses *below* B." A crossing above a person or object is spelled out. Thus, Figaro goes DL, X-ing table to DL of it:

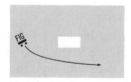

And Figaro goes L, X-ing above table to UL of it:

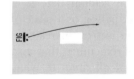

Finally, to pinpoint the moment when a given change of position is to occur, we add, near the shoulder line, a number that shows the singer the exact measure during which the movement indicated by the arrow should start. The notation shows that Figaro should start walking left in measure 47 of whatever musical number is being charted:

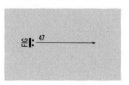

The sign X at the end of an arrow ──────────▶ is used to represent a character's freedom to turn in one or more directions before embarking on his next move. In the following example, Figaro, who goes down left in measure 47, can make several turns before proceeding to the right in measure 65:

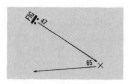

Having developed a method for notating stage movement, we are ready to deal with the special characteristics of the proscenium stage as it relates to operatic behavior.

Facing the audience

We do not behave on the stage as we do in real life. Some differences are only quantitative. For instance, because the audience watches us from a distance, we often have to make facial expressions more pronounced and gestures larger. In respect to positioning and movement, however, the adjustments are more fundamental. Because we are observed from only one direction on the proscenium stage, it is not easy to insure both visibility and proper highlighting. To make the action clear, all characters must be plainly seen, and special prominence must be given to important characters and activities. These considerations profoundly affect the singing actor's positions and movements, both when he is alone on stage and when he is in a group.

In ordinary life we do not give preference to any one direction. We do not face north rather than south or west rather than east. When singing on the proscenium stage, however, it is important not to turn away from the audience. The favored direction is therefore downstage.

Opera singers usually imagine that the reason for facing the audience is musical or acoustical. They are afraid that unless they sing straight out, their voices will not be heard to best advantage. This is not necessarily so. As we have all had ample opportunity to observe, acoustical effects can be very deceptive. It is fruitless to argue over the extent of vocal losses caused by departures from the "song recital" position, when the vocalist stands downstage center and faces the auditorium four-square. There is no need for such arguments. The best reason for showing one's face to the audience is that it is the most expressive part of the body. The simple, common-sense theatrical rule has always been: When an actor has important things to communicate, his face should be clearly visible. Since important communicative moments in opera are usually those when the actor is singing, the old rule has always been interpreted quite properly as: *Do not turn away from the audience while singing.* A few pages above I said that it was so often essential to look at one's partner. This is indeed true, and the singer must learn to find positions on the stage where he can do *both*: look at his partner and show his face to the audience.

The most obvious and comfortable position for this purpose is upstage and sufficiently to one side of the partner so as not to be obstructed by him. This brings us to the next rule of visibility on the proscenium stage: *You cannot be seen by those in the audience whom you cannot see.* This is known as the rule of sight-lines, and it is important to remember that the non-singing partner (if he stands downstage of you) cannot tell whether or not he is obstructing you. It is you, the singer (standing upstage), who must notice the obstruction and move further to one side to become clearly visible to everyone in the audience.

This basic position for singing and listening works well until the singing line is taken up by the other character. Then a realignment must take place or else the new singing character will be forced to turn his back on either the audience or his partner. One way out of this predicament, a method used extensively in duet situations, is to have the singing partner move downstage at the end of his lines and then turn to listen to his singing colleague. He thereby creates a favorable position for his partner, who in turn moves downstage when he finishes his sentence, and so on.

This alternating downward zigzag is very useful, but it comes to an abrupt end as soon as both partners reach the edge of the stage platform. It then becomes necessary to return to the upper section of the stage, a basic procedure known as *gaining depth* or *taking the stage.* During orchestral interludes the singer can safely turn his back on the audience and walk upstage, but while singing, or during short vocal rests, he cannot do this without "losing face." The most obvious alternative to walking upstage is backing up, or simply backing. Backing is something that people do infrequently and unwillingly in everyday life. It is a perfectly natural manner of walking, but it is not popular because it is unpleasant not to see where one is going. Nevertheless, backing is enormously useful on the proscenium stage. Because it is relatively unfamiliar, however, it must be practiced.

Not only must the singing actor learn how to back, but he must also review his habits of walking and turning. Since, by the age of three, most of us have completely mastered the art of getting from place to place, talking about it seems as pointless as analyzing how we breathe, an activity which we mastered even earlier. But just as breathing while singing is not at all the same as ordinary breathing, so changing position onstage is by no means identical with everyday walking. No one becomes an accomplished actor without practicing the muscular processes connected with keeping one's balance, walking, backing, and turning. Trying to describe these activities in words is hopelessly long-winded and cumbersome, if not impossible. I shall endeavor to point out the most common errors of stage behavior and movement, but for more effective and practical help, the student will have to turn to dramatic coaches who specialize in the teaching of characteristic theatrical movement and the correction of individual faults and mannerisms. Visual aids, such as instant replay television tapes, have also proven to be very revealing and useful.

Singing on stage

Before continuing with a more detailed discussion of operatic stage behavior, it is necessary to point out that its execution is intimately connected with vocal and musical techniques. The procedures recommended in this volume are not intended for the type of singer who is unable to produce good vocal tones unless he gets set, or stiffens into immobility; nor are they meant for those whose musical accuracy is totally dependent on visual cueing and continuous guiding by prompters and conductors.

A competent opera singer must be able to walk, back, or turn while singing, and in general to move freely without losing track of the music sung by his colleagues or played by the orchestra. Obviously, no singer would be wise to attempt, and no stage director to demand, complicated stage movements during passages that feature particularly taxing and tricky vocal or musical problems, but having worked with several thousand aspiring opera singers, I can vouch that relatively few of them are incapable of combining musical accuracy with freedom of movement. With those who lack the minimum musical machinery, it is useless to hope for anything approaching theatrical believability.

Assuming that a singer is flexible vocally and competent musically, he can claim to have mastered the techniques of the proscenium stage if: (a) he is able to move to any part of the stage without looking clumsy; (b) he does not obstruct the audience's view of his colleagues and knows how to avoid being obstructed either by them or by stage props; (c) he is familiar with several techniques for "taking" and "giving" the stage; and (d) he is aware of the traffic problems that arise in the process of regrouping and knows how to handle them.

One of the most disturbing things about many operatic productions is the general clumsiness of the singers. Much of this clumsiness originates in the orientation of the singer's torso and shoulders towards the audience. It is the same tendency that produces that "magnetic needle" habit we discussed earlier. When an actor whose shoulder line is parallel to the footlights starts walking to the right without first turning his torso in that direction, he is quite often tempted, in taking his first step, to move his left leg across his entire body and place it to the right of his right leg. This twisted movement is known as a *cross-step*, and a series of them is called a *cross-walk*. It is a most awkward method for changing one's location on stage, but I regret to say that it is still widely practiced, particularly on very large operatic stages where singers, who worry about being heard, gravitate to the downstage area and are reluctant to walk with their profiles to the audience. To avoid cross-steps and cross-walks, follow two simple rules:

1. Always turn your shoulders slightly *before* taking the first step.
2. Start with your right foot when going right and your left foot when going left.

This second rule is sometimes called the rule of the *name* foot, because the direction and the starting foot have the same name. This applies not only to forward walks, but also to backing. Here is the typical RSB turn extended into a backing to up left:

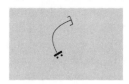

Even though the actor turns to face down right, the direction of the next movement is up left. Therefore, after turning the shoulders slightly, the first backing step should be taken with the left foot. Both when walking and backing, it is well to keep the first step fairly close to the body. This step connects the turn with the larger movement and is really an auxiliary link between the two.

When practicing these turns and initial steps, the student will notice that their smooth execution depends largely on the ease with which he controls the shifting of the weight of his body from one foot to the other. This activity is known as *footwork*, and it is the key to all graceful and effortless bodily movement, be it in sports or in the arts. No tennis player or dancer could get very far in his profession without highly developed footwork, and although to a lesser degree, it is also a basic tool of the opera singer.

Obstructions and crossings

A special problem of the proscenium stage is that of avoiding *obstructions*. As long as changes of position consist only of realignments, the singer should encounter no special difficulties in keeping both himself and his partner in full view of the audience. During regroupings, however, temporary obstructions cannot be entirely avoided. Obviously, when one actor crosses below another, he will block the view of his partner for a few moments; and if he crosses above him, he himself will become temporarily invisible. It is therefore advisable to follow the rule: *Do not cross below a singing character and, while singing, do not cross above a partner.*

We must remember, however, that on the proscenium stage there are two different dimensions: the horizontal and the vertical. The rule just stated is valid when two singers move horizontally on the same stage level, but when one of them is raised above the floor level or brought closer to it, the situation changes. If two participants (or rather their faces) are visible on sufficiently different vertical levels, they can cross freely without ever obstructing each other.

Among the various devices used for "raising" performers are platforms, ramps, and steps, but a singer can also stand on flat rocks, benches, chairs, or tables; to "lower" himself he can sit, kneel, crouch, or lie on the ground. Imaginative stage directors and experienced singers take advantage of all these possibilities for facilitating stage movement during regroupings. There are other procedures for handling obstructions. For example, an actor who is being temporarily masked by another crossing below him, may shorten the duration of his obstruction by moving in the opposite direction.

The student should also develop an awareness of the weakening effect of partial obstructions. Many opera singers get into the habit of using a chair or a table as if it were a shield between themselves and the public. By partially concealing themselves, they lessen the impact of their performance. An actor can avoid being partially hidden by furniture if he trains himself to be aware at all times of the picture he is presenting to the audience. Not all partial obstructions are necessarily harmful, however. When performing with a fairly short girl, a man who is over six feet tall can safely stand and move directly above her.

Rules regarding the singer's facial visibility are not sacred, and can be broken occasionally. Short, casual sentences can often be "sacrificed," i.e., uttered while facing away from the audience. Even important lines can sometimes be sung in this manner. I shall always remember Lothar

Wallerstein's staging of the first act of *Lohengrin*, when he had the Herald sing his third and final call for Elsa's defender facing directly upstage. Since Lohengrin and the swan appeared from this very direction shortly afterward, the Herald's unusual stage position produced a very strong dramatic impact.

The singing actor must master thoroughly the techniques for *taking and giving the stage*. The rules for these procedures are:

1. Whenever a performer is singing while in direct rapport with his partners, he must move to upstage (right or left) of them.
2. Those giving the stage must not impede this process by upstaging their colleague; in other words, they must either remain in the same stage position or move slightly downstage of it.

The three methods for taking the stage are: (a) motivated walks, (b) cheating approaches, and (c) backing. When musical timing permits it, a motivated walk upstage offers the simplest solution to the problem of taking the stage. The singer may be driven upstage by strong feelings: simple joie de vivre, or a crying spell. If the character's frame of mind is not appropriate or the music not compelling enough to justify such energetic movements, the singer taking the stage must be provided with a sensible reason for walking upward. This reason must be carefully planned and, if necessary, planted ahead of time. A door may have been left open for the singer to close; a letter, a book, or some other prop needed for the action may have been planted in the upstage area; or it may be possible to arrange for a *false exit*, when the singer begins to leave through an upstage door, then changes his mind and turns to address his partners.

When a singer who stands in the same stage level as his partner, but some distance away from him, wants to walk toward his colleague, he can choose one of three different approaches: (a) the straight line, (b) slightly upward, and (c) slightly downward. The first method is used when both participants continue to sing and share the stage as equal partners.

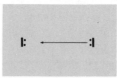

The other methods are known as cheating approaches. Cheating upward

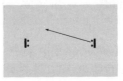

is done to take the stage, and cheating downward

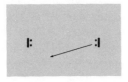

is the preferred method for relinquishing the stage to one's colleague.

When a singer who is sharing or giving the stage in the immediate vicinity of his partner wishes to take the stage rapidly without losing face, backing is the best way to do it. There are three possibilities:

1. Taking the stage, after having shared it, by means of a straight backing to up left:

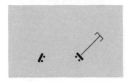

2. Taking the stage, after having been in indirect rapport with the partner, by means of an RSB turn extended by a backing to up left:

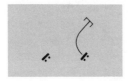

3. Taking the stage, after having given it to the partner, by means of an LSB turn extended by a backing to up left:

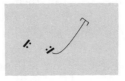

The greater the number of participants, the more complex their inter-relationship in terms of grouping and rapport; and this brings us to an examination of the behavior of operatic choruses, which is notoriously stilted and clumsy. This touchy subject is perhaps best approached by pointing to the two most objectionable habits of chorus singers: ranging themselves in military formations, and crowding in the center of the stage. Even after the director has carefully arranged them so as to form a picturesque and nicely distributed tableau, these masses of humanity will soon again face the audience four-square and stand in straight lines with their shoulder angles roughly parallel to the footlights. To counteract their unfortunate tendency to assemble in such groupings as those seen in Diagrams 1–6 or 1–7, choristers should be trained in techniques of indirect rapport and taught to cluster in smaller, well-separated groups.

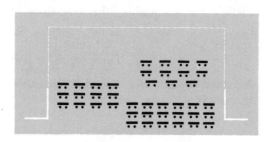

Diagram 1–6

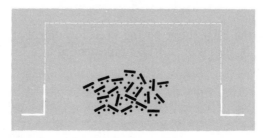

Diagram 1–7

It is often desirable to divide the chorus into several, self-contained "families" who address only each other and remain aloof from strangers. One or two of the family members can then be placed downstage of the others and act as focal points for the eyes of their colleagues. In Diagram 1–8, there is a grouping in which six choristers (1 through 6) focus their attention on two other chorus members, one of whom (7) faces them, while the other (8) is in indirect rapport with them. An assemblage of thirty-six singers (Diagram 1–9) could well be broken up into eight family groups of different sizes, some having as many as nine individuals and others as few as two, or even one.

Members of the chorus should also be made aware of the more elementary and obvious methods of creating a well-balanced stage picture. One of these, known as *dressing* the stage, consists of making certain that the sides of the stage platform—and most particularly the corners

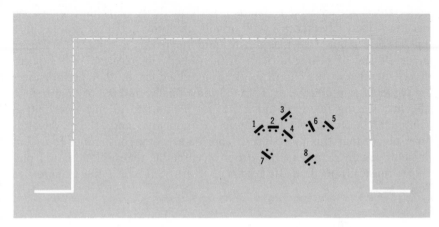

Diagram 1–8

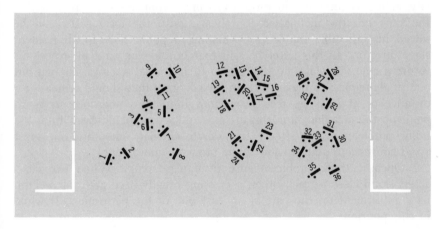

Diagram 1–9

closest to the audience—are not left unoccupied and, visually speaking, unprotected. Additional variety in grouping can of course be accomplished by a judicious use of elevations and stairways, and by having some choristers kneel, sit down, or embrace each other.

It may be well, at this point, to repeat what was said earlier concerning the musical dependability of opera singers. None of the techniques mentioned here can be employed by a chorus tenor or a soprano who is not certain about the pitches he is to sing unless he is surrounded by a mass of other tenors or sopranos. Similarly, it is useless to bring up such matters as direct or indirect rapport when working with choristers who cannot attack their lines unless cued by a conductor or a prompter. A well-trained singer, who is familiar with methods of achieving musical accuracy (see Chapter 6) will usually perform better if placed in a mixed-voice group (see Chapter 8) and treated as a competent singing actor worthy of belonging in a distinguished congregation of his peers. Every member of the chorus in all my productions, be they performances by students or professionals, is tested individually, and is not admitted to the first staging rehearsal unless he has memorized all his lines and is completely certain of his music. Conductors and stage directors may object that this procedure is enormously time-consuming. It is, but it saves equally enormous quantities of ensemble rehearsal time and produces musical and dramatic results that are well worth the trouble one has taken.

Stage traffic problems

A story is told of a famous opera singer who traveled from city to city, acting as guest star in various provincial companies. He had neither the time nor the inclination to rehearse with the local casts, and he solved his ensemble problems by mailing a polite note to all resident stage directors. In this letter he said that he did not want or expect his future partners to make any changes in their normal stagings. He had but one single request to make of them: at all times they should remain at a distance of at least six feet away from him! This anecdote serves to point up the fact that problems of stage traffic are not different from the traffic problems in city streets. In order to circulate smoothly, one must avoid congestions and provide ample room for movement.

Operatic traffic problems arise from regroupings. When two characters stand close to each other, a crossing usually necessitates a preliminary adjustment on the part of at least one of the performers. If while in this position:

character A is directed to "go right, X-ing B," he will either collide with B ("slice" him) or have to walk around him in a very obvious and unsightly "hook" movement:

If, however, A backs first and separates himself slightly from B:

then the crossing movement can be performed smoothly and comfortably:

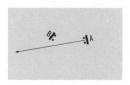

The same result can also be achieved by having character B back slightly, separating himself from character A and giving his partner more room for his crossing:

Both methods are perfectly sound. The first one has the slight advantage of being more autonomous in the sense that the character performing the crossing does not have to depend on his partner, but can rely solely on his own resources.

In congested situations involving regroupings of three or more singers, I like to use a procedure that, because of its suggestive stretching and contraction, I have nicknamed the *accordion*.

Three or more characters standing close to one another constitute a *tight* group. The characters in this group located farthest right and left are called *right end* and *left end*; the partner standing next to the end is known as the *neighbor*; and the singer who executes the regrouping is the *crosser*. In using the accordion, one starts out by detaching the end and sending him a little distance away in his "name" direction, i.e., the right end is told to go to the right, or the left end is sent to the left. This creates a gap between the end and his neighbor, and the regrouping is accomplished by having the crosser move into this gap.

To avoid unnecessary complications, we shall disregard all matters of shoulder lines and rapport to observe the regrouping possibilities of a tight group formed by the three singers A, B, C. Singer A is the right end, C is the left end, and B is the neighbor. If C is directed to go left, it creates a gap between him and the neighbor: AB C. Character A, who now acts as the crosser, crosses B and moves into the gap, thus forming a new tight group BAC. The next accordion move could be initiated by making B the right end and C the crosser. This results in the new grouping BCA. Detaching A to go left, leads to CBA, and the following regrouping with C as the right end produces CAB, and so on.

With more than three singers there is a correspondingly greater choice of crossers. After Character F (as the left end) detaches himself from the tight group consisting of ABCDEF, the director can choose any one of four singers (A, B, C, or D) to be the crosser. If he designates C, this not only leads to the regrouping AB DECF, but also creates an additional gap between B and D and permits either A or E to fill this space. It is clear that the accordion permits a great number of possible permutations. Furthermore, with either three or more characters there is no special reason why one should always end up with a tight group.

To create variety, a director can obtain fine effects by using diagonal directions (up left, down right, and so on) and circular movements around fountains or pieces of furniture. He should see to it, however, that leading characters do not move simultaneously in parallel lines. This change of location looks better if character A does not make his move until his partner has reached his destination, below the table.

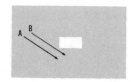

Just as with city traffic, stage traffic is also prone to jamming and collisions. The stage director is responsible for the orderly movement of his actors and, whether he relishes the task or not, he must perform the duties of a traffic policeman. Furniture props—benches, tables, and chairs —are comparable to the traffic islands and median strips of highways. If the thirteen choristers seen grouped around the table in Diagram 1–10 are to move past the two armchairs and land on stage right, the director must assign to each the route he is to take, the moment he is to depart, and the exact location he must occupy after completing his transit. The armchairs serve as traffic islands. Route 1 runs below the downstage chair, Route 2 between the chairs, and Route 3 above the upstage chair. If the change of position is to be made rapidly, all choristers must move at the same time. Character J, followed by I, H, G, and F, could take Route 3; A, B, C, and D might travel along Route 2, while choristers E, M, L, and K, crossing below the table and the downstage chair, proceed along

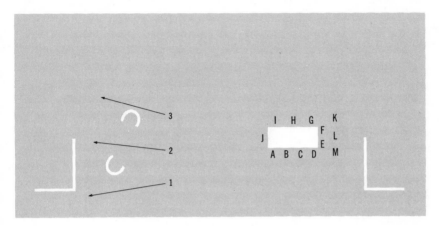

Diagram 1–10

Route 1. If the move can be made in a more leisurely fashion, the director may create a more varied form of movement. J, I, H, and G could leave first and take Route 1; A, B, C, and D would wait until this group gets out of the way and then go up right along Route 3. The rest of the choristers might be divided into two subgroups, so that E and M go above the table and K and L move below it. Having crossed the table, they could converge and take Route 2. To avoid confusion and collision, all decisions regarding these matters must be made beforehand, and the movements themselves must be carefully rehearsed.

~~2

The language of music

A YOUNG SINGER may have acquired enough theatrical experience to know how to remain in character and how to make dramatic sense, but when he turns to opera, he is baffled by the high-handed manner in which music seems to push him around and interfere with his desire for normal stage behavior. Most of all he is bothered by the many orchestral passages that precede, separate, and follow his lines, and by an inability to make theatrical sense out of the endless repetitions of words and sentences in his vocal line. This omnipresent music keeps him off balance; it makes him stand around waiting for his cue, wondering whether to twirl his thumbs, and then it drives him into an unnatural, repetitive delivery of his lines. When he asks for help, he often finds that his stage director is similarly puzzled by the overabundance of vocal lines and orchestral interludes. These complaints are fairly universal. Yet once one learns the language of music, which is as clear and precise as the language of words, these very same orchestral interruptions and vocal repetitions offer a highly detailed and immensely valuable blueprint for staging and acting. Singers and directors who understand the information provided by orchestral and vocal music will find that within the pages of a score the composer has given them precise and precious suggestions as to how each character should utter words, behave, move, laugh, cry, show unhappiness or despair, make love, and even kill or be killed.

It is true that musical tones cannot express everything, but words and music complement each other, music being strongest where words are weakest. It is extremely difficult to describe the gradations of an emotion in words—the difference, for example, between the tenderness a child feels for his grandfather and for his pet dog. But a musical description can convey the most subtle nuances of emotion instantly. And, music provides the exact timing and intensity of every mood and action.

Consider, for example, the act of sobbing. A dictionary defines it as "weeping and crying with convulsive catching of the breath and spasmodic contractions of the throat." Clear as this definition is, it is hardly useful for distinguishing and defining individual variations of sobbing in specific operatic situations. Obviously, an attempt to describe the differences in frequency, depth, rhythm, and emotional color of these convulsions and contractions would be hopelessly verbose. But Verdi was able to express in music each sobbing breath of his characters with the most accurate precision and unmistakable individuality. Given below are the sobs of six of his unhappy men and women, the personal aspect of their suffering portrayed with sublime musical mastery and almost clinical accuracy.

Example 2–1. LA TRAVIATA, II, sc. 6. Violetta's tears

Example 2–2. AIDA, I, sc. 1. Aida's tears

Example 2–3. SIMON BOCCANEGRA, III. Fiesco's tears

Example 2–4. OTELLO, III, sc. 8. Desdemona's tears

Example 2–5. RIGOLETTO, II, no. 9. Rigoletto's tears

Example 2–6. OTELLO, III, sc. 2. Otello's tears

Just as Verdi was supreme in giving musical expression to weeping and sobbing, Mozart was the master of musical caresses. It would be impossible to duplicate in words the exactness of Mozart's "stage directions" for amorous gestures. For example, if Da Ponte, the librettist of *Don Giovanni*, had wanted to show Zerlina how to console her bridegroom Masetto as he lies on the ground moaning and complaining of having been beaten up by Leporello, he would have had to write a stage direction something like: "Zerlina caresses Masetto twice in quick succession. Her behavior is flirtatious without being too provocatively sensuous. Her first caress begins about two-thirds of a second after the last note of her first phrase. Each caress lasts about four-thirds seconds, and the interval between the two is two-thirds of a second." But there is no need for such clumsy and verbose instructions—Mozart's music conveys all this and much more in a "stage direction" which is concise, elegant, and completely lucid (Example 2–7).

Example 2–7. DON GIOVANNI, II, no. 18

Mozart's operas are filled with such orchestral acting instructions. In *Così fan tutte*, for instance, when Guglielmo sings of his moustache, the instruments tell him exactly when and how long to twirl it (Example 2–8).

Example 2–8. COSÌ FAN TUTTE, I, no. 15

There are many ways in which music can stimulate theatrical thinking and serve as a point of departure for staging ideas. Some musical passages have a very distinctive character and stand out from the surrounding musical landscape. Whether these musical "events" occur in the orchestra or in a voice part, whether they consist of a melodic phrase, a short motif, or even a single note, they inevitably seem to illustrate specific dramatic ideas, and singers and directors must learn to find suitable stage activities for them. Some composers, like Wagner and Strauss, indicate clearly the dramatic meaning of these significant musical passages. Others—Mozart, Rossini, and Verdi—leave the interpretation of musical events to individual choice, but in every case these unusual passages should be accounted for and highlighted by some appropriate theatrical business.

The duet between Donna Anna and Don Ottavio in the opening scene of *Don Giovanni* contains a significant orchestral passage just before Donna Anna's words tell us that her thoughts have turned suddenly from grief to vengeance (Example 2–9). If the Commendatore's sword, which had been knocked out of his hand earlier by Don Giovanni, is left lying on the stage for Donna Anna to find just as this passage is played, her discovery at that moment, that her father had been killed in cold blood, will give new strength to the cry for vengeance that she then utters.

Example 2–9. DON GIOVANNI, I, no. 2

When an operatic text offers no explanation for an unusual musical event, it becomes necessary to invent a motive for some appropriate stage business. In Zerlina's duet with Don Giovanni, "La ci darem la mano," she sings a sustained high F-sharp that is quite unlike the rest of her vocal line, and in the *Rigoletto* quartet Gilda has a high B-flat that produces an equally startling effect. I like to justify Zerlina's vocal excitement by having her suddenly embraced by Don Giovanni, and to explain Gilda's high note by having her observe her lover, the Duke, caress Maddalena at that moment.

These examples touch upon only a few of the ways in which music imparts dramatic information. Certain aspects of the language of music are "universal," and others are highly individual with certain composers, so that in general an operatic score is like a secret message that must be decoded before it can be completely understood. Since music and theater constantly mesh and influence each other in opera, no operatic presentation can be satisfactory if the interpreters have not known how to make the music yield up its dramatic secrets to them. From a theatrical point of view, the most important musical values are: (*a*) energy and mood, (*b*) informative devices, (*c*) timing, and (*d*) formal construction.

Energy and mood

All music consists of a succession of episodes that vary in mood and in the degree of energy they express. Generally speaking, loud sounds are more energetic than soft ones, accented passages more energetic than smooth ones. Dissonant harmonies and all startling combinations of sound also create an increase in energy values. These musical energies take hold of both the performer and the listener; they affect the entire body. They make one want to move around, to march, dance, shout, or clap one's hands. What is generally referred to as tempo in music is also an element of energy. The faster and louder the music, the more energetic it is. When it becomes softer and slower, the energy values subside. One can almost measure the temperature of the energy in each musical moment. Matching the rise and fall of these musical energies with stage activities is one of the most fundamental rules of the operatic theater. One should not even contemplate theatrical possibilities that contradict or do not fit with the changes of energy in the score.

In opera one must see what one hears and hear what one sees. It is not enough for music to be played in the pit while the drama is acted on stage; there must be a recognizable relationship between these two activities. The orchestra does not merely accompany and support the characters on stage; it also reflects their thoughts, feelings, and actions. Consequently, singers' actions must justify the music, as if they themselves were causing the music to be what it is. And, for his part, the director must consider only those possibilities of staging that will justify the mood and energy dictated by the score.

In the second act of *La Traviata*, Violetta's pleading with the elder Germont is punctuated by three vigorous orchestral outbursts. The breathless excitement of her vocal lines shows she is fighting for all that is dear to her. The orchestral sections are also *her* music, and their vigor must be matched by the energy of her behavior. In my staging of this scene, I help Violetta justify these interludes by providing her with subtexts. When this section begins, I place her far enough away from Germont so that she has plenty of room for her movements. "Don't you know," she sings, "the burning love, the immense love that fills my heart?" She approaches him during the first interlude (Example 2–10), thinking her subtext ("Don't you know it?"). With her second sentence— "Don't you know that I have no one, neither friends nor relatives, among the living?"—her thoughts turn to her lover, and she acts out the second interlude (Example 2–11) by backing and gazing away from Germont, as if seeing Alfredo's image in the distance ("I have no one, no one but

Alfredo!"). She then sings, "Don't you know Alfredo has sworn to me
that I shall find everything in him?" Toward the end of this sentence,
Father Germont moves as if to interrupt, but Violetta, during the third
interlude (Example 2–12), stops him with a gesture ("No, please do
not interrupt me!") and walks away with great determination.

Example 2–10. LA TRAVIATA, II, sc. 5. First interlude

Example 2–11. Second interlude

Example 2–12. Third interlude

Certain types of short, energetic orchestral passages are so reminiscent
of muscular movements that they can be said to belong to the special
category of "action music." These passages not only give the singer a
blueprint of just how an action is to be performed, but on occasion they
also help to determine what gesture or other action should take place at
a given moment. Such help can be very welcome, especially with eight-
eenth- and early nineteenth-century composers, whose scores often lack
even the most essential stage directions.

An interesting case in point occurs in the third act of Verdi's *Masked Ball*, where Renato informs Samuel and Tom—who are involved in a plot to assassinate Riccardo—that he has letters in his possession which contain proof of their complicity and guilt. Renato, however, is not planning to turn these papers over to Riccardo. On the contrary, he wants to join the plotters, and in reply to their doubting words and looks, he assures them that he will prove his change of heart and dispel their suspicions "not with words, but with deeds!" What deeds? Neither the full score nor any of the Italian or American editions of the piano-vocal score that I have consulted contain any clarifying remarks on this subject. Verdi and his publishers must have felt that the three short passages played here by the strings (Example 2–13) were such obvious examples of "paper-tearing music" that no verbal instructions were necessary. I regret to say that I have seen performances of this opera where instead of destroying the evidence at this point, the baritone shook hands with the conspirators!

Example 2–13. UN BALLO IN MASCHERA, III, sc. 1

Renato's act of tearing up the incriminating documents is essential in this situation. Without it, his reference to "deeds" simply does not make sufficient sense. "Gesture music," however, does not always refer to an action which has this compelling necessity. As a rule, music offers many dramatic alternatives and lets the stage director use his imagination much more freely.

There are, for instance, two passages near the beginning of the second act of *Tosca* that I like to treat in a rather unconventional manner, although I am not at all certain that other directors (or for that matter the composer) would agree with my interpretation. Yet I believe these passages are worth discussing here because they show different kinds of dramatic clues that can be found in the orchestral sections of an opera.

Near the very beginning of the second act, Scarpia, whose office is located on the second floor of the Palazzo Farnese, asks his henchman, Sciarrone, if Tosca has arrived in the palace. After Sciarrone tells him that "one of the chamberlains has gone to fetch her," the orchestral strings embark on a two-bar "hippety-hoppety" phrase (Example 2–14), the meaning of which is not explained either in the libretto or the score. It is possible that Puccini intended the instruments to imitate the

Example 2–14. TOSCA, II

chamberlain's galloping through the streets of Rome on his way to Tosca's
dwelling, but musical illustrations seldom refer to invisible actions by
characters who are total strangers to the audience. Agitated operatic
music is primarily the expression of things that happen here and now.
In my staging of this string passage, Scarpia gets up from his chair behind
the desk and goes rapidly to the main entrance of the room. He is on
his way to the lower floor of the palace, where he hopes to intercept
Tosca before the beginning of the concert in which she is scheduled to
participate. Just before he gets to the door, however, he glances at the
window and changes his mind. The rest of the mise-en-scène need not
concern us here. The point is that a vigorous orchestral passage cannot be
left without a dramatic equivalent. It calls for a fitting visible expression,
and in this case I feel that Scarpia, rather than the invisible chamberlain,
is the person who should act it out.

The other passage occurs a few minutes later. It follows Scarpia's
monologue, in which the all-powerful chief of the Roman police reveals
his craving for every form of enjoyment from lovely women to fine wine.
When Sciarrone announces the arrival of Spoletta, Scarpia shouts:
"Splendid! Bring him in!" and the stage direction informs us that Scarpia
is "eccitatissimo"—most excited. The orchestral phrase that is played on
the heels of Scarpia's shout (Example 2–15) is marked "crescendo e strin-
gendo," soon becoming "rapidamente." The stage direction for Scarpia
says "si siede"—sits down—but it seems a shame to waste this exciting

Example 2–15

music solely on the entrance of the relatively unimportant Spoletta. In my staging of this passage Scarpia remains standing. He lifts the bottle to which he referred earlier and pours into his glass a stream of red wine that seems to converge with the sparkling stream of sixteenth notes that cascade down from the violins in the last two measures of this passage.

Of course, such orchestral passages can be acted out in many different ways, but the music invariably tells us at least four things that must be closely reflected in any satisfactory staging: (*a*) something must happen here, (*b*) this is where it begins, (*c*) this is how long it lasts, and (*d*) this is the mood and the amount of energy with which it must be performed.

Informative devices

Instrumental music has no *direct* means of conveying specific information, but its suggestive power is so great that the merest hint of a word or a picture is often sufficient to give it a precise meaning. The various devices composers have used to give specific theatrical meaning to their instrumental music can be put into three categories, which I call *imitations, analogies,* and *associations.*

Imitations

From Monteverdi to Alban Berg there is hardly an opera composer who has not imitated man-made and natural sounds in his music, who has not succumbed to the temptation of composing orchestral heartbeats, bird calls, storms, or the whirring of a spinning wheel. Convincing as these imitations may be, they are not apparent to the listener unless a clue to their identity is given by words, a title, or a scenic picture. For example, the call of the cuckoo can be copied from nature with almost complete accuracy. When this pattern (Example 2–16) is played in

Example 2–16.

the last movement of Beethoven's *Second Piano Concerto*, it is not associated with a cuckoo, yet the same notes in corresponding passages of Beethoven's *Pastoral Symphony,* the Forest Scene of Humperdinck's

Hansel and Gretel, and Delius' *On Hearing the First Cuckoo in Spring* are unmistakable bird calls. Similarly, the sound of thunder can be quite perfectly imitated by the roll of the kettledrums, but if a scenic picture or a title does not suggest that a storm is taking place, the kettledrum roll is nothing more than a musical effect.

Composers have zealously explored the possibilities of such musical imitations, which have ranged from locomotives and nightingales to telephone dials. It is virtually impossible to think of a noise which has not been orchestrated by such rabid imitators as Moussorgsky, Richard Strauss, and Ravel. These instrumental imitations are often immensely effective, but when overdone they can become as ludicrous as a singer who illustrates every word with a gesture. Richard Strauss used this device at times to the point of obsession. When Elektra, for example, tells her mother that she will be "at her heels like a dog," it hardly seems appropriate to emphasize this sentence by sounds of barking in the orchestra.

Analogies

Unlike imitations, which are restricted to actual resemblances in sound, analogies can convert ideas or happenings into tonal counterparts that are not related to sound. This method of giving precise meaning to various tone combinations is rooted in our habit of discussing music in terms borrowed from other fields. We speak of related and remote tonalities, white and dark voices, harsh and heavy chords, brilliant and mysterious passages, smooth melodies, high and low pitches, rising and descending scales, and sharp and flat keys. These terms are not taken literally in purely instrumental music. No one hearing a "deceptive" cadence imagines that some mischief is being perpetrated or suspects that every "descending" scale leads down a staircase. In opera, however, these descriptions are often taken seriously and used for a variety of dramatic purposes.

In the second act of Gounod's *Faust,* one of the students, Wagner, climbs onto a footstool before singing the Song of the Rat and descends from it after he is interrupted by Mephisto. The orchestra describes both the "up" and the "down" of his actions by corresponding passages, first toward the treble (Example 2–17) and then toward the bass (Example 2–18). For some unknown reason, the two stage directions referring to these climbing activities have been omitted from all scores of the opera. They are found only in the original French libretto, and even there the position of the second action is slightly misplaced.

In this instance, just as in many of our earlier examples, orchestral music must serve in lieu of printed stage directions. But even if these directions had been accurately inserted in the score, they could not begin to be as graphic and informative as Gounod's purely orchestral "descriptions."

Example 2-17. FAUST, II, no. 4

Example 2-18

Listening to this "upward" and "downward" music, we can clearly visualize the loud and domineering Wagner as he picks up the stool, places it in a favorable position, and climbs up on it with the self-assurance of a peacock; later we can see him descend meekly from his perch, all the starch taken out of him by Mephisto's commanding personality.

It is fascinating how the logic of a dramatic situation or the nicety of an argument can be paralleled in music by the use of analogies. Some of my students have questioned the value of these parallels on the ground that audiences are seldom aware of their existence. I remind them that many important theatrical details escape the attention of audiences. Matching such musical subtleties as analogies with appropriate stage behavior gives performances a greater richness of texture and depth of characterization. Audiences can always distinguish a performance that is filled with life and meaning from one that is one-dimensional, even if they are unable to analyze what lies behind it.

From a dramatic point of view, the analogies found in opera which seem to be most useful are those based on *melodic contour, harmonic progressions, tonalities,* and *instrumental timbres.*

Analogies based on melodic contour have their origin in vocal music, where words and moods are intimately connected with characteristic melodic lines. When typically "vocal" effects are imitated in the orchestra, they not only create an emotional effect, but also convey actual information. Mignon's crying spell in the instrumental interlude of her second-act aria (Elle est là! près de lui!) could not be more explicit in this respect: these are certainly musical sobs and tears (Example 2–19), and Mignon's actions must justify them.

Example 2–19. MIGNON, II, sc. 2

Mozart excelled in the use of melodic fragments to convey information: his operas abound in caresses, giggles, sighs, little heartaches, and gestures of yearning, all represented by appropriate orchestral passages. Time and time again he used the same violin figure (Example 2–20) to represent sighs. In certain dramatic situations these sighs develop into sobs, as when Elvira's or Countess Almaviva's unhappiness brings them close to tears. With Cherubino or Count Almaviva this same melodic figure represents sighs of amorous impatience. Verdi and Tchaikovsky also employed this method to depict emotionally excited breathing.

Example 2–20. THE MARRIAGE OF FIGARO, I, no. 6

Other melodic patterns have been used by composers with great consistency. The ascending fourth is often used to invoke the deity, and innumerable operatic prayers begin with this interval. More curious is the use of the descending major seventh in association with violent death. We find it not only in *Don Giovanni* and Beethoven's *Fidelio*, but also in such sophisticated scores as Richard Strauss' *Till Eulenspiegel,* where, according to the composer's own testimony, this interval played by the trombones represents Till's death verdict.

Analogies based on harmonic progressions are more subtle than those which use melodic contour. To understand the principle behind them, we must bear in mind that for the greater part of the last three hundred years a certain order of chord successions was regarded as mandatory and constituted the backbone of all harmonic movement. Progressions of the type tonic-dominant-tonic or tonic-subdominant-dominant-tonic were the rule within a given tonality, and modulations to other keys were similarly standardized. These procedures changed somewhat with each generation of composers, but if we know the style of a given composition, we can usually predict the direction in which the harmony is going to move. Consequently, any drastic deviation from the expected harmonic sequence can highlight a sudden interruption of activity or an unexpected change of mood.

An orchestral passage from the opening scene of *Don Giovanni* will serve to illustrate how analogies of harmonic progression can affect the execution and timing of fairly extended stage actions. As the Commendatore dies at the end of the trio, there is an orchestral postlude of five measures (Example 2–21). The key of F minor has been firmly established.

Example 2–21. DON GIOVANNI, I, no. 1

During the first two measures the oboe plays a sorrowful, descending chromatic scale. This phrase is picked up by a flute and a bassoon and is repeated in the third and fourth measures. At the end of the fourth measure something strange takes place. The last G of the flute and the bassoon remains stationary and the leading tone (E-natural) in the other flute and the second violins fails to resolve into the tonic. The whole harmonic structure slides down, hovers on the brink of a mysterious new tonality, and then evaporates into thin air. The orchestra is silent: the Commendatore's soul has left his body. The metaphysical mystery of death could not be presented with greater musical clarity. These five measures suggest an obvious theatrical equivalent. The Commendatore, who was half reclining on the ground while he sang, begins to sink down with the oboe scale. As the flute and bassoon move up to the C, his old body lifts itself in one last flicker of life; but as this scale descends, his energy is spent, and by the end of the fourth measure he is dead. The stage direction in the score ("muore"—dies) is unfortunately printed immediately after the last note of the vocal trio, so that in many performances Donna Anna's father is lifeless long before his music stops breathing. Singers and directors who develop the habit of listening to the dramatic values of music will not be guilty of such an error.

Another harmonic analogy occurs later in the same scene. Just before Donna Anna faints, the harmony is clearly moving toward D minor. However, instead of the final and seemingly inevitable dominant-tonic cadence in that key (Example 2–22), Mozart introduces a totally unexpected excursion into A minor (Example 2–23). This violent musical interruption must be given a corresponding theatrical equivalent. When fainting, Donna Anna must not be permitted to complete her fall and reach the D-minor destination of her musical phrase. Instead, the surprising harmonic deviation can be justified by having Don Ottavio catch her in his arms.

Example 2–22

Example 2–23. DON GIOVANNI, I, no. 2

The linking of different tonalities with specific mood values is one of the most interesting and subtle connections between music and non-musical phenomena. We know, for instance, that composers almost invariably choose F Major to represent a pastoral scene or mood. Similarly, D Major has a quality of joyful celebration, C minor is pathetic, and C Major possesses a strong brilliance. If we know that a given composer consistently associates the same keys with the same moods, we can be sure that a modulation to a particular key serves as an indication that he is thinking in terms of certain emotions or actions. For example, we know that for Mozart (as for most musicians in the eighteenth century) there was an affinity between tears and the key of F minor. Consequently, when the music takes a turn into this key in the finale of the second act of *The Marriage of Figaro* at the point when the Count accuses his wife of infidelity, the Countess' unhappiness can well take the form of sobbing and weeping. Our guess about Mozart's intentions here is further reinforced by the Countess' broken vocal line and the typically Mozartian "sighs" in the violins (Example 2–24). Neither the score nor the libretto has a stage direction at this point, nor are tears mentioned in the text which is being sung. All our evidence is circumstantial, and the two most important clues—the tonality and the "sighing" violins—are given in the form of analogies. Thus the knack of recognizing and understanding these musical hints can be of great help to singers and directors, often leading them to imaginative, musically correct, and dramatically valid solutions.

Example 2–24. THE MARRIAGE OF FIGARO, II, Finale no. 15

Analogies based on instrumental timbres relate the characteristic sound of certain instruments to the special activities for which they are used. Composers have long used the French horn to suggest the idea of a hunt or a forest, and the oboe, clarinet, and English horn—with their resemblance to the shepherd's pipe—to evoke pastoral life. Another obvious connection is that of the pipe organ with the idea of a church or with religious sentiments. The use of the organ in operatic church scenes goes back to Meyerbeer's *Robert le Diable* and has been used extensively ever since, as in *Faust, Die Meistersinger, Manon,* and *Tosca.* Instrumental imitations of the organ are employed freely with operatic allusions to churches or holy ideas, as when Micaela refers to the chapel in the first act of *Carmen* or when Siebel dips his finger into Marguerite's font of holy water in the second act of *Faust.*

The meaning of these analogies based on timbres varies from generation to generation. The sound of trumpets was once associated exclusively with royalty and they were used, as in *Lohengrin,* to announce the arrival of kings and queens. Later this association with nobility ceased to exist, and today the trumpet, together with the snare drum, has become the war instrument par excellence. The trombones, although they no longer carry any special associations, were once considered to have a mysterious tone particularly suited to portraying supernatural events. Mozart used them for this purpose in both *Idomeneo* and *Don Giovanni.*

According to a legend which dates from antiquity, the husband of a faithless wife is supposed to grow horns. Because the same word is used for the French horn and a betrayed husband's frontal ornament in Italian, German, and English, many composers connected the musical instrument with the idea of cuckoldry. Outstanding examples of such musical punning are the amusing French horn solos accompanying Figaro's lament over the fate of all husbands in the last act of *The Marriage of Figaro,* the chord played by four horns in Nicolai's *The Merry Wives of Windsor,* and the passage played by two horns in the second act of *Falstaff.*

Many analogies of instrumental timbres can be converted into stage actions. In the third act of *Aida,* Radames should listen intently to the soft fanfares of muted trumpets playing in his imagination as he describes his future war-like exploits to his beloved. The incipient cuckolds, Figaro and Ford, can touch their itching foreheads or illustrate by gestures the shameful horns that will soon grow on their heads. The timing and the intensity of these actions will, of course, be governed by the music.

Associations

Composers often set up purely musical associations without any reference to the world of common experience. These associations are based upon our ability to recognize and remember short musical phrases, provided they are repeated a sufficient number of times. If, for example, a musical phrase recurs often enough during a love scene, an association is created, and the phrase then stands for the idea of love. If it is constantly used to allude to this emotion, it becomes the love motive. By creating such artificial associations, a composer can attach a specific musical phrase to almost any conceivable object, person, or idea. These associations are often combined with imitations or analogies of instrumental timbres. In Wagner's *Ring* the motive of the Valkyries imitates the galloping of horses, and the motive of the sword is entrusted to the war-like trumpet.

When associations are based on melodic contour, they become very flexible. A motive can be harmonized in many different ways, played at varying speeds in the treble or the bass, and under all these guises it can still be easily recognized as the same melodic phrase. It is even possible to change the actual intervals of a motive and have it retain its identity as long as its general contour is preserved.

The different melodic, rhythmic, and harmonic shapes assumed by a motive can be very useful in indicating characteristic behavior or even suggesting specific gestures. There is, for instance, the majestic theme of "Elektra, the Princess" in Strauss' opera (Example 2–25). The same theme shows her when she first appears on stage as a frightening demon, deformed by suffering and devoured by hatred (Example 2–26). The sudden snake-like striking and spitting which is so clearly audible in this phrase should be at least suggested in Elektra's movements.

Once a leading motive has been well established, it can be used not only to support the ideas expressed on stage, but also to clarify, change, or even contradict the words of the text. When Isolde addresses Tristan in the first act and speaks of having "reached the goal," she ostensibly means the shores of Cornwall, but the orchestra makes it absolutely clear that she is really referring to her own and Tristan's impending death. Associations can also be used for comic purposes as in *Der Rosenkavalier*, when the Marschallin apologizes to Baron Ochs for having kept him waiting. The orchestra, by playing the same music that accompanied her passionate embraces with Octavian, gives the lie to her words: "I had a headache this morning."

Example 2–25. ELEKTRA *   Example 2–26

Composers have used the technique of associations in many different ways. Often an operatic character is given his "own" tune by which he can always be recognized. In *The Marriage of Figaro* both Figaro and Cherubino announce themselves to the audience from offstage with strains from their songs. Associations can also be very effective when they occur in changed dramatic circumstances, as they inevitably do in operatic mad scenes. When a heroine whose mind has become deranged by some tragic development "relives" scenes of former happiness, the return of once joyous music always produces the poignant effect of irreparable loss.

Once a motive has been sufficiently well-connected with a dramatic personage, it becomes symbolically representative of him. When played in the orchestra, such an "associated" phrase identifies the person as clearly as if his name had been sung onstage. This technique often per-

mits the audience to read the thoughts of silent characters. Thus in the
second act of *Fidelio,* when Florestan stirs in his sleep, the oboe melody
(Example 2–27) tells us that he is dreaming of his beloved Leonore.
During the wedding procession in the second act of *Lohengrin* the appearance of this phrase (Example 2–28) pinpoints the exact moment when
Elsa's thoughts turn to her future husband. The facial expressions of
these performers must reflect the tender thoughts revealed by the instruments of the orchestra.

Example 2–27. FIDELIO, II, no. 12

Example 2–28. LOHENGRIN, II, sc. 4

Recurring orchestral themes can often stimulate the dramatic imagination of stage directors and singers. The orchestral phrase from
Carmen is usually thought of as the "fate motive" (Example 2–29). To
me, this theme symbolizes the basic incompatibility between the gypsy's
lawless freedom and the soldier's stern discipline. In my staging of this
opera, I bring Don José and Carmen close to each other every time this

Example 2–29. CARMEN, Prelude

"fate motive" appears in the score. The music then seems to emerge spontaneously from the juxtaposition of these two personalities as from a magnetic field generated by two opposite electric poles.

All of the informative devices found in the orchestral portions of a score have a significant bearing, direct or indirect, on operatic staging. The music can provide us with new information or it can simply reinforce the words, emphasizing them in much the same way that a gesture heightens the effect of a line in a spoken play. Consequently, musical duplications can often be effectively synchronized with appropriate gestures and actions. Even when the instrumental portions of a score do not add any new information, they still offer valuable clues for the characterization of a role. Baron Ochs' vulgar elegance or Bartolo's crotchety craftiness can, of course, be deduced from the text, but their music adds another dimension which sharpens and clarifies these characteristics as words alone never could.

Before ending our discussion of informative devices in music, I should like to draw the attention of the reader to two operatic episodes that in my opinion do not ordinarily receive a correct musical-dramatic interpretation. The first of these occurs in the final act of *The Marriage of Figaro*; the second, in the Garden Scene of Gounod's *Faust*.

In Susanna's Recitative and Aria No. 27 (Deh vieni, non tardar), the romantically languishing recitative sentences and the gaily whispering orchestral passage that precede and follow them are so far apart in mood and energy values that, at first glance, they seem to contradict each other completely. I feel, nevertheless, that this contrast is intentional and that it constitutes a perfectly logical musical equivalent of Susanna's feelings at this moment. The dramatic context makes it abundantly clear that Susanna is about to indulge in a bit of clever teasing. Her yearning for the embraces of Count Almaviva, which she voices here, is obviously an "act" meant to excite Figaro's jealousy and to punish him for his unworthy suspicions. I am convinced that the laughter and amusement portrayed by the orchestra (Example 2–30) represent Susanna's real feelings, while the passion of her opening sentences (Example 2–31) is pure

Example 2–30. THE MARRIAGE OF FIGARO, IV, no. 27

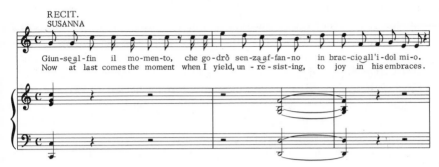

RECIT.
SUSANNA

Giun-se al-fin il mo-men-to, che go-drò sen-za af-fan-no in brac-cio all'i-dol mi-o.
Now at last comes the moment when I yield, un-re-sist-ing, to joy in his embraces.

Example 2–31

pretense. Having been told of Figaro's suspicions by Marcellina, and see-ing him hovering nearby, Susanna cannot resist the temptation to play a practical joke on her fiancé. It is then only natural for her to act out her own amusement during the gay orchestral passages and to feed the flame of Figaro's jealousy in her vocal sentences.

Although the interpretation of this recitative seems so obvious, sopranos entrusted with the role of Susanna invariably object that the aria itself, which is so tender and sincere, would be spoiled by even a hint of affectation or exaggerated emotion. This is perfectly true, but it does not in the least weaken my argument concerning the opening bars of the recitative. The evidence supplied by Mozart's musical language—and of every other first-rate operatic composer—is completely trustworthy. The gist of it can be summarized in a few words. In the beginning of the recitative the instruments laugh and Susanna's utterances show an exag-gerated—and totally uncharacteristic—affectation; soon the orchestral laughter subsides, and, beginning with the aria proper, the vocal and orchestral lines coalesce in a completely unanimous expression of amorous tenderness, proving that at this point Susanna stops pretending and be-comes thoroughly sincere. I see no conflict in this succession of events. After all, Susanna is yearning for the embraces of her beloved, and even though she has tricked her bridegroom into believing that she is sighing for someone else, she knows, and we know, that this beloved person is none other than Figaro himself. Treated as an expression of Susanna's love for Figaro, this aria becomes the very epitome of a young bride's amorous impatience. To borrow Albert Einstein's famous re-mark about the Almighty: "Mozart's music may be subtle, but it is never illogical!"

The transition from the recitative, with its contrasts of laughter and melodramatic declamation, to the sincere tenderness of the aria calls for a considerable skill both in pantomiming and in acting with the voice.

To facilitate Susanna's task, I ask the Countess to remain on stage for a while so that the two women can keep in fairly close rapport during the opening bars of the recitative. Susanna laughingly points to the corner of the stage where Figaro is hiding and then draws her mistress' attention to her almost comically romantic fervor. At first, the Countess smiles and shakes her head at Susanna's naughtiness. During the more subdued third orchestral passage, while Susanna is forcing herself to become more serious, the Countess withdraws into the wings with an expression that seems to say: "It is all very well for you to joke about marital infidelities. For me, alas, this is no longer a laughing matter!"

An example from *Faust* demonstrates the point that although instrumental music may not always tell us exactly what to do, it very often tells us what *not* to do. Music has absolute veto power in opera, and disregarding it in staging or acting can only lead to serious errors. In the Garden Scene most Marguerites spin and keep the spinning wheel turning lustily while they sing the song of the King of Thule. The whir of the spinning wheel is one of the sounds that can be most successfully imitated in music and is, in fact, illustrated by the orchestra in *Faust* during the vision of the Prologue and the spinning aria (which is often omitted) of the third act. But spinning is *not* depicted musically in the Garden Scene, and to have Marguerite rotate the spinning wheel during her song is to ignore completely the prohibition inherent in the orchestral music of this scene.

Musical timing

We have seen that the music played by the orchestra determines the degree of energy with which the stage action must be performed. We have also learned that on many occasions this instrumental music can tell us what action to perform and can suggest many important details not indicated in the text or the stage directions. We shall now turn our attention to the one aspect of stage behavior where music has absolute dictatorial power: the *timing*, the exact pacing and spacing of dramatic action.

When the theater, dealing mainly with thoughts, words, and characteristic visual images, becomes associated with music, it has to relinquish to its new partner full control over the timing of almost all activities. Only when the orchestra is entirely out of the picture (as in keyboard-accompanied, secco recitatives) or when the instruments stop or play long, sustained notes, can the singer be free, like the actor in the spoken drama, to choose the tempo of his behavior.

Stage directors who come to opera from the legitimate theater are usually appalled by the timing restraints imposed on them by the music. They will often beg the conductor to shorten, speed up, repeat, or slow

down sections of the music that do not adjust comfortably to the stage
business they have imagined. Needless to say, their pleas are seldom, if
ever, heeded. The composer and his immediate representative, the conductor, always claim the privilege of establishing all the durations in
opera.

It is taken for granted that the tempo of the vocal lines sung on
stage must coincide exactly with that of the music played in the pit.
The singer must attack his lines at certain precise moments and continue
to sing in time with the orchestra. This coordination of all speeds between
the vocal and instrumental portions of the score is of such cardinal importance in opera, and is so beset with subtleties and dangers, that it
deserves a detailed discussion of its own (see Chapter 6).

It is equally important to coordinate the action with the music.
When a gesture or stage movement must coincide exactly with an accent or some other feature of the music, we shall speak of *synchronization*. The term *contouring* will be reserved for acting sequences that
follow the outline of the music more loosely, without having obvious
moments of exact coincidence.

Synchronizing *single* actions with musical accents is one of the most
common forms of the timing coordinations that take place between stage
and pit. To execute it, the singer first makes certain that he "feels" the
beat of the music accurately; then he performs a preparatory movement
immediately preceding the actual synchronization. This auxiliary gesture,
which is usually made to begin one full beat ahead of time, is always
aimed in the opposite direction from the movement itself. Because of its
close rhythmical kinship with the similar movement performed by the
conductor, we shall call it the *upbeat gesture*. The conductor's arm moves
up before he gives the down beat; the leg of the kicker draws away from
the object before he kicks it; the fist is lifted before it knocks at the door
or pounds on the table. A few examples will help to demonstrate the
practical values of upbeat gestures in the synchronization of single actions.

There is a moment in the third act of Verdi's *Masked Ball* when
Renato realizes that to avenge his honor he must kill not his wife, but
her lover Riccardo. "It is not *her* blood that must flow," he sings, ". . .
that blood is your blood!" (Example 2–32). The picture of Amelia's pre-
sumed lover hangs over the center-wall fireplace of Renato's study, and
the aroused husband points to it as he utters the otherwise unidentified
pronoun in the phrase: "*Your* blood!"

Example 2–32. UN BALLO IN MASCHERA, III, sc. 1

To give this gesture maximum energy and dramatic impact, Renato should be facing away from the picture. Using the words "that blood is" as an upbeat, he then turns and lifts his arm so that he can glare and point to the picture at the precise moment when he thunders forth the climactic high F-sharp of his final sentence.

Another example of a synchronization that requires very precise timing occurs in the first act of *Der Rosenkavalier*, in the scene of the Marschallin's levee. While the Italian Tenor entertains the lady of the house, Baron Ochs becomes involved in an argument with the Marschallin's notary. Enraged at the notary's stubborn refusal to accept his interpretation of a certain paragraph in the wedding contract, the Baron slams the palm of his hand on the table, thus interrupting the concert and causing a minor scandal. The crashing noise of Och's gesture and the explosive chord of the orchestra come together on the third beat of the measure (Example 2–33).

Example 2–33. DER ROSENKAVALIER,* I

Many years ago I attended a staging rehearsal in which a famous Baron Ochs had an endlessly hard time trying to master this synchronization. It was obvious that the principle of upbeat gestures had never been explained to this otherwise capable singer. If the Baron lifts his arm on the second beat of this measure, just as the notary sings "oder" and the Tenor attacks his high G-sharp, he should have no difficulty in timing the movement of his arm so that his hand hits the table at precisely the right time.

Many synchronizations will not function well unless the singer is placed in just the right location on stage. Renato, for instance, must be at some distance away and sufficiently upstage to face Riccardo's picture without turning his own face away from the audience. Baron Ochs cannot hit the table if he is not sitting or standing in its immediate vicinity.

When the synchronizer has to come into physical contact with people or props, he must be located near them or able to approach them in time to perform the actions. In situations where the music—and consequently the behavior of the character—is lively or agitated, these approaches have to be timed with particular care. In the pantomime section of this volume the reader will find numerous examples of synchronizations that depend on precisely executed approaches.

In synchronizations involving physical contact with other singers, the actions should be closely supervised by the stage director. Such moments as Scarpia's amorous pursuit of Tosca just before she stabs him and Figaro's simulated escape movements before he is collared by the Count in the final scene of *The Marriage of Figaro* require particularly careful direction.

The preceding examples dealt with synchronized stage actions that were indispensable and intrinsic features of given dramatic situations. Many actions, less obviously necessary, are often added for emphasis, illustration, or simply to achieve variety. Some of these optional synchronizations originate in the creative minds of individual artists; others result from suggestions made by stage directors. It is true that not every accent in the score needs a corresponding muscular exertion, and one must be careful not to overload the action. There is nevertheless an undeniable affinity between musical energies and the movements of the singer's body, and the sensitive operatic artist learns to listen to music with his muscles as well as his ears.

When selecting suitable equivalents for the synchronization of single actions, one must make certain that they are (a) dramatically appropriate, (b) in accord with the corresponding musical energies, and (c) properly prepared by well-timed upbeat movements.

The following three examples are taken from my staging of *Hansel and Gretel*. They demonstrate how the ebullient spirits of a young boy can be made more apparent by a judicious use of characteristic actions inspired by the musical energies of the score.

1. Hansel is hungry and impatient. To emphasize his frustration, he hits the table with his fist (Example 2–34).
2. Hansel is nearly in tears. He acts out his angry aggressiveness by kicking furiously at a broomhead which he had tossed on the floor earlier in the action (Example 2–35).

3. Hansel warns his sister good-humoredly by shaking an admonishing finger (Example 2–36).

Notice how carefully each action was chosen to conform to the musical energies: the vigorous crescendo leading to the explosive chord in Example 2–34, the solid *forte* of the full orchestra in Example 2–35, and the gentle accent of the strings in Example 2–36.

Example 2–34. HANSEL AND GRETEL, I, sc. 1   Example 2–35

Example 2–36. HANSEL AND GRETEL, II, sc. 1

Although *multiple* synchronizations consist basically of a series of single actions, they nevertheless present some special problems of their own. When the synchronized actions produce audible noises, such as repeated knocking on a door, these sounds become part of the total musical texture, and a singer must be able to execute them with the precision of a percussion player in the orchestra. An example from the last act of *Rigoletto* will help to demonstrate how a singer can achieve this goal by mastering the technique of upbeat gestures.

Having overheard Sparafucile's and Maddalena's argument about killing the Duke, Gilda realizes that the only way she can save her lover's life is

to provide the hired assassins with a substitute victim. Pretending to be a
guest seeking shelter from the storm, she knocks at the tavern door.

Altogether there are nine separate knocks, arranged in three groups
of three knocks each. The final group comes considerably later, after the
extended ensemble sung by the three principals, but the first two groups
occur in close proximity and will illustrate our point. The positions of
these six knocks as they are indicated in the score are shown in Example
2–37. Since these knocks also serve as cues for the vocal lines of Maddalena and Sparafucile, it is essential that they be carried out with absolute

Example 2–37. RIGOLETTO, III, no. 13

accuracy. I have been told that in many opera houses Gilda only pretends to do the knocking while the actual noises are executed offstage by a musical assistant. Quite apart from the fact that the direction
from which stage sounds originate can never be successfully simulated, I
would never dream of offending a soprano by implying that she is not
musical enough to perform this synchronization to my complete satisfaction. As with all other complicated timing sequences, I recommend that
Gilda use an auxiliary subtext immediately following her singing lines.
Since her last sentence before knocking is an aside, it is advisable to have
her stand some little distance away from the tavern and sing facing in
the opposite direction. With the word "die" she turns toward the tavern
so that she can begin her approach with her last word, "sake."

Here is the complete subtext which should be thought (or silently recited) at the speed of quarter notes. Observe that the upbeat to the synchronized actions falls on the word "and" (Example 2–38).

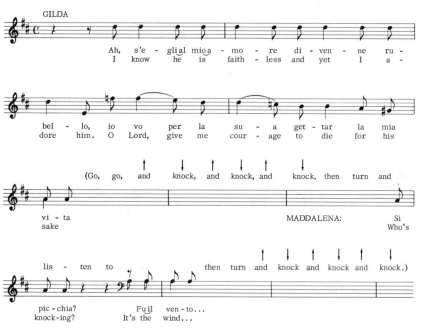

Example 2–38

Multiple synchronizations must be executed with care and taste if they are not to have certain undesirable effects. An overly exact enacting of musical beats and accents can have unwelcome consequences: it can dehumanize the characters of the drama by making them seem artificial and it can even make them appear comical.

This dehumanizing occurs when singing actors give the impression of being dancers. Singers should not behave and move like dancers unless the character being portrayed has a special tendency toward muscular plasticity. In *Rigoletto*, Maddalena, who is a professional street dancer, naturally carries a certain "dancy" bias into her everyday life. To a lesser extent this may also be true of Carmen and other operatic ladies addicted to dancing. Certain male characters—the matador Escamillo, for instance—can also justifiably display a leaning toward plasticity. I advise singers, in general, to avoid walking in time with the music. Exceptions, of course, can always be made. When the page, Oscar, enters at the end of the third act of Verdi's *Masked Ball*, his elegance and gaity are in such complete contrast to the tragic and conspiratorial mood of the preceding episodes that it does not seem out of place to have him strut in time with the brisk, tiptoeing march played by the orchestra (Example 2–39).

Example 2–39. UN BALLO IN MASCHERA, III, sc. 1

When dehumanizing is *desired*—in the portrayal of supernatural beings or in dream visions, for example—precise plastic execution is all the more recommended.

Everyone knows that unplanned comedy and unexpected laughter are highly embarrassing theatrical experiences. It is well to keep in mind, therefore, that a string of precisely synchronized gestures or movements often appears funny to present-day audiences. This is probably caused by the general popularity of motion-picture cartoons, and by the use of this technique in television advertising. Precise movements in time with the music, particularly in fairly normal everyday situations, can remind the spectator of these very amusing mechanical drawings. In opera this kind of synchronization is referred to as "mickey-mousing," and it must be watched very carefully by the director if he wishes to avoid audience laughter where none is desired. This is true even when such precise synchronization had originally been planned by the composer himself. There is a moment in the first act of La Bohème where Mimi faints and Rodolfo sprinkles some drops of water on her face in order to revive her. This action is accompanied by four pizzicato chords in the violins which are intended to be an exact counterpart of the four sprinkles (Example 2–40). Puccini had no way of guessing that later audiences would consider a precise execution of this music hilariously funny, but because they do, exact synchronization should be avoided in this serious moment.

Example 2–40. LA BOHÈME, I

Continuous synchronizations of stage actions occur mostly in dancing and marching. Marching steps and dancing movements are always performed in time with the individual beats of the musical rhythm. In order to keep track of the music, dancers usually count the beats, number them, and train themselves to remember which step, turn, or other movement coincides with a particular number.

Many operatic characters (Carmen, Dalila, and Salome, for instance) are required to perform fairly elaborate dances. It is clear that for best results these dancing sequences should be pre-set and rehearsed by expert choreographers.

When dealing with less complicated dances, the stage director may prefer to do his own choreography, especially in scenes where the dancing movements occur side by side with words of the vocal line. In this situation dancing and singing have to be combined into a single, well-integrated dramatic unit. A competent stage director should be able to handle simple dancing sequences and make them fit closely with the rest of the action. An example of such a staging will be found in Chapter 9, in the section dealing with the minuet, country dance, and waltz from *Don Giovanni*.

Contouring means following the outline of the musical phrases and seeing to it that the movements and gestures of the singers are executed in such a manner that the ebb and flow of the stage action correspond to the distribution of the peaks and valleys of the music. Whereas synchronizations are based primarily on the singer's ability to feel beats and upbeats, contouring depends upon his comprehension of complete musical phrases.

Singers and stage directors who acquire the habit of thinking in terms of phrases and combinations of phrases will find all musical forms much easier to analyze and to convert into their theatrical equivalents.

Understanding the interplay of synchronizations and contouring is vital in operatic staging and acting. It can be adequately demonstrated only in a fairly long operatic excerpt in context with the general problems involving the timing of the music and the drama. An analysis of an episode from the third act of Verdi's *Masked Ball* (Example 2–41) will serve this purpose and will introduce us to still another function of musical time: its influence on stage locations and distances and on various kinds of theatrical business.

It is rather fascinating to contemplate the variety of ways in which one could approach the task of timing this music. An intermission commentator for a radio broadcast of the opera would probably want to know its total duration and, after timing it with a stop watch, would discover that this episode lasts one minute and five seconds; a violinist in the orchestra (who, it so happens, has nothing to play during this scene) would count each downbeat of the conductor's baton and find that this episode consists of 27 bars; a choreographer, who might want to arrange this musical excerpt for some expressive rhythmical exercise, would learn that it is composed of 108 danceable beats; the conductor would be eager to see if his own tempo in this scene comes close to the speed of 100 quarters per minute, which is the metronome mark indicated by Verdi at this point.

For purposes of acting and staging, however, none of these measurements would be as helpful as the knowledge that this scene can be divided into six distinct musical phrases, each of which features a number of significant orchestral events:

1. A four-bar fortissimo melody entrusted to the cellos and doubled by the clarinets and bassoons;
2. A three-bar episode highlighted by forceful exclamations from the trombones and trumpets in the first and third bars;
3. A threefold repetition of a two-bar pianissimo sentence, combining the melodic opening of the first phrase with a very soft echo (by a flute and a clarinet) of the trumpet-trombone exclamations of the second phrase;
4. A threefold repetition of a shortened single-bar version of the preceding phrase;
5. A barely audible kettledrum roll, followed by Renato's anxious questioning of Samuel; and
6. Another kettledrum roll leading to Samuel's answer and Renato's exuberant expression of gratitude.

Looking at this scene from the point of view of the drama, we observe that it is part of the "Congiura," or Conspiracy, scene. Earlier in the act folded slips of paper were deposited in a vase. They bear the names of the three conspirators—Renato, Samuel, and Tom—who are eager to repay Riccardo for the wrongs he has committed against them.

Amelia, who came in unexpectedly to announce the arrival of the page Oscar, is now commanded by her husband, Renato, to draw the name of the avenger out of the vase.

The stage direction reads: "The trembling Amelia walks slowly to the table on which the vase is placed. Renato's eyes are fixed relentlessly on her. At last, with a shaking hand, she pulls out one of the papers. Renato takes it from her and hands it to Samuel."

These remarks take us as far as the fifth musical phrase, after which the verbal indications in the libretto refer only to the vocal tone colors in Renato's questions and in Samuel's answer: "dark and agitated," and "with exaltation," and then "trembling with joy" for the former, and "sorrowfully" for the latter. There are no further instructions for gestures or movements.

It becomes immediately apparent that the music calls for, or rather assumes the existence of, a number of dramatic actions not mentioned in these stage directions. Certainly some way must be found to justify such important musical events as the two forceful trumpet-trombone exclamations, their quintuple echo by the flute and clarinet, and the brass explosion in the sixth phrase.

What we find here is typical of what one discovers in most of the operas one studies, produces, and performs. The composer does not simply follow the story as it is presented in the vocal text and the acting directions; he reads between the lines and elaborates on the drama with his music. Where the stage direction reads: "at last . . . she pulls out one of the papers," Verdi interprets this to mean: "She does not take it at first, not for a while!" At first Amelia obviously vacillates and perhaps tries to disobey her husband. Verdi's Renato is not content to fix his eyes relentlessly on his wife or even to "wither her continually with his glances," which is a more accurate translation of the Italian. Instead, he commands her with two unmistakable gestures portrayed by the trumpet and the trombone.

The librettist describes the next action as: "Renato takes it from her and hands it to Samuel." Verdi expands this moment musically to such an extent that we are forced to presuppose some other dramatic activities. What activities? It is the stage director's duty to determine what additional dramatic details would fit the music best, would make the situation more believable and the action more varied.

To choose these additional activities, I put myself in the place of the participating characters and try to relive the situation. The conspiracy is supposed to be a secret from Amelia. "Don't fear," Renato whispered earlier to Samuel and Tom. "She knows nothing!" If I were Renato, after taking the paper I would motion my wife to move away, so that she would be less likely to guess the exact purpose of the paper and could

Example 2–41. UN BALLO IN MASCHERA, III, sc. 1

Example 2–41 (continued)

not hear the name when it was finally announced. If I were Amelia, I would take the vase and put it back on the mantle of the fireplace from where Renato had removed it. If I were Samuel, I would want Tom to see Renato's name written on that paper, and I would hand it to him after reading it, but before announcing what I had read. Finally, were I Renato hearing my name read by Samuel, I would want to see it written down on the paper and feast my eyes on it.

Using these dramatic insights, one can now adjust the action to make it conform with the exact shape of the music. The six musical phrases described earlier can now be juxtaposed with an equal number of dramatic concepts which might be labeled: (*a*) approach, (*b*) confrontation, (*c*) obedience, (*d*) hesitation, (*e*) revelation, and (*f*) gratitude.

In setting up the mise-en-scène for this episode, I first decide which musical moments demand synchronization and then determine their dramatic content. I equate the two short trumpet-trombone exclamations with Renato's commanding gestures as he points to the vase. To motivate them, I have Amelia contour her behavior in such a way that she looks imploringly at her husband during the bars preceding his two gestures. Then I interpret four of the five soft repetitions of this trumpet motive as glances which the different characters direct at the fateful paper. A general contouring is fully sufficient here. During the third of these echoing repeats Renato looks at Amelia and orders her to move away. This more peremptory look, which is coupled with a movement of the head, deserves to be synchronized with some precision, as does the explosion of the full brass in the sixth phrase. This, I feel, is best enacted by having Renato tear the paper out of Tom's hands. Everything else should be contured with a gentle correlation of action and music, devoid of any violent or overly precise movements.

We know that subtexts enable the singer to remain in close touch with the progress of instrumental music, and for this reason they are particularly valuable as aids in synchronization. In contouring, where the correspondence between the action and the music is much less rigid, it is seldom necessary to rely on this device.

Because in this episode we are confronted with a combination of synchronizations and contouring, I have provided a complete subtext. To avoid confusion, however, all the portions of the subtext which relate to precise synchronizations are in slanted type. The words and sentences which are not italicized can be treated as almost completely free rhythmical entities. The parenthetical remarks provide additional stage directions.

First phrase ("Approach")
AMELIA (*approaching the table on which the vase is placed*): Turn and slowly go to it, then turn to him: I beg you!
Second phrase ("Confrontation")
RENATO (*pointing to the vase*): You must!
AMELIA (*with an imploring gesture*): Mercy!
RENATO (*pointing to the vase*): You must!
Third phrase ("Obedience")
AMELIA (*taking the paper out of the vase*): Take it out and look at it. (*handing it to Renato*) Here it is!
RENATO (*taking the paper*): I take and look. That is all I need. *Get out!* (Amelia picks up the vase and takes it to the fireplace.)
Fourth phrase ("Hesitation")
RENATO (*handing the paper to Tom*): For you!
TOM: I look. (*He takes it and hands it to Samuel.*) For you!
SAMUEL: I look. I take.

Fifth phrase ("Revelation")

SAMUEL: Unfold the paper and look at it.

RENATO (*singing*): Let us hear what you read there!

(*Samuel hands the paper to Tom, who takes it and looks at it.*)

SAMUEL (*singing*): Renato!

Sixth phrase ("Gratitude")

RENATO (*singing*): I am chosen! (*tearing the paper out of Tom's hands*) I want to see! (*singing*) O, you heavenly powers! Now his life will atone for my grief!

Observing the distribution of dramatic events in this scene, one quickly becomes aware of the considerable difference in time that is available for the various actions. In the opening phrase Amelia is given at least three bars in which to approach the table. In the fourth phrase, on the other hand, Renato, Tom, and Samuel must each perform several actions —look at the paper, take it, and hand it to the next person—within a space of less than three bars. The mood of suspense and tragedy that pervades the first five phrases of this episode calls for a solemn and evenly spaced stage movement. The simplest and best way to accomplish it under these varying timing conditions is to have Amelia begin her action from a point located at some distance from the table, while the three men stand so close to each other that the paper can be passed among them without hurry or delay.

We now see that by governing the timing of actions, music also exercises a considerable influence on the distance between characters and on the location of props. As a matter of fact, special problems connected with contouring and synchronizations can be so pervasive as to affect even the design and planning of an entire scenic picture.

From a purely practical point of view, it is clear that singers and directors run into difficulties only when the composer has provided too much or too little music for the comfortable execution of an action. It is fairly obvious that the less music there is, the closer the singer should be to the place where the action is performed. We encountered this problem with the *Rosenkavalier* example. In order for the Baron to hit the table in time with the orchestral chord, he obviously had to be located in its immediate vicinity. All this becomes much less obvious, however, when extended to actions not involving synchronizations. In the first act of *La Bohème*, for instance, there is only a rest with a fermata between the time Mimi leaves the garret carrying her lighted candle and the moment she returns to look for her key. If, after Rodolfo's "good evening," she is still far away from the door, the ensuing silence can last an embarrassingly long time! Equally critical from the point of view of distances and locations is the action that follows upon Mimi's return to the room. Rodolfo notices that the flame of her candle is flickering in the draft.

"Don't stand there in the doorway," he warns her. "The wind is blowing out your candle!" Less than five seconds later he remarks that his own candle has also gone out. During these seconds Rodolfo must be able to pick up his candlestick, carry it to the door with the intention of relighting Mimi's flame, and see to it that his own candle becomes extinguished before he sings his next lines. All this is carefully notated in Puccini's score and is by no means difficult to execute provided that Rodolfo is placed close enough to the table on which his candlestick is resting. In short, musical proximity requires stage proximity.

The lack of sufficient music to execute an action is something of a rarity in opera. Such mismatchings are normally caught during the preparation for the first production, when the composer can still furnish additional music. A study of Bizet's manuscript reveals, for example, that he had originally provided too little music for the exit of the gypsy chorus in the third act of *Carmen*. He rectified this by adding ten bars, so that now, before Micaela's entrance, the stage can remain quiet and empty for just the right length of time.

The real and persistent problem of operatic timing arises not from lack of music, but because on so many occasions there seems to be too much. In the situations where, from a dramatic point of view, there appears to be an excess of music, the singer needs help. Finding a way to achieve believable behavior under these circumstances may require considerable ingenuity and is a task that belongs to the stage director. A number of the staging examples in the third part of this book deal with the problem of "too much music." Stage directors, however, should not be the only ones concerned with these conflicts between theatrical and musical timing. I suggest that singers—especially since they cannot always count on competent guidance—should try to acquire at least a nodding acquaintance with the two main methods that have proven beneficial in resolving these conflicts: (*a*) learning how to increase the distance to the next place of action, and (*b*) using delaying tactics to postpone the next action.

Increasing the distance to the place of the next action is often merely a matter of simple foresight. If, immediately preceding the *Masked Ball* episode discussed earlier, Amelia uses her aside to walk away from the table that holds the vase, she will automatically create an additional distance required for a comfortable contouring of her next action. She motivates this walk by her desire for privacy, her fear that her thoughts might otherwise be overheard by her husband and the two courtiers.

With the help of such motivations a singer can always, if need be, arrange to make a logical detour to another location, thus increasing any given distance as desired. Observe, for example, Rosina's movements in my staging of the introduction to her aria in *The Barber of Seville*.* She enters downstage right, coming from her room and intending to tiptoe

* The complete staging is given on page 188.

to the balcony located in the center of the upstage wall of the set. She is anxious to discover whether the young man who was serenading her earlier is still waiting on the square. She stops, however, before she gets too close to the balcony and runs downstage left to the door that leads to the apartments of Dr. Bartolo. After listening there for a moment, she again starts out for the balcony. She changes her mind a second time and goes to listen at the main entrance, which is located upstage left. It is only then that she feels safe enough to run toward the balcony and satisfy her curiosity by lifting the blinds and peering outside. Her fear of being caught by her guardian has enabled her to increase by several lengths the original distance to the balcony and has helped her immeasurably to contour the five phrases of Rossini's graceful orchestral introduction.

Quite often a singer's ability to increase a stage distance depends on a preliminary action performed by his partner. When, in the final scene of *Hansel and Gretel,* the children decide to escape from the witch, they need all the space they can get if they are not to find themselves a considerable distance offstage before the witch has an opportunity to stop them. Gretel, who has no singing lines during the preceding forty-two bars, can easily find a reason to walk to the stage location that, when Hansel joins her and urges her to run away, will afford both children maximum running space.

Delaying tactics are those that slow down the progress of events without necessarily depending on additional distance for stage movements. A musical delay can often be justified simply by hesitation or unwillingness to go ahead with an action. This is what we saw happening during the early part of our *Masked Ball* example. By filling the three bars of the second phrase with Amelia's imploring looks and Renato's commanding gestures, we were able to postpone the drawing out of the paper until the pianissimo that initiated the third phrase of this episode.

The end of the second-act duet between Carmen and Don José contains a typical example of an action that can easily lose its proper degree of energy unless it is stretched out logically by some specially devised delaying tactics. After his angry argument with the fiery gypsy, José is ready to leave Lillas Pastia's tavern. The enormous orchestral energies that Bizet unleashes at this point make it clear that José starts running to the door with his last word, even before Carmen's final "goodbye." However, if he performs this action at this moment and gives it the energy so clearly implied by the orchestral instruments, he will reach the door much too early. The plot demands that José's headlong flight be interrupted by a knock on the still closed door. We are dealing here with a so-called "false exit," a fairly common theatrical situation where a character intending to leave the stage is prevented from completing his action. As we saw in the *Hansel and Gretel* example, having too much exit music can prove quite embarrassing in these circumstances. A singer can find himself caught between the Scylla of a premature exit and the Charybdis of having to wait helplessly at the door, or some other point of egress, until the music permits his action to be arrested. I solve Don José's dilemma by having him leave his military cap on the table near which Carmen is standing. As she sings her final words, she grasps the cap and hurls it after José. It does not matter if the cap hits the departing soldier or flies past him. He becomes aware of having left it behind, and by the time he has picked it up, the music has run its course and Zuniga's knocking stops José in his tracks long before he has a chance to open the door.

So far we have been discussing only relatively minor discords in the marriage of music and drama. I have tried to demonstrate that by arranging for longer distances on stage and by occasionally using auxiliary dramatic actions one can easily compensate for the presence of a few bars of music that would otherwise create some uncomfortable blank spots in the dramatic continuity. One unfortunately encounters much more serious discrepancies between musical and dramatic durations, discrepancies not of a few bars or a few seconds, but of scores and even hundreds of bars that can last several minutes. These *tableaux vivants*, where the action comes to a virtual standstill are the outcome of certain musical forms, and they are responsible for that unfortunate impression of dramatic intermittence that is such a persistent and discouraging trait of the operatic theater.

There is no cause for despair, however, for a reconciliation between the structure of music and drama is by no means an impossible task.

Musical form

One does not have to be a trained musician to feel the impact and interpret the meaning of musical mood and energy values, but an understanding of musical form requires a more exact knowledge, and stage directors who are not musicians should spend some time studying this aspect of music.

Musical compositions are put together according to a precise structural plan. Musicians speak of phrases, periods, phrase groups; of the song form, the rondo form, or the sonata form. All these terms indicate long or short blocks of musical patterns with sections that repeat, alternate, and develop in various combinations. From the point of view of the drama this aspect of music need not constitute a disadvantage. These blocks of music correspond to complexes of ideas, and the stage director can clarify the succession of both the musical and the dramatic ideas by creating visual counterparts between the form of the music and the grouping and movements of the actors on stage. For instance, when the form is a simple one like A-B-A-coda—main subject (A), subsidiary subject (B), return to the main subject (A), and ending (coda)—one may use different portions of the stage to correspond with relative sections of the music: one could decide to play both A sections on one side of the stage, the B section on the opposite side, and the coda in the center.

A good example of a simple analogy between musical structure and stage locations can be observed in the first chorus scene of *Don Giovanni* (see page 300). The music consists of an introduction, three stanzas, and a postlude. The introduction serves to bring in the wedding party which, at first, congregates upstage right; the first stanza is sung only by the women, who move to stage left; the second stanza, which belongs to the men, plays on stage right; during the third stanza the entire company proceeds to stage center; and the postlude is used to return them all to the area near which they entered.

Unfortunately, musical patterns are rarely so simple, and it is not always possible to find such convenient analogies between the music and the action. This is especially true in long, repetitious ensembles, when the music contains complicated forms but little change in energies. All too often these ensembles are given "concert form" presentations with no attempt at action. In such situations, when both the plot and the musical energies remain quite static, the musical form itself can often point the way to a sound dramatic idea.

At first glance the trio that ends the first act of *The Abduction from the Seraglio* seems to present an almost insoluble dramatic problem. There is only one theatrical idea: the tenors, Belmonte and Pedrillo, want to enter the palace and the bass, Osmin, is determined to stop them. "Get out of here," says Osmin, "or I will smack you one!"* "That would be a pity," retort the two tenors. "Get away from the door; we are going in!" The trio has 133 measures of almost uniformly excited music (going from "allegro" to "allegro assai") during which these and only slightly different words are repeated over and over. Five measures before the end of the trio, just as the curtain begins to descend, the score gives its single stage direction: "Belmonte and Pedrillo push Osmin away and enter." With so little help from the plot, the words, and the musical energies, we must turn to the form of the music for the thread that will lead to a reasonable stage solution.

The first section of the trio is an allegro in 2/4 time, which begins in C minor but soon gravitates toward E-flat Major, the key in which it ends 64 measures later. The second section of 33 measures begins with the same C-minor music as the first, goes through a period of uncertainty, and eventually culminates in the jubilant C Major of the "allegro assai, alla breve," which lasts 36 measures. This sequence of keys gives us a

---

* The original German is just as colloquial.

strong feeling of inner conflict, as though the C-minor tonality were strug-
gling to decide whether it should give preference to its relative major,
E-flat, or to C, its parallel major. If we relate this musical conflict to the
quarrel on stage, the indecision of the key of C minor is clearly akin
to the uncertainty of the outcome of the onstage battle. But which side
is to be equated with E-flat Major? Since the scene ends in C Major
with the victory of Belmonte and Pedrillo, it is Osmin who must represent the E-flat-Major side of the trio. Once this has been decided, the
general outline of the stage action begins to emerge. In the first C-minor
section, after a period of indecision (when he is afraid to venture too far
from the palace door), Osmin has an inspiration: he will lock the door,
hang the key around his neck, get a club, and chase the intruders away.
By the time the music reaches E-flat Major, Osmin appears to be in control of the situation. During the second C-minor section Belmonte and
Pedrillo find two lengths of rope, harass Osmin from different sides, and
finally succeed in lassoing him. During the C-Major "allegro assai" the
tenors put the crowning touches on their victory by disarming Osmin,
tying him up, and taking away his key. As the curtain falls they enter the
palace, leaving their enemy helpless and defeated.

⁓ 3

The motivations of operatic characters

IN THE PRECEDING CHAPTERS we have discussed stage actions from the point of view of their meaning, timing, and execution. From the libretto and from the director, the singer learns what to say and do; the music helps him determine not only when to start his actions and how to contour them, but also how to apportion their mood and energy values. It is now time to approach the singing actor's final and perhaps most important problem: the reasons for his actions. A singer must continually ask himself: Why do I make this gesture or this turn? For what reason do I go from one place to another? The answers to these questions are known as *motivations*. It is essential for a performer to have a clear and vivid understanding of the reason behind every action he makes. To be convincing, furthermore, these motivations must become his own personal reasons rather than activities performed merely because they have been notated in the score or arranged by a stage director. One can invariably tell when an actor is executing a stage movement out of an inner personal compulsion and a sincere conviction, and when he is merely following directions and making a "move."

Reasons and urges

It is useful to differentiate between two types of motivations: intellectual reasons and predominantly emotional urges. This distinction is particularly important because it affects the direction or focal point of every movement. Reasoned motivations invariably induce specific, direction-focused movement; urges lead to a more random, unfocused type of stage behavior. For example, a character may go toward a door because he intends to open or close it, or to eavesdrop near it. All these are reasons for approaching the door. But the same character could also go near the door because his nervous pacing accidentally happens to take him there.

Under the influence of emotional stress, or purely as a result of vitality and joie de vivre, an actor can move to any area or corner of the stage and his move will be equally convincing wherever he goes. This freedom of direction is typical of the urge type of action and is one of the main differences between reasons and urges. There are other distinctions. Because of their intellectual basis, reasoned movements can often be performed coldly, without much emotional excitement. Urges, on the other hand, are likely to have a very pronounced emotional tone. When analyzing motivations, one must bear in mind that most stage movements depend upon a combination of reasons and urges. It is usually possible to determine at which point the pure urge begins to predominate by asking oneself whether the actor could have moved just as naturally in some other direction. If the direction is immaterial, then the motivation is most likely to be one of the urge type. If, on the other hand, the action makes no sense unless it takes the actor to a specific stage location, then we are probably dealing with a reasoned motivation.

The difference between reasons and urges can be equated with the difference between thought processes and emotional states. When an action results from a reasoned motivation, the audience should be well aware of the thought process behind it. In order for spectators to accept an action originating in an urge, the actor must be able to convince them of the sincerity and strength of the feeling behind it. Reasoned motivations are usually related to specific persons or objects on stage or in a certain direction off stage. For the execution of urges the actor must call upon his resources of imagination and feeling. Here he is concerned with his inner vision and his emotional state rather than with external stimulants.

The influence of music

The distinction between reasons and urges acquires a special importance when applied to opera, where the presence of music has a very particular effect upon stage behavior. It tends to create an atmosphere of heightened emotional tension, and it raises the level of muscular energy beyond the point usually encountered in the spoken drama. The theatrical interpretation of energetic orchestral passages demands stage movement possessing a comparable degree of emotional and muscular forcefulness. It is not surprising, therefore, that emotionally motivated urges play a vital role in operatic acting. Movement based solely on emotions is not sufficient, however. A good mise-en-scène should provide the singing actor with a considerable number of reasoned motivations. Some of these, of course, are given in the stage directions of the score or can be easily deduced from the words sung by the characters. There is a point, however, where the operatic performer is likely to run into difficulties.

Since musical forms rely so heavily on the development and repetition of individual phrases and on the recapitulation of entire sections, the more obvious reasons for acting and for the changing of positions are soon exhausted and the singer is forced either to perform in concert style or to rely entirely on motivations based on urges. In these repetitious moments he must be helped by the stage director, whose business it is to devise additional reasoned motivations where they are needed.

Before we proceed with a discussion of these specially invented motivations, it is important to point out that, even in the absence of an imaginative director, a competent singing actor should be able to work out a certain amount of sensible stage movement based on standard procedures and on sufficiently persuasive reasoned motivations.

Motogenic ideas

Among the many possible thoughts and emotions a character can have, only certain ones tend to produce muscular movement. As we have observed earlier, thoughts and feelings are useless, theatrically speaking, unless they are converted into visible actions. The actor must learn to seek out those dramatic ideas which generate movement, which are, to coin a word, *motogenic*.

One of the most useful of these motogenic ideas is the wish to turn toward or approach a person or object. The object may be a stage flat representing a rock or a door; it may be a piece of furniture or a book or flower. The desire to come closer may be induced by the most diverse ideas and feelings. Certain characters come closer to inspect, caress, or cherish; others, to insult or threaten. What matters is that the actor have a strong reason, akin to an inner compulsion, for moving or turning toward the object of his attention. If the object is a person, the actor may wish to address him, point to him, touch him, strike him, or embrace him; if it is an inanimate object, he may want to kneel beside it, or perhaps sit or lean on it; if it is a piece of paper, he might write on it, tear it up, or perhaps fold it and hide it.

Just as common is the opposite wish: to turn or move away from somebody or something. Here again we encounter a wide variety of motivations. Among the many possible reasons for moving away are hatred, fear of giving away one's secrets, nervousness, shame, and terror.

These two ideas—moving *toward* and moving *away from* something —furnish the impulse for a great number of stage movements, and it is important to understand that the people and things in the actor's thoughts need not be present on stage, nor do they necessarily have to have a physical reality. Abstract concepts—one's native land, death, jealousy, love or hatred for a person not present on stage—can all serve as objects of motogenic ideas.

There is, however, one attribute that all these persons, things and ideas (whether real, imaginary, present, or absent) have in common: in relation to the actor they must have a clearly identifiable position on or off stage. Seeing or imagining these people, things, or ideas, the actor turns toward them or away from them, and once the meaning of these directions is clearly established, a pattern of motivated stage movement can begin to emerge.

In Aida's first-act aria, "Ritorna vincitor," for example, the heroine is torn between her loyalty to her native Ethiopia and her love for Radames, who has just been chosen to lead the Egyptian armies against the Ethiopians. Left alone, Aida gives vent to her conflicting emotions and then asks the gods to have pity on her. If Radames was last seen leaving the stage to the right, this direction should logically be assigned to represent Aida's love for him. Ethiopia must then be conceived as lying in the opposite direction, toward stage left, while the gods are imagined as having their abode in heaven, toward downstage. This enables Aida to direct her lines and movements in three different symbolic directions, which serve as a point of departure for developing a sensible stage composition.

In the mise-en-scène of the Countess' aria which opens the second act of *The Marriage of Figaro* (discussed in Chapter 7), we shall observe a much more elaborate collection of motogenic ideas. The absent husband will be symbolized by both the main entrance and the window; the God of Love will be imagined toward down left, and Death toward down right. The couch, the table, and the chair, as well as the smaller props— the embroidery screen, the hand mirror, and the handkerchief—will also be exploited for motogenic purposes and will help the Countess perform a great variety of turns, walks, and other visible and meaningful actions.

Repeated words and sentences

Another very valuable source of motogenic impulses can be found in the repetitions of words and sentences. These repetitions are a common feature of operatic texts, and I do not share the attitude of those of my colleagues who consider them theatrically embarrassing. Strong emotions are enormously persistent and lend themselves perfectly to musical and verbal reiteration and elaboration. When treated with the respect they deserve, these repetitions become completely valid dramatic expressions.

We must not forget that language serves more than one purpose. Words are used not only to impart information, but also to express emotion. Specialists in the field of semantics refer to these two sides of language as its *informative* and its *affective* aspects. In acting and staging opera, where word repetitions occur with such great frequency, these concepts have proven to be very helpful. While many of these repetitions represent merely an increase in emphasis, one should always consider the possibility that a sequence of identical or very similar sentences may fit into a typical and very useful informative-affective pattern.

To understand the mechanism of these repetitions, we must bear in mind that when we become emotionally involved, a change of topic is difficult to achieve and we are apt to keep repeating—and reliving—the thought that gives us such intense pleasure or pain. It is as if the mind is hypnotized in a way that keeps out every other emotion or idea. Just as a person who suffers from a violent toothache is unable to think of anything except his pain, so a man in the throes of an intense passion keeps repeating the same thoughts in identical or very similar terms. The passion of love, whether shared or unrequited, tends to banish all other ideas except: "I adore you!" or "She no longer loves me!"

When informing others, an actor naturally faces them and addresses them, but when his intense feelings induce him to repeat his words, he tends to turn away and speak to himself. This technique of emotionally induced changes of direction can be applied to almost any operatic episode featuring repetitions and possessing a sufficiently high degree of agony or ecstasy.

Santuzza's aria in *Cavalleria Rusticana,* when she tells her lover's mother of her predicament, provides an example of an entire series of directional changes derived from such emotional nuances. Here is the complete Italian text of what the unhappy girl says following the ten-measure orchestral introduction. The literal English translation pinpoints the verbal repetitions, of which there are no less than seven. The positions of the fairly short orchestral interludes are indicated by the letters in parentheses.

Voi lo sapete, o mamma,   prima d'andar soldato,   Turiddu
You know, mother, that before he was called to military service, Turiddu

aveva a Lola eterna fè giurato, aveva a Lola eterna fè giurato. Tornò,
swore eternal faith to Lola,   swore eternal faith to Lola.   Upon his return
    1. *(informative)*   *(affective)*

la seppe sposa,   e con nuovo amore volle spegner
he discovered she was married, and with a new love he wanted to extinguish

la fiamma che gli bruciava il core. M'amò,
the flame that burned his heart.   He made love to me. . . .

l'amai,   l'amai,   ah! l'amai.   Quell'invida d'ogni delizia mia,
I loved him,   I loved him, oh, I loved him! Envious of my every happiness
2. (*informative*) (*affective*)   (*affective*)
         (A, 6½ meas., and B, 2 meas.)   (C, 2½ meas.)

del suo sposo dimentica, arse di gelosia,   arse di gelosia.
and forgetting her husband, she burned with jealousy, burned with jealousy.
         (D, 1½ meas.)   3. (*informative*)   (*affective*)

Me l'ha rapito,   me l'ha rapito.
She stole him away from me, she stole him away from me!
      4. (*affective*)   (*informative*)
                     (E, 3 meas.)

Priva   dell' onor mio, dell' onor mio rimango.
Deprived of my honor,   of my honor,   I remain.
      5. (*informative*)   (*informative*)

Lola e Turiddu s'amano,   Lola e Turiddu s'amano,
Lola and Turiddu love each other, Lola and Turiddu love each other . . .
      6. (*informative*)   (*affective*)

io piango, io piango, io piango!
I weep,   I weep,   I weep!
7. (*affective*) (*affective*)   (*affective*)

    During the first half of the orchestral introduction to this aria
Mamma Lucia sits down at the right side of the table, which is located in
RB2. The exclamatory instrumental phrase that fills the second half of
the introduction is acted out by Santuzza, who first looks in the direction
of Lola's house (offstage in the UL direction) and then runs to the
table, sits down facing Mamma, and has a short weeping spell.
    I find this scene particularly educational because it not only illus-
trates the dramatic advantages of word repetitions, but also features most
of the possible ways in which motogenic ideas can be applied. Four of
the seven repeated phrases—numbers 1, 2, 3, and 6—follow the normal
pattern, in the sense that Santuzza first faces right toward Mamma to
address and inform her, and then turns to face either toward Lola's dwelling or to speak to herself, facing DL. The emotional impact of the second series of repetitions is so intense that Santuzza is forced to say "I
loved him" a third time with a rise in emotional intensity that finds its

outlet in the added "oh" and the ringing, high A-natural supported by the orchestral fortissimo. This type of increase in emphasis can be notated by writing the appropriate term or its abbreviation (in this case *affective*, or *aff*). The emotional energy displayed here is so great that it is best if Santuzza not only turns away from Mamma, but also gets up and makes it clear that she is on the verge of an hysterical outburst. During the following orchestral passage (interlude A) she again turns toward Mamma, collapses in the chair, buries her head in her arms, and weeps bitterly.

In the fourth sequence of repetitions we find a reversal of the normal order. The initial vocal and orchestral exclamations make it clear (at least to me) that here the affective element erupts immediately and the informative segment follows later. I ask Santuzza to get up and go left during the affective repetition of the third sequence, so that at the time she sings the first half of the fourth sequence she is still facing away from Mamma and turns to her only for the quieter, informative repeat of "she stole him away from me!"

Having Santuzza in this location (near CC) at this point facilitates the staging of the orchestral passage (E) that comes now. During this interlude she can go UR, crossing above the table to UL of Mamma, and stand quite near the older woman for the intimate confession that follows. Since the loss of her virginity is something the unhappy girl can bring herself to mention only in a very subdued tone of voice, the singer must observe the carefully notated piano in the vocal line. It is only when Mamma shakes her head in horrified disbelief that Santuzza repeats the information with an increase in emphasis and intensity. This type of emphatic repetition of an informative section is quite common, but it must always be stimulated by an appropriate reaction such as surprise, contradiction, or inattention on the part of the supporting partner. Santuzza's three final affective exclamations can be handled as pure urges, and it really does not matter in which direction they are sung.

In teaching this entire sequence I have often made the experiment of explaining to the singer the principle of the informative-affective treatment of repeated words and sentences and then leaving her to her own devices. The staging arrangements that resulted, while not particularly original or imaginative, were usually entirely acceptable and occasionally quite exciting.

Useful as it may be, the method illustrated in the staging of Santuzza's monologue is rather primitive. Devices of this type can produce adequate results in very short scenes and in fairly obvious dramatic situations, but in more complicated theatrical sequences the singer most definitely requires the guidance of a stage director.

I would like to state emphatically that it is not the business of the singer to invent dramatic ideas any more than it is his business to compose music. But just as the singer interprets the score and gives it the stamp of his personality, so must he absorb, digest, and interpret the staging ideas of his dramatic guide. The mise-en-scène is created by the director, but the reasons and urges that govern the behavior of the characters must be re-created by the singing actor and must become the spontaneous and vivid expressions of his own mind and heart. The composer notates his intentions in the score; the stage director explains, analyzes, and demonstrates; but it is the singer who brings their ideas to life, and he must work at them until he has made these ideas completely his own.

When imparting his ideas to the singer, the stage director must keep in mind that it is not enough to indicate what should be done, and when and how the actions should be performed. The motivations which may be crystal-clear to the director are often not readily apparent to the actor. In my own work as a director I have found it advisable not to assume that the singer will always know or guess just why I want him to perform a certain action. It is best to be very specific about both the thoughts that lie behind the reasons and the feelings that activate the urges.

Analysis of motivations in two operatic scenes

The following detailed discussion of two operatic scenes gives a complete analysis of the motivations underlying every move of the characters involved and illustrates the difference between motivations based on reasons, and those resulting from urges.

The two scenes—Cherubino's first-act aria, No. 6, from *The Marriage of Figaro* with the preceding recitative, and the duet, No. 20, from *Così fan tutte* with the preceding recitative—were chosen because they represent widely contrasting possibilities regarding the need for special invention on the part of the stage director. The plot of *The Marriage of Figaro* is so rich in important details of theatrical business that very few additional reasons need to be added. The duet from *Così fan tutte*, on the other hand, has a text that is almost entirely devoid of external allusions. In order to create logical motivations for changes of position and to justify the fluid and varied movement that would seem to be an indispensable adjunct of Mozart's score, the director has to provide a complete set of reasons based on a freely invented scenic environment and on specially devised characteristic activities.

Cherubino's aria

In the first act of *The Marriage of Figaro* the stage represents a room in the castle. The main entrance is in the center. There are two other doors, the one on stage right leading to the apartments of the Countess, the one on the left to those of the Count. The properties used during Cherubino's aria, "Non so più cosa son," and its preceding recitative are: (*a*) a small table and stool located in RB2; (*b*) a large armchair in LB2; (*c*) a woman's dress, nightcap, and ribbon, which are on the table; and (*d*) Cherubino's song, a folded sheet of paper hidden in his belt or in his cuff. There are other objects present on the stage, but since they do not pertain to this particular scene, there is no need to enumerate them. All these properties except the table and the stool are specifically indicated in the score. The table and the stool are not absolutely necessary for enacting the plot, but they serve many useful purposes and permit a more natural handling of many sequences. The armchair must be large enough to permit various characters to hide behind it and inside it. The dress,* nightcap, and ribbon belong to the Countess and were brought in earlier by Susanna when she returned from her mistress' room. Since neither Beaumarchais nor Da Ponte furnish any clues as to why Susanna has to occupy herself with these objects, adequate motivations must be supplied by the stage director. I assume that this is the dress that the Countess intends to wear for the wedding ceremony, and I recommend that one actually use the dress which the Countess later wears in the third act, or, what is probably safer, an identical one. The dress needs some minor repair job, such as a stitch or two to mend the hem. The nightcap is a freshly laundered one, and Susanna has it in order to thread the ribbon into its stiffly starched slits or folds. During the recitative preceding her duet with Marcellina, Susanna placed the cap and the ribbon on the right side of the table and the dress on the left side. The ribbon is at first folded inside the cap, for it is advisable not to have Cherubino see the ribbon until the moment he becomes curious and inquires about it. Cherubino's song is inscribed on a single sheet of paper. One often sees musical characters written on that paper, but this is surely based on a misunderstanding. Cherubino is not a composer, but a budding poet. According to the fashion of the time, his poem is meant to be sung to one of the well-known tunes of his day. In Beaumarchais' comedy Cherubino performs his song to the strain of "Marlbrough s'en va-t-en guerre," and Mozart's "Voi che sapete" is intended to be an imitation of a simple popular ditty. Susanna, who takes music lessons from Basilio, is certainly capable of strumming a guitar accompaniment to a familiar tune without needing a score to guide her.

At the end of Duet No. 5, Marcellina left the room in a huff and Susanna followed her to the center door, laughing triumphantly. For the moment Susanna has won out over her elderly rival, but Marcellina's nasty remarks are still rankling in her ears. Even though Susanna is still fuming over Marcellina's nastiness, she knows that she must hurry up if she is to help her mistress and get ready for the wedding herself. Now

---

* Mention of the dress is omitted in many scores, but it is included in the Complete Edition and there is no reason to doubt its authenticity.

that she is left alone she must get on with the domestic duties which were interrupted by her spat with Marcellina. Here are all the moves that she and Cherubino make in my staging of the forty-two measures of recitative preceding his aria:

1. (measure 1) Susanna turns Clw, goes to the table, picks up the dress, and goes to DR of the armchair. These moves illustrate the difference between a reason and an urge. In order to pick up the dress, Susanna must go to the table, but she has no apparent reason for continuing to the armchair. Her immediate intention is to inspect the condition of the dress, and this could just as easily be accomplished without moving away from the table. She keeps going because she is too excited to stand still. Notice, however, that since she is moved by anger, she does not necessarily have to go to the armchair—she could just as easily move in any other direction. One might argue that Susanna goes toward the left because she intends to hang the dress on the back of the armchair, but somehow it does not sound convincing. It seems to me that Susanna is in a mood to strangle Marcellina and that she gives vent to her wrath by walking and shaking the dress.

2. (measure 4) Cherubino appears at the center door. He has been lurking in the vicinity for a long time, waiting for a propitious opportunity to be alone with Susanna.

3. (measure 5) Cherubino glances offstage, to the right and the left, to make sure that no one is approaching. Susanna addresses Cherubino over her right shoulder as she shakes the dress.

4. (measure 6) Cherubino runs to above Susanna. He is in trouble and needs both sympathy and help. He has all sorts of reasons and urges for coming close to Susanna.

5. (measure 7) Cherubino embraces Susanna from behind, his head over her right shoulder. The pageboy is still a child who wants to be comforted, but he is also an adolescent who craves to put his arms around every girl whom he dares to embrace.

6. (measure 8) Susanna turns to get out of Cherubino's embrace. Holding the dress in her right hand, she gently, but very firmly, pushes Cherubino slightly UR with her left hand and backs away from him. Susanna has good reasons for not wanting to be embraced by Cherubino. She likes him well enough, and of course he is still a child, but in recent months his boyish embraces have assumed a rather alarmingly passionate flavor and she has no intention of encouraging anything of the sort.

7. (measure 10) Susanna shows her amusement at Cherubino's plight (the Count was furious at finding him alone with Bar-

barina). Susanna has calmed down considerably by now and has begun to forget about the episode with Marcellina. She has reassured herself that the hem of the Countess's dress can be repaired in a few moments and in the meantime she is curious to learn more about Cherubino's "misfortune."

8. (measure 12) Cherubino turns toward the Countess's door. He is motivated by what one would call "a passionate reason." He seems to want to look through the wall to behold the queen of his dreams.

9. (measure 14) Cherubino goes right to the stool and sits down. Susanna goes to the armchair and carefully hangs the dress over the back of it. This is a good example of a "business" move which is performed without any particular feeling tone.

10. (measure 15) Cherubino puts his arms on the table and buries his head in them. He does this because he is sorry for himself at the idea of being "sent away" from the castle. Susanna also feels sorry for him and, although she cannot resist teasing him, her words are also meant to cheer him up. She goes right, crossing above Cherubino to the corner of the table, picks up the nightcap with the ribbon inside it, and goes left again, crossing above Cherubino and passing the nightcap into her left hand. While Susanna chatters, she is busy taking care of her chores. She has only the simplest and most prosaic of reasons for her passage to the table and back to the armchair— she wants to fetch the nightcap and ribbon and sit down some place where she can weave the ribbon into the folds of the cap. If Cherubino were not sitting at the table, Susanna would most likely fix the cap there, but as he is, she goes to the armchair.

11. (measure 18) Susanna pinches Cherubino's left ear playfully as she crosses above him and continues to the armchair. It might be worth mentioning at this point that since Cherubino is a distant cousin of the Countess, he belongs, from Susanna's point of view, to the upper classes, and one does not push the upper classes around (except when they get too free with their hands!). Susanna does not go to the table because she wants to tease Cherubino; she simply pinches his ear while she is in the process of fetching the cap. Her allusion to Cherubino's worship of the Countess revives the boy's spirits, and he sits up to address Susanna.

12. (measure 19) Susanna sits in the armchair. Cherubino gets up and goes slightly left. He goes closer to Susanna in order to emphasize how much he envies her intimacy with his adored one.

13. (measure 22) Susanna takes the ribbon out of the nightcap and

attempts to thread it into the slits. Cherubino turns and goes to the table as he begins dreaming about the Countess and imagining her being "dressed in the morning and undressed in the evening" ("che la vesti il mattino, che la sera la spogli"). He is driven by a sensual urge, and here again the direction is optional.

14. (measure 24) Cherubino sits on the downstage side of the table and turns toward Susanna. His sitting is a more or less unconscious physical comment on the hopelessness of his desires.

15. (measure 26) Susanna, imitating Cherubino's rapturous tone of voice, first holds up the ribbon with her right hand and then the nightcap with her left hand.

16. (measure 27) Susanna puts the ribbon down in her lap and then starts working at the slits of the starched nightcap to soften them so she can thread the ribbon through them.

17. (measure 28) Cherubino runs toward Susanna in order to get the ribbon.

18. (measure 29) Cherubino snatches the ribbon with his left hand, turns clockwise, and goes UR to CC.

19. (measure 30) Cherubino kisses the ribbon passionately. Susanna throws the nightcap into the armchair and follows Cherubino. She throws down the cap because she fully intends to use force to retrieve the ribbon and needs both hands for the purpose. Cherubino kisses the ribbon a second time, notices Susanna's approach, turns and goes left, crossing above Susanna and the armchair to UR of the Count's door. He escapes toward the left because he wants to keep Susanna at bay with his stronger right hand while he holds the ribbon out of her reach on the other side. Susanna follows Cherubino.

20. (measure 31) Holding the ribbon as far away as possible with his outstretched left arm, Cherubino turns and with his right arm wards off Susanna, who stops UL of the armchair.

21. (measure 32) Susanna goes downstage to DL of the armchair. Her walk is an emotional expression of her annoyance with Cherubino. It is also induced by the energy of the chase and is mixed with an "I-refuse-to-fight-with-naughty-boys" motivation.

22. (measure 33) Cherubino goes to Susanna's left, stuffing the ribbon in his belt with his left hand, then nudging Susanna with his right elbow. All of his moves from here to the end of the recitative are governed by his determination to keep the ribbon and yet remain in Susanna's good graces.

23. (measure 34) Cherubino reaches into his belt and takes out a folded paper that has the words of the song he has written on it.

24. (measure 35) Cherubino gives Susanna the song. Susanna turns and takes the song with her left hand.
25. (measure 36) Cherubino backs slightly left to emphasize his next words.
26. (measure 41) Cherubino goes to Susanna and embraces her around the waist. Feeling that he has been forgiven for the theft of the ribbon, he does not neglect the opportunity to snuggle up to Susanna once more.
27. (measure 42) With an air of saying "How can one be angry with this darling little scamp?" Susanna gives the boy a push on the left shoulder with her right hand, causing him to reel in a complete counterclockwise circle, ending up halfway between the armchair and the Count's door, facing Susanna. She looks at the song Cherubino has given her, wondering what to do with it. Then she turns, goes to the table and leaves it there before returning to the chair. The song must be "planted" on the table so that Basilio can find it there during the recitative that follows Cherubino's aria. Susanna must be careful not to give away the fact that her action has a stage director's reason behind it. Without overstressing the point, she must make it clear that the table is the only logical place for the song. Susanna returns to the chair in order to pick up the nightcap. Instead, she becomes fascinated with Cherubino's youthful ardor and sits down in the armchair without taking her eyes off him.

As the recitative neared its end, Cherubino gradually became more and more excited: He succeeded in obtaining possession of the ribbon that touched the hair of his beloved Countess, he gave his poem to Susanna, and furthermore, he pressed the body of the pretty chambermaid close to his own. As he reels around, he feels intoxicated and dizzy. The orchestral accompaniment of the aria must appear to be generated by rapturous sensuality, by the beating of this adolescent heart, throbbing excitedly with the pangs of the sweet awakening of Eros. All of Cherubino's moves in this aria are primarily the expression of his urge to project both in words and in action the pleasure and pain of his youthful passions. But he is telling it all to Susanna, and quite a few of his moves are motivated by his desire to be near her, to touch her, and to embrace her. Naturally, Susanna is affected by Cherubino's confessions and advances, and her reactions provide additional reasons for his movements:

1. (measure 9) Cherubino backs slightly UL.
2. (measure 12) He backs slightly again.
3. (measure 15) Cherubino goes DR toward Susanna.
4. (measure 19) Cherubino rapturously turns slightly Cclw.
5. (measure 22) Cherubino turns Clw to address Susanna.

6. (measure 26) Cherubino sits on the left arm of the armchair and addresses Susanna.

7. (measure 31) Cherubino embraces Susanna. His embrace invokes the suspension of the G-flat by the second violins in the thirty-second measure.

8. (measure 33) Susanna gently pushes the boy away toward the left and, laughing, turns Clw in the chair. As a result of her push, Cherubino gets up to UL of the armchair.

9. (measure 36) Because Susanna has turned away from him, Cherubino goes right, crossing above the armchair to its UR corner, so that he can continue to tell her his story face to face.

10. (measure 37) With his shoulders still facing right, Cherubino looks over his left shoulder to address Susanna.

11. (measure 41) Cherubino gazes DR.

12. (measure 45) Cherubino goes DR as far as CC.

13. (measure 48) Cherubino turns LSB and backs UR to the left of the stool.

14. (measure 51) Cherubino goes DL to Susanna. The "sighs" of the first violins in measures 51 through 57 must be justified by Cherubino's own breathlessness.

15. (measure 56) Cherubino sits on the right arm of the armchair.

16. (measure 65) Immediately after the "fermata" in this measure (which adds two extra half-note beats) Cherubino gets up and goes slightly DR.

17. (measure 68) Cherubino turns LSB and backs UR.

18. (measure 69) Susanna laughs during the quarter rest and, still sitting, turns Cclw.

19. (measure 70) Cherubino goes left, crossing above the armchair to the left of it, to address Susanna face to face.

20. (measure 76) Cherubino sits on the left arm of the armchair.

21. (measure 84) After the fermata (which adds two additional half-note beats) Cherubino gets up and goes slightly DL.

22. (measure 87) Cherubino turns RSB.

23. (measure 93) Cherubino goes slightly right toward Susanna.

24. (measure 96) Cherubino backs slightly.

25. (measure 97) Cherubino turns Cclw away from Susanna in embarrassment. Of particular interest is the "piano subito" on the downbeat of the ninety-eighth measure. Here Cherubino tells Susanna that when there is no one with whom he can share his passions, he "speaks of love alone" ("parlo d'amor con me"), and his realization that he is giving away the secret of his solitary amorous pursuits makes him catch himself and blush. This is one of the supreme examples of Mozart's unsurpassed gifts for the musical depiction of subtle psychological details.

26. (measure 98) During the quarter rest with the fermata (which, like the preceding fermata in this measure, adds an extra half-note beat) Cherubino looks at Susanna over his right shoulder.

27. (measure 99) Cherubino turns Clw, goes right, and kneels at Susanna's left side. This final rapturous kneeling is equivalent to an exclamation of "Oh, I don't care if you know *everything* about me!"

28. (measure 100) At the conclusion of his final note Cherubino puts his head on Susanna's lap.

The duet—Fiordiligi and Dorabella

In Beaumarchais' and Mozart's *The Marriage of Figaro,* producers and directors have at their disposal an intricate and masterfully constructed plot with a great number of finely drawn characters and a wealth of detailed stage directions. No so in *Così fan tutte.* Here, we are pretty much on our own and have to supply not only the major part of the motivations, but also most of the details of individual characterization. The following psychological analysis of the dramatis personae is one that I consider logical, theatrically valid, and in keeping with Mozart's music. I am well aware, however, that entirely different interpretations can be imagined and defended with arguments of equal strength.

I think of Fiordiligi as the older sister who sets the tone for the younger Dorabella and who makes all the important decisions. Fiordiligi resists temptation longer than her sister, and when she finally gives in, her passion has a more sincere and pathetic ring. Dorabella is a much flightier person, quite playful and possibly even a bit giggly. Throughout the first act Dorabella seconds her sister's heroics, but then she begins to be bored with this rather tiresome pose of eternal fidelity and is ready for something less heavy and more entertaining.

The setting for the first scene of the second act is described by Da Ponte simply as "a room," leaving all the elaboration up to the individual taste of the producer. I think of it as the dressing chamber of the sisters with two practically identical tables placed symmetrically in RB2 and LB2 facing slightly away from each other. There are two hand-mirrors, one on each table, and Fiordiligi, who sits on the left, also has a small *etui* containing some beauty spots. Boxes with jewelry and various bottles of toiletries are visible on the dressing tables. A number of other objects are present in the room, but since they are not used here, there is no need to describe them.

At the beginning of the second act the sisters listen in virtuous silence to Despina's dissertation (Aria No. 19) on what is right and proper for the modern, emancipated woman. As the saucy maid departs toward the right, Dorabella turns to watch her go. Fiordiligi remains adamant in her

rejection of such worldly philosophy. Dorabella, however, is quite impressed, although she feels that a strong initial word of condemnation
might prove to be a good point of departure and would give her subsequent arguments a more solid basis. It would be terribly nice, she
feels, if Fiordiligi could be induced to consent to a bit of innocent
flirtation. If only Fiordiligi would stop being so aggressively virtuous and
stuffy, those exotic young men could prove to be very amusing, and the
whole thing would surely turn out to be quite a lark. The entire recitative
preceding Duet No. 20 is devoted to Dorabella's efforts to persuade her
sister to relax her intransigent attitude toward Tizio and Sempronio. There
are five verbal and bodily moves by Dorabella, and each of them is par-
ried with appropriate arguments from her sister. It is only after Dorabella's
sixth attempt that Fiordiligi begins to give in. Since the older sister plays
a more passive role in this exchange, she remains seated at the table. It
is Dorabella who takes the initiative, and each of her verbal thrusts is
emphasized by an additional energy output in the form of a bodily
movement. During the forty-one measures of this recitative Dorabella has
ten changes of position. Fiordiligi participates in only one of these—
the final one.

1. (measure 7) Dorabella gets up rather languidly to begin the
   important argument. She is beginning to get set for the campaign.
   Fiordiligi wants none of it.
2. (measure 10) Dorabella goes slightly left, opening her mouth
   to contradict her sister's statement that "the joke could be dangerous," but she is stopped by Fiordiligi's gesture and words.
3. (measure 14) Dorabella goes further left to Fiordiligi's right in
   order to emphasize the part of the plan involving Despina.
   Fiordiligi dismisses the argument with what she considers the
   final word, concerning the need to avoid all gossip. She seems
   to be slightly bored by the conversation and turns away to apply
   a recalcitrant beauty spot and to watch the effect in the mirror.
4. (measure 16) Dorabella crosses above the chair to UL of
   Fiordiligi. She wants to face her sister while she continues to
   present her case. Fiordiligi is not impressed.
5. (measure 25) Dorabella goes right, crossing above the chair to
   UR of Fiordiligi. In order to emphasize Despina's contribution to
   the success of her plan, she looks, gestures, and walks in the
   direction where the maid was last seen. "And what of our
   engagements?" asks Fiordiligi.
6. (measure 27 or 28, depending on the size of the stage) Dorabella
   goes slowly DR. There is no reason why she should go in this
   particular direction. The walk is motivated by an urge to move.
   Dorabella is pouting, and the emotional tone could be described
   as: "It is very difficult to live in the same house with such an

unreasonable person." Dorabella knows that her sister prides herself on her clear thinking, especially in matters of higher morality. She has been known to be impressed occasionally by a logical construction such as: "An innocent diversion is not equivalent to a breach of faith." Dorabella tries it, and Fiordiligi *is* impressed. "That is true," she says. This is the turning point of the entire plot. From here on everything runs downhill to the inevitable denouement.

7. (measure 31) Dorabella whirls around to face her sister—almost unexpectedly, she has won her case. "Do as you please," Fiordiligi says.

8. (measure 32) Dorabella runs toward Fiordiligi. Now that the main point has been conceded, there are a few subsidiary details to be arranged. Also, she feels grateful to Fiordiligi and wants to hug her. Dorabella's enthusiasm seems somewhat unseemly to Fiordiligi, who stops her sister's progress by pointing out that she has warned her and disclaims responsibility for possible consequences.

9. (measure 36) Dorabella runs to Fiordiligi and kneels close to her. She brushes off Fiordiligi's last remark. The thing to decide is how to divide the two cavaliers. Fiordiligi does not care one way or the other. She has consented to participate in this "innocent diversion," but only to oblige her sister.

10. (measure 41) Dorabella gets up, pulling Fiordiligi with her. Dorabella is full of playful energy and wants to put her sister in the right mood for the adventure. Fiordiligi decides that, having consented to humor Dorabella, she might as well be a good sport and show some enthusiasm.

In the third measure of Duet No. 20, Dorabella turns Fiordiligi around and leads her downstage. Then in the fifth measure she turns to hug Fiordiligi and presses her head on her sister's shoulder, giggling at the prospect of the good time they will have flirting with the two cavaliers. All of this is motivated by Dorabella's bubbling vitality. In the seventh measure Dorabella looks up at her sister.

Beginning with the ninth measure, when Dorabella backs upstage, much of the activity performed by the two sisters is of a type that could be called "illustrative." They anticipate and act out in advance the way they and their adorers will behave at their forthcoming meeting. In measure 11 Dorabella walks downstage, and in measure 12 she turns to face Fiordiligi. Her walk should be "gay and bright."* Then in measure 15 Fiordiligi walks to the left, turning to face Dorabella in measure 17.

---

* My singing translation for Dorabella's "io di quel risponderò" is "I will be so gay and bright."

Her walk, on the other hand, should be "so demure."* In measure 19
Dorabella kneels and gestures with exaggeration, obviously imitating
Tizio's (Guglielmo's) fervent declarations in the first act. This imitation
continues in measure 20, when she gets up and makes a big Clw semicircle
to the table on the right. By contrast, when Fiordiligi goes to the right
and gestures with gusto (measure 21), she must be sure to mimic the
more ethereal Sempronio (Ferrando).

In measure 22 Dorabella picks up a hand-mirror and sits down on
the right side of the table, facing left. Fiordiligi goes to her sister, takes
the mirror, and turns to sit down on the left side of the table. In measure
24 Fiordiligi holds the mirror so that both sisters can admire themselves.
All of this business with the mirrors—both here and later—was invented
to supply additional reasons for the young ladies' moves. Thus, in measure
25, Fiordiligi gets up and goes slightly left, admiring herself in the mirror, and two measures later she turns and holds the mirror toward Dorabella so that her sister can do likewise. Pleased with what she has seen,
Dorabella gets up with the downbeat of measure 19 and walks a little to
the right, while Fiordiligi puts the mirror down on the table and backs
to up left of the right chair. Two measures later Dorabella turns LSB
and backs a little to face her sister so that, during the long sustained
note of measures 32 and 33, Fiordiligi can go to the right, crossing the
chair, to join Dorabella.

Fiordiligi's arpeggio, which descends to an extraordinary low A-
natural, should be sung in a suitably exaggerated manner and accompanied by the shaking of an admonitory finger, as though the older sister
is good-naturedly berating the younger one and saying: "Oh, you naughty,
naughty girl!" The vocal imitations in measures 35 through 38 should be
seen as well as heard. To make them visible, Dorabella, who acts as the
ringleader throughout this scene, takes the initiative and, crossing Fiordiligi, walks to the down left corner of the table. Once there, she stops and
looks over her right shoulder, inviting her sister to follow. Fiordiligi does,
and this imitative movement, which is repeated in measures 37 and 38,
takes the two sisters all the way to CC. In measure 39 Dorabella turns
to face Fiordiligi, and after her sister pats her playfully on the shoulder
(with "sospi*retti*"), she turns and goes beyond the table at the left. As
Dorabella walks in this direction, she remembers her sister's recent excursion to the lowest reaches of her vocal range and decides to attempt
something similar. This takes the form of an almost grotesque portamento
down a major ninth, a vocal joke that Dorabella combines with a large
clockwise turn and an extravagant bow in Fiordiligi's direction. The
older sister, who finds this quite amusing, turns and walks down right,
crossing the table and continuing to imitate Sempronio's sighs. In the
meantime, Dorabella picks up Fiordiligi's mirror, which is lying on the

* I render Fiordiligi's "io dell'altro imiterò" as "so demure I'll be tonight."

left dressing table. Inspecting her reflection, she walks in a counterclockwise semicircle around the table to up right of it so that with her next sentence (measure 47) she can wave the mirror in the air, indulging in a rather violent bit of gesturing.

Fiordiligi, who interprets Dorabella's vigorous waving as an invitation to come and admire herself in the mirror, hurries around the table, but as she arrives near her sister, Dorabella presses the mirror to her bosom and goes down left to complete her circle around the left dressing table. Not to be outdone, Fiordiligi decides to make a similar circle around the right table, so that by measure 51, when Dorabella turns to look at Fiordiligi, the older sister is well on her way toward RA1. Now Dorabella puts down her mirror, and as soon as her sister turns around (measure 52), starts walking toward her. This walk must be timed so that Dorabella puts her hand into Fiordiligi's on the accent of the horns, cellos, and basses at the beginning of measure 54. With the repeat of this accent two measures later the sisters come closer together. Then (measure 58) Dorabella backs left, pulling Fiordiligi with her. After stopping below the right table (measure 59), Dorabella backs again, still pulling Fiordiligi.

By measure 61 both sisters have arrived in the general area of CC. In measure 62 Dorabella turns away from her sister, but continues to sing to her over her right shoulder. Fiordiligi then turns away (measure 64), continuing to sing to Dorabella over her left shoulder. The sisters are back to back. They turn face to face and back away from each other in measure 67. In measure 70 they approach and hold hands. They separate in measure 71, still facing. In measure 73 they join outstretched right hands and, dancing, exchange right-left positions, with Fiordiligi passing above Dorabella. In measure 75 they turn face to face, join outstretched left hands, and again exchange right-left positions. In the last measure of the orchestral postlude they curtsey to each other.

During the entire final section, beginning with measure 62, the sisters assume the roles and looks of a pair of porcelain shepherdesses. Generally speaking, their behavior throughout this duet is filled with joie de vivre, and an almost dance-like expression of girlish vitality and good humor.

Motivations and movement patterns

Looked upon purely from the point of view of the actor, the direction of movements motivated by urges was described as optional. It must not be imagined, however, that the execution of these movements is left to chance or to a last-minute decision on the part of the performer. On the contrary, all stage movements, whether based on reasons or urges, are carefully pre-set by the stage director. He is the artistic organizer of all stage activities, including motivations. The skillful director takes advantage of the opportunities offered by urges and reasons, using them to move the characters of the drama to the different locations where in his opinion the various sections of the piece should take place. He mixes and interrelates various types of motivations so as to avoid obvious procedures that the audience can recognize as technical devices.

Just as the composer strives for a harmonious musical form, so should the stage director endeavor to devise a visual pattern of movement that satisfies his artistic feeling for unity, diversity, and balance. The analyses of the two Mozartian scenes in this chapter were undertaken to show how various types of motivations affect the singing actor. A discussion of the same scenes, from the point of view of the stage director, will illuminate a different facet of the relationship between staging processes and motivations.

The general scheme of movement in Cherubino's aria is relatively simple: it is based on a pattern resembling the swing of a pendulum. Susanna remains in the armchair throughout the aria, while Cherubino plays consecutively in five fundamental positions:

1. Stage left to the left of the armchair
2. In the center, up right of the armchair
3. Stage right to the left of the table
4. In the center to the right of the armchair
5. Stage left to the left of the armchair

The obvious similarity of positions 1 and 5 and of positions 2 and 4 is modified and disguised by additional movements that are superimposed on this simple pattern:

1. Stage left to the left of the armchair
   a. The boy backs twice (measures 9 and 12), emphasizing the musical excitement values of the melodic rise to the high G.
   b. He walks toward Susanna (measure 15) and turns twice, left and right (measures 19 and 22).
   c. He sits on the left arm of the chair (measure 26).
   d. He embraces Susanna (measure 31, highlighting the suspension of the G-flat in the second violins). Susanna pushes him away (measure 33).
2. In the center, up right of the armchair
   a. He crosses above the armchair to up right of Susanna (elaborating the tension of the long B-flat).
   b. He turns to downright (measure 41).
3. Stage right to the left of the table

    a. He walks down right (measure 45); turns and backs (measure 48). Same musical emphasis as in 1*a*.

4. In the center to the right of the armchair
    a. He returns to the right of the armchair in measure 51 ("sighs" of the first violins).
    b. He sits on the right arm of the chair in measure 56 (continued "sighs" of the first violins).
    c. He walks down right slightly in measure 65, then turns and backs in measure 68 (first vocal climax).

5. Stage left to the left of the armchair
    a. He returns to the left of the armchair, crossing above it (measure 70).
    b. He sits on the left arm of the chair (measure 76), highlighting the countermelody in the first violins.
    c. He walks slightly down left in measure 84, then turns and backs in measure 87 (second vocal climax).
    d. In the final section (coda: measure 92 to the end) he elaborates his confession and embarrassment, then kneels at Susanna's side.

Several of the musical-dramatic connections in this aria were discussed earlier. At this point I should like to draw attention to such structural features as the echoing of the musical excitement in sections 1*a* and 3*a*, and the mirror treatment of the sections leading to the two vocal climaxes (measures 65 to 68 and 84 to 87). The mechanics of motivation are simple in the extreme. Urges and "inner-vision" motives draw Cherubino away from Susanna; the desire to approach and face Susanna is always the reason that induces him to return to her. Susanna's turns, which are primarily urges, set the stage for Cherubino's two crossings above the armchair.

The general scheme of the *Così fan tutte* duet is somewhat more complicated. The nature of the subject matter and the arrangement of the stage properties favor a symmetrical design. I take advantage of the areas adjoining the dressing tables to separate the sisters and to bring them together again in a number of varying patterns.

The overall composition of the movement is built around five basic positions:

1. The sisters are together at stage left.
2. They separate.
3. They get together at the right and move to the center.
4. They separate.
5. They get together at the right and move to the center.

A number of more intricate patterns are superimposed on this fundamental design:

1. The sisters are together at stage left.
    a. Two moves are initiated by Dorabella.
2. They separate.
    a. Dorabella moves to the right, illustrating her future behavior. Fiordiligi follows suit, moving left.
    b. Dorabella returns to the center and kneels, illustrating her swain's future behavior. Fiordiligi follows suit, but remains near the left table.
    c. Dorabella moves to the right table and initiates the business with the mirror.
3. They get together at the right and move to the center.
    a. Fiordiligi joins Dorabella at the right table to share in the business with the mirror. Fiordiligi continues and elaborates this business.
    b. Dorabella moves to the down right corner. Fiordiligi joins her.
    c. Dorabella crosses Fiordiligi and both sisters move to the center.
4. They separate.
    a. Dorabella moves to the left, illustrating her future behavior.
    b. Fiordiligi follows suit, moving to the right while Dorabella moves around the table.
    c. Dorabella completes her circle around the left table while
    d. Fiordiligi imitates Dorabella's earlier move by circling around the right table.
    e. Fiordiligi completes her circle around the table.
5. They get together at the right and move to the center.
    a. Dorabella joins Fiordiligi at the down right corner.
    b. Dorabella pulls Fiordiligi to the center.
    c. The sisters have fun imitating a flirting couple.

In studying the design, one notices immediately that section 4 is a variation of section 2 and that a similar relationship exists between sections 3 and 5. This basic resemblance of structure is camouflaged by reversing the left-right positions of the sisters and by various embellishments of the movement patterns, such as the added circling of the tables in section 4.

Constructing a varied and balanced pattern of movement is only a part of the story, however. It is of the utmost importance that the essential characteristics of the plot and the music be reflected with the greatest possible fidelity in all staging compositions. Dramatically speaking, all the moves in the sisters' duet come into being as a result of Dorabella's efforts to persuade Fiordiligi to agree to an innocent flirtation. She is in very high spirits and her urges set the tone for Fiordiligi, who is content to follow her sister's lead. The special musical events—the canonic imitations in measures 35 to 40, the accents on the downbeats of measures 57 and 59, the chuckles in measures 63 to 67, and the dance-like character of the orchestral postlude—are all faithfully mirrored in the behavior and movements of the two sisters.

Discussing these scenes from the points of view of both the singing actor and the stage director may seem a roundabout and somewhat repetitious process, but it helps to clarify their respective jobs. The stage director converts both the musical and the dramatic values of an opera into a carefully thought-out and well-balanced theatrical activity, devising visual shapes that reflect and reinforce both the content and the form of the music; the accomplished actor brings all these ideas to life through the power of his individual vocal and histrionic talent.

4

Operatic pantomimes

NO YOUNG SINGER can hope for a successful career in opera today unless he undertakes a systematic study of voice, music, and acting. This extensive training program is complicated by the fact that the student must master all these necessary skills in a relatively short time. Piano or violin lessons are often started when a child is seven or eight years old, but singers generally have to wait at least another ten years before they can start studying voice in earnest. Once they have begun, it usually takes two more years until they are ready to tackle even relatively simple operatic excerpts.

While musical competence in the form of sight-reading, harmony, and piano playing can be acquired right along with vocal schooling, this is not true of operatic acting skills. Most voice teachers feel, justifiably, that a study of opera dramatics, which normally involves a combination of singing and acting, should be deferred until the pupil's vocal technique is firmly established. A premature concern with theatrical actions is apt to harm the voice and lead to poor singing habits. This desire for unhampered vocal development is reflected in the curriculums of conservatories and colleges, where students majoring in voice are not encouraged, and often not permitted, to attend opera classes until they become juniors.

When I went to Boston many years ago to head the opera school of the New England Conservatory of Music, I began searching for methods that would enable students to learn operatic stage techniques without straining their voices and, in fact, without having to use their voices at all. I considered it extremely important that young singers combine this part of their training with their other studies, instead of waiting until they were vocally and musically mature to begin the study of operatic acting, thus wasting much valuable time. Courses in spoken drama were useful up to a point, but they did not touch upon the crux of the operatic problem, which lies in a close integration of music with the specific thoughts and feelings of a stage character. I felt that future singing actors needed a preparatory training based on an understanding of the language of instrumental music as it was practiced by distinguished operatic composers and on the interaction of this music with dramatic events that were specifically operatic in origin.

Extended pantomimes taken from standard works finally turned out to be the answer. They offered opportunities for vocally immature young singers to develop skill in operatic acting, and wherever they were introduced on an experimental level, proved popular with both teachers and students. Furthermore, these pantomimes help to teach young opera singers one of the most difficult aspects of their art: remaining in character when they are not singing in a way that does full justice to the accompanying music.

One of the great advantages of these pantomimes is that they provide the entire membership of a class with the opportunity for active participation. Whenever the subtext of a pantomime lends itself to an exact duplication with the rhythm of the accompaniment, one member of the group can perform the actions while the others recite the words in unison or think them silently in time with the music. Since there are no problems of pitches or vocal registers, I find it very valuable to have each pantomime studied and performed by all members of the class, regardless of whether the operatic character in question is a man or a woman. To facilitate this type of class work, one prepares appropriate mimeographed material of the type shown in Example 4–1 from the *Cavalleria* pantomime.

Is he at | home? I wish I could be | cer - tain... but not a soul must |

see me... there's no one | here. Let me | look... all is | quiet...

Example 4–1

There are five pantomimes presented in this chapter. The first two (one for a woman, one for a man) are concerned solely with *leading* action; the third contains two leading actions and four *supporting* ones; and the last two are devoted to supporting action.

Other excerpts suitable for pantomimes will be found in later chapters of this volume. For additional practice of silent leading action, see the orchestral introductions to Rosina's aria (Chapter 5), to the Countess' Cavatina (Chapter 7), and to Marguerite's "Song of the King of Thule" (Chapter 9). The Susanna-Figaro and the Guglielmo-Don Alfonso-Ferrando scenes analyzed in Chapter 9 are also appropriate for studying ensemble actions in pantomime form.

The student should not neglect the supporting pantomimes presented in this chapter. The importance of the supporting actor cannot be stressed too much, and it is essential for every opera singer to learn the most effective ways to assist whichever of his colleagues has the leading action.

The most common form of interaction between the leading actor and his supporting partner is that of addresser and addressee: the leading actor sings, the supporting actor listens. "When in doubt, listen to those who sing" is an old and reliable operatic maxim. This rule, however, is not as simple as it may seem, for listening can mean a number of things. It can be active, passive, or even downright malicious.

Fortunately, malicious behavior on the part of the listening partner is quite rare. It is true that singers occasionally accuse their colleagues of willfully upstaging them. I suspect, however, that most of the time this happens not because of ill will, but rather out of ignorance and inexperience. A singer who has not been taught the techniques of taking and giving the stage can make things very uncomfortable for his colleagues, and he may often do so without having the slightest awareness of the trouble he is causing.

It is undeniable, on the other hand, that some theatrical bigwigs indulge in the most ludicrous antics in order to remain in the limelight. Their egoism and discourtesy can reach truly monumental proportions. I shall never forget a particularly glaring example of such behavior which I witnessed many years ago. It was during the first act of *Tosca*. While the prima donna was extolling the delights that awaited her and her lover Cavaradossi that night, he, impersonated by a famous tenor, walked upstage and embarked on a vigorous and extended pantomime directed toward the chapel where Angelotti had taken refuge earlier in the act. "Go ahead and eat, you poor hungry fellow," was the gist of the tenor's gesticulated message. "I will get rid of this woman as soon as I can, and then we will find a way to spirit you out of here!" This appalling exhibition went on in steady counterpoint with the soprano's solo and lasted until the tenor was ready to trumpet forth his high B-flat. It was only then that he deigned to acknowledge the presence of his lady love. I am happy to report that this gentleman's operatic career came to a well-deserved halt not long after this disgraceful performance, when all the sopranos of the company notified the management that they would resign rather than continue to share the stage with him.

Passive listening, while not as objectionable as the malicious variety, can also be very harmful. An air of absent-minded boredom on the part of the listening colleague affects the audience and makes it lose interest in the words and movements of the leading actor. Many beginners imagine that it is sufficient to face the singing partner and pretend to pay attention. These passive listeners are often only dimly aware of what is being sung, and they do not begin to come to life until they hear their cue.

Active listening, on the other hand, is one of the most valuable theatrical skills, and no one who has not mastered it has any right to call himself an accomplished actor.

The active listener constantly digests the import of what he hears and evaluates it in the light of what it means to his stage personality. This produces visible reactions caused by such thoughts as: Do I approve or disapprove? Do I believe or disbelieve him? Is this something that I knew before? Is it a surprise or perhaps a shock to me? Does it please me? Does it annoy, upset, anger, or provoke me? Should I try to contradict or interrupt him? The true supporting actor functions almost like a prompter by helping to elicit, stimulate, and provoke the succeeding words and actions of his partner.

Various ways in which stage directors can use the supporting actor's movements to achieve changes of grouping and stage locations will be discussed in Chapter 9. A well-trained performer, however, must not rely solely on the guidance of his director, and I hope that a careful study of the examples of leading and supporting action found here will help and stimulate him to master his art.

Acting was defined earlier as the communication to the audience of a character's thoughts and feelings. This is done with words, with voice color, with the singer's appearance, and with the movements of his body. A singer also reveals ideas and emotions by relating himself to other characters, objects, and abstract concepts. Some of these are real and visible; others are imagined and invisible. But before a singer can focus his attention on any of them, he must know what they are and where they are located. He will, therefore, find it very useful to make a list of focal points and to learn their position on and off stage by studying diagrams of the settings. These diagrams include all the scenic elements and furniture props needed for the enactment of a given scene. Inventories of focal points, on the other hand, should list only items on which the actor actually fixes his attention and should omit objects, such as chairs or doors, which he uses only with an absent-minded automatism. Such an inventory can be arranged in many different ways, but I recommend the following scheme:

Focal points

Onstage	Description	Locations
Other characters		
Scenic elements		
Furniture props		
Hand props		

Offstage (real or imagined)	Description	Direction and connecting scenic elements
Other characters Other objects Abstract ideas		

When making such a list it is well to distinguish between focal points that are written into the libretto and score, and those that are invented by the director, derived by inference, or transposed from other portions of the work. Those in the first category are intrinsic and are, generally speaking, applicable to all staging arrangements; the others are superimposed and subject to change depending on individual settings and the wishes of different producers.

The young singer should also bear in mind that the locations of all ingredients, not only those that are superimposed by a director, are subject to change from production to production. For example, in my inventory for the aria from *A Masked Ball*, Amelia and the portrait of Riccardo are intrinsic items; but Amelia's placement at the beginning of the recitative, the direction in which she leaves the stage, and the location of the portrait may be different in each and every mise-en-scène.

Here again, as in all other sections of this volume, my intention is not to furnish a ready-made solution, but to demonstrate a method that can be usefully applied not only in these operas, but in most others.

Before presenting the actual staging of each pantomime, I shall discuss its problems from several points of view: its dramatic content, musical aspects, the focal points in the setting, and the stage actions.

CAVALLERIA RUSTICANA: Pantomime for Santuzza's entrance

The drama

Santuzza, a simple Sicilian village girl, has fallen in love with the handsome young soldier Turiddu, who has promised to marry her. After seducing her, he seems unwilling to keep his word, having been lured away by his former flame, Lola. In the opera, Santuzza's feelings are expressed in her aria "Voi lo sapete, o Mamma."* They are presented even more clearly and fully in Verga's play, on which the opera is based. Here, slightly condensed, is what Santuzza says to Turiddu's mother in the play:

Before Turiddu went to the army, he had an understanding with Lola. Then, when he returned, he found her married to Alfio, and at first he put her

* For the full text and a discussion of this aria, see pp. 111–113.

out of his mind. But she did not forget him. She managed to walk by every time she saw him at my door, and the trollop stole him away from me with her pagan eyes. She would always start a conversation with him: "Friend Turiddu, what are you doing in the neighborhood? Don't you know that it was not the wish of God? Now leave me alone, for I am a married woman!" The "wish of God" was to tempt him! He started courting me just to spite her, because she had married someone else. How true it is that an old love is never forgotten! When he purred sweet words to me, with those honest eyes of his, I felt my heart would jump out of my breast! I was crazy, yes! How could I refuse him when he begged me: "Let me in, Santuzza; let me in if it is true that you really care for me!" How could I refuse him? But I said to him: "Listen, Turriddu. Swear first, swear before God that I shall be your wife!" He swore! Then, when that wicked woman found out, she became insanely jealous and took it into her head to steal him away from me. She changed my Turiddu just like that . . . He denies it because he is sorry for me, but he does not love me any longer. And now I am in this condition . . . I think my brothers would kill me with their own hands if they knew . . . But this is not important. If Turiddu didn't love her, I would die happy. Yesterday evening he came and said: "Goodbye, I am going on an errand." His face was so kind . . . Oh, God! Is it possible with a face like that to have the treachery of Judas in one's heart? Later, a neighbor who was going to confession told me that she had seen Turiddu in our vicinity, in front of Lola's door.

Santuzza's actions during this pantomime must reflect her total emotional state, as well as her immediate concerns and desires. Her general frame of mind can be summarized as unhappiness over Turiddu's behavior, jealousy of Lola, and worry over her own condition. Her immediate concerns are: an urgent need to learn whether or not Turiddu spent the night with Lola, the fear of being rebuffed by Turiddu or his mother, the desire to keep her inquiries secret, and her shame at being driven to this extremity.

The music

The general character of the music reflects the down-to-earth and almost primitive psychology of the wretched village girl who finds herself on the verge of being abandoned by her lover. The two contrasting sections appear to correspond to Santuzza's two main preoccupations: her worried unhappiness and her religious fervor. The first part is set in the minor mode and is entrusted to the cellos, accompanied by the upper strings. These thirteen measures portray the darker side of the girl's present state of mind. In contrast to this, we have the major mode and the surging woodwind phrases of the second part, which express so well the hope that Santuzza derives from her faith.

The echo effect in the cello melody in Sections 8 and 9 of the first part should be interpreted and staged with great care, while the flute phrases of the second part (Example 4–2) seem to lend themselves partic-

Example 4–2. CAVALLERIA RUSTICANA

ularly well to an association with a specific gesture, such as the sign of the cross (see below, p. 141).

The paucity of dynamic markings in the piano-vocal score should not be misinterpreted by the accompanying pianist. This type of music favors a straightforward approach with nuances that follow quite unashamedly the upward and downward flow of the melodic line.

Focal points

Onstage	*Description*	*Location*
Scenic elements	1. Door to Mamma's house	
	2. Window in Mamma's house	
	3. Church Window	

Offstage (real or imaginary)	*Description*	*Directions and connecting scenic elements*
Other characters	4. Villagers who might see her	Left wing, upstage and downstage. Right wing downstage.
	5. Mamma and Turridu	Inside Mamma's house (beyond the door and the window)
Abstract ideas	6. Appeal for the Madonna's help	Church window
	7. Hatred for Lola	In upstage left wing

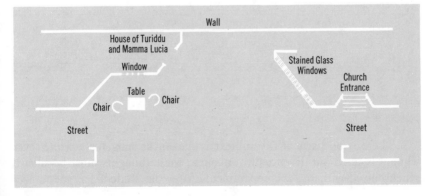

Diagram 4–1. The setting for Santuzza's entrance

Santuzza's actions explained

The twenty-eight-measure orchestral interlude that accompanies Santuzza's entrance in the opera consists of two contrasting sections of approximately equal length. Before the student is introduced to the mise-en-scène of the first section, I ask her to memorize the following subtext: "Is he at home? I wish I could be certain . . . But not a soul must see me! There's no one watching. The square is so quiet. The service must have started. I must find out, I must find out, I must find out the truth! But what if Mamma's there? The window's closed. What am I doing?"

These sentences fit exactly with the music played by the cellos (Example 4–3), and by compressing the melody to less than an octave and a half, we enable the student to sing or hum it right along with the words.

Example 4–3. First part

There is no harm if the subtext is spoken or sung for a while, even while it is acted out. Eventually, of course, these thoughts must be silently synchronized with the accompaniment. After the student has memorized

the music and the subtext, I point out to her that most of her thoughts
refer to such real or imaginary focal points as Turiddu's house, its door
and window, the church entrance, and various offstage directions from
where she could be observed. Santuzza's movements and motivations, as
well as the focal points of her attention, can be listed as: (*a*) a walk to
Turiddu's house in order to knock at the door; (*b*) a series of movements
to assure herself that she is not being watched from offstage; (*c*) a return
to the house; (*d*) hesitation due to the fear of facing Mamma Lucia; (*e*)
an attempt to look through the window to see if Turiddu or Mamma are
at home; and (*f*) shame at behaving in such an unworthy and prying
manner.

In the second section of the pantomime (measures 14 to 28, Example
4–4) the mood changes. The sequence of thoughts are written beneath the
music.

Example 4–4. Second part

Santuzza's movements are now governed by the religious fervor of
her appeal to the Virgin and her determination to regain Turiddu's love.
The visual presence of the church and the unmistakable meaning of
such symbolic gestures as making the sign of the cross, kneeling, and folding her hands in prayer, enable the actress to convey Santuzza's mental
processes with great clarity.

Putting all these elements together, we can allocate a specific action for each musical phrase and its corresponding thought. The roman numerals above the various phrases in the preceding musical illustrations correspond to the following stage movements.

FIRST PART (MEASURES 1–13)

1. Santuzza enters from up left and goes right toward the door of Turiddu's house. She takes five or six steps.

ii. She stops, hesitating.

iii. She turns Cclw and looks in the direction from which she came.

iv. She assures herself that there is no one coming from up left.

v. She turns Clw and goes down right to slightly left of CC, looking into the right wing. She wants to make certain that no one from that direction will see her knocking on Turiddu's door.

vi. She looks over her left shoulder at the church entrance and down the street that goes off down left.

vii. She turns Clw, and with some agitation, goes up right to the door of the house, raising her arm to knock.

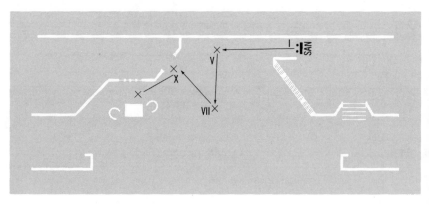

Diagram 4–2

viii. She suddenly realizes that the door may be answered by Turiddu's mother.

ix. Afraid and ashamed to discuss things with Mamma Lucia, she drops her arm and then turns slightly Cclw, away from the door.

x. She wishes she could find out if Mamma has already gone to church. She looks at the window and goes down right toward it with the idea of looking inside.

xi. Ashamed of her behavior, she turns Cclw, so that she faces the church.

SECOND PART (MEASURES 14–28)

I. She looks at the church and the stained-glass window portraying the Virgin Mary, whom she regards as her special protectress.

II. Drawn toward the church by her feeling for the Madonna, she goes down left as far as CC.

III. She stops and makes the sign of the cross.

IV. She continues down left toward the church.

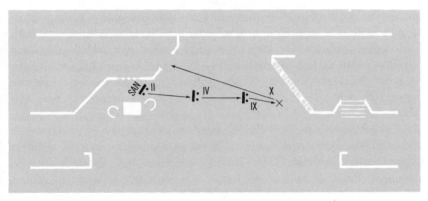

Diagram 4–3

v. She goes down on both knees, bends her head, and folds her hands to her face.

vi. She prays fervently, asking the Madonna to make Turiddu forget Lola.

vii. Her hatred for Lola gets the better of her.

viii. Still on her knees, she makes the sign of the cross.

ix. She gets up and takes another step or two toward the church.

x. Strengthened by her prayer and determined to speak to Turiddu, she turns Clw and goes up right to the door of his house.

xi. She looks quickly over her left shouler to reassure herself that she is alone on the square.

xii. Turning back, she knocks at the door.

DON CARLO: Pantomime preceding the aria "Ella giammai m'amò"

The drama

Before she became the wife of King Filippo of Spain, the French princess, Elizabetta of Valois, was engaged to Filippo's son, Don Carlo.

She has retained a tender affection for the young man who is now her stepson. Filippo, on the other hand, mistrusts and mistreats his son, whom he regards as a threat to both his throne and his marital happiness. Knowing all too well that his marriage was the result of a political arrangement intended to secure the peace between France and Spain, Filippo is afraid that Elizabetta's heart will never belong to him. To make matters worse, the king suspects that she and Carlo are involved in an illicit affair.

Eboli, the queen's lady-in-waiting, is passionately attracted to Carlo, but is rebuffed by him. Guessing correctly that the prince is desperately in love with his stepmother, Eboli decides to take revenge on both Carlo and Elizabetta. She steals the queen's jewel box, which contains a medallion with Carlo's portrait, and gives it to the king, hoping thereby to prove Elizabetta's guilt. When Filippo discovers his son's picture among his wife's treasured possessions, his doubts become a near certainty.

In Schiller's play *Don Carlos*, from which the plot of the opera is borrowed, the king's suspicions are based on a much more solid chain of circumstantial evidence. His closest associates—his father confessor, Domingo, and the Duke of Alba—are only too eager to serve up various items calculated to turn the monarch against his son and the queen. Filippo learns of their clandestine meeting in the gardens of Aranjuez and of the widespread rumor that little Clara Eugenia may in reality not be his daughter, but the fruit of the much feared adultery.

To steep himself in Filippo's self-inflicted tortures, the singer enacting this role should study the scene in the play where the king, caressing the little girl, compares her features with the reflection of his own face in the mirror and wonders whether the startling resemblance is the result of little Clara's being his daughter or his granddaughter. Since the child, the Duke of Alba, and Domingo have all been omitted from the libretto of the opera, none of this valuable, character-revealing information can be conveyed to the audience. I have endeavored to strengthen the evidence against the queen by including in the mise-en-scène another item left out of the text of the opera: Carlo's love letters to Elizabetta dating from the period of their engagement.

The music

The thirty-two measures of this orchestral introduction are made up of four different musical themes:

(A) Repeated half notes entrusted mainly to the French horns (Example 4–5).

(B) A descending cello passage (Example 4–6).

(C) An expressive melody sung by the cello (Example 4–7).

(D) A succession of quasi-circular phrases played by muted violins (Example 4–8).

Example 4–5. Theme A

Example 4–6. Theme B

Example 4–7. Theme C

Example 4–8. Theme D

Themes A, B, and C are at first presented separately. The muted violin phrases, however, do not appear alone. They are heard in conjunction with theme A, and later in combination with themes A and C. All told, there are seven musical sections presented in the thematic order: A, B, A, C, D–A, B, and D–C–A.

Theme A seems to have had a curious fascination for Verdi. It appears in a great many of his operas and always as a sort of signal that the curtain is about to rise.* The student of Verdi's musical mannerisms will find practically identical phrases at the start of the second acts of *Nabucco* and *Attila*, of the third acts of *I Lombardi* and *I Due Foscari*, and of the fourth act of *La Battaglia di Legnano*. I have the feeling that these heavy, thrice-repeated notes were associated in Verdi's mind with the relentless power of an adverse destiny, a guess which is well supported by the composer's use of this theme for the fateful horn signal in *Ernani*, and for the opening of the overture to *La Forza del Destino*.

* Perhaps it is an unconscious musical equivalent of the three loud raps that, in the ancient French and Italian theaters, used to warn the audience that a new act was about to begin.

Focal points

Onstage	Description	Location
Scenic elements	1. Window (in connection with 9)	Along 34, straddling LBC
Furniture props	2. Table	In RC2
Hand props	3. Casket	Held by Filippo, later on the table
	4. Jewels	In the casket
	5. Medallion	In the casket
	6. Letters	In the casket

Offstage (real or imagined)	Description	Direction and connecting scenic elements
Other characters	7. The Queen	In the right wing
	8. The Prince	In the left wing
Abstract ideas	9. Death and burial in the Escorial	Beyond the window

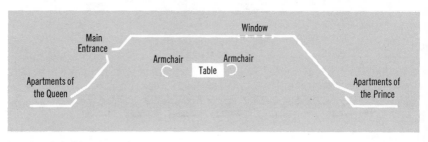

Diagram 4–4. Filippo's study

Filippo's actions explained

The pantomime takes place at the beginning of the third act in the King's study. It is dawn, and Filippo, seated at a table, is examining the contents of the jewel box given to him by Eboli. The candles on the table have burned down almost to the ends, indicating that the King's unhappy thoughts have kept him awake the entire night.

Of particular interest are the contrapuntal episodes of this passage, where several musical ideas are presented simultaneously. In section IV of the pantomime we hear a combination of two musical ideas. Filippo's mind turns to Elizabetta's jewels, but at the same time he is still haunted by the thought (in parentheses) which dominated the first section:

Jewels, lovely jewels that adorn her, so regal, so feminine and
        (My wife . . .   my son . . .

yet so full of mystery . . . and here's the string of pearls that she
      in love!)   (My wife . . .

wears around her shoulders, as cool and remote as her feelings for her husband . . .

      my son . . .   in love!)

In the final section of the pantomime, three themes from previous
sections are combined—a primary thought (shown in capital letters) and
two secondary thoughts:

Jewels, lovely jewels that adorn her, so regal, so feminine and
    HER   HEART RE——JECTS   ME
          my wife . . .   *my son . . .*

Of course, the performer is expected to center his attention only on the
primary thoughts, but the meaning of the secondary themes will still be
felt and is incorporated in the stage action. The idea of the jewels, for
example, is expressed in Filippo's almost unconscious fingering of the
necklace, while the third thought sequence ("My wife . . . my son . . . in
love!") is shown by the slight movement of his eyes and head toward the
stage areas associated with Elizabetta and Carlo. Example 4–9 shows the
way Filippo's thoughts fit the music and describes his actions in detail.

Example 4–9. DON CARLO

Example 4–9 (continued)

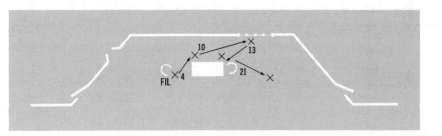

Diagrams 4–5 and 4–6

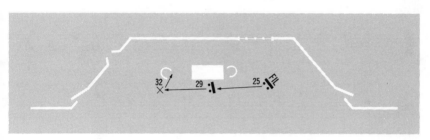

Jew - els, love - ly jew - els that a - dorn her, so re - gal, so femi-nine and yet so full of

Her heart re - - jects me. I'm left

My wife... My son...

He goes slowly to R . . . as he X's............................ table .... he .... stops, puts down the medallion
and picks up the pearls. ....

my - st'ry, and here's the string of pearls that she wears around her shoulders as cool and re-

out_____ locked out like a stran - - - ger. They're

in love! My wife... My son...

He .... then continues to walk R, ... X's armchair, ...

Example 4–9 (continued)

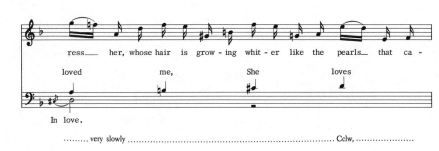

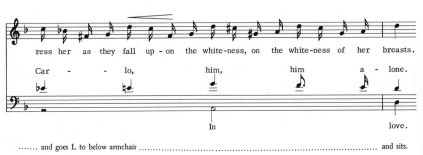

Example 4–9 (continued)

THE ABDUCTION FROM THE SERAGLIO:
Pantomime preceding the aria "Martern aller Arten"

The drama and music

The Turkish ruler, Pasha Selim, seems determined to add the English lady, Konstanze, to his harem. He threatens her with torture unless she submits to his desires. This is spelled out in a spoken dialogue* wherein Konstanze refuses the Pasha's demands and finally challenges

* Selim has no singing lines in the opera.

him: "Torture me if you must, but I shall never be yours!" This is followed by an extended, sixty-measure orchestral introduction. In the vocal portion of her aria Konstanze continues to assure Selim of her determination to resist him. Her argument is divided into four parts:

1. Defiance of Selim ("I laugh at torture and pain!");
2. Firm resolve not to be unfaithful to her fiancé, Belmonte;
3. Gentle supplication, promising Selim the blessing of heaven should he prove merciful; and
4. Violent reaction to Selim's intransigence ("I shall be firm and wait for death to liberate me from your threats and tortures!").

We do not know what prompted Mozart to preface this aria with an orchestral concerto grosso of such extraordinary dimensions. Perhaps it was done at the request of the prima donna of the Vienna premiere of this work, Katherina Cavalieri, who, having just sung the extended cantabile aria "Traurigkeit ward mir zum Loose," needed time to rest before embarking on the coloratura fireworks of "Martern aller Arten." Also, Mozart may have been tempted by the purely musical opportunity to juxtapose four solo instruments (a flute, an oboe, a violin, and a cello) with an orchestra composed of clarinets, bassoons, horns, trumpets, kettledrums, and strings. Whatever his reasons for composing it, the length of this introduction, to say nothing of its mood and energy contrasts, offers a real challenge to the actors and the stage director.

The musical and dramatic content of the introduction is clearly related to the themes and ideas of the following aria: defiance of Selim, tenderness for Belmonte, appeal for pity, and willingness to die. The initial matching of these theatrical ideas with the music does not offer any particular problems. Selim's violent threats and Konstanze's defiance obviously fit the more energetic musical phrases, while the sections played softly can be used to accompany the young woman's gentle pleas for mercy. From here on, however, the path is less smooth. One must find a way to identify and express Konstanze's devotion to Belmonte and—what is much more difficult—achieve a sufficient variety in the actions, keeping in mind that the same ideas are later duplicated in the sung portion of the aria.

I try to solve these problems by giving Belmonte a symbolic presence in a medallion that Konstanze wears around her neck and by adding four Janissaries, whom Selim summons to escort Konstanze to the torture chamber. Thanks to these "elaborations" and "extensions"* Konstanze can address herself to several new focal points. Placing the Janissaries on opposite sides of the stage makes it possible, furthermore, to provide visual equivalents for the musical repeats in sections vi and xii (Example 4–10), and to arrange for a detailed staging of the scales played in section ix by the four solo instruments.

* For a detailed discussion of these staging techniques, see Chapter 10.

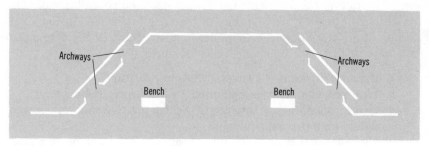

Diagram 4–7. The setting for Konstanze's aria

Focal points

Onstage	Description	Location
Other characters	1. Pasha Selim	Various positions on stage
	2. Four Janissaries	Various positions on stage
Hand props	3. Medallion with Belmonte's picture	Carried by Konstanze

Offstage	Description	Direction
Abstract ideas	4. Appeal for strength	Heavenward, beyond the walls of the auditorium

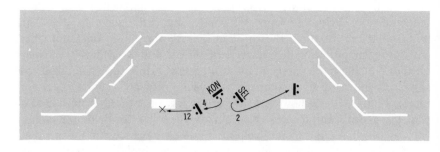

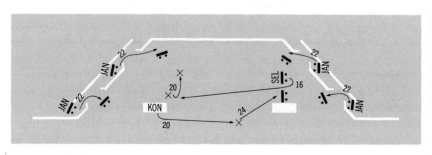

Diagrams 4–8 and 4–9

●* Kon and Sel stare at each other defiantly.

● Sel turns Cclw and goes UL to above L bench (facing L).

● Kon turns slightly Clw and takes out medallion which hangs around her neck on a chain. .....

She caresses it, admires, and kisses it.

● She goes DR to below R bench and sits ....

...... facing DR, looks again at the medallion and ......

...... returns it to her bosom.

● Sel turns Clw, goes R ......

....to slightly UL of Kon and R bench ......

● Sel grips Kon's L wrist with his LH . . and drags her to her feet, turning her Cclw. ......

..... Kon defies Sel and goes L, X'ing him and rotating him Cclw. He lets go, and goes U slightly R of CC and .....

..... Kon stops slightly L of CC and DR of L bench, rubbing her wrist and glowering over her R shoulder at Sel.

● Sel claps his hands.

....then turns Clw and goes slightly DL to CC.

● Kon (hearing claps) turns to face Sel (UR).

● Four Janissaries enter through arches and bow to Sel.

● Kon turns further Clw and goes UL (X'ing above L bench) to the Jan's on L.

...... She looks from one to the other, pleading for mercy. (They ignore her.)

● Kon turns Clw and goes R to DL of Sel who eyes her lecherously and advances toward her as if to embrace her.

*This symbol indicates that action is to begin precisely at this point.

Example 4–10. THE ABDUCTION FROM THE SERAGLIO

• Kon goes R (X'ing Sel) to plead with
the other two Jan's.   ...... Sel follows her slightly R.

• Kon turns Cclw to Sel
and stretches out her
hands, pleading for mercy.
..... Sel takes her hands
and tries .... to pull her towards him.

• Kon pulls away, turns LSB, drawing Sel
with her DR a bit (towards R bench)......
...... Sel breaks, then follows her DR a
bit and tries to embrace her.

...... Kon again breaks with Sel and X's him
to L (landing UR of L bench).

...... Sel turns Cclw and follows her, puts his
hand on her shoulders and ......   • Sel turns
Kon to   • Kon cowers
face him.   away from
Sel.

• Kon escapes DR to DR of R bench (X'ing Sel and
R bench).
   • Sel follows as far as CC and motions to the
Jan's to come closer.

• The upstage Jan's advance two steps.
   • Kon (facing R) looks wildly
around, then, turning Clw,

starts out on a large Clw
semi-circle, appealing to each
Jan as she passes him and   arriving above L bench at ....
   ...... Sel watches her and turns as she X's above him.
         ...... As he turns, he backs D towards CC a bit.

.... • Kon
above L
bench.
   • Kon turns RSB and goes R to UR of L bench
begging Sel to dismiss the Jan's.
         ...... Sel refuses
         and turns away,
         Cclw. ......

Example 4–10 (continued)

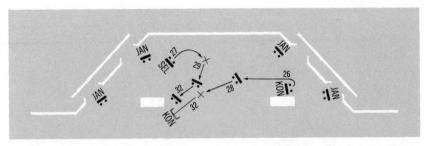

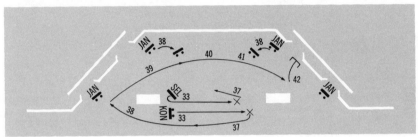

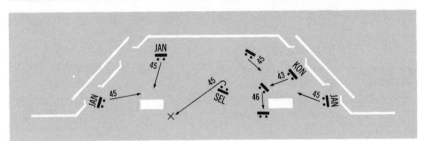

Diagrams 4–10, 4–11, and 4–12

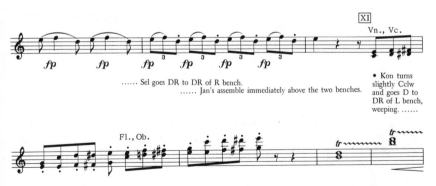

...... Sel goes DR to DR of R bench.
...... Jan's assemble immediately above the two benches.

• Kon turns slightly Cclw and goes D to DR of L bench, weeping. ......

• Kon draws herself upwards and calls on heaven for courage. ......

Example 4–10 (continued)

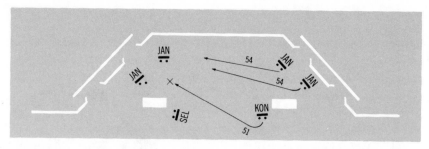

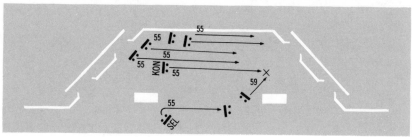

Diagrams 4–13 and 4–14

• Kon, preferring torture to dishonor, turns
Clw, goes UR to Jan's, and offers them
her two arms, fists clenched, palms down.

...... The two R Jan's take her R arm and she turns LSB and offers her
L arm to the two L Jan's who approach and take it.

• Sel turns Clw to watch.

• Kon and Jan's start L.

• Sel, amazed at her courage,
follows L to DR of R bench. ......

• Sel
stamps
his foot.   .... Jan's release Kon and all five
turn to face Sel. ......

...... Sel dismisses the Jan's who
bow and leave UL.

• Kon advances R to UL of Sel.
......They stare at each
other defiantly.

Example 4–10 (continued)

The next two scenes have been chosen to demonstrate the great variety of expressive nuances that are available to, and expected of, an accomplished operatic actor when he performs as the silent collaborator of a singing partner. These exercises should be analyzed in terms of:

1. The supporting actor's share in the leading action
2. The incentives and stimulants he offers to the words and actions of his singing partner
3. His ability to justify orchestral interludes and special instrumental "events," such as sudden changes in dynamics, rhythm, or tempo
4. The difference between precise synchronizations and the more leisurely contouring of stage actions

THE TELEPHONE: Ben's pantomime during Lucy's first aria

Since Menotti's charming one-act opera is perhaps not as widely known as the other works discussed in this volume, here is a short synopsis of its contents:

Ben's train is scheduled to depart in one hour. He is in love with Lucy and wants to ask her to marry him before he leaves. While groping for the right words he is interrupted by the ring of Lucy's telephone, and she becomes involved in a lengthy conversation. As the opera progresses, there are several amusing variations of this interruption idea. Finally, Ben realizes that he cannot compete with his electronic rival. He leaves Lucy's apartment, rings her up from a phone booth, and his proposal is accepted by telephone.

The drama

Ben's actions during Lucy's first telephone conversation are motivated by a variety of attitudes and feelings: politeness, mild impatience, concern over Lucy's health, desire to make her aware that he is in a hurry, temporary resignation and willingness to be patient, amazement at the topics of her conversation, joy that the interruption is about to terminate, disappointment, nervousness, and frustration. All this provides Ben with many urges to move around the room, while Lucy is happily ensconced on the sofa. She is very fond of Ben and reassures him occasionally that she is aware of his presence, but these attentions are quite secondary to her fascinated preoccupation with the invisible and inaudible Margaret at the other end of the telephone.

This pantomime is particularly instructive because for once the supporting, non-singing actor is entrusted with all the larger movements, while the singing partner remains throughout in the same basic location.

Ben's efforts to shorten Lucy's conversation elicit a certain number of her responses, but otherwise her chatter and laughter have no particular dramatic significance and acquire importance only to the extent that they motivate Ben's behavior. Nevertheless, Ben's actions, reactions, and his growing frustration must be handled with great delicacy so as not to distract the attention of the audience from Lucy's vocal line.

The music

This scene begins with two introductory measures during which Lucy's telephone rings for the first time. The aria that follows is composed of two stanzas, each featuring three separate musical ideas: the opening allegro, A (Example 4–11), the more leisurely "meno mosso," B (Example 4–12), and the "allegro con brio," C (Example 4–15, p. 161). Sections A and B of the first stanza are separated by a transitional section of fifteen measures that starts out as a variation of A (Example 4–13), but then introduces a completely new and nonrecurring Prase D (Example 4–14).

The second stanza is considerably shorter than the first. The words of its A section are a sort of mirror image of what Lucy said in the first stanza: instead of "Hello! Hello?" we hear "Well then, good-bye." The order of events in the second stanza is ACB rather than the earlier ABC, and the aria ends with a nine-measure coda, which starts out with a variant of C and continues with a presto version of the opening section. The 105 measures of this scene thus fall into seven clearly defined sections—four in the first stanza and three in the second—framed by an introduction and a coda. The distribution is as follows:

INTRODUCTION (2 MEASURES)

FIRST STANZA (60 MEASURES)

Section A ("Hello! Hello?")—14 measures
Transition ("Hello! Hello?")—5 measures
Phrase D ("I heard the funniest thing")—10 measures
Section B ("And how are you?")—14 measures
Section C ("Ha! Ha!")—17 measures

SECOND STANZA (34 MEASURES)

Section A ("Well then, good-bye")—14 measures
Section C ("Ha! Ha!")—10 measures
Section B ("And how are you?")—10 measures

CODA (9 MEASURES)

This musical structure is closely reflected in the activities of the mise-en-scène. The *ritenuti* and fortissimo chords in sections A of both stanzas are identified with corresponding actions: reassuring gestures by Lucy in

Example 4–11. THE TELEPHONE.* Section A

Example 4–12. Section B

Example 4–13. Variation of Section A

Example 4–14. Phrase D

* Selections from *The Telephone* are used by permission. Copyright 1947 by G. Schirmer, Inc.

measures 12 and 72, and tussles over the telephone receiver in measures 16 and 76. The nonrecurring portion of the transition is dedicated to a similarly unrepeated business with the boutonniere. During both B sections, Ben's attention is diverted to the candy box and the area around the right table, while the energetic allegro con brio sections and the presto of the coda are connected with activities centering on the chair.

Focal Points

Onstage	Description	Location
Other characters	1. Lucy	Sitting or reclining on the couch
Furniture props	2. Chair	Up right of the table in LB3; later, carried by Ben to various locations
Hand props	3. Telephone receiver	In one or the other of Lucy's hands
	4. Statuette	On right table in RB2
	5. Wrist watch	On Ben's left wrist
	6. Flower vase	On left table in LB3
	7. Bouquet of flowers, including one removable flower for Ben's boutonniere	In vase on left table
	8. Candy box	On end table left of couch; later, carried by Ben to right table in RB2
	9. Chocolate candy wrapped in tinfoil	In candy box; later put into flower pot by Ben
	10. Cradle of the telephone	On the end table, left of couch
Offstage	Description	Location
Abstract ideas	11. Impatience gradually turning into irritation	Heavenward, beyond the walls of the auditorium

Ben's actions explained

Lucy and Ben are sitting on the couch. She sits to his left. The phone rings.

LUCY: Excuse me. (*She takes the phone in her right hand, puts the receiver to her right ear, and faces slightly down left.*)

Ben gets up, thinking: "Go ahead, I'll wait." He nods politely and goes up right toward the table.

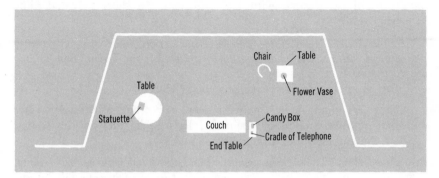

Diagram 4–15. The setting for Ben and Lucy

LUCY: Hello! Hello? Oh, Margaret, it's you. I am so glad you called, I was just thinking of you.

Ben seems apprehensive until he hears Lucy mention "Margaret." Relieved that she is not talking to a man, he turns his attention to the statuette.

LUCY: It's been a long *time* since you *called* me.

With "time," Ben looks at his watch. After "called me" he goes down right, crossing the table.

LUCY: Who? I? I cannot come tonight. No, my dear, I'm not feeling very well. *(She coughs.)*

Concerned about Lucy's health, Ben turns Cclw and goes up left toward her.

LUCY *(reassuring him with a gesture)*: When? Where? I wish I could be there!

Ben continues up left to up right of Lucy, above couch.

LUCY: I'm afraid I must not. *(Two fortissimo chords.)*

Ben takes Lucy's right wrist with his left hand and on the word "not" pulls away her arm. Then, on the two fortissimo chords, he

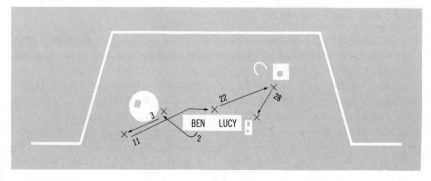

Diagram 4–16

points to his wristwatch with his right hand to show her that time is getting short.

LUCY: Hello? Hello? (*Surprised by Ben's action, Lucy turns Clw, takes the receiver with her left hand, and puts it to her left ear, leaving Ben holding her right wrist.*)
Ben drops Lucy's wrist on her second "Hello."

LUCY: What did you say (*she turns Cclw*), my darling? What did you say?
Ben gestures imploringly behind Lucy's back, and on the second "What" he embraces her around the shoulders.

LUCY: Hello? Hello? (*She removes Ben's left hand with her right hand, passes the receiver to her right hand, and puts it to her right ear while turning slightly Clw.*) *Please speak louder.*
On "Please speak louder" Ben turns Cclw, sees the flowers, and decides to pick a boutonniere.

LUCY: I heard the funniest thing!
Ben goes to the down right corner of the left table and picks a flower.

LUCY: Jane and Paul are going to be married next July. *Don't* you think it is the funniest thing you ever *heard*?
On "Don't" Ben turns Clw and adjusts the flower in his lapel. On "heard" he goes down right to the left of the telephone table and motions Lucy to hang up.

LUCY: I know. (*She notices and misinterprets Ben's gesture*). Of course. (*She picks up the candy box.*) (Example 4–14.)
(Lucy hands Ben the box in the first measure; in the second measure she giggles.)

Ben takes the box reluctantly, looks at it, and decides that he might as well have a candy while he waits.

LUCY: And how are you? And how is John? And how is Jean? You must tell them that I send them my love.
Ben goes right to the right table, crossing above the couch and opening the box as he walks. He puts the box and its lid on the table, selects a chocolate, and unwraps it.

LUCY: And how is *Ursula,* and how is Natalie, and how is Rosalie? I hope she's gotten over her cold. And how is your mother, and how is your father, and how is dear little *Granny?*
On "Ursula" Ben bites into the chocolate and makes a face (it's a mint!). He looks over his left shoulder at Lucy to see if she is watching him, rewraps the chocolate, and starts to put it back in the box. He hesitates, starts to put it into his coat pocket, changes his mind, and turns Cclw, wondering where to hide it. On the word "Granny" he looks at the flower vase and decides to drop the candy inside it. (Example 4–15).

Example 4–15. Section C, Allegro con brio

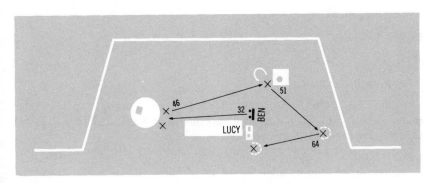

Diagram 4–17

Ben goes left, crossing above the couch and the chair to above the left table. He separates the flowers and drops the chocolate inside the vase.

LUCY: Oh dear! *(She puts the receiver to the left ear.)*

During these twelve measures, Ben picks up the chair, takes it down left to LA1, places it facing Lucy, and sits down. Annoyed with her good humor, he sulks, but her last laugh is so contagious that he can't help chuckling.

LUCY: Well then, *good-bye*. Good-bye, my dear, good-bye. I am so glad you called. I was just thinking of you. It's been a long time since you called me.

On "good-bye" Ben gets up excitedly, steps to the right of the chair, picks it up with his left hand, and goes right, crossing the left table. He puts the chair down at the down left corner of the sofa, picks up the phone from the little table, and offers it to Lucy, holding it in both hands.

LUCY: Of course, I won't forget! (*She reassures Ben, gesturing with her right hand.*) Yes, my darling, good-bye . . . (*She is about to hang up.*)

Ben pulls at Lucy's left wrist with his right hand to help her hang up.

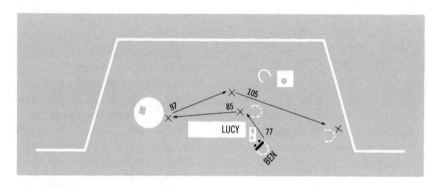

Diagram 4–18

(*Fortissimo chords*)

LUCY: Yes! (*On the fortissimo chords she hears Margaret's comment, becomes excited, retrieves the receiver with her right hand, and puts it to her right ear, leaving her left arm with Ben.*)

Seeing that Lucy is at it again, Ben begins to lose his temper.

LUCY: That's the funniest thing I ever heard.

During this interlude, Ben puts the cradle of the phone on the little table, gets up, turns Clw to face the chair, picks it up by the seat, and carries it up to half way between the sofa and the left table. He puts it down and, on "That's the funniest thing I ever heard," looks angrily over his left shoulder. (Example 4–16).

LUCY: And how are you? And Bets and Bob and Sara and Sam? You must tell them that I send them my love.

Ben goes right to the right table, crossing above the sofa, and replaces the lid on the candy box.

Example 4–16

LUCY: And how is the *pussy cat*, and how is the *dog*? Oh, I'm so glad.
On "pussy cat" Ben looks at her in disbelief. On "dog" he strikes his forehead, ready to burst.

LUCY: *Good-bye! (Fortissimo chords) Yes, Margaret!*
Ben approaches Lucy after "Good-bye" on the fortissimo chords, wondering if she is actually going to hang up. Her "*Yes, Margaret*" is the last straw. He decides to do something drastic to make her stop. (Example 4–17).

Example 4–17

Ben goes left, crossing above the couch, and picks up the chair and brandishes it in the air, as if about to bring it down on the cradle of the telephone.

LUCY: All right, all right, good-bye! All right, all right good-bye. . . . (*She waves her left hand to calm him down.*)
Ben remains with the chair in the air.

LUCY: Now, *Margaret*, good-bye! So long.
With "Margaret," Ben carries the chair down left, turns Clw, and puts it down so that the chair faces toward Lucy. As she says "So long," he stares at her grimly, gripping the back of the chair.

DON GIOVANNI: Donna Elvira's pantomime during Leporello's catalog aria

The drama

Donna Elvira is a young noblewoman from the Spanish city of Burgos who considers herself the lawfully wedded wife of Don Giovanni. He abandoned her three days after their wedding, and she has been trying to find him ever since. Later, when she runs into him in a square of another city, she angrily demands an explanation of his behavior. The Don assures her that his reasons for leaving can best be revealed to her by his faithful Leporello. As Elvira turns to listen to the servant, Don Giovanni manages to escape. Leporello's double-talk that "to wit, inasmuch as in this world the square is not round" is an obvious impertinence, but when Elvira turns to complain, Don Giovanni has vanished, and she tearfully asks Leporello to show her where she can find her husband. Leporello assures her that his master is not worthy of her love and parades before her a catalog of the Don's amorous adventures.*

---

* The original Italian text identifies the catalog as a single sizeable volume ("questo non picciol libro"), but I prefer to let Leporello use several books, one for each country he mentions. This allows him a wider variety of actions and also greatly enhances the effect of the ridiculously large Spanish volume (containing the thousand and three names), which does not make its appearance until the musical climax of "In Ispagna" (In Spain).

At first, Elvira's reaction is pure indignation. She still smarts from Leporello's recent quip about "squares that are not round," and she will not again be the victim of his coarse jokes. Besides, she is not interested in what went on in Italy, Germany, Turkey, or France. Why should she care how many affairs Don Giovanni had in foreign countries before he met and married her? It is only when Leporello produces the Spanish volume with its "thousand and three" names that she begins to wonder whether there may not be some truth in his jabbering. Near the end of the allegro section of the aria she actually touches the book, suspecting that her own name might be included in it, but she soon puts it down again, pretending not to be interested. In true feminine fashion she now begins to take things personally: she reacts quite violently to the idea that Don Giovanni "likes brunettes for their faithfulness," since she herself, alas, is a faithful brunette; she is disgusted by Leporello's vulgar outlining of the large-bosomed figure, horrified at the thought of the "old women," and humiliated at having to hear about her husband's predilection for virgins. The cold-blooded statement that Don Giovanni will sleep with anything that wears a skirt infuriates her to the point of wanting to attack Leporello, but his final references—to her knowledge of Don Giovanni's way with women—takes the wind out of her sails. When he again points to the Spanish catalog, she can no longer resist the temptation: she picks up the volume, leafs through it (with his help), finds her own name, hurls the book down, and leaves the stage to the accompaniment of his triumphant laughter.

The music

In Lucy's aria from *The Telephone*, Ben was allotted most of the larger moves. This, as I pointed out, is quite exceptional. The theatrical interplay between Elvira and Leporello in the "Madamina" aria belongs to the much more common variety of collaboration: the singing actor carries the main burden of the scene, while the silent participant's chief function is to help the singer motivate both his actions and his words. In apportioning the various stage movements one begins by deciding which of the actors should be entrusted with the interpretation of significant instrumental interludes and "special events."

In this instance, I imagine that, at first, Elvira's indignation makes her more aggressive and energetic than the quietly malicious Leporello. It is she, consequently, who is asked to "justify" the vigorous interludes in measures 16, 17, 20, 21, 24, and 25 of the "allegro," as well as the one in measure 11 of the "andante." During the interludes of the allegro, Elvira traverses the stage from its down-right corner to the left bench; the sparkling passage in measure 11 of the andante takes her to the center. The loud fanfare-like accompaniments in measures 29 and 30 of the andante pack enough energy values to support not only Leporello's high sustained tone, but also to "move" Elvira to the area of the right bench. Particularly important, from the point of view of Elvira's participation, is the final coda with its spectacular six-fold repetition of "voi sapete" (you know). During the first "voi sapete" Elvira is almost ready to attack Leporello for his impertinence and is stopped only by the rude allusion of the final word of his "quel che fa" (what he does). Mozart highlights this moment with the unexpected appearance of a high D in the flute. This whistling high tone (which, unfortunately, is omitted in most piano-vocal scores of the opera) should stop Elvira in her tracks like a sudden jet of cold water. It is important that she be watching Leporello again when he points to the catalog during his fourth "voi sapete," so that she can cross below him and be on her way to the left bench during the interlude between the fourth and fifth repetitions of this phrase. Elvira's preoccupation with the Spanish section of the catalog and her pathetic search for her own name are of enormous help in the total staging of this aria.

Focal points

Onstage	Description	Location
Other characters	1. Leporello	Various positions on stage
Hand props	2. Volume listing the Spanish women	Carried by Leporello; later, placed on left bench

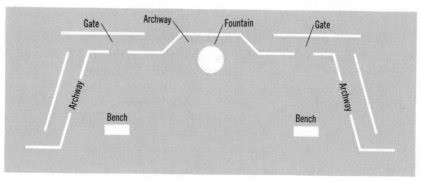

Diagram 4–19. The setting for Elvira and Leporello

Elvira's actions explained

Before turning to the following stage directions and subtexts, the singer should study the analysis of the dramatic content of this scene from Leporello's viewpoint, found in Chapter 5, p. 219 ff.

When this scene begins, Leporello is standing upstage center and Elvira is downstage right of him, facing him. Her main motivating forces are disbelief, humiliation, curiosity, and horror. Her first five actions are motivated by a determination not to listen.

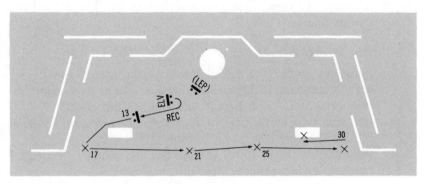

Diagram 4–20. End of recitative and allegro, measure 1

RECITATIVE (FINAL NINE MEASURES)

1. After Leporello's "sue belle" Elvira turns Clw and goes slightly down right. (I've had enough of your jokes!")

ARIA

Allegro: Section 1 (measures 1–15)

2. (measure 13) She goes further down right, crossing above the right bench to RA1. ("I would not dream of reading anything with you!")

Allegro: Section 2 (measures 16–48)

3. (measure 16) Turns Cclw, looks at Leporello ("How dare you!"), and then goes left, crossing him and the right bench, almost to CC. ("I refuse to listen!")

4. (measure 20) Looks at Leporello over her right shoulder ("What nonsense!"), then goes further left, beyond CC. ("Stop annoying me!")

5. (measure 24) Looks to heaven ("Good Lord!"), then goes still further left, to below the left corner of left bench. ("I am leaving!")

(Actions numbered 3, 4, and 5 require careful contouring. Elvira's "looks" should coincide with the high D's in the violins. She "goes" with the explosive scales in the flutes and bassoons, and stops only when she hears Leporello's next sentence.)

6. (measure 29) Turns Clw and goes very slightly right. ("Did you say Spain?") Her interest is aroused in spite of herself.
7. (measure 33) Sits down on bench, looking at Leporello. ("Shame on you! What a dreadful joke!")
8. (measure 35) Turns Cclw (while seated) to face left. (What disgusting manners!")

Allegro: Section 3 (measures 49–84)

9. (measures 49–69) During all this time she listens, turning her head occasionally in Leporello's direction. ("This is a monstrous invention! Still, I wish I could look through this book!")
10. (measure 69) Turns Clw to face right. ("How can Giovanni tolerate such behavior in his servants!")
11. (measure 72) Turns Cclw, touches Spanish volume ("Perhaps I can just catch a glimpse while this man faces the other way."), but then immediately turns Clw and faces downstage. ("No! It's impossible!")

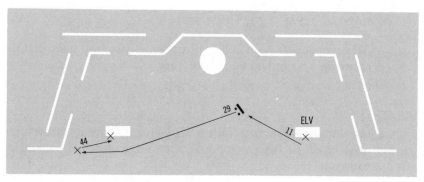

Diagram 4-21. Andante con moto, measures 1–50

Andante con moto: Section 1 (measures 1–31)

12. (measure 10) Gets up and goes up right to CC. ("Don't you dare point at me!") She stands there, facing down right. ("Well, I guess I *am* a faithful fool as well as a brunette!")
13. (measure 29) Turns Cclw to look at Leporello. ("Vulgar, disgusting man!") Then turns Clw and goes down right, crossing bench to down right of it. ("How humiliating all this is!")

Andante con moto: Section 2 (measures 32–62)

14. (measure 40) Turns Cclw and goes slightly left to below the right bench. ("Old women too? No! You're lying to me! It's impossible!")

15. (measure 47) Turns Clw and sits down near right corner of bench, facing down right. ("If it's true, it's just too monstrous!")

16. (measure 51) Gets up and goes right. ("Beginners? He means virgins, of course! Is it for this that I have kept my chastity?")

17. (measure 59) Turns Cclw to face Leporello. ("Ugly ones, also? No, it's not true, not true!")

18. (measure 62) Goes up left toward Leporello, crossing above bench. ("Stop it, you impudent boor! Stop it or I'll slap you!")

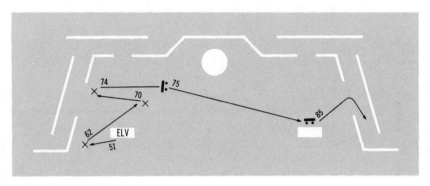

Diagram 4–22. Andante con moto, measures 51–88

Andante con moto: Section 3 (measures 63–88)

19. (measure 63) Stops, still facing Leporello. ("Me? What do you mean by that?")

20. (measure 66) Turns Clw to face right. ("Yes, of course. He's right! I know it only too well!")

21. (measure 70) Goes slightly right, crying. ("It is true! All of it is true!")

22. (measure 74) Turns Cclw to face Leporello. ("No, it's *not* true! Stop it at once!")

23. (measure 75) Goes left, crossing Leporello to above left bench and picks up the volume. ("Yes, this book will prove it, one way or another!")

24. (measure 78) Goes slightly right, opening book. ("My name should be the last one!")

25. (measure 80) Holds book, while Leporello turns back several pages. ("All these names after mine, in this short time? It cannot be!")

26. (measure 82) Holds book while Leporello points to her name. ("I will die! No! I will have vengeance!")

27. (measure 85) She throws the book on the bench and leaves the stage down left. ("Monster! Monster!")

5

The singing actor

IT IS SO CUSTOMARY to hear operatic characters sing instead of speak that few people are aware of the complications caused by this departure from theatrical normality. Yet all singers (and their mentors) must remember that, from the listener's point of view, singing functions on three separate levels: the words that are sung appeal to his intellect, the beauty of the vocal tones gives him a physical pleasure, and the musical nuances of a well-executed performance satisfy his artistic sense.

From the singer's point of view, this creates unfortunate discrepancies: the elongated vowel sounds of sustained singing interfere with verbal clarity, and crisp enunciation disturbs the smooth legato that is the basis of beautiful vocalization.

Yet both parlando and cantabile are indispensable ingredients of opera. There are many operatic sequences where it is absolutely essential that words be understood, just as there are other moments where the unique sensual appeal of the human voice makes us forget the very existence of words. At one end of this spectrum we have the clearly enunciated parlando of the secco recitatives, or of the modern Sprechstimme; on the other, we find the intensively sung vocal cadenzas uttered entirely on the "ah" or "oh" vowels. Between these two extremes lies the vast area of "ordinary" vocal lines, where the sensible and the sensuous must somehow learn to adjust their differences.

Some opera lovers complain incessantly about the impossibility of understanding anything that is sung on stage, while others are equally vociferous on the subject of the decline of *bel canto* singing. I find it more realistic to say simply that—except in the extreme situations mentioned earlier—a singer should strive to achieve the mixture of parlando and cantabile best suited to the particular passage he happens to be singing. The need to distinguish between these various mixtures was preached

171

very eloquently by Richard Strauss, whose eminence as a practicing operatic conductor makes his opinions on the subject particularly authoritative. In the preface to his *Intermezzo*, Strauss asks conductors who prepare this opera to "pay the greatest attention to the subtle transitions from the purely spoken word to the sung and half-enunciated word . . . until one finally reaches to so-called *bel canto*, where absolute clarity may be somewhat sacrificed to favor beautiful vocal sound (*zugunsten schoener Tongebung*)."

When a singer is looking for the correct ratio between the word and the tone, it is useful to distinguish four main types of gradations which I call: (*a*) crisp parlando, (*b*) sung parlando, (*c*) enunciated cantabile, and (*d*) full cantabile. In the first, the performer concentrates solely on distinct verbal communication; in the second, he produces a clearly understandable, yet musically continuous, line; in the third he aims at a sensuous legato effect and does not worry if an occasional word is not clear; and in the fourth, he is completely willing to sacrifice verbal clarity as he gives his full attention to vocal intensity and splendor.

I first thought of this series of gradations when I noticed the curious way that Verdi annotated his music for the singers. Most other composers use dots and slurs over their vocal lines in much the same way as in their instrumental music, namely, to indicate the difference between a disconnected (staccato) and a smooth (legato) execution. But Verdi consistently used four different symbols: notes with dots (Example 5–1), notes without dots (Example 5–2), notes with slurs and dots (Example 5–3), and notes with slurs only (Example 5–4). This highly individual notational mannerism may well have been intended to designate the desired parlando-cantabile relationship, so that Example 5–1 corresponds to crisp parlando, Example 5–2 to sung parlando, Example 5–3 to enunciated cantabile, and Example 5–4 to full cantabile. I have found that this approach often produces convincing results when applied to Verdi's operas.

Examples 5–1, 5–2, 5–3, and 5–4

Enunciating the text

Whichever of these four gradations is being used, the important thing for singers to remember is that even though a character's feelings can usually be communicated by the tone of his voice and by his actions, only a few of his thoughts can be transmitted if his words are not under-standable. Given a strong enough incentive, most singers can be persuaded to enunciate more clearly. It is well to remember, however, that a singer's normal advisers—his coaches, vocal teachers, accompanists, and conductors —are seldom trustworthy judges of verbal clarity. As a rule these ladies and gentlemen know the words so well that they "hear" them even if they are not well pronounced.

To insure verbal clarity in my own opera productions, I always set aside special rehearsals (which my friends call "clapping sessions") to which I invite outsiders who are not familiar with the text that is being sung. At every word or sentence the meaning of which escapes them, these guests are asked to clap their hands and interrupt the rehearsal. After each interruption the obscure passage is sung again, and the process is repeated as often as necessary. This method produces salutary effects on both sides of the footlights. The singers, who at first are shocked and dismayed by the number of interruptions, begin to realize that com-municating their words requires a considerable effort. Those of the inter-rupters who are particularly "hard of understanding" become aware that keeping track of sung speech requires a trained and alert ear. During these sessions, incidentally, I also make it my business to explain which passages in the score would suffer from excessive singing and which from ex-cessive enunciation.

Musical nuances

Changes of dynamics or tempo in the vocal lines of an opera must be interpreted in the light of their dramatic meaning. Since these musical nuances are attached to words, their meaning is inevitably obvious. Whether the reason for a pianissimo phrase is found in embarrassment, secrecy, fear, illness, or exhaustion is something that can always be readily determined from the words and the theatrical situation.

The only purely musical effects in singing which may require special discussion are those connected with short, staccato tones. In instrumental music, legato and staccato have equal standing, but in the realm of sing-ing, continuous speech in the form of a legato vocal line is the only accepted and normal form of utterance. A sentence that is to be spoken or sung with pauses between words or individual syllables requires special justification. True staccato singing is used, as a rule, only to illustrate something that is abnormal or not of strictly human origin. The en-chanted bells in Lakmé's aria, Titania's magic flight through the air in her *Mignon* aria, and Olympia's musical clock mechanism in *The Tales of Hoffmann* are typical examples of theatrical concepts that lend them-selves to staccato execution. We also readily accept the presence of such effects when a character is mad or overcome by excitability, as in the almost insane raging of the Queen of the Night. Otherwise, separated words and syllables in opera generally belong to a *non*-legato variety of execution that occurs when a character who would normally express himself in an ordinary, connected vocal line finds that he is unable to do so because of an emotional condition that interferes with smooth breathing. The most common causes of non-legato singing are sobbing, sighing, and laughing.

Mozart and Verdi, both masters of this vocal and dramatic "breathlessness," managed on occasion to include both laughter and crying in the same musical ensemble. The most notable examples are found in the first-act quintet of *Così fan tutte*, where Fiordiligi and Dorabella weep disconsolately while Don Alfonso tries his best to suppress his laughter, and in the quartet from *Rigoletto*, where the sobbing is done by Gilda and the giggling by Maddalena.

In executing such passages, the singer must convince the audience that his inability to sing a legato line is the direct result of muscular contractions caused by his emotions. Dramatically speaking, nothing is more disenchanting than the cackled vocalization which one occasionally hears in such rapturous moments as when Gilda sings her "Caro nome."

Vocal nuances

Perhaps even more important than the ability to handle musical effects dramatically is the invaluable art of coloring the voice. The human throat is capable of producing an almost endless variety of tonal shadings. Think how drastically our tone of voice changes depending on whether we give orders to servants, dictate letters, ask for favors, quarrel with members of our family, plot vengeance, or whisper secrets. In opera a soprano may be called upon on successive days to enact a young girl, a mature woman, and an old lady. Naturally, her voice cannot be permitted to have the same sound in these three roles. Even in different portions of a single operatic scene she may have to express indifference, love, and hatred; or to sound gay, tender, melancholy, and despairing. Consider Amneris who displays no less than five different aspects of her personality in the opening scene of the second act of *Aida*. For each of these she must be able to find a suitable tone of voice. Her vocal color must characterize in turn:

1. A passionate girl expressing her amorous yearning (Example 5–5);

Example 5–5. AIDA, II, sc. 1

2. A proud princess addressing her slaves and dismissing them from her presence (Example 5–6);

AMNERIS

Si – len – zio!   A – i – da ver – so noi   s'a – van – za...
Be   si – lent!   I think I hear A – i – da's foot-steps...

Example 5–6

3. A young woman tormented by jealous suspicions and "dreadful doubts" (Example 5-7);

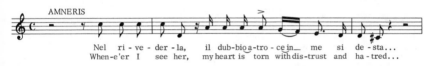

AMNERIS

Nel   ri – ve – der – la,   il dub-bio a-tro – ce in_   me   si   de – sta...
When-e'er I   see her,   my heart is torn with dis-trust and ha – tred...

Example 5–7

4. A scheming female setting a deadly trap under the cloak of friendship and sisterly sympathy (Example 5–8); and

AMNERIS

I tuoi se – gre – ti   sve – la-mi,   al – l'a – mor
If se-cret trou-bles wor – ry you,   share_ them_ A-

mi – o, al – l'a-mor mio t'af – fi – da.
i – da, con-fide in   me and trust   me.

dolce

Example 5–8

5. A raging tigress who hates her rival and racks her brain to devise
the most cruel and humiliating punishment (Example 5–9).

Example 5. 9

In the course of this scene Amneris has ample opportunity to characterize
the various features of her personality by using all the histrionic means at
her disposal. But even if she possesses a sonorous voice, a regal figure, and
a fine dramatic talent, her portrayal of this role will not be complete
unless she is also an accomplished mistress of vocal nuance.

Many operatic sequences call for even more rapid alterations in
the timbre of the voice. This is particularly true in secco recitatives,
where these contrasting shadings of tone color are usually accompanied
by simultaneous changes of dynamics and tempo. An instructive example is furnished by the recitative that precedes the Marcellina-Susanna
duet in the first act of *The Marriage of Figaro*. Here each of Marcellina's
opening three sentences must be sung with sharp differences in tone of
voice, degree of loudness, and speed of delivery.

In the beginning of the recitative Marcellina is alone and talks to
herself in a business-like tone of voice with moderate speed and loudness
(Example 5–10). As she notices Susanna approaching, Marcellina's tone
becomes conspiratorial and drops to a hurried whisper (Example 5–11).
After Susanna enters, Marcellina's delivery becomes offensively sarcastic,
and since she does not want her rival to miss a single word, she enunciates

everything that follows very slowly and with an exaggerated loudness
(Example 5–12). This final series of observations is a masterpiece of
scurrilous innuendo. It not only slanders Susanna's reputation and virtue
by hinting that she has let herself be seduced by Count Almaviva, but
it also manages to imply that she has been paid for it and that Figaro
had consented to this transaction for the sake of the dowry he will receive
for marrying the girl.

Example 5–10. THE MARRIAGE OF FIGARO,* I, Recitative preceding no. 5

Example 5–11

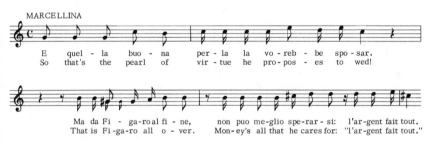

Example 5–12

Within a span of less than thirty seconds Marcellina has to act
out three different personalities: a sedate, business-like planner; a hurried
whispering conspirator; and a loud-mouthed, slandering gossip. Without
corresponding changes in vocal color, this sequence of characterizations
loses all its pungency and zest.

While not all vocalists are equally talented in the ability to color
the voice, every aspiring opera singer should be fully aware of its supreme
importance. A performance devoid of contrasting inflections and hues
soon deteriorates into a collection of tones that no matter how pleasant
they may be in themselves, become monotonous. The ability to change
vocal color is indispensable in opera.

* Lorenzo Da Ponte, *Le Mariage de Figaro*, English version by Edward J. Dent (New York:
Oxford University Press, 1937). Used by permission.

Vocal disguises

Just as the accomplished actor must be able to transform himself into many different dramatic characters and to assume many kinds of disguises, the opera singer must have a vocal mastery that permits him not only to sing expressively a wide variety of roles, but also to camouflage his voice occasionally so that it is unrecognizable.

When an episode in a role calls for such a vocal disguise, the singer must ask himself if his new voice is supposed to sound merely like a certain type of person or if he must give an actual imitation of another member of the cast. The first category of vocal disguises we shall call a *masquerade*; the second, an *impersonation*.

There are quite a number of vocal masquerades and impersonations in operatic literature, and every singer must learn how to deal with them. Their respective problems are by no means identical. When confronted with a vocal masquerade, the singer must look for what is typical; when required to do an impersonation, he has to attempt to duplicate the voice of a specific artist.

For example, in the last act of *Rigoletto* when Gilda knocks at the door of Sparafucile's tavern and asks to be admitted, she is not attempting to imitate the voice of a person known to Sparafucile, Maddalena, and the audience; she is simply trying to sound like any young boy lost in a storm, begging for shelter. She will therefore look for the most typical qualities in a boy soprano's voice and will aim for a straight, vibrato-less production and a whimpering, imploring kind of sound.

When, on the other hand, Don Giovanni decides to hide his identity in the opening scene of the second act, he should not merely endeavor to disguise his own voice and sound like somebody's servant. He must definitely strive to match the vocal timbre of the artist who is actually singing Leporello; he must realize that Masetto and his peasant friends, as well as the audience in the theater, have become intimately familiar with the real Leporello's voice and will surely spot any inaccuracy in the Don's imitation of it. If he is wise, he will ask the real Leporello to demonstrate how *he* would sing the words in the impersonation scene so that the master can learn to imitate his servant's voice with the greatest possible precision.

In searching for the most typical traits to be used in vocal masquerades singers are usually assisted greatly by the librettists and composers. In the opening and closing acts of *Der Rosenkavalier*, for instance, the librettist, Hugo von Hofmannsthal, helps Octavian to act the part of a flirtatious servant girl by providing the singer with the additional disguise of a heavily spiced Viennese dialect. When Falstaff masquerades as a female fortune-teller in Nicolai's *The Merry Wives of Windsor*, the composer makes him sing this entire scene in a very funny high falsetto. When Gianni Schicchi pretends to be Buoso Donati, Puccini sets his vocal lines in such a way that they can be uttered in a tremulous, tenor croak which fools even Buoso's own physician, Spinelloccio.

There are times, however, when the librettist and composer fail to provide any specific suggestions, and it is then up to the singer and the director to find the most convincing form of vocal camouflage. For example, the score of *Così fan tutte* gives no clue as to how Despina should execute her vocal masquerades. Besides singing her regular role of the sassy servant girl, she also appears as the "magnetic" doctor and the giddy notary. She can help herself greatly if she uses an outlandish and generously dosed guttural accent for the first disguise and if she flavors her second masquerade with noisy, asthmatic gasps and an exaggerated nasal twang.

Another role that calls for great vocal versatility is that of Count Almaviva in *The Barber of Seville*. The tenor enacting this part disguises himself successively as a drunken soldier and as a music master. The difference between the vocal characterizations of these two masquerades must be sufficiently pronounced to deceive the sharp ears of Rosina's watchful and suspicious guardian, Dr. Bartolo. Moreover, the Count also pretends to be the impecunious student, Lindoro. The purpose of this particular deception is to make certain that Rosina loves him for his own sake, rather than for the sake of his wealth and noble title. As a result of this conglomeration of assumed personalities, Almaviva must continually switch from one voice to another. This is particularly true in the big ensemble scenes where he reserves his "Lindoro voice" for Rosina, his "Almaviva voice" for Figaro, and his "drunken soldier voice" (or his obsequiously humble "Don Alonzo voice") for Dr. Bartolo.

The ability to sing with several voices must have been a rather common accomplishment in the operatic world of the eighteenth century. This is clearly reflected in the prevalence of doublings which we find in so many original playbills. The normal complement of leading singers of Italian companies of that time numbered seven: three women and four men. Most of the librettos were carefully fashioned to conform to this standard, but if the plot called for the services of an additional personage, one of the singers was always ready to oblige by undertaking two different roles in the same performance.

Such doubling of roles can serve as an excellent test of an artist's ability, from the physical as well as the vocal point of view, and I have observed some quite extraordinary accomplishments. Many years ago, because of a last-minute illness, I asked Mike Ryan, a fine Cleveland tenor blessed with an excellent acting talent, to sing the two contrasting roles of the half-brothers, Jenik and Vašek, in a performance of *The Bartered Bride*. No public announcement was made, and Ryan was able to camouflage both his voice and his appearance to such an amazing extent that the audience had not the slightest inkling that both brothers had been impersonated by a single performer.

The purpose of impersonations is not merely to hide one's identity, but to persuade the listeners (and beholders) that they are confronted by another member of the cast. The execution may be difficult, but the task is crystal clear: the impersonator must try his best to match not only the looks, but also the voice of another character.

The visual part of an impersonation is usually helped along by changes in costume and, even more, by darkness. Voices, however, do not change their quality when the lights get dimmer. Even though it is dark at the end of the first act of *Die Götterdämmerung*, Siegfried must still sing in Gunther's voice; otherwise, Brünnhilde would become aware of the deception as soon as she heard the real Gunther. Even under the protection of Don Giovanni's feathered hat, Leporello must imitate his master's voice sufficiently well to deceive Donna Elvira, just as Cyrano de Bergerac (in the night scene under the balcony) must make Roxane believe that she is listening to Christian.

Perhaps the most difficult of all impersonations is that required of the Countess in the last act of *The Marriage of Figaro*. Pretending to be Susanna, she must fool three men—Cherubino, Figaro, and her own husband—all of whom are thoroughly familiar with the voices of both the mistress and the maid.

In all these instances I strongly urge the singers to put their pride in their pockets and ask the prototypes who are to be imitated to demonstrate how they would sing the lines in question. Just as with the painter who uses a real model, the likeness will be much more exact if the impersonator works from life rather than from memory.

No discussion of vocal disguises would be complete without mentioning quotations and reminiscences, those short references by one singer to something that has been said earlier by another. Although in these situations there is no desire to deceive anyone, these forms of imitation are closely akin to impersonations and should also be, as often as possible, copied from nature. Italian and French composers were very fond of this technique. Rigoletto quotes his master, the Duke, sleepily commanding him to be amusing; Manon Lescaut's brother gives her a verbatim report of the amorous complaints of Des Grieux; Mimi and Marguerite relive their first meetings with Rodolfo and Faust by quoting the words and music sung on these occasions by their lovers.

It is only rarely that singers get the full vocal and dramatic value out of these priceless opportunities to act with the voice. Of the many times we have heard Alfredo's aria in the second act of *La Traviata*— with its lovely vocal phrase where the amorous tenor quotes Violetta's tender assurance: "I will spend the rest of my life being faithful to you!" —how many Alfredos have given, or attempted to give, this sentence a touch of vocal color and inflection that would be even remotely reminiscent of Violetta?

Too few singers try to act with their voices. Many of them seem to feel an obligation to stick to what might be called their "best voice." Perhaps this should not surprise us. An opera lover, trying to follow dramatic events in a language he does not fully understand, is likely to interpret vocal disguises and other changes in vocal color as—to quote from a recent newspaper article—"strange and unbeautiful blemishes in the vocal technique of an otherwise fine singer." A remark of this type, after it finds its way into a couple of printed reviews, will often discourage the aspiring artist. He will decide that a more consistent dependence on his "Con amore" voice will be less likely to get him into trouble. There is no need to be pessimistic, however. As the appreciation and enjoyment of the dramatic elements of opera increases—and there is not the slightest doubt that it is on the increase—acting with the voice, as well as with the body, is certain to come more and more into its own.

Aria stagings

The aria stagings included in this chapter are not offered as final or definitive solutions but as school exercises and practice pieces. Obviously, the moves notated here can be used only when the distribution of scenery and properties is as indicated on my diagrams. Every individual scenic arrangement requires its own sequence of theatrical events and movements. A complete analysis of the situations, characters, and actions is not possible. All that I hope to achieve here is to stimulate the thinking of young singers and directors by showing them a variety of approaches, perspectives, and points of view.

When fitting words to music, my main concern is to provide singers with an English text* that fits very closely with the contour of the vocal phrase. Absolute textual fidelity to the original is not, in my opinion, a

---

* The English texts included in the *Barber*, *Carmen*, and *Rigoletto* discussions are based on the versions I made many years ago in collaboration with Sarah Caldwell. The English words of the Leporello aria are by Ruth and Thomas Martin who have graciously given me permission to make a few minor adjustments in order to conform more closely with my staging of this scene.

crucial consideration. When these arias are sung in Italian or French, singers should familiarize themselves with the exact meaning of the original, either in a literal translation, or in a close approximation. Literal translations are appended to the arias from the *Barber, Rigoletto,* and *Don Giovanni;* an approximate translation is appended to the aria from the *Masked Ball.*

Before presenting the actual staging of each aria, I shall discuss its problems from three different points of view: the theatrical, the musical, and the vocal.

A character in a play is seen by the audience for only part of the duration of the drama. There are invariably times when he is not on stage, times which he spends either in his dressing room or in the wings, watching the action and waiting for his next entrance. Let us call the moments when the character is on stage his *visible* life and the others, his *hidden* life.

From the musical point of view, the hidden life of an operatic role is either non-existent or restricted to a few bars of offstage singing. Seen in the light of the drama, however, this unseen portion of a role is by no means negligible. It almost invariably motivates or in some way colors the return to visibility. What a character thinks or does while not on stage can seriously influence his behavior when he re-enters. As a rule, singers and operatic stage directors are so preoccupied with the difficulties and complications of the visible life of the characters that they have neither the time nor the energy to bother with the hidden. Yet once a singer has mastered the mechanics of the visible sections of his part, it is relatively easy to "fill it out." This task, once done, can improve tremendously the onstage portions of the role.

THE BARBER OF SEVILLE, ACT I: Rosina's cavatina "Una voce poco fa"

Let us "fill out" the role of Rosina in *The Barber of Seville* from the time the Count's serenade wakes her up to the opening of the second scene, when she is ready to embark upon her cavatina "Una voce poco fa." We can do this by imagining her thoughts. We will assume that the reader is familiar with the basic facts of Rosina's relationship with the other characters of the opera: her guardian, Dr. Bartolo; her music teacher, Don Basilio; the barber, Figaro; and the two servants, Berta and Ambrogio. It also seems unnecessary to describe in great detail what occurs in the visible portions of Rosina's role, since this can be learned easily by studying the score or libretto.

ROSINA'S HIDDEN LIFE

Section 1 (from the time she wakes up to her appearance on the balcony)

What is this? A band playing at this hour of the night? The sun hasn't risen yet! Sounds like a serenade. I wonder if it's something arranged by that handsome young man who kept staring at me on the Prado in Madrid and who seems to have followed us to Seville. What a shame that the windows of my bedroom do not face the square! Well, you can trust my guardian to see to that! I hope they don't wake him up. That would make him even more sour! Fortunately, his room is in the other wing and he is a little hard of hearing. Let me see if I can tiptoe to the living room and look outside. No, in this darkness I will be sure to trip over a chair or something; and then what will I say? I'll light a candle; that will be safer! Careful now . . . just listen to that music. How gay! They must have seen the candlelight through the window and want me to realize that they know I can hear them. Darn it! Bartolo has noticed the light and is yelling down to Berta to go and see if I am sick. I *am* sick . . . of him! That man has a thousand eyes! No use . . . back to the bedroom. There must be some way of letting *him* know that I am *very* interested and *very* unhappy. Could I write him a note? Dangerous! My guardian suspects everyone and everything, and he inspects every scrap of paper. Perhaps if the note looked innocent enough like . . . like words to a song . . . let me try. Yes, if I use a piece of music paper Basilio gave me yesterday, it might work. What shall I write? Let's be very formal. "Your assiduous attentions have excited my curiosity. When my guardian leaves the house, find some way of informing me of your name, your occupation, and . . ." Let's see . . . yes . . . "your intentions. I am guarded like a prisoner. Please help me break my chains. Your unfortunate . . ." Shall I sign it? Well, since I ask him for his name, I might as well tell him mine! If I am caught, all is lost anyway, so . . . "your unfortunate Rosina." I will fold it like this and it will look quite innocent. If Bartolo asks me what it is, I'll tell him it is a song Don Basilio wants me to learn. No! I'd better tell him that these are the words for the aria of a new opera. He hates new operas so much, he will never think of looking at the paper. Oh, it's time to get dressed and have breakfast . . . Even now while we're eating, Bartolo can't leave me alone. He's asking me with an insinuating smile if it was a dream that woke me up. If I flirt with him a little, he will give me permission to go on the balcony with him. Flirt with him . . . ugh! But it's the only way to get anything out of him. Listen to that Figaro singing away outside. What a gay and nice fellow he is! I think I'll do a little embroidering before asking about the balcony. This way Bartolo won't wonder why I am in such a hurry.

ROSINA'S VISIBLE LIFE

Section 1 (on the balcony)

All works out as she has planned it. Rosina manages to drop the letter. She asks Bartolo to fetch it and while her guardian is on his way down,

Figaro retrieves the note. The Count and Figaro hide again. Unable to find the letter, Bartolo realizes that he has been duped. Angrily, he orders Rosina to come in from the balcony.

ROSINA'S HIDDEN LIFE

Section 2: (from her exit to just before the Count's second serenade)

That nasty old man! Now, I guess, the balcony will be locked forever! But at least I managed to let *him* have the note. Imagine Bartolo telling Berta to stay in the living room to see that I don't go near the balcony doors! I'll just remain in my own room until he is ready to leave the house. I know he is planning to fetch those silly marriage documents. How ridiculous! As if he could ever force me to marry him! I'll wait until he leaves and then I'll find some way to get rid of Berta. Aha! He is going. I can hear him giving orders to Ambrogio. Very well. I'll join Berta in the living room and do a little work on that embroidery screen. I just remembered that today is laundry day, Bartolo will make Berta count and write down every single piece of dirty linen. I will ask Berta to make a list of the things in my room and while she is there I'll peek from behind the blinds. Maybe my young admirer and I can get acquainted by singing a song to each other!

ROSINA'S AUDIBLE AND PARTLY VISIBLE LIFE

Section 2 (behind the balcony blinds)

The Count sings to Rosina, accompanied by Figaro's guitar. She answers once. In the middle of her second answer she is surprised by Berta, who orders her to return to her room.

ROSINA'S HIDDEN LIFE

Section 3 (from the end of her offstage singing to her entrance in the cavatina "Una voce poco fa")

Now I have to stay in my room! How annoying! Well, at least I know his name—Lindoro! What a pretty name! He said he was poor. I don't care. When I come of age, I will have my own money, unless that wicked old man squanders it all before then! I wonder if Berta will tell Bartolo that she caught me at the balcony. It really doesn't matter! Let him scold and rant and rave. One way or another, I'll win Lindoro. I wonder if Bartolo has returned. What a nuisance to have to sit here without knowing what goes on! Lindoro and Figaro were together. They must be friends. Perhaps Figaro can help us. I like Figaro—he is always gay!   [End of first scene.]

Figaro has entered Dr. Bartolo's house to administer "medicines"—a sneezing powder for Berta and a sleeping potion for Ambrogio—to put Bartolo's household in disarray. Rosina's hidden life continues through the intermission.

Wait a moment . . . that's Figaro's voice. I hear him calling Ambrogio and Berta. If Berta leaves the living room, I can look again through the shutters. I wonder if Lindoro is still outside. If Bartolo has returned and catches me, I think I'd better find some pretext for going into the living room. Suppose I take this skein of wool. I can always pretend that I wanted to match the color on the embroidery screen. I hope that Figaro keeps those servants busy for a good long while. Let me peek to see if anyone is in the living room.

[Curtain opens on Scene 2] All is quiet! There is no one here! I must have courage! [Orchestra plays the introduction to the cavatina]

The music

In the thirteen measures of the orchestral introduction we are presented with a shortened version of the ideas that are later spelled out in the vocal portion of the andante. The initial four notes (Example 5–13)

Example 5–13. THE BARBER OF SEVILLE, I, Cavatina no. 4

enunciate the central thought of the cavatina: "la vincerò" (I'll win the day). There are three phrases of approximately equal length in this introduction. The opening and closing ones refer to Lindoro. The whispering sotto voce of the middle phrase is associated with the danger posed by Dr. Bartolo and the tactics required to outwit him. The remaining twenty-nine measures of the andante elaborate on this contrast between the young admirer and the old guardian. They are highlighted by four bursts of vocal and orchestral energies on "Si, Lindoro" (see measures 21, 25, 34, and 38), which must receive their proper share of muscular excitements.

The orchestral opening of the moderato section is noteworthy for its triumphant repetition of the "I'll-win-the-day" motto in the eighth measure and the scrambling violin figures in measures 10 and 11.* I hear and interpret these as music for Rosina's "excited writing." There are

* The measures of the andante and moderato sections of this cavatina are numbered separately here, so that the andante goes from measure 1 to measure 42 and the moderato from measure 1 to measure 78.

additional violin passages to finish the writing of the letter in measures 41 through 46.

The juxtaposition of Lindoro and Bartolo heard in the andante was only the first set of contrasts to be found in this cavatina. In the moderato section there are two other pairs of conflicting notions: the docile lambkin versus the angry viper and lying quietly in ambush as opposed to springing a trap suddenly. Observe particularly the musical development (in measures 32–41 and 56–65) of "e cento trappole prima di cedere farò giocar," which means literally: "and a hundred traps, before I yield, I will spring!" Rossini supplies musical equivalents for both the setting and the springing of the traps. The first he does with cunningly insinuating vocal chromatics and the use of the fairly remote key of F-sharp minor. The traps are sprung with energetic sixteenths in the vocal line and the unmasking of the underlying tonality of E Major. This sequence of events suggests staging parallels: a casual relaxation for the setting of the traps and an impulsive bodily movement for springing them. The musical energies of the orchestral postlude call for some corresponding muscular exertions. Activities connected with fetching, folding, and hiding the letter serve this purpose to perfection.

Vocal aspects

Rosina's tone of voice must change with each of her thoughts: her love, her heart, her cleverness, and her determination to battle Bartolo to win Lindoro. As she thinks of her beloved, her voice must reflect all the naiveté and innocent rapture associated with a girl's first love. When she refers to Bartolo, her vocal attitude can be that of almost brazen self-confidence. Comments on her docility and obedience should have a slightly ironic tinge; references to the viper must be angry, while the plans for setting and springing traps must reflect, in turn, slyness, the sound of laughter, and triumph. All runs, skips, and other vocal ornaments are meant to mirror and emphasize the mood of the moment, to express rapture, amusement, anger, or triumph. Under no circumstances may they sound like exercises for perfecting vocal fluency!

Singing version, text, and translation

Andante

When he sang, my heart stood still. What could I do,   what could I say?
Una   voce   poco   fa   qui nel   cor   mi   risuonò.
A   voice   a while   ago here in my   heart   resounded.

It is useless to resist. Love commands, we must obey!   Yes, Lindoro,
Il mio cor   ferito e già, e   Lindoro   fu che il piagò.   *Sì, Lindoro*
My heart   is wounded and Lindor   was who struck it.   Yes, Lindor

I am yours. Yours, forever, let　come what may! Should my guardian interfere,
mio sa-　　　*rà,*　　　*lo giurai, la　vincerò.*　　　*Il tutor　　ricuserà,*
mine shall　be,　　I swore it,　I shall win.　　The guardian shall refuse,

he will very quickly find— and I'll make it very plain—　　that Rosina knows
io　　l'ingegno agguzerò, alla　　fin　s'accheterà　　e　　contenta io
I will　sharpen my wits.　　In the end he will calm down and contented I

her mind. Yes Lindoro, I am yours, yours forever,　let come what may!
resterò　　Si, Lindoro mio sarà,　　lo giurai,　　la vincerò!
shall be.　　Yes, Lindoro will be mine, I swore it.　　I shall win the day!

Moderato

I'm sweet and ladylike, as is expected;　I know that guardians should
Io　sono　　　docile,　　son rispettosa, sono obbediente, dolce
I　　am　　　docile,　　I am respectful, I'm obedient, tender

be respected. I am obedient as any girl should be, I can be kind
amorosa.　　Mi lascio reggere, mi lascio reggere,　mi fo guidar,
and loving.　　I can be ruled,　I can be ruled,　　I can be led.

and so polite. But those who cross my path will quickly feel my wrath,
mi fo guidar. ma se　mi　toccano　　dov'è il mio debole
I can be led, But if I'm　　touched　　where it hurts,

my girlish charm will turn to spite. And Doctor Bartolo, you'll
sarò una vipera,　　　　sarò.　　E cento trappole
I become a viper,　　　　I become. And a hundred traps

very shortly know, Rosina's bound to win her fight!
prima di cedere　farò giocar,　　farò giocar!
(before I give in)　I shall spring,　　I shall spring!

Focal points

Onstage	Description	Location
Scenic elements	1. Balcony door	Along 34, straddling CC
Furniture props	2. Table	In LB2
Hand props	3. Skein of wool	Carried by Rosina
	4. Inkwell and quill	On table (LB2)
	5. Sheet of paper	In table drawer
	6. Sander	In table drawer
	7. Saucer for excess sand	In table drawer

Offstage (real or imagined)	*Description*	*Direction and connecting scenic elements*
Other characters	8. Lindoro	Up center, beyond balcony door
	9. Bartolo	Along 12, beyond left archway

| Abstract ideas | 10. Love for Lindoro and determination to win him | Down right, heavenward |

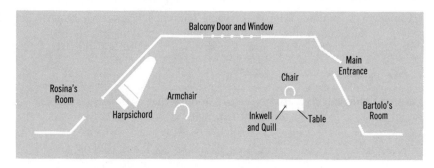

Diagram 5–1. The setting for Rosina's cavatina

Rosina's actions explained

During the orchestral introduction of the andante, Rosina enters from her room and looks around to make certain that she is alone. She is anxious to peek through the shutters of the locked balcony door to see if the young man who serenaded her earlier is still waiting outside in the square. In order to have an excuse for coming to this room, she has brought with her a skein of wool and is ready with the lie that she came merely to match up a color in a half-finished flower on the embroidery screen. Finding herself unobserved, Rosina cautiously closes the door to her room and tiptoes halfway to the balcony. At this point she glances at the archway leading to Bartolo's quarters and decides that it would be wiser to check whether by any chance he has managed to return home

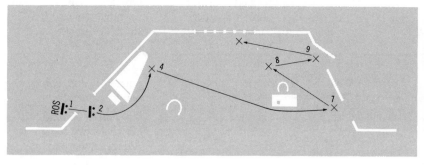

Diagram 5–2. Andante, measures 1–21

earlier than expected. She puts the skein of wool on the piano and runs to the archway to look and listen. Having reassured herself that her guardian is not in his rooms, she turns and starts out again toward her goal. As she passes near the main entrance, she imagines hearing a noise and makes a slight detour to be sure that no one is approaching from that direction. There is no one! Delighted to be rid of her various chaperons, she makes a beeline for the balcony shutters and looks eagerly to the right and left. The square is empty. No matter. Love will find a way! She turns around and is ready to sing.

For the first eight measures of the vocal section (measures 14 through 21) Diagrams 5–3 shows the recommended angle of the shoulder line in relation to the balcony door. This position allows Rosina to distinguish between two focal points:

1. Her recollection of Lindoro and his singing: indirect rapport, over her right shoulder and
2. Herself and her heart.

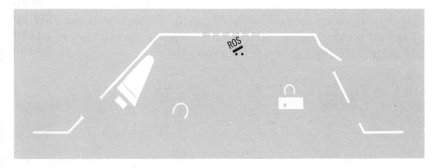

Diagram 5–3. Andante, measures 14–21

The next two walks are motivated by the intensity of Rosina's ardor, which is translated into an urge to move. The direction, down right, is the one that is reserved for her determination to win Lindoro. For the "guardian" section of the andante, Rosina goes slightly left. Referring to Bartolo, she faces the archway; referring to herself, she turns away from it. When using the Italian text, she changes direction with each measure: left, right, left, right. In the English version given here (see page 187) she sings two measures toward the archway and two toward the right. The walks that follow are quite similar to the earlier "determination" moves. Since they start further downstage, they take Rosina closer to her room, so that she ends the andante in almost the same location she began it.

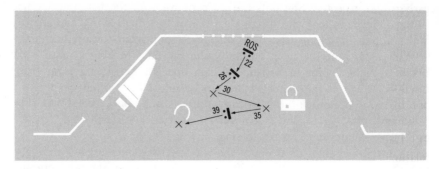

Diagram 5–4. Andante, measures 22–42

During the orchestral introduction of the moderato (measures 1 through 12) Rosina has a sudden inspiration: she is going to write Lindoro another, and even more encouraging, letter. She runs to the table and takes from its open drawer space* the necessary writing utensils.

She puts the stack of six sheets of paper in front of her. She places the sander to her right and the saucer to her left. All this should be accomplished in the eight opening measures of the introduction. With the orchestral forte at the end of the eighth measure, Rosina looks up with determination and gets hold of the quill. She spends measures 10 and 11 in brisk writing, and in measure 12 she replaces the quill in the inkwell and is ready to sing.

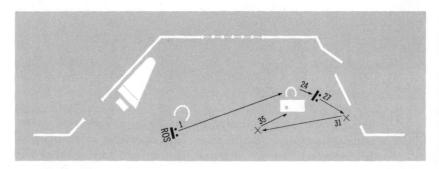

Diagram 5–5. Moderato, measures 1–38

In the first section of the vocal portion of the moderato (measures 13 to 24) the two flute scales, which come in measures 14 and 18, deserve to be highlighted by means of a synchronization. I have Rosina lift the sander on "*docile*" and shake it lightly over the paper as soon as she

---

* When a table is placed in the manner shown on the diagram, it is much safer not to risk having to open a real drawer, which could stick and interfere with the accurate timing of an action.

finishes singing this word. She puts the sander down again on "rispet*tosa*."
With "obbediente," she lifts the paper and moves it gently back and
forth to make sure that the sand has blotted all the ink. With the second
flute scale she empties the sand into the saucer, then she replaces the
paper in front of her.

On the fermata (measure 24), which is usually embroidered by a
vocal portamento to the upper octave and an anticipation of the word
"ma," Rosina gets up and steps slightly to the left of the table.

The four changes of location in the next section (measures 25 to
41) are associated with the vocal energies displayed on the words "vipera"
and "giocar." The two cantabile F-sharp-minor phrases (beginning on
measures 32 and 36) should be sung as if intended for the ears of Bartolo
beyond the archway. During the second and more ornamented of these
"entrapment" promises, Rosina can perch on the front edge of the table
in an almost provocatively relaxed posture.

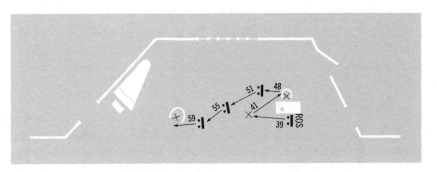

Diagram 5–6. Moderato, measures 39–62

During the next section (measures 41 to 48), which is a paraphrase
of measures 13 to 24, Rosina returns to the table and finishes writing the
letter. The fermata at the end of this segment of the moderato is ornamented much more richly than its predecessor, but it ends in the same
manner and is accompanied by a similar acting maneuver, although, instead of stepping out to the left of the table, Rosina moves to the right.

Since both musically and vocally the next section (measures 49 to
65) represents a repetition with variations of what was heard between
measures 25 and 41, the stage actions must reflect a corresponding pattern.
All the energy outputs and relaxation spots occur in the same musical
places as in the earlier section. However, they are enacted in a different
stage area, so that the four walks, instead of being concentrated in the
vicinity of the table, are now acted out toward and around the right armchair.

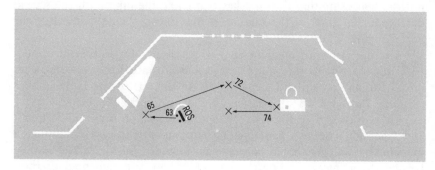

Diagram 5–7. Moderato, measures 63–78

For the vocal portion of the coda (measures 66 to 78) Rosina proceeds to the center of the stage. During the orchestral postlude she runs to the table, folds the letter, returns to the center, dances around in a circle, kisses the letter, and hides it in her bosom.

CARMEN, ACT III: The Card Song

The drama

The character of Carmen is so well known that only a few words are necessary to describe the immediate situation in the third act. The beautiful and capricious gypsy girl is passionately dedicated to the men with whom she happens to fall in love. But she tires of them rather quickly, and when the amorous magic has run its course she has no further use for them. In the past these separations seem to have been effected without too much difficulty. José's predecessor was dispatched quite unceremoniously. As Carmen says in the Seguidilla: "Je l'ai mis à la porte, hier." Her current lover, however, the soldier who has become a deserter for her sake, seems determined to hang on to a relationship which for Carmen is now a distasteful nuisance.

It is night-time in a gypsy camp in the mountains near Seville. Bales of illegal merchandise, waiting to be smuggled into the city, are stacked in the clearing. While the two leaders of the expedition, Dancairo and Remendado, have gone ahead to Seville to make sure that there will be no unforeseen complications at the receiving end, most of the members of the gang are resting and gathering strength for the next lap of the journey. Two of the young gypsy girls, Frasquita and Mercedes, pass the time by reading their fortunes in the cards and, after a while, Carmen, who has come closer to watch them, also decides to consult the cards to discover what fate holds in store for her.

Before analyzing the music and the stage movement of this scene, perhaps I should say a few words about this particular manner of predicting the future. Young Americans have only the vaguest notion of what is involved in telling fortunes, and their ignorance handicaps them when they are entrusted with such roles as one of the gypsy girls in *Carmen* or that of the Fortune-Teller in Strauss' *Arabella*. As a young boy in Russia, I had many occasions to observe women using playing cards to read fortunes. My grandmother was a confirmed card prognosticator, and by watching her I was able to pick up quite a bit of knowledge which later came in very handy, at least operatically speaking. The thing to remember is that while a few cards have a permanent meaning—the queen of diamonds is a young unmarried woman, the king of spades an old gentleman —the prediction of the future is based mostly on combinations and juxtapositions. The ace of spades, for example, is a very dangerous card, especially when surrounded by any red cards: it means "death" (with hearts) or "imminent death" (with diamonds). Lying in a nest of clubs, this ace becomes less threatening and is equivalent to "impending bankruptcy" or merely "severe reverses in business matters." When it appears in a threesome with the king and queen of spades, the same ace loses all its malevolence and is "read" simply as "the home of a dignified elderly couple." I cannot guarantee that the Spanish gypsies of Carmen's generation followed the same system as my grandmother, but I have been assured by experts that this general principle applies to all systems of fortune-telling in cards,* and Carmen's (and the orchestra's) reaction to the combination of diamonds and spades ("Carreau! Pique!") leaves no doubt about it. As for the strength of the superstition, I imagine it may be safely compared to our present-day reliance on weather forecasting: something to be taken as a serious probability, but not as an absolute certainty. There is no question but that for Carmen and her friends reading the cards is not just a game, but a very real look into the mysteries of the future.

Singers impersonating Carmen, Frasquita, and Mercedes must bear in mind that gypsies are professional fortune-tellers to whom the handling of playing cards is as familiar as the use of a typewriter to an American office girl. Consequently, Carmen and her colleagues may not display any clumsiness in shuffling or manipulating the cards.

To facilitate matters, I recommend reducing the size of Carmen's deck to twenty cards, made up in about equal numbers of diamonds and spades. It does not matter particularly how she holds these cards when shuffling them. Before reading the future, however, she should

---

* This is supported also in the section entitled "Fortune-telling by Cards," found in W. G. Benham's *Playing Cards*, published by Spring Books, London.

transfer them to her left hand, making certain that the face of the deck is turned toward her palm. Then, using her right thumb, she peels the cards off, one by one, from the top of the deck.

To put a card down with its face showing, Carmen should first flip it up with a slight counterclockwise turn of the wrist. If its face is to remain hidden, the top card is lifted without turning the wrist. Both of these procedures are used in this scene. The terms *flip* and *show* describe the up and down motions of the first method, while *lift* and *hide* indicate the respective movements involved in the second procedure.

The music

Although Carmen's "Card Song" is not an aria, but part of an ensemble involving Frasquita and Mercedes, I have included it in this chapter because it happens to be one of the best possible exercises for the coordination of singing with the manipulation of hand props. Since there are very few changes in focal points and locations in this scene, and since our main concern here is the study of musically synchronized movements, we can dispense with inventories and diagrams and treat the musical and vocal aspects and all questions of Carmen's actions in a single presentation.

We begin our staging of the "Card Song" twelve measures before the "andante quasi allegretto" in 6/8 time. At this point Frasquita is kneeling above a wooden chest in LB2 and Mercedes is sitting on the ground to the left of the chest. Carmen, who was standing above her companions and watching them read their fortunes, now starts shuffling her cards. Her friends notice her presence, and Frasquita picks up her own cards and moves slightly to the right, inviting Carmen to take her place above the chest. Carmen stops shuffling for her opening sentence: "Let's see what my fate holds in store." With her last word she kneels down so that, on the first beat of the new tempo, she can kiss the deck for good luck and start putting down her cards.

The "Trio of the Cards" may have started out at a slightly slower speed, but by the time our staging begins, the tempo has usually reached the frequency of approximately $\quarternote = 120$, or one bar per second: $\halfnote = 60$. A slight acceleration in the last four measures preceding the andante quasi allegretto leads directly and smoothly into the new rhythmical pattern, where each of the dotted quarters equals the preceding half note: $\dottedquarter = \halfnote = 84$.*

Combining two acting subtexts with Carmen's first singing line, we have the sequence shown with Example 5–14. Note the transition from the 2/4 section to the one in 6/8 time.

* For a more detailed description of the mechanism of smooth tempo changes of this type, see Chapter 6, page 255.

Example 5–14. CARMEN, III, no. 19

As soon as Carmen begins to lay down the cards, she lifts her head and closes her eyes. She does not want to see the individual components of her fortune, but waits until she can inspect the completed group of three cards all at once. As soon as the third one is showing, Carmen looks down and discovers at her dismay that she has uncovered a highly un-lucky combination of diamonds and spades.

The rushing scale of the strings that culminates in the fortissimo brass chord reflects Carmen's startled reaction to the dire prophecy the cards have spelled out for her. The musical impact of this orchestral pas-sage is so powerful that I find it necessary to provide additional dramatic emphasis by having Frasquita, who was reading the cards along with Carmen, rise and back away in horrified fascination. Carmen becomes aware that the two gypsy girls have been watching her, and during the prolonged ominous silence that follows "diamonds . . . spades!" she glances defiantly at each of her companions in turn.

The next five measures are an almost exact replica of the preceding ones, except that Carmen does not kiss the deck a second time, and it is Mercedes who gets up with the fortissimo chord and walks away to the left. During the next five measures the strings play a very soft descending arpeggio of dotted half notes. On each of these, Carmen inspects one of the newly opened cards and puts them one on top of the other, ending up with a neat stack containing five cards. Frasquita, in the meantime, tiptoes down left, crossing above Carmen to join Mercedes, who moved earlier to the down left corner of the stage. On the word "death" Carmen puts the sixth card on the stack and, at the same time, turns left to glare at her companions, whose silent sympathy begins to annoy her. With the crescendo that follows "death" Carmen passes the rest of the deck into her right hand and lifts it, so that on the sustained sforzando of the brasses she can slam it (also face up) on top of the small stack lying in front of her. She slides the full pack off the top of the chest into her left palm, gets up at once, and walks toward the right, away from Mercedes and Frasquita. Carmen's attitude must make it plain that when cards insist on foretelling disaster and death, she prefers to consult them in strict privacy. The synchronization pattern of the six measures that precede the andante in 3/4 time can be practiced with the subtext (Example 5–15).

Example 5–15

The andante section can be treated as a solo aria. Although Frasquita and Mercedes are still present, they should sit on the ground, facing upstage, and pursue their fortune-telling activities so discreetly as to be unnoticed by the audience.

During the two introductory measures of the orchestra, Carmen kneels down in the general area of LB2 or LB1. In some productions Carmen spreads out her shawl at this point, but I feel that the muscular energy involved in this action tends to contradict the *ppp* of the string accompaniment.

Vocal aspects

The dramatic impact of the next sixteen measures depends almost entirely on the manner in which they are sung. Bizet's direction here is "très également et simplement" (very evenly and simply). Carmen's tone of voice must reflect her fatalistic acceptance of the future as it is foreshadowed by the cards. The formal arrangement—two similar stanzas, ending respectively in F minor and A-flat Major,—deserves to be mirrored by appropriate changes of posture. The stage directions (they are not Bizet's) that I have added to the following text show what I have in mind. The English translation given here is not literal, but a version intended for singing.

Text, singing version, and Carmen's actions

En vain pour éviter les résponses amères,
It's useless to persist, in vain is all endeavor . . .

En vain tu mêleras,   *(Carmen begins to shuffle the cards*
Why should I try again?   *very slowly.)*

Cela ne sert à rien, les cartes sont sincères
No matter what I do, it is the same forever

Et ne mentiront pas!   *(Still kneeling, Carmen sits back on*
The answer's all too plain!   *her heels.)*

Dans le livre d'en haut si ta page est heureuse,
The future won't be changed, no mercy will be granted,

Mêle et coupe sans peur   *(She slides over to rest on her left*
I'll have the same reply,   *hip.)*

La carte sous tes doigts se tournera joyeuse,
The cards will not deceive, their magic is enchanted,

   (She continues the preceding action until she rests on her left elbow.)

T'annonçant le bonheur!
They will not tell a lie!

In the next section of the andante, Bizet introduces a completely new musical idea: an orchestral countermelody entrusted to an oboe and doubled first by a trombone and later by a clarinet (Example 5–16). These undulating chromatics add an undercurrent of eery tension to

Example 5–16

the vocal line. A feeling of apprehension keeps growing, at first slowly
and then more rapidly, until it explodes into a vocal fortissimo, supported
by a brass chord and an ominously growling timpani roll. To illustrate
this unusual musical concept with an equally distinctive stage action,
Carmen, still holding the deck in her left hand, starts peeling off and
dealing out a fanlike succession of ten cards. She puts them on the
ground, face down, and synchronizes the placement of each card with
the dotted half notes of the orchestral melody. Here is the position of the
cards in relation to Carmen and the order in which they are spread out:

Diagram 5–8

To practice the coordination of her arm and body movements with
the orchestral melody and the vocal line, the singer can use the following subtext. The numbers above it correspond to the card numbers indicated on the diagram. The subtext with the original words, an English
version, and the music of the orchestral melody is seen in Example 5–17.

While placing the cards, Carmen moves from left to right and gradually returns to her earlier kneeling posture. After putting down the tenth
card, she leans backward and supports herself on her outstretched arms,
singing the long fortissimo note in this position. Two measures later she
leans forward again and starts picking up and turning over the cards that
she had placed face down in front of her. During the last six measures
of the andante Carmen discloses three cards in this fashion. I interpret
the figurations played here in turn by the violins, violas, and cellos as
"pick-up-turn-and-look" music. The descending chromatic scale in the
bassoons accompanies Carmen's analysis of the meaning of each card in
relation to its position in the circle. Her reaction to the third card comes
so quickly that, in her anxiety to find at least one "fortunate" card, Car-

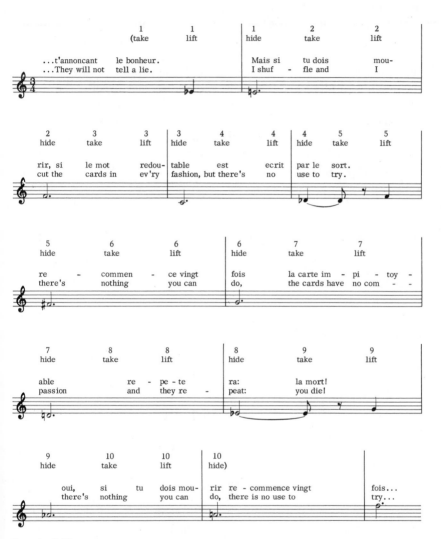

Example 5–17

men has it fully opened ahead of the rhythm indicated by the strings, thus justifying her unhappy response to it in the beginning of the sixth measure. It is best, therefore, if for the second and third of these "readings," Carmen uses cards that lie next to each other. With the word "die," which falls on the first downbeat of the tempo primo, Carmen slides over on her right thigh, sinks down toward down right to rest her head on her outstretched arm, and remains in this position for several measures.

In the meantime, Frasquita and Mercedes have imperceptibly returned to dramatic life. During the last six measures of the andante they
work themselves into a position where they are sitting to the left of the
chest, facing the audience. They open their own cards and sing gaily,
without paying the slightest attention to their unlucky companion. Beginning with the eighth measure of the tempo primo Carmen sits up
and resumes reading her future by uncovering, one by one, the rest of
her cards. The order in which she does it is not important, except that
it is better to leave cards 1 and 2 until the very end. Before she sings
the low E-flat, she picks up the fifth card and compares it with the other
uncovered ones to make certain she has made no mistake. She drops it
on the ground only after finishing the expansive sentence of Example
5–18.

La mort!   la mort!   en - cor...   la   mort!__
It's death!   It's death!   once more...   it's   death!__

Example 5–18

She turns over cards 6, 7, and 8 immediately thereafter and holds
on to card 8, treating it in the same manner as card 5. During her two
measures of rest—measures 11 and 12 before the end of the trio—Carmen
turns over cards 1 and 2.

When presenting a complete production of this opera, I have Don
José re-enter the stage at this point. He appears on a tall rock, far
upstage in the approximate vicinity of line LBC. Having noticed Dancairo and Remendado approaching from far away, he is on his way downstage to meet them. Seeing Carmen, he stops to watch what she is doing.
As she sings her last note, she becomes aware of his presence and stares
at him as if he were the very personification of the death she has seen
in her cards. This tableau is fittingly accompanied by the fate motive
played by the lower strings. In the last three measures of this piece Carmen turns toward the cards and sweeps them up with a vigorous movement of her right arm, synchronizing this gesture with the final chord in
the orchestra.

RIGOLETTO, ACT II: Scene and aria "Ella mi fu rapita"

This scene, which opens the second act of Verdi's opera, presents
some rather intricate and intriguing musical-dramatic problems. It begins
with a fast and very agitated orchestral introduction. There is a succession

of two eight-measure pianissimo phrases of breathless excitement. A crescendo at the end of the second phrase leads to a new five-measure section featuring heavy chords, at which time the spendidly attired Duke enters in extreme agitation (the stage direction in the score says "agitatissimo.") As soon as the orchestra stops playing, the Duke begins his "Ella mi fu rapita!" (She has been abducted!) He then proceeds to tell us that driven by an obscure premonition, he returned to Gilda's dwelling and found "the gate open and the house deserted."

In Victor Hugo's play, upon which the opera is based, this particular situation does not occur. There, King Francis (who is the counterpart of Verdi's Duke of Mantua) has no inkling of the preceding night's violent events, and he learns of the abduction only when the courtiers bring in the girl whom they have stolen and whom they believe to be Rigoletto's mistress.

We do not know whether it was Verdi's librettist, Piave, or the composer himself who recommended this change from the original play. Operatically speaking, the new version has a very great advantage: it serves to generate the kind of emotional turmoil which forms the basis of all Verdi's dramatic scenes. The recitative first expresses the unhappy lover's agitation, which leads quite naturally to his tender recollections of Gilda's loveliness. Then his renewed outburst of anger and desire for revenge against the unknown abductors culminates in the aria where he imagines the scene of the kidnaping and laments the fact that he was unable to help "this heavenly being whose beauty rivals that of the angels."

In spite of the musical and dramatic effectiveness of this scene, it introduces a break in the logical development of the plot, a flaw which becomes apparent when we try to retrace the Duke's steps and ask ourselves just when he returned from the house of his beloved Gilda. His extreme agitation has all the earmarks of immediacy: he has obviously just now discovered the disappearance of the girl and is eager to vent his anger and disappointment. But if that is true, how is it possible for him to enter wearing his royal robes? We know that he went to see Gilda on the preceding evening in his middle-class disguise, that he overheard her say: "I feel that he is poor, but I will love him all the more!" We have heard him pretend to be a needy student. It certainly is not conceivable that he would wish to destroy the illusion by visiting her the very next morning dressed in a nobleman's garb. On the other hand, it would be even less possible to have him dressed as a poor student when he greets his courtiers, who enter immediately after his aria. In other words, the costume in which the Duke appears in this scene is inconsistent with the known facts of the story and with his mood as indicated by the music and the words.

Although audiences have been witnessing this scene for more than a hundred years without being aware of anything illogical or disturbing, the alert stage director should notice such admittedly minor dramatic flaws and see not only how they can be corrected, but how, in general, he can improve the believability of the drama and the music. In this case, it is possible to imagine that the Duke visited Gilda in his student outfit and then changed to his ducal attire in some other place before the curtain rises, but to my ears the breathlessly agitated orchestral introduction completely contradicts this reasoning. Some other solution must be found. In our search for it, let's again try to identify with the personage in the play.

If you were the Duke and were driven to revisit Gilda the very next morning after your romantic meeting, how would you go about it? You would certainly want to continue with your "poor student" act and wear the appropriate clothing. As soon as you had discovered the tragedy of the abandoned house, you would return to your palace and would immediately change into something more suitable to your rank. Well then, why not let the audience in on this sequence of events? Let them see the Duke both as a student and as a nobleman. Of course, if he entered the stage at the point indicated in the score, changing his costume in the five remaining measures would be clearly impossible. But what about the preceding sixteen measures? Certainly these are also "his" music. Even so, to undress and dress on stage at the speed which the orchestra is playing these twenty-one measures, he would have to be a quick-change artist and give a very ignoble impression. But in Hugo's play, when the King enters in this scene, he is described as wearing "un magnifique négligé du matin" which, literally translated, means "a magnificent dressing gown of the type worn in the morning." A dressing gown can be easily worn over a student's boots, trousers, and shirt. Furthermore, a Duke has pageboys hanging around the palace whose duty it is to assist him. As a matter of fact, one of these pages appears looking for him later in the act. Let the Duke enter as soon as the orchestra begins to play and clap his hands to order the pages to fetch his dressing gown? Then he can peel off his jacket and throw it on the table along with his student's hat. During the second eight-measure phrase, the pages can return and busy themselves around him. One of them helps him with the dressing gown while the other picks up the things he threw on the table. At the end of the orchestral introduction, the pages disappear offstage while the Duke, wearing his magnificent dressing gown, is ready for his recitative.

All this constitutes a noticeable gain in musical and dramatic truth, both for the singer and for the audience. There is, I believe, an additional advantage. In operas where the plot demands that important characters appear in different types of attire, the audience can easily become confused and fail to recognize the same stage personality in his different guises. In such works it is desirable to let the audience witness changes of costume whenever it can be arranged. Since the Duke in *Rigoletto* later appears in still another disguise (that of a cavalry officer), showing his transformation from "student" into "nobleman" helps to delineate him even more precisely as a restless philanderer and makes the dramatic continuity that much easier to grasp.

The music

The orchestral introduction has twenty-one measures and is marked "agitato assai" (very agitated). Not counting the opening measure, which establishes the key of D minor, it consists of five phrases of equal length. Since the second and the fourth of these are repetitions of the first and third, there are only three musical ideas, arranged in the order A, A, B, B, C. The A's and B's are marked "pianissimo," the C is marked "forte." The whispered softness and the almost impossibly fast speed indicated by Verdi's metronome mark make it clear that the actions performed here must be executed hurriedly and rather stealthily. This applies however only to the A and B phrases. Once the introduction has reached phrase C, the character of the music changes drastically, and this contrast between the softly running eighth notes and the heavy quarters must be reflected in the behavior and the attitudes of the Duke and the two pageboys that I use in this introduction.

The structure of the following vocal section is rather unusual. It seems to consist, in fact, of two separate recitatives, both beginning with the same sentence—"Ella mi fu rapita"—but then following different paths. The first of these recitatives begins with an account of Gilda's disappearance and leads into the F-Major aria section, wherein the Duke contemplates the possibility of changing his mode of life. These virtuous resolutions are soon interrupted by the second recitative, angrier and more vengeful than the first, which gradually works its way into the principal G-flat-Major aria, in which the Duke's thoughts turn to tender memories of his beloved. All this serves to illuminate his flightiness and suggests that, while his heart may be capable of sincere and generous impulses, his good intentions are not too firmly rooted.

The unconventional structure of the G-flat-Major aria should be mirrored in a correspondingly asymmetrical sequence of stage locations. Its basic scheme is simple: two eleven-measure stanzas framed by a fairly short orchestral introduction and a seven-measure vocal and orchestral coda. Although the stanzas are equal in length, they are not identical in content. Curiously enough, it is their opening sentences that feature different thematic material, and only the longer answering phrases run in a parallel manner. This unconventional arrangement can be represented by the scheme AA′ BA′. These A′ phrases, which are almost double the length of their mates, become the twin pillars supporting the structure of this adagio. Their special importance is further enhanced by a number of word repetitions and by vocal and orchestral embellishments.

In my staging of this aria I have tried to find visual counterparts not only for the fluctuation of energy and mood elements and the repetitions of words and sentences, but also for the irregularities of the basic framework of the composition.

Vocal aspects

The special notations that Verdi has added to the vocal line should be studied with great care. A respectful observance of all crescendos, diminuendos, and accented notes contributes greatly to emotional credibility and variety in the execution of this piece. Also important are the dolce markings in the transitions from the declamatory to the cantabile sections and the dolcissimo at the end of the final cadenza. In addition to following all these indications, singers may find it useful to analyze the differences in inflections and tone colors that must be attempted in an intricate vocal composition of this type. For example, the feeling behind the first "Ella mi fu rapita" could be described as "indignant," while the second one is "angry." The flavor of sincere repentance that is suitable for the F-Major andante should be quite different from the more visionary and sensuous mood of the adagio in G-flat Major.

I wish that tenors would be more willing to try the optional ornaments that the composer has provided for them in this aria. Even though it is printed in all the scores, one almost never hears the charming variation that Verdi has suggested as an alternative cadenza in the ninth measure before the end of the piece.

Singing version, text, and translation

Recitative

She was no longer there! What could have happened? Early this morning
Ella mi fu rapita! *E quando, o ciel?* *Ne' brevi istanti*
She was abducted! And when, o heaven? In that short time

some dark and strange foreboding made me return to the home of my beloved.
prima che il mio presagio interno sull'orma corsa ancora mi spingesse . . .
before my foreboding drove me to retrace my steps . . .

The door stood open . . . the garden was deserted! Who carried you away
Schiuso era l'uscio! *E la magion deserta!* *E dove ora sarà*
The door was unlocked! And the house was deserted! And now where could

my dearest angel? When I beheld you, so innocent and trusting,
quel angiol caro?   Colei che prima potè in questo core
she be, the dear angel? She, who first knew to kindle in my heart

I felt the flame of a new and pure emotion! To make you happy, I would
destar la fiamma di costanti   affetti?   Colei si pura,   al cui
   the   flame of a constant devotion.   She, so pure, she, whose

change my way of living, I would choose the path of virtue and devotion!
modesto   sguardo quasi   spinto a virtù   talor mi credo
virtuous   gaze could drive me to virtue   I believe!

They carried her away! They dared to touch her!
Ella mi fu rapita!   E   chi   l'ardiva?
She was abducted!   And who dared it?

O, I shall find her and avenge this insult!
Ma ne avrò, ma ne avrò vendetta!
But I shall be, I shall be avenged.

Yes, I shall find her, I shall find her and console her!
Io chiede il pianto   della   mia diletta.
I owe it to the sobs   of   my darling!

Aria

Dearest, can I forget you? So fearful, yet so tender . . . when in that
Par mi veder le lagrime   scorrenti   da quel ciglio,   quando fra
I can imagine the tears   flowing down her cheeks, when, torn by

modest garden, you opened the gates of heaven, gave me the blessed memory,
il dubbio el l'ansia del subito   periglio,   del amor nostro memore,
doubts and fears of the sudden   danger,   remembering our love

of your first kiss of love! Dearest, where have they taken you,
il suo Gualtier chiamò.   Ned ei   potea soccorrerti,
she called for her Gualtier. No, he could not help you,

frightened and broken with sorrow? They seized you while you were dreaming
cara fanciulla amata; ei che vorria   coll'anima
dearest, beloved girl;   he, who would wish with all his heart

dreams of a bright tomorrow, trusting your faithful lover to guard
farti   quaggiù beata, ei che le sfere agl'angeli
to make you ever happy, he who does not believe heaven's

your peaceful dreams!
per te no invidio!
angels are comparable to you!

Focal points

Onstage	Description	Location
Other characters	1. Two pageboys	First in the archway at RB3; later around the table and left chair
Scenic elements	2. Archway to inner apartments	In RB3
Furniture props	3. Table	In RC2
Costume props	4. Student's hat	Carried in by the Duke
	5. Student's Jacket	Worn by the Duke at his entrance
	6. Splendid dressing gown	Carried in by one of the pages

Offstage (real or imaginary)	Description	Location
Other characters	7. Gilda	Left, along 23, at eye level, beyond the walls of the set
	8. Unknown abductors	Down-left, at eye level beyond the walls of the auditorium
Abstract ideas	9. Gilda as the embodiment of beauty and charm	Down-right, heavenward, beyond the walls of the auditorium

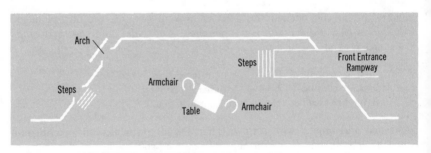

Diagram 5–9. The setting for the Duke's actions

The Duke's actions explained

As soon as the curtain opens and the orchestra begins to play, the Duke enters hurriedly from the up left platform and claps his hands. One of the two pageboys who are loitering in the up right archway

runs off to fetch the Duke's dressing gown, while the other remains onstage ready to assist his master. The Duke flings his hat on the floor
and goes down left, crossing above the table. During the second A and
the first B phrase he takes off his jacket and throws it down. The page
picks up the discarded garments from the floor and the table; the other
boy returns from up right so that, with the beginning of the C phrase,
they can both help the Duke into his dressing gown. He then motions
the pages to leave the room, and by the time the orchestral introduction
has run its course, they have disappeared through the up right archway.

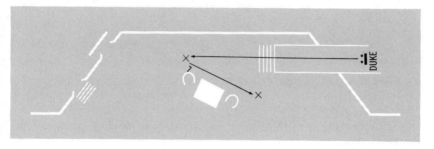

Diagram 5–10. Measures 1–28

Taking advantage of the three brief orchestral interludes, the Duke goes
around the table in a counterclockwise circle, arriving at the left armchair
just in time to sing his adagio-dolce sentence. He then sits down in the
chair for the andante cantabile and remains seated until the next allegro.
At this point he gets up and, during the energetic passages played by the
first violins, cellos, and basses, goes down left toward LA1, stopping there
to sing the second transitional section marked adagio dolce.

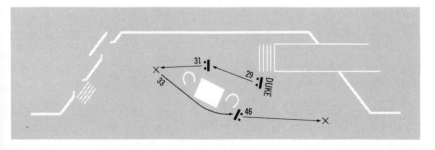

Diagram 5–11. Measures 29–56

The rippling sextuplets of the orchestral introduction to the G-flat-
Major aria are "filled out" by a leisurely walk to RB2. It is in this general
location that the Duke sings the first stanza of the aria, accompanying all
vocal expansions and repetitions of words and sentences with appropriate
movements and gestures, and by an interplay of focal points between the
direction of the "real" Gilda (left, along 23) and the "ideal" Gilda (down
right and heavenward).

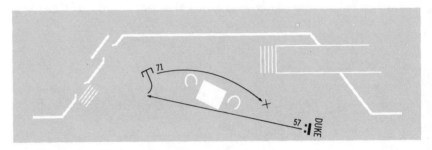

Diagram 5–12. Measures 57–80

The parallelism of the two A' phrases is best brought out by having
the Duke repeat his actions—with variations—in an analogous area: to the
left of the left armchair. He goes there, crossing above the table and both
chairs, during the four measures of the B phrase of the second stanza.
The seven measures of the coda then give him enough time to return to
the right—this time crossing below the table—so that with the last note
of the aria he can sit down and relax in the right armchair.

Diagram 5–13. Measures 81 to the end

Most of the walks performed in this aria are motivated by urges.
The Duke's feelings of indignation, anger, pity, and love are mainly responsible for his moves, both in the recitative and in the aria. Since the
locations to which urges move a person are basically optional and inter-

changeable, singers can easily become confused and forget whether the next walk is supposed to take them to the right or the left, to upstage or down.

To remember staging patterns not based on logical reasons, it is useful to think of them in terms of geometrical figures, such as circles, zigzags, triangles, or pendulum-type movements. This scene from *Rigoletto*, for instance, consists fundamentally of two basic patterns: a succession of counterclockwise arcs for the recitative and a series of overlapping clockwise circles for the aria. In relation to the table and the armchairs, these patterns can be traced in two simple lines, the first going from X to Y (Diagram 5–14), and the second from Y to Z (Diagram 5–15).

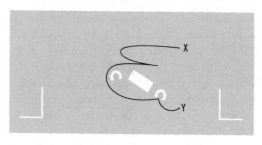

Diagram 5–14. Recitative

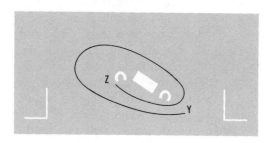

Diagram 5–15. Aria

Singers should acquire the habit of tracing similar patterns whenever it is difficult to remember the sequence of staging movements.

THE MASKED BALL, ACT III: Renato's recitative and aria
"Eri tu"

The drama

It is always useful to put yourself into the shoes of unusual operatic characters and to decide whether you might not behave in the same manner under similar conditions. Often we think of characters acting in an exaggeratedly operatic manner when in reality their behavior in the given circumstances turns out to be perfectly understandable once we have truly identified with them. Let us apply this method to the role of Renato in the scene immediately preceding his recitative and aria "Eri tu."

Imagine that you are married to a beautiful and tenderly responsive woman who has always been morally and socially above reproach. You have a little son whom you adore and you are firmly convinced that yours is a blissfully happy household. You are also very close to the ruler of your country; in fact, you are his most intimate friend. For some time you have been aware of the existence of a plot threatening your friend's life, and one evening you discover that conspirators are proposing to strike that very night. It seems that your friend has been followed to a desolate spot in the country where he is pursuing an amorous adventure. Here is a perfect situation for an assassination. Enveloped in a dark cloak, similar to that worn by his enemies, you manage to forestall events and to warn your friend. Putting your cloak around him, you urge him to escape unrecognized. You are not particularly concerned about the presence of a heavily veiled woman. As long as she remains behind, your friend will not be spotted by his enemies, and neither she nor you are in any real danger of being harmed by the approaching conspirators who are interested only in getting rid of the ruler. After some hesitation, your friend agrees to your plan for his escape, but only if you swear to escort the lady back to the city without exchanging a single word and without in any way trying to discover her identity. You can readily understand his predicament, and you gladly undertake to protect his and his lady's secret. Your friend escapes safely, but when the plotters arrive, things do not proceed according to plan. Frustrated at having missed their prey, the men insist on unmasking his inamorata. When you draw your sword to protect the lady's honor, you are immediately surrounded by more than a dozen armed and angry assailants who seem intent on getting their way at any cost. At this moment, the woman rushes forward to protect you and pulls down her veil. It is your wife! The tableau is so unexpected and startling, in fact so ridiculous, that the anger of your opponents turns into merriment. Truly, nothing could be funnier to them than this domestic confrontation in a remote and unlikely spot, particularly when it is fairly clear that your wife is someone else's mistress! Imagine your own feelings. The evidence is overwhelming, the guilt is undeniable. Your love, your self-respect, your position at court—everything lies in ruins. Nothing remains except hatred and the thirst for revenge. Since you have sworn to escort the woman to the city, you do so. You bring your wife home and are about to kill her. She is ready to die, but begs for a delay just long enough to bid her little boy a last farewell. At this moment you begin your recitative.

The dramatic interest of this scene lies in the rapid succession of many conflicting emotions. The deadly hatred and lust for vengeance that motivated Renato in the beginning of this scene has been tempered during Amelia's touching aria, so that at the beginning of this scene he gives her permission to bid farewell to their little son. During her exit music some of his former tenderness for his wife begins to return, and he suddenly realizes that his revenge must fall on a different person: Riccardo, the guilty lover. When his eye falls on a dagger lying on the table, he feels an unholy delight at having discovered the instrument of revenge. Next he comes face to face with Riccardo's portrait, and this leads to the accusation which culminates in the bitter remark that the man who betrayed him was his best friend. The next section is filled with self-pity, memories of bliss and lost happiness. The coda sums up his emotions: deadly hatred for the betrayer and hopeless mourning for his lost love.

From the point of view of the stage movement, we have here an instructive example of a situation where one of the main focal points of the aria is located at the rear of the stage. The "tu" of the "Eri tu" is represented by a life-sized portrait of Riccardo hanging in the center of the upstage wall of the room. Renato must give the impression that the picture dominates his mind, and yet while he sings of it and even *at* it, he must not turn his back on the audience.

As a rule, one avoids placing important focal points (people or objects that must be addressed by singers) in the upstage center area. It puts a great strain on believability when (as sometimes happens with the King in the Triumphal Scene of *Aida*) everyone turns his back on the person who is presumably being addressed. It is much wiser to place these important objects of attention in one of the downstage corners of the stage. Pictorially speaking, however, the upstage center position of an important personage is very advantageous. This is one of the many bones of contention between the designer and the stage director. As always, one should evaluate the relative merits of two conflicting possibilities, each having certain advantages and disadvantages, and choose between them on the basis of whether one gains or loses more. In this particular scene of *The Masked Ball*, we can safely retain the pictorial advantage of placing Riccardo's portrait in the central position because the dramatic problem in this act occurs only in Renato's aria and can be easily solved by the method of indirect rapport.

The music

Most opera lovers think of Verdi as a composer who relied chiefly on the expressive powers of the human voice and on what he called "parola scenica": the trenchant theatrical wording of the vocal text. This scene offers eloquent proof that, in his search for total credibility, Verdi knew how to utilize many other resources of the language of music.

In the recitative alone, Verdi makes use of a thematic association and of analogies based on harmonic progressions and characteristic tonalities. Amelia's exit is accompanied by a quotation from the aria that she has just finished singing. The reappearance of this phrase has a twofold significance. It not only paints anew the unhappiness of the woman who has been rejected by her husband, but it also tells us what is passing through Renato's mind. He thinks of the words that Amelia sang to this musical phrase: "Morrò, ma queste viscere consolino i suoi baci" (Permit my little son's kisses to be my last consolation before I die) It is this image of the child embracing his doomed mother that softens Renato's attitude toward his wife and induces him to search for the real culprit responsible for the tragedy that has befallen him. His sudden change of mind is reflected in the violent enharmonic substitution of sharps for flats. The F-flat and G-flat are transformed into an E-natural and an F-sharp respectively, enabling the avenging dagger to make its appearance in B minor, the classical tonality of death.

This imaginative use of musical metaphors is not restricted to the recitative. The D-minor and F-Major sections of the aria are associated with the ideas of turbulence and lost happiness. F minor, the "key of tears," is heard at an appropriate and suggestive moment, and the rhythm that earlier accompanied Renato's loathing of Riccardo is heard again in connection with the word "hatred."

Vocal aspects

An artistic performance of this scene calls for a considerable repertoire of vocal inflections and shadings. They must illuminate the different facets of Renato's personality, allot the proper degree of emotional intensity to the repetitions of words and sentences, and highlight particularly sensitive ideas.

In the recitative we must hear the tones of voice of the proud and humiliated man who is intent on punishment, the man of action who is eager to deal with an attack on his honor, and the avenger who anticipates the joy of killing the person responsible for his tragic predicament. In addition to these states of being, the vocal colors in the aria must reflect the feelings of a man who hates his rival, is betrayed by his best friend, lacerates himself by recalling the raptures of his lost happiness, and finds he has nothing to live for.

Within each of these tone categories the singer must be careful to give individual attention to the loudness, softness, and emotional intensity of the various sets of repetitions. Even where the central aspect of personality remains the same, the baritone must discriminate between the more subtle tinges of meaning required by certain words and ideas. For instance, even though in the first section of the recitative Renato's voice remains basically cold and distant, there must be a considerable difference between the tone colors given to "your son," and "your shame," and "my disgrace."

Text and translation

Recitative

Alzati! là   tuo   figlio a te concedo riveder.
Get up! over there I shall let you see your son once more.

Nell'ombra e nel silenzio, là,   il tuo rossore e l'onta mia
In darkness and in silence, over there, your shame and my disgrace

nascondi.   (Amelia parte) *Non è su lei,   nel suo fragile petto*
you can hide. *(Amelia leaves)* It is not on her, on her fragile breast

che colpir degg'io.   Altro,   ben altro sangue
that my punishment must fall. A different, very different blood

a terger dessi l'offesa . . .   (fissando il ritratto del Conte)
must cleanse this insult . . . *(fixing his eyes on the Count's portrait)*

il sangue tuo! E lo trarrà il pugnale   dallo sleal tuo core:
your blood!   And my dagger will draw it from your disloyal heart:

delle lacrime mie vendicator, (fremente) *vendicator,* (cupo) *vendicator!*
my tears shall be avenged,   *(raging)*   avenged   *(darkly)* avenged!

Aria

Eri tu che macchiavi quell'anima, la delizia dell'anima mia . . .
It was you who defiled that angel, my soul's delight . . .

che m'affidi   e d'un tratto esecrabile
whom you entrust to my care and with one abominable stroke

l'universo avveleni per me,   avveleni per me! Traditor!
you poison the universe for me, poison it for me! Traitor!

che compensi in tal guisa dell'amico tuo primo,
to reward in such a way the trust of your best friend,

dell'amico tuo primo la fè!   O dolcezze perdute!   o memorie
the trust of your best friend! Oh lost happiness!   oh memories

d'un amplesso che l'essere india!   quando Amelia sì *bella,*
of embraces   that transported my being! when Amelia,   so lovely,

sì *candida sul mio seno brillava d'amor!   quand'Amelia sul mio seno*
so pure,   in my arms glowed with love! when Amelia in my arms

brillava d'amor,   brillava d'amor!   È finita!
glowed with love, glowed with love!   It is finished!

non siede che l'odio,   non siede che l'odio,
nothing remains except hatred, nothing remains except hatred,

che l'odio   e la morte   nel vedovo cor!
except hatred and death in my mourning heart!

O dolcezze perdute! o speranza d'amor, d'amor, d'amor!
Oh lost happiness! oh hopes of love,   of love, of love!

Focal points

Onstage	Description	Location
Other characters	1. Amelia	First kneeling and stand-ing up right of the table; then exiting through the door in RA2
Scenic elements	2. Door to inner living quarters	In the right wall at RA2
	3. Life-size portrait of Riccardo	Over the fireplace in the center wall along 34
Hand props	4. Dagger	On the table

Offstage (real or imagined)	Description	Direction and connecting scenic elements
Other characters	5. Amelia's and Renato's son	Beyond the door in RA2
	6. Amelia	Beyond the door in RA2
Abstract ideas	7. Lost friendship with Riccardo	Down left, in the dis-tance, far beyond the walls of the auditorium
	8. Lost happiness with Amelia	Same

Renato's actions explained

At the beginning of the recitative Renato sits behind the table and stares in front of him. Amelia, who has just finished pleading for per-mission to say farewell to her son, is kneeling dejectedly up right of the

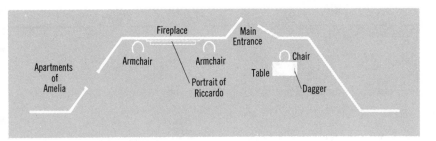

Diagram 5–16. The setting for Renato's actions

table. The stage direction in the score makes it clear that Renato should address his wife without looking at her.

On "over there" he motions with his head toward the door in RA2. The second "over there" is more emphatic and suggests an arm gesture in the same direction. With "my disgrace" Renato turns away to face down left, and with "hide" he waves Amelia away, indicating that he has nothing more to say. She rose from her knees after his initial "Get up!" and now she walks sadly toward the right. When she reaches the door, she gives her husband one last look over her left shoulder. This should be timed so that she sees him precisely on the climactic G-flat of the oboe and clarinet melody. Immediately afterward she turns away and disappears through the door. Reacting to the impact of the G-flat as if her glance had been an invisible arrow, Renato rotates in his chair to look in her direction. Their eyes must not meet, however. He should barely see her "fragile" figure moving into the right wing.

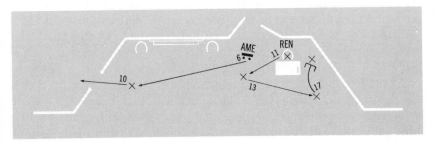

Diagram 5–17. Recitative, measures 1–27

This is the moment when he realizes that his desire for vengeance must find another outlet. Overcome with emotion, he gets up and begins to transform the descending flats of her melody (Example 5–19) into the

Example 5–19. UN BALLO IN MASCHERA, III, sc. 1

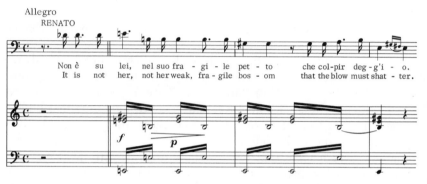

Allegro
RENATO

Non è   su   lei,   nel suo fra - gi - le pet - to   che col-pir deg - g'i - o.
It is   not   her, not her weak, fra - gile bos - om   that the blow must shat - ter.

Example 5–20

reverse-direction E-Major line of the opening words of his allegro (Example 5–20). With "punishment must fall" he takes two or three steps to the right.

Not only must all repetitions of words in this scene be handled with very pronounced changes of vocal color, but they must be accompanied by physical actions of one sort or another as well. On "different, very different" Renato turns and goes down left, crossing the table so that, with the two orchestral chords that follow "insult," he can veer around in a vigorous RSB turn and, from a position to the left of the table, be ready to point at Riccardo's picture. I recommend placing the dagger on the down-left corner of the table. This enables Renato to pick it up with his left hand, gesture toward it on "dagger," and point again at the painting with "disloyal heart." On "my tears" he turns away toward down left. Each of the three exclamations—"avenged!"—must have a meaning and an interpretation of its own. Verdi specifies "fremente" (raging) for the second one and "cupo" (dark and somber) for the third one. It is best if they also have their own individual focal points. I have Renato address the first "avenged" almost gratefully to the dagger; he then turns Clw so that he can hurl the second "avenged" to heaven and sing the third one while replacing the dagger on the table, staring with grim and murderous intent at the portrait of Riccardo.

During the five measures of the orchestral introduction to the aria Renato's eyes do not leave Riccardo's picture. Whether he is standing, walking, or turning, he remains in direct, almost hypnotic, contact with the man who has become the object of his hatred and vengeance. Having gotten rid of the dagger, Renato steps back slightly and then walks to the right, crossing the table and going as far as CC. Here he turns his back on the audience, and—with the third and last of the trumpet-trombone-timpani phrases—raises his fists and shakes them at the portrait of his enemy. Renato must make us feel that he has thoroughly memorized Riccardo's features so that, when he addresses his rival over his shoulder, he can visualize him as clearly as if he were facing him.

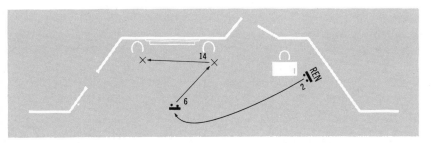

Diagram 5-18. Aria. Andante sostenuto, measures 1–17

After the long silence in the fifth measure of the orchestral introduction Renato lowers his arms and starts going up left, as if meaning to return to the chair above the table. He stops, however, after taking two or three steps and begins his denunciatory sentence ("It was you"), singing over his right shoulder. The mention of Amelia ("that angel") makes his thoughts and eyes focus beyond the door in RA2, and with "the universe" he turns away to concentrate on his own suffering. Remembering how, a few hours earlier, Riccardo had "entrusted" Amelia to her own husband, Renato again gets into indirect, over-the-shoulder rapport with the picture on the wall. The repetition of "poison it for me" seems to give an irresistible urge to move. He walks halfway to the right door, so that the word "traitor" can be sung over the left shoulder. The first mention of friendship makes Renato gaze heavenward toward down left, and with the repetition of this sentiment he walks in that direction, going beyond CC.

The melody played by the flute during the next orchestral interlude indicates that Renato's thoughts are centering on Amelia. He turns to look toward the right door, then wanders upstage and sits down in the armchair that stands left of the fireplace.

As Renato begins the next vocal portion of the aria, he rotates Cclw in the chair so that he can sing of his "lost happiness" facing heavenward, toward down left. With "Amelia'" he focuses his attention again on the door, and he stands up for "so lovely, so pure." The recollection of holding Amelia in his arms moves him toward the right. The sustained high G is directed to heaven, and the third mention of Amelia's "glowing with love" makes him gaze at the focal point for lost joys, toward down left. The sobbing F-minor tonality moves Renato left, past the center line, so that with "hatred" and the repetition of the rhythm we heard when he was denouncing Riccardo, Renato can again face the man who caused all his sorrow. With the second "nothing remains" the distracted husband turns away and starts walking to the table. The mention of death should be synchronized with a look at the dagger.

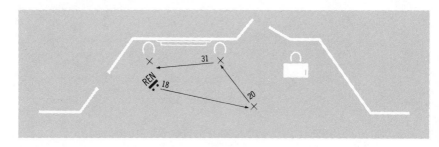

Diagram 5–19. Andante sostenuto, measures 18–33

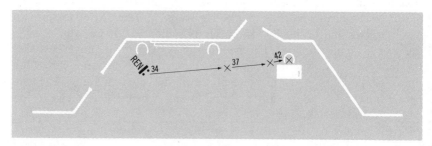

Diagram 5–20. Andante sostenuto, measures 34–45

The flute melody in the coda serves as another reminder of Amelia and motivates Renato's unhappy glance over his right shoulder. The "hopes" make him concentrate again toward down left, and with the first "love" he should move to above the table in preparation for his eventual collapse in the chair. If Renato picks up the dagger on the second "love," this prop can help to emphasize and justify the crescendo on his last note. Not every Renato I have worked with likes this idea. To be sure, it cannot be performed comfortably unless the dagger is placed in such a manner that it can be picked up without having to reach for it, and this must be prearranged at the end of the recitative. When Renato finishes singing, he sits down and buries his head in his arms.

DON GIOVANNI: Leporello's catalog aria

The drama

In the final measures of the recitative preceding the aria, Leporello advises Elvira to give up her attempt to recapture Don Giovanni's affections. As proof of his master's unworthiness, he shows her a catalog containing the authentic records of the Don's amorous adventures.*

The main point of this scene is that Leporello, while pretending to enlighten Elvira, embarks on a pungently salacious and detailed account of Don Giovanni's lifelong hobby of seducing women. This Catalog Aria is a sort of abbreviated version of the *Memoirs of Casanova*, beginning with a statistical analysis and proceding to more intimate revelations of what special feminine qualities the Don savors and what types of women he prefers for the various seasons of the year. Leporello becomes more and more daring, adding such tidbits as that although his master occasionally has affairs with old women (just for the satisfaction of augmenting his collection), he really prefers virgins. The servant caps his recital with the insinuating observation that it is not necessary for him to tell Elvira just what Don Giovanni does with all these women since she, of course, knows better than anyone else.

The singer portraying Leporello must keep in mind that Elvira is a member of the upper classes and that, while an eighteenth-century male servant was occasionally allowed to kiss the hem of a noble lady's skirt, he would never permit himself anything even remotely suggesting physical familiarity. While it is true that insolent servants were stock theatrical characters of that period, their impertinences always remained purely verbal. Intimacies between noblemen and servant girls were fairly common in the eighteenth-century theater, but bodily contact between a male servant and a lady was out of the question. It could only occur as a result of mistaken identity, as in the second act of *Don Giovanni*, when Elvira embraces Leporello, believing him to be the Don. Unaccustomed to rigid class distinctions, American singers often commit rather shocking lapses

* See footnote on p. 164.

of respect when playing such Mozartian servants as Pedrillo, Figaro, or Leporello. The comic as well as the pathetic sides of the Catalog Aria are greatly enhanced if Leporello's impertinences are uttered in an outwardly respectful manner.

The music *

In the aria, which consists of an allegro and an andante con moto, Leporello's explanations proceed from the general to the specific: the allegro presents the geographic, numerical, and social (ranging from chambermaids to princesses) data about his master's women, while the andante concentrates on Don Giovanni's special perferences for individual feminine types.

The allegro has three sections: (a) an introduction where Leporello claims to be the originator of the catalog and invites Elvira to read it with him; (b) a statistical review of the Don's conquests; and (c) an expanded repetition of the preceding section.

The andante con moto is also in three parts. In the first, Leporello acquaints Elvira with Don Giovanni's feelings about blonde, brunette, fair-skinned, plump, thin, tall, and majestic women; in the second part, he deals with little girls, old hags, virgins, and with the fact that Don Giovanni does not care whether a woman is rich, ugly, or beautiful provided that she wears a skirt; in the third and last part, Leporello becomes more personal and reminds Elvira that she, being one of the Don's victims, should have no illusions as to how he treats the women whom he seduces.

Since Leporello sings almost continually in this aria, there is no point in burdening him with subtexts. It is essential, however, to match the powerful orchestral energies of the allegro, to justify the many significant instrumental phrases in both parts of the aria, and to arrange for a sufficient variety of positions and groupings. Several of the verbal and musical repetitions also deserve special treatment. Since Elvira's supporting action is invaluable in helping Leporello to accomplish all this, the singer working on this scene should also study the discussion of Elvira's part in it. By refusing to listen and by walking away, Elvira provides the necessary motivations for Leporello's five pursuing movements in the first twenty-seven measures of the allegro. By turning away while seated on the left bench, she furnishes the reason for his sixth walk when he crosses above the bench to address her face to face. His seventh and eighth walks (shuttling back and forth above the bench) are motivated by his desire to display the various books he has left lying to Elvira's right and left. His extended pendulum movement in the last section of the allegro is

* Compare the section on the musical aspects of Elvira's supporting action on pp. 165 and 166.

the only action that must be handled as an urge: Leporello is just too excited about all of his master's noble and ignoble conquests. He must convince us that he could not stand still even if he wanted to.

Donna Elvira's looking and walking away take care of the orchestral interludes in measures 16–17, 20–21, and 24–25. The remaining instrumental phrases of special significance (those in measures 33–36, 67–70, and 77–78) are illustrated by Leporello when he licks his thumb, turns the pages of the Spanish volume, and imitates his master's strumming the mandolin.

The more sustained nature of the andante con moto is reflected in the absence of extended and rapid stage movements. The motivations are again provided by Leporello's desire to move closer to Elvira. The only exceptions are the second illustration of the "tall, majestic woman" (which is in the nature of a strut) and Leporello's wicked glee in connection with the "virgins" (which is an "urge"!).

Vocal aspects

Leporello's tone of voice must faithfully reflect the different facets of his personality as it manifests itself in this scene. In the final measures of the recitative, he pretends to be a kind and sympathetic counselor. In the allegro section of the aria, he reveals himself as a statistician, a world traveler, and a biographer. In the andante con moto, where he identifies himself with his master, he must appear to savor the various qualities of feminine charms, and sound as if he also were an accomplished connoisseur and seducer of women. While pointing out the various characteristics of the women favored by Don Giovanni, Leporello's tone of voice must betray the vicarious sensual pleasure he finds in being able to communicate all this to a young and beautiful lady. It is only near the end of the aria that his lower-class instincts gain the upper hand. In his references to Elvira's own involvement in the Don's adventures, the mocking twang of Leporello's voice should expose the cynical insolence of the coarse servant.

Singing version, text and translation

Final nine measures of the recitative

Please take my word for it, you're by no means the first one,		
Eh, consolatevi!	*Non siete voi, non foste,*	
Come, console yourself.	You are not, you were not,	

nor the second, and you won't be the last one.		I'll show you.
e non sarete ne la prima, ne l'ultima.		*Guardate.*
and you won't be either the first or the last.		Look here.

These quite impressive volumes contain the faithful account
Questo   *non picciol libro*   *è tutto pieno dei nomi*
This   good-sized   book is filled with the names

of his adventures. Ev'ry village, ev'ry province, yes, ev'ry nation
di sue belle.   *Ogni   villa,   ogni borgo,*   *ogni paese*
of his conquests.   Ev'ry village, ev'ry town,   ev'ry country

can give you proof of Don Giovanni's occupation.
è   testimon   di sue donnesche imprese.
bears witness   to his adventures with women.

Aria

My dear lady! Here are valid statistics of his conquests
Madamina!   Il catalogo è questo   delle belle
Dear Lady.   This is the catalog   of the women

from border to border,   in the best geographical order.
che amò il padron mio;   un catalogo egli è che ho fatto io.
who were loved by my master; a catalog   made by me.

If you want to, go through them with me, if you want to, go through them
Osservate,   leggete con me,   osservate,   leggete
Look at it,   read it with me,   look at it,   read it

with me. Here in Italy, six hundred and forty;   and one hundred
con me.   In   Italia sei cento   e quaranta, in Lamagna
with me.   In   Italy   six hundred and forty;   in Germany

in Greece which is plenty. Germany's share is two hundred and twenty;
due cento e trenta;   cento in Francia,   in Turchia novant'una,
two hundred and thirty;   a hundred in France, in Turkey ninety-one,

but look at Spain here: Spain supplied him a thousand and three,
ma in Ispagna,   in Ispagna son gia mille e   tre,
but in Spain,   in Spain already a thousand and   three,

thousand and three, thousand and three! There are peasants
mille   e tre,   mille   e   tre.   V'han fra queste
a thousand and three, a thousand and three.   Among them are

by the dozens, here's a queen with all her cousins,   here's a countess
contadine,   cameriere,   cittadine,   v'han contesse,
country girls,   chambermaids,   city girls,   there are countesses,

and a duchess who have fallen in his clutches, ev'ry type of female gender,
baronesse,   marchesane,   principesse, e v'han donne d'ogni grado,
baronesses,   marchionesses,   princesses,   women of ev'ry class,

plump or slender, young or old, plump or slender, young or old.
d'ogni forma,   d'ogni età. d'ogni forma,   d'ogni età,
ev'ry shape,   ev'ry age,   ev'ry shape,   ev'ry age.

Little Sicily compares well with Turkey: eighty-seven if added together,
In Italia   sei sento e quaranta. In Lamagna due cento e trent'una,
In Italy   six hundred and forty. In Germany, two hundred and thirty-one,

England has fifty   in spite of the weather, but, but, but Spain is leading:
cento in Francia   in Turchia novant'una, ma, ma, ma in Ispagna,
a hundred in France, in Turkey ninety-one,   but, but, but in Spain,

Spain supplied him a thousand and three, thousand and three, thousand
ma in Ispagna   son gia mille e tre,   mille e tre,   mille
but in Spain,   already a thousand and three.   thousand and three, thousand

and three. From Toledo to Gibraltar, without blessing from the
e tre.   V'han fra queste contadine, cameriere,   citta-
and three.   Among them are country girls, chambermaids,   city

altar he has lured a thousand beauties from their homes and moral duties.
dine, v'han contesse, baronesse, marchesane,   principesse,
girls, there are countesses, baronesses, marchionesses,   princesses,

Whether destitute or wealthy, weak or healthy,   short or tall,
e v'han donne   d'ogni grado,   d'ogni forma, d'ogni età,
and women   of ev'ry class,   of ev'ry shape, ev'ry age,

Don Giovanni loves them all, Don Giovanni loves them all!
d'ogni forma,   d'ogni età,   d'ogni forma,   d'ogni età.
of ev'ry shape,   of ev'ry age,   ev'ry shape,   ev'ry age.

Andante con moto

His affections change with the season, his selections have rhyme and reason
Nella   bionda egli   ha   l'usanza di lodar la   gentilezza,
In   blondes   he   usually   praises   the gentleness,

Spanish ladies or Eurasian, all depending on the occasion.
nella bruna la constanza,   nella bianca la dolcezza.
in brunettes the constancy,   in fair-skinned girls the sweetness.

He likes round ones when it's wint'ry, and in summer slim and splint'ry.
Vuol d'inverno   la grassotta,   vuol d'estate la magrotta.
In the winter   he wants the plump one,   in the summer, the skinny one.

Comes the autumn, then my patron likes a large, imposing matron!
È la grande   maestosa,   è la grande   maestosa,
The tall one is majestic,   the tall one is majestic,

But in springtime, in the springtime, he prefers them very tiny, very tiny,
la piccina   la piccina,   la piccina,   la piccina, la piccina,
the little one,   little one,   little one, little one,   little one,

very tiny, very tiny, very tiny, very tiny; he likes the sweet ones,
la piccina, la piccina, la piccina, la piccina è ognor vezzosa,
little one, little one, little one, little one, will always charm him,

he likes the sweet ones, and the petite ones!
è ognor vezzosa,   è ognor vezzosa!
will always charm him,   will always charm him!

Haggard spinsters, gray-haired donnas,   in his favor share equal honors.
Delle vecchie   fa conquista   pel piacer di porle in lista.
He seduces even old women just for the pleasure of adding them to his list.

But his fav'rite form of sinning is the girl who's just beginning!
Sua passion predominante   e la giovin principiante.
But his foremost passion   is   the young   beginner.

He adores them weak or healthy, plain or pretty, poor or wealthy.
Non si picca   se sia ricca,   se sia brutta,   se sia bella,
He does not care if she's rich,   or ugly,   or lovely,

All the girls receive the same caresses, just as long as they wear dresses.
se sia ricca, brutta, se sia bella, pur che porti la gonnella,
if she's rich, or ugly, or lovely;   as long as she wears a skirt,

You should know it best of all, you should know it best of all.
voi sapete   quel che fà;   voi sapete   quel che fà.
you know what he does with her, you know what he does with her.

Just as long as they wear dresses, you should know it best of all.
Pur che porti   la   gonnella voi sapete quel che   fà.
As long as she wears a skirt,   you know   what   he   does   with   her.

You should know, you should know it best of all,   best of all,
Voi   sapete,   voi sapete   quel che fà,   quel che fà,
You know,   you know   what he does with her, what he does,

best of all, you should know it best of all!
quel che fà, voi   sapete   quel che fà!
what he does, you know   what   he   does!

The setting

The stage setting is identical with the one described in Chapter 4
(page 166). When the scene begins, Leporello is standing upstage center
and Elvira is downstage right of him, facing him.

Focal points

Onstage	Description	Location
Other characters	1. Elvira	Various positions on stage
	2. A number of other women whose presence he imagines as he describes them	
Hand props	3. Several small volumes listing names of women from various countries	Carried by Leporello in his vest pockets
	4. A large volume listing the names of Spanish women	Carried by Leporello in a pouch by his side; later, placed on left bench

Leporello's actions described*

RECITATIVE (FINAL NINE MEASURES)

1. After "I'll show you" Leporello throws open his jacket to expose
   the four inside pockets, each containing a small book.

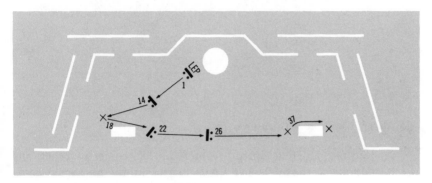

Diagram 5–21. Allegro, measures 1–48

ARIA

Allegro: Section 1 (measures 1–15)

2. (measure 1) Goes DR to UL of Elvira.
3. (measure 5) Pats his jacket to draw Elvira's attention to the books.
4. (measure 14) Goes DR, crossing above right bench to UL of
   Elvira.

Allegro: Section 2 (measures 16–48)

5. (measure 18) Takes a small book out of his pocket and goes
   left, crossing above bench to UR of Elvira.
6. (measure 22) Extracts another small book, and goes further left
   toward Elvira.
7. (measure 26) Takes out third and fourth books and goes left to
   right of the left bench.
8. (measure 28) Puts the four books on right corner of the bench
   and takes out a very thick Spanish volume from a large pouch
   hanging at his left hip.
9. (measure 33) Sticks out his tongue and wets his right thumb by
   passing it (on the long orchestral note) from his nose to his chin,
   and then turns a page.
10. (measure 35) Repeats previous action.
11. (measure 37) Holding Spanish volume, goes left, crossing above
    Elvira to UL of her.

* Compare the section describing Elvira's actions on pages 166–169.

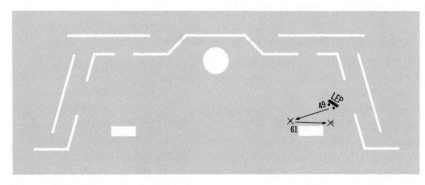

Diagram 5–22. Allegro, measures 49–70

Allegro: Section 3 (measures 49–84)

12. (measure 49) Puts Spanish volume on left corner of bench and goes right, crossing above Elvira to pick up the four small books lying on the right corner of the bench.
13. (measures 51–60) Shows the books to Elvira one by one, shuffling them in his hands.
14. (measure 61) Replacing all four books in his pockets, goes left, crossing above Elvira to UL to her.
15. (measure 64) Picks up Spanish volume.
16. (measure 67) Licks thumb and turns pages as in No. 9.
17. (measure 69) Repeats preceding action.

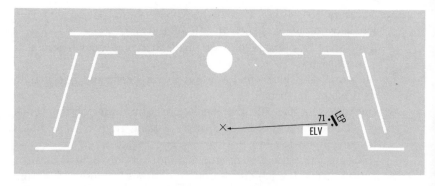

Diagram 5–23. Allegro, measures 71–73

18. (measure 71) Puts Spanish volume down on left corner of the bench and goes right, crossing above Elvira, continuing quite a distance beyond the bench (almost to CC).

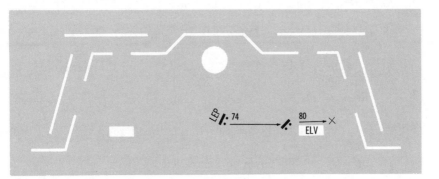

Diagram 5–24. Allegro, measures 74–84

19. (measure 74) Turns Cclw and returns to UR of Elvira.
20. (measure 77) Pantomimes the strumming of a mandolin.
21. (measure 80) Goes left, crossing above Elvira, to UL of her, as if serenading her.

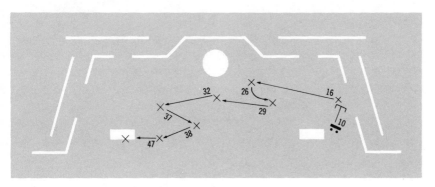

Diagram 5–25. Andante, measures 1–50

Andante con moto: Section 1 (measures 1–31)

22. (measure 10) Points a finger at Elvira and backs up.
23. (measure 16) Goes UR toward Elvira.
24. (measure 23) Illustrates "the tall one" by raising himself on tiptoe.
25. (measure 25) Illustrates "majestic" by indicating with both hands, a protruding bosom.
26. (measure 27) Illustrates "the tall one" by turning Cclw and walking slightly on tiptoe.
27. (measure 29) Turns Clw and illustrates "majestic" by going toward Elvira and indicating an exaggeratedly large and protruding bosom.

Andante con moto: Section 2 (measures 32–62)

28. (measure 32) Goes DR to UL of right bench, illustrating "very tiny, very tiny."
29. (measure 37) Illustrates "the sweet ones and the petite ones" by walking left and (measure 38) right.
30. (measure 44) Nods his head to assure Elvira that what he says is true.
31. (measure 47) Looks around conspiratorially and then goes still closer to bench.
32. (measure 50) Sits down on bench, left of Elvira.
33. (measure 51) With "beginning," he almost nudges Elvira with his right elbow and then gets up and goes UL, laughing gleefully.
34. (measure 55) Turns Clw to face Elvira and backs up slightly.

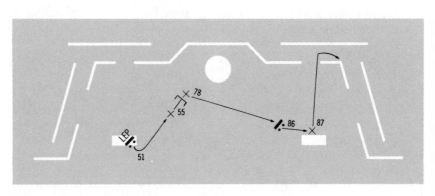

Diagram 5–26. Andante, measures 51–88

Andante con moto: Section 3 (measures 63–88)

35. (measure 62) Curtsies archly, imitating a girl wearing a skirt.
36. (measure 63) Points an accusing finger at Elvira.
37. (measure 75) With his left hand, he points at Spanish volume, which is lying on left bench.
38. (measure 78) Goes DL to UR of Elvira.
39. (measure 80) While Elvira holds the volume, he turns a few pages backward.
40. (measure 82) Points to Elvira's name on the page and backs up to UR.
41. (measure 86) Goes DL to above bench, picks up the Spanish volume, and exits to UL, laughing.

~ 6

Achieving musical accuracy

WHEN I WAS A YOUNGSTER studying piano in Budapest, my teacher, Ernst Dohnànyi, had a standard piece of advice for his students who were about to play in public. "Remember, children," he always said, "there are mistakes that are noticed only by us, and there are mistakes that are noticed by the audience. Be sure to avoid the latter!"

This may be sound advice for the solo performer, but the opera singer must consider the effect of his mistakes not only on his audience, but also on his fellow artists in the pit and on stage. While some mistakes may result in nothing more than a momentary scowl from the conductor, others may turn out to be real bloopers that upset the whole musical applecart. The English language has no special word for this sort of mushrooming mistake, but in German it is known as a *Schmiss,** which can be approximated by our word "crack-up." A typical crack-up is initiated when the leading soprano, entrusted with the main melodic passage in a complicated ensemble, attacks her most important phrase half a measure earlier than indicated in the score. If the unfortunate lady continues to sing unmindful of her offence (and this does happen), the rest of the company—singers, orchestra members, and the conductor—are faced with a painful dilemma: should they skip back half a measure or should they stand their ground in the hope that she will notice the discrepancy and correct herself? Since there is no standard rule for dealing with such incidents, it often happens that half the performers choose to join the lady while the others wait for her to join them. The resulting cacophony may be called a "full-blown crack-up," a condition which seems to last an eternity until some shouted direction by the conductor or some lucky musical accident pulls things together and saves the day. Sometimes it even becomes necessary to stop and start over again in the hope that things will go better the second time.

* Literally, an "overthrow."

The thought of such a crack-up is frightening to all musicians, but it is particularly nightmarish to the man responsible for the smoothness of the musical ensemble, the conductor. It is true that total collapse is quite rare, but the prospect of it is so terrifying that even a singer's most harmless musical mistake can remind the conductor that disaster may be imminent. What is more, frightened singers cannot act and worried conductors won't let them act for fear that it will increase the chances of a musical catastrophe. The one stares at the other, intent only on avoiding musical mistakes, and apprehension becomes so overpowering that a singer in this state of paralysis will often start to imagine he is wrong when in fact he is completely accurate. In the constant expectation of being scolded, he stands ready to apologize as soon as a coach or conductor interrupts a rehearsal to make a correction.

"I am sorry, Maestro" is a sentence that drives me wild in rehearsals because it is so often said by singers who have done nothing at all to be sorry about. I may be stopping to make some general observation or I may want to ask for a special nuance from a group of singers to my left when some guilt-ridden tenor on my right, who imagines that he is about to be torn to pieces, chimes in with his propitiating "I'm sorry, Maestro." This constant preoccupation with real and imaginary errors produces such an emotional wear and tear in many singers that it quite seriously interferes with the quality of their performance. I have made it a rule in all my educational and professional dealings with singers that when one of them begins to apologize for a mistake during rehearsals, he must correct himself by saying: "I am *not* sorry; I am *glad* because this gives us a chance to go over this place once more." It is important to instill the idea that even the best coordinated and most musical person is subject to momentary malfunctions of muscular control and to occasional slips of memory. In that sense, one can truthfully maintain that the occurrence of mistakes is a mathematical certainty. The singer must be made to understand that these occasional malfunctions on his part are simply a reminder that he is a member of the human race, and it is also very useful to make him aware that other members of the company—instrumentalists, coaches, and even conductors—are also human beings and, as such, are also entitled to occasional mistakes. This attitude will lead to a more relaxed frame of mind and will permit us to look more calmly into the cause and cure of musical errors. For while "to err is human," it is also undesirable, and it would be nice to do away with mistakes or, at least, to reduce their number to an absolute minimum.

What causes musical mistakes

Many conductors are convinced that musical mistakes are the inevitable results of the stupidity of singers. By "stupidity" they mean, of course, musical ineptness or, more specifically, a low sensitivity to such musical values as rhythm and time. I will readily admit that some singers are congenitally unmusical, just as some others are stupendously gifted musicians. Among the several thousand singers with whom I have worked in the last thirty years, there have been some musical morons and also a few geniuses, but really very few in either of these categories. The vast majority were simply sufficiently musical, and once the methods of insuring accuracy were explained, most of them became reliable performers. The morons should be urged to abandon the field of music, the geniuses do not need any special methods, and the rest of the singers, hopefully, will profit from the ideas and devices described here.

Let us return to the scene of our recent crack-up. What caused the soprano to make the initial error that started the fatal chain of events? The answer is simple: she was lost. She had probably sung her last phrase more than half a page earlier. She had waited. Then it seemed as if her time had come, and she sang. She was not quite certain; she guessed, and she guessed wrong. She was like a driver in a strange city. All the streets looked vaguely familiar, and she took the wrong turn. What she needed was a good landmark and a clearly marked signpost. The landmark and signpost were there all the time, but she had not been trained to recognize and follow them. There are so many singers who spend their lives in poorly marked musical surroundings that one wonders why this happens only to them and not to accompanists, coaches, or conductors. The answer is that not only does the singer, unlike the others, have to memorize his part, but, perhaps more important, his activities are discontinuous. In an opera he usually spends more time not singing than singing, and it is when he is silent that he needs musical help in the form of landmarks and signposts which will show him exactly when his singing should begin and how it must mesh with the music made by his colleagues.

Musical beats, signals, and landmarks

The timing of music is based on beats which are heard by the ear and felt in the form of muscular contractions. Ensemble performing is possible only when all the participants feel these beats at the same time and remain synchronized through all the changes of frequency which the beats may undergo in the course of the music. In order to achieve this, only two things are necessary: the moment of each beat must be clearly identified, and intermediate signals must be provided to warn of any changes in the frequency of the beat. The workings of these principles can be readily understood by performing a simple exercise. Have someone play the passage in Example 6–1 on the piano or any other musical instrument. Let us agree that the beats of the music will fall on the lowest and highest notes of this sequence. We then ask every member of the group (they do not have to be musicians, incidentally) to say "tah" at the moment of the beat (Example 6–2).

Example 6–1

Moderato

tah   tah   tah   tah   tah   tah   tah   tah

Example 6–2

At first, some of the participants may feel a little diffident, but they will soon catch on and join the others in perfect unanimity. Very soon the beat will become firmly established and it will be possible to eliminate the three notes connecting the beat notes to each other (Example 6–3). It is a characteristic of musical beats that the muscular contractions which they generate will continue at the same frequency without additional stimulation.

Moderato

tah   tah   tah   tah   tah   tah   tah

Example 6–3

Now let us see if we can maintain a good synchronization in our group of performers when the beat frequency is changing. Have the person playing the passage start it slowly, then speed it up, and finally slow it down again (Example 6–4). You will notice that the participants in the experiment will have little difficulty in adjusting their responses. The intermediate notes  in each ascending sequence and in each descending one serve as signposts and indicate with sufficient precision whether the next beat note will appear a little sooner (as in measures 1 and 2) or later (as in measure 3).

Example 6–4

Now have the player vary the values of the notes at random (Example 6–5). It is at this point that some members of the group will respond with greater ease and precision than others. When the passage is played rapidly, a change to a slightly slower speed may not be noticed by the less alert participants in time to make the correction. And it is not only a matter of alertness. In judging small differences between time intervals, some people are simply better equipped by nature. This is what makes some pianists fine accompanists and ensemble players and why certain conductors can *follow* so much better than others.

Example 6–5

It is quite certain that the members of the group will be completely unable to predict the position of the beats if the intermediate signals are (*a*) inaudible, (*b*) too rapid, or (*c*) erratic. To see how our ensemble will collapse if these signals are inaudible, we can omit the intermediate notes and the last example and play it as in Example 6–6. Likewise, the ears and muscles of the listeners will not be able to

Example 6–6

adjust quickly enough and the ensemble will be thrown into confusion if the intermediate notes in the passage are suddenly too rapid, as in Example 6–7. The machinery of synchronization can also be defeated by another trick. The members of the group will utter their fifth "tah" long before the player hits his fifth beat note if the passage is performed in an erratic manner, as in Example 6–8.

Example 6–7

Example 6–8

The last three experiments demonstrate that musical signals will not function if they are inaudible, too rapid, or do not conform to reasonable expectations. These principles for establishing musical synchronization have a general validity for all forms of ensemble. For instance, the conductor's baton must pinpoint the moment of a musical beat; it must also provide some form of warning for the moment of the next beat. The exact timing of beats is usually indicated by a clearly visible change of the baton's direction, and the following beat can be readily predicted by observing the speed with which the conductor's arm moves to the next beat position. As in our last experiments, synchronization will break down if the conductor's arm moves too fast, if his beat is erratic, or if it is invisible.

Musical beats are felt as muscular contractions, but the opera singer must learn to keep this beating of time completely hidden from the spectators. Some singers keep time by tiny contractions of the body muscles, others rely on mental images of muscular movements, but nothing is more disturbing from the theatrical point of view than a Countess Almaviva who taps her foot in time with the music or an Aida who wiggles her toe. Equally if not more objectionable is the habit certain male singers have of marking time with their whole body somewhat in the manner of a rider on horseback.

To summarize what we have learned about musical beats and signals:

1. A clear perception of musical beats (by eye or ear) is essential in keeping time and in achieving musical synchronization.
2. Notes occuring between beats can be regarded as signals that help both to establish the beat and to predict changes in beat frequencies.
3. This signal system will not work if the intermediate signals are inaudible, erratic, or too rapid.
4. Opera singers must learn to keep time without in any way making it visible to the audience.

Problems of timing and intonation

When we discussed the unfortunate soprano in the crack-up incident, we pointed out that what the lady needed was a musical landmark together with clearly defined musical signposts. The reader has probably guessed that signposts are fashioned out of the signals we have been discussing here, but what is a musical landmark and why is it needed? As its name implies, a landmark is something which stands out clearly from the surrounding territory. To be useful, a musical landmark should be located fairly close to one's destination: the vocal entrance. It should say in effect: "Watch out! And from here on, follow the signals!" In the succeeding examples, we shall study how to use musical landmarks and signals for the prevention of musical mistakes.

Let us suppose that a baritone studying "Eri tu" from Verdi's *Masked Ball* has learned the recitative, and now wants to be absolutely certain not to miss his first entrance in the aria itself. Between the end of the recitative and this entrance there is a fairly long orchestral introduction. As a conscientious performer, he wonders how thoroughly he should familiarize himself with it, and is puzzled by the silent measure near the end. How many beats can he allot to this measure which, to make matters worse, is elongated by a fermata? All of a sudden he realizes that he does not have to know every detail of this introduction and that it does not matter how long the fermata lasts. *The long silence itself is the landmark* that will help him get to his vocal entrance accurately. The only beats that need concern him are those after the silence. He starts singing on the fourth beat of the measure after the fermata. The silence of the preceding measure is devoid of signals so that he cannot predict just when the first beat of the next measure will occur. But it does not matter. The second and third beats are indicated with such overwhelming clarity by the intermediate rhythms and harmonies that it is virtually impossible to miss the vocal entrance.

In this example we have the perfect combination of an unmistakable landmark, a very short distance from the landmark to the vocal line, and the clearest possible signals indicating the position of the beats. The musical setup is so favorable that even the least experienced beginner can be trusted to attack the opening sentence correctly. It may be instructive nevertheless to see how we can best utilize the final signals that precede the vocal line. The conventional way would be to count the beats, but saying (or thinking) "two, three" just before taking a breath to sing does not add anything of value; one might as well say "tah, tah." Instead of wasting signals, one should try to make them carry some useful information. It is often desirable, for instance, to remind oneself of the words to be sung next. In this case, one can superimpose the rhythm and words of the opening sentence on the orchestral music preceding the vocal attack (Example 6–9).

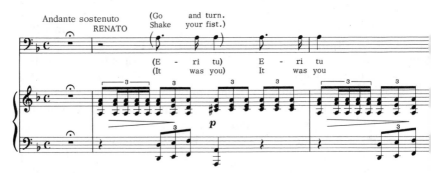

Example 6–9. UN BALLO IN MASCHERA, III, sc. 1

In this particular instance the singer would hardly need this reminder, but in many other places this sort of "self-prompting" subtext can be very helpful indeed. Other aids to one's memory are stage-movement and gesture subtexts, such as "Go and turn" and "Shake your fist." Used between vocal phrases, these various subtexts not only provide the timing of the transition but are invaluable in helping the singer create a convincing dramatic personality. To be most useful, they should be sung full voice in early rehearsals. They are, of course, only thought in performances, but the sensations the singer experienced when practicing them remain very vivid and survive to produce the desired beneficial results.

The opening scene of Humperdinck's *Hansel and Gretel* offers an example of a seemingly simple vocal entrance which is often missed by very dependable singers. The repetitious music with its unvaried harmonies tends to confuse the ear by its very unpretentiousness. The main difficulty lies in the absence of a clearly defined landmark. One has to backtrack ten full beats from the vocal entrance to find anything resembling a musical event of sufficient individuality. At this point the French horn plays an accented C-natural which is tied over to the next measure. This is repeated in the following two measures (Example 6–10). The horn then leads to the vocal line by playing four more C-naturals, this time right on the beats (Example 6–11). The subtext I recommend here is shown in Example 6–12. The first C-natural of the horn, which has the same shape as the following "look outs," serves as the landmark. The singer need not be able to predict the exact moment of its appearance. It is enough for her to recognize the landmark when it is played by the horn. She climbs on the signal train as soon as possible and rides along on the subtext all the way to her destination. At first the singer may complain that the landmark (the first accented C-natural of the horn) cannot be distinguished clearly enough. This is not unusual; many musical cues appear to be hidden in the surrounding sound, but once a singer knows what he is looking for, he develops a knack for identifying the desired cues. Let me remind him that during rehearsals it helps enormously to sing the notes which make up the landmarks and signals. This in itself greatly strengthens his ability to hear them.

Example 6–10. HANSEL AND GRETEL, I, sc. 1

Example 6–11

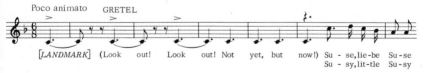

Example 6–12

The words of Gretel's subtext seem at first glance to be somewhat irrelevant, but they have been chosen with care. Obviously, they refer to her difficult entrance and help her to prepare for it. Furthermore, since the landmark is not too easy to hear, it is better at this point not to get the singer involved in complicated stage business. Earlier in the orchestral introduction she can safely gambol with her brother, but here it is better to have her sit quietly, perched on her stool, seeming to devote her full attention to the knitting of her sock. She is not too expert at this occupation, and so the look on her face as she thinks the subtext ("Look out! Look out! Not yet, but now!") is interpreted by the audience as referring to her fear of losing a stitch. Thus Gretel's musical worry is neatly converted into expressive acting.

It may be better for the singer to familiarize herself with the entire orchestral introduction of *Hansel and Gretel* than "live in the dark" and wait for landmarks. But the problem is not of what is desirable, but of what can reasonably be expected. The singer cannot and should not have to memorize every orchestral introduction or interlude. I wonder how many coaches or conductors really know their operas that well. It is enough for the soprano portraying the role of Gretel to be able to act out this introduction while looking and behaving like a little girl. The opera singer's task is sufficiently difficult, and we must do all we can to make it as easy as possible.

Two final points must be made regarding landmarks. First, they are needed only when the singer has been silent for a fairly long time. When dealing with short orchestral interludes between two vocal phrases, the singer does not need a landmark, but simply musical signals, since his last words themselves serve as a point of departure. Second, one must not imagine that only orchestral music can serve our purpose. Vocal lines, even prominent single words sung by other participants, make excellent landmarks, since they are often more clearly audible than the music emerging from the pit. It is only when vocal cues are not available (as in our preceding examples) that one must rely upon orchestral signals. The singer should always select the clearest landmark, regardless of its origin. Then, once he has been alerted, he should immediately get his own musical "clock" going in a manner that assures him the greatest accuracy of attack and tempo.

Musical connecting links in one form or another should be used whenever a singer feels the slightest uncertainty about his next entrance. Uneasy feelings of this kind come about for a variety of reasons. One of the most common is the seeming disappearance of the musical beat during long notes and rests. The musical clock which has been ticking so reassuringly suddenly seems to stop, and the singer loses track of the timing. What disappears, of course, is not the beat, but the intermediate notes that provide signals for the easy recognition of the beat. During such long notes and silences the singer must learn to keep the beat alive by using his own time-keeping machinery. I have found that I can help the singer if, during piano rehearsals, I occasionally add repeated notes or some other type of rhythmic bridge to fill out the rests and the long notes. The singer's ear and his muscles become stimulated by these auxiliary signals, and he keeps hearing and feeling them even when they are no longer actually played. Example 6–13, for instance, is a rather primitive example from the first act of Puccini's *Tosca*, where the added notes appear inside the circle.

Example 6–13. TOSCA, I

In the middle of Rodolfo's first-act aria "Che gelida manina" in *La Bohème*, there is a place where a surprising number of tenors misjudge the timing of a short orchestral interlude and attack their next phrase too soon. As a matter of fact, many opera conductors, having given up all hope of correcting this error, speed up the orchestra to be sure to catch up with the tenor. Of course, mistakes of this kind are very insidious, but they are not beyond repair. I am convinced that here the trouble lies in the absence of intermediate eighth notes, so that the quarter notes of the interlude seem long to the singer and fail to convey a precise succession of beats. This difficulty, like all others of this type, is easily cured by having the tenor practice a specially devised connecting passage attached to suitable words. Example 6–14 shows my own suggestion.

Example 6–14, LA BOHÈME, I

The next example involves an error which is more unusual than the preceding one, and which demonstrates how, in often unexpected sections of a score, a subtext can be helpful even to singers who do not normally require it. On one of my opera tours a very gifted and musical soprano suddenly developed a mental block whenever she came to the place in *La Bohème* where, during the café scene, Mimi shows Rodolfo's friends the little bonnet which he bought her at the beginning of the act. Throughout her solo she is accompanied by eighth notes which indicate the beats with perfect clarity. The first section of her solo ends with a long note punctuated by the harp (Example 6–15). During the

Example 6–15. LA BOHÈME, II

next three measures of the orchestral interlude Mimi is silent, and it was in her next entrance that my otherwise excellent soprano kept making her mistake. It was caused, I believe, by the combination of her long C-sharp and the sustained E-natural in the oboe and English horn. In some strange way, these two long notes made her forget that there was still another phrase in the orchestra before she was to resume her singing. Giving her an acting subtext at this point cured her completely and permanently (Example 6–16). Obviously, this subtext was fashioned to fit the action used in this particular production. It could easily have been changed to "Admire the bonnet and turn to them; give them a smile" or whatever else might fit both the music and a given piece of stage business.

Example 6–16

Up to this point, the subtexts have helped the singer to avoid musical mistakes, to remember his stage movements and gestures, and to recall the opening words of his next singing line. One can also select sentences that represent the thoughts and feelings of the character in the drama. These "inner-feeling" subtexts are similar to those we have used in the pantomimes which were studied earlier.

We can take a passage from the second act of *Aida* to show how an inner-feeling subtext can be used to measure the duration of an extended interval of time. Princess Amneris sees Aida approaching and decides to try to discover whether or not her slave and the victorious general Radames are having a love affair. Amneris' final words before Aida enters are: "But I swear that today I'll learn her secret!" Then the strings play a few soft transitional chords and the bassoons and horns attack a sustained A-natural (Example 6–17). This A-natural pinpoints

Example 6–17. AIDA, II, sc. 1

the first beat of a measure containing four beats. Amneris does not sing until the second beat of the next measure, and from the beginning of the A-natural to her vocal entrance there is not a single intermediate signal. The subtext, "I shall soon learn the truth," represents most appropriately Amneris' thoughts at this point in the opera (Example 6–18). Notice that the subtext has been constructed so that it is rhythmically identical with Amneris' first singing line. In situations where the orchestra is silent or has only long sustained notes, this procedure is very much to be recommended. It prevents the singer's sense of time, rhythm, and tempo from becoming disorganized and neatly prepares him for the music that follows.

Example 6–18

Vocalists also have problems not related to matters of timing. Occasionally it is the beginning pitch that is the source of uncertainty and worry. To help the singer, one constructs a specially arranged melodic line that leads from the last pitch of his preceding phrase to the note that is causing the difficulty. This melodic "bridge" is sung in rehearsals with a suitable subtext and, as a rule, cures the trouble in a very short time. Any musical passage, vocal or instrumental, can serve as a point of departure for building a melodic bridge. The very first words sung by the Marschallin in Strauss' *Der Rosenkavalier* provide a good illustration. The orchestral introduction to this opera begins and ends in the key of E

Major. After the curtain rises, the music continues in this key and remains in E Major until the very end of Octavian's opening sentence, which culminates on a G-sharp (Example 6–19). Less than two measures later the Marschallin has to begin her first line on two notes completely unrelated to the key of E Major (Example 6–20). At first glance, the connecting melody played by the violins (Example 6–21) does not seem helpful. But by singing this melody an octave lower and stopping on the F-natural, the singer has an excellent bridge which easily leads her to her opening notes (Example 6–22).

Example 6–19. DER ROSENKAVALIER, I

Example 6–20

Example 6–21

Example 6–22

A passage from the first act of *Tosca* will illustrate a melodic bridge with a subtext that not only solves a pitch problem and serves as a self-prompting device, but also combines elements of stage movement and inner feeling. Tosca's lover, Mario Cavaradossi, has just asked her to leave so that he can continue to work on his painting. Before departing, she wants to take a look at the picture he has been working on. The discovery that it portrays a beautiful blonde shocks Tosca (who is a brunette) and reawakens her earlier jealous suspicions. Tosca's surprise at seeing the picture is accompanied by an equally surprising orchestral chord, the harmonies of which mirror her sudden alarm. This sudden harmonic change can present a problem. I once worked with a soprano who had difficulty adjusting to the new harmony and hearing the seemingly unrelated B-flat with which she had to begin her next phrase. A simple melodic bridge helped her find this pitch and removed all uncertainty. The subtext attached to this bridge also helped her time her reaction to the picture so that it was simultaneous with the corresponding orchestral chord (Example 6–23).

Example 6–23. TOSCA, I

   Until now we have been dealing primarily with situations where the singer must synchronize his activities with the orchestra. Duets and ensembles present similar problems, but often permit slightly different remedies. Instead of inventing special subtexts, one can let the singer supplement his own part with the vocal line and the words of his partner. This procedure always helps to prevent any embarrassing delay or jerkiness. When rehearsing the scene of Mimi's initial appearance in the first act of *La Bohème*, I have the soprano and the tenor practice a vocal line that combines both of their parts (Example 6–24). After a while they get the feeling of smooth continuity that persists even when they begin to omit the added lines. Singers should be encouraged to learn and sing the lines of other characters, especially those that precede their own. It is surprising how many pitch and timing difficulties disappear once a singer understands precisely how his lines are related to those of his partners on stage. Consider the general problem of rhythmic sluggishness, for instance. Many singers seem to drag their feet when joining

Example 6–24. LA BOHÈME, I

others who are in the midst of a merrily galloping musical passage. This is a natural result of the basic discontinuity of operatic roles which we discussed earlier. No one can start racing from a standing start. When a singer isn't "alive" rhythmically speaking, it naturally takes him a little while to warm up. By singing the lines preceding his, a singer simply winds himself up ahead of time and joins his companions without the slightest hitch.

Secco recitatives

At this point I would like to discuss a special subdivision of opera which seldom receives the attention it deserves. There are extended sections of certain operas where all accepted rules of musical discipline should be broken. These sections occur in eighteenth- and early nineteenth-century comic operas of the type known as *dramma giocoso*, or *opera buffa* (exemplified by the three famous Italian operas of Mozart and *The Barber of Seville*). Works of this genre contain keyboard (secco) recitatives which represent a topsy-turvy, no-man's land of music where all normal standards of operatic behavior are suspended. Vocal lines are more spoken than sung, and they are not accompanied by the orchestra, but by chords played on a keyboard instrument. The mathematics of note values are completely disregarded: quarter notes may be sung faster than sixteenths and these, in turn, slower than eighth notes. Notes are grouped in measures of equal length only to present a more orderly visual aspect. The chords in the accompaniment are not necessarily played where they appear in the score, and they can be embellished, multiplied, or omitted. The tempo is slowed down or speeded up at will. Even the pitches of the notes are not sacred, but are often altered by *appoggiaturas*, which are added in strategic places to produce the desired inflections.* Dramatic sense and theatrical reason are the only considerations that govern the execution of these musical dialogues. Clearly, secco recitatives obey rules of their own. What interests us here, however, is how one gets back to normality and establishes a beat.

---

* A detailed discussion of unmarked vocal *appogiaturas* would lead us too far afield. For more information, consult the list of authoritative writings on page 248.

The earliest sign that a secco is about to return to musical reason is the beginning of a rhymed couplet. In contrast to usual operatic texts, the words of the seccos are not rhymed. However, at the very end of every secco section (just as in the couplets which often end prose sections in Shakespeare's comedies) we invariably find two lines of verse, and it is immediately after the word which is to be graced with a rhyme that the secco begins to mend its disorderly ways. At this point the parlando changes to a more cantabile vocal sound, and the timing begins to coalesce into a regular musical beat. As we have seen in our synchronization experiments, all that is needed to establish a tempo is a short series of regular beats which impress themselves, one way or another, on the members of the ensemble, and which then continue to function by themselves. Chords played on a keyboard instrument (either a harpsichord or a piano) are so ideally suited for this purpose that a succession of only two of them is sufficient to set up a perfectly clear beat frequency. Since opera buffas were ordinarily conducted by the person who sat at the keyboard accompanying the seccos, these final chords were invaluable in setting up the coming tempo for the pit as well as for the stage. They also enabled singers to start out without having to wait until the orchestra established the beat.

When a composer and his librettist wanted a character to begin singing at the very start of an orchestrally accompanied number, they allotted the final sentence in the recitative to the same character. The reasoning here was eminently practical: since this singer knew the speed of the coming beat, he could be trusted to anticipate it. If a recitative ends in the same key in which the orchestral number begins, one can set up the orchestral attack with just a single keyboard chord, having the last chord coincide with the orchestral attack. But this method succeeds only if the singer is able to establish the exact beat during his last words in the secco. For practical purposes, such a musical bridge should consist of no less than one full measure containing four beats. In the three versions of the recitative measures preceding the "La ci darem la mano" duet from *Don Giovanni*, we can observe the actual notation of the musical bridge (Example 6–25) and two possible executions: one where the orchestral attack is prepared by two keyboard chords (Example 6–26), and one where the last chord coincides with the orchestral attack (Example 6–27). There is no question but that the latter method should be employed whenever possible, as it permits a much smoother transition and is much more musical. In Example 6–26 the customary *appoggiaturas* are shown, and in Example 6–27 the chord marked with an asterisk could also come on the last eighth note of the measure.

Most of these bridges connecting secco recitatives with regular musical numbers are simple, and today's singers take them in stride. Once in a while, however, there is a tricky transition that demands careful

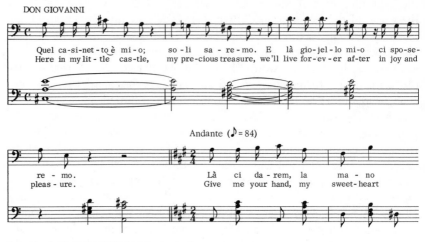

Example 6–25. DON GIOVANNI, I, no. 7

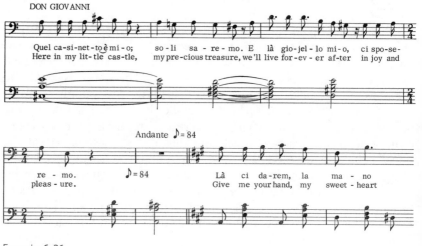

Example 6–26

Example 6–27

handling. An example is Dr. Bartolo's aria in the second scene of *The Barber of Seville*. Unless the tempo of this aria is well prepared ahead of time, the orchestral accompaniment will lack precision. The baritone performing Dr. Bartolo must be able to make the beats of his last recitative sentence equal to that of his opening sentence in the aria, and the space between these two sentences must be timed with great care. With the help of keyboard chords and a subtext (Example 6–28), a baritone can manage this task, but the special synchronization problems of this transition ought to be explained to him first.

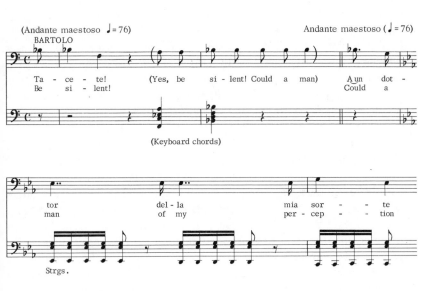

Example 6–28. THE BARBER OF SEVILLE, I, no. 7

Before we leave the topic of seccos, I would like to add a few more words regarding their special musical nature. Once in a while one hears them sung in time, exactly as notated, and without inflections or *appoggiaturas*. These are grave stylistic errors which rob these recitatives of all their musical and dramatic meaning. Many musicians, used to the precise notation of vocal lines in operas written in the last hundred years, are tempted to assume that the same accuracy can be imputed to composers of earlier generations. But the historical facts contradict this assumption. My esteemed colleague and former pupil, Ross Reimueller, has done exhaustive research in this field and has established beyond the slightest doubt that, even though they were not written out, "inflected" endings of vocal phrases were considered *obligatory* until the middle of the last century.*

Problems involving tempo changes

Earlier we spent several anxious moments delving into the details of a musical calamity which we identified by the colorful German word *Schmiss*. Another type of musical upset occurs when some of the instrumentalists or singers misunderstand the tempo and start performing at different and unrelated speeds. Although this can happen at any time, it is much more likely to occur at certain specific moments in the music; when these moments approach, the conductor begins to feel a perfectly natural apprehension. Most opera singers do not understand what causes his anxiety. In a way, this is only natural. Each profession has its own technical niceties which are of no particular interest to outsiders. Oboe players are fascinated by subtle differences in reeds; singers can spend hours discussing the position of the soft palate; lighting designers worry about shades of gelatins; and conductors argue about metronome marks. Each expert has his own special headaches. It is essential for members of the operatic fraternity to recognize this and to refrain from aggravating each other's headaches. A conductor may not know or care too much about the mechanics of a singer's breath support, but when he notices that a singer is short of breath, he speeds up the music slightly to help him. A singer who is aware that a lighting designer has spent hours in creating a moonlit scene will not want to spoil his efforts by choosing to remain in total darkness just inches away from the spot that has been so carefully illuminated. In the same way, it is important for the singer to understand the reason for the conductor's concern and help to dispel it. The wise conductor, on the other hand, can help everybody if he

---

* To dispel any doubt a singer (or his repertoire coach) may have in this regard, I refer them to any or all of the following selected list of authoritative writings that treat this subject:

AGRICOLA, Johann Friedrich, *Anleitung zur Singkunst*, Berlin, 1757.
MANCINI, Giambattista, *Pensieri e riflessioni sopra il canto figurato*, Vienna, 1774.
HILLER, Johann Adam, *Anweisung zum musikalisch-zierlichen Gesange*, Leipzig, 1780.
MANFREDINI, Vincenzo, *Regole armoniche*, Venezia, 1797.
LASSER, Johann Baptist, *Vollständige Anleitung zur Singkunst*, München, 1798.
TOMEONI, Florido, *Théorie de la musique vocale*, Paris, 1799.
SCHUBERT, Johann Friedrich, *Singe-schule oder gründliche und vollstänige Anweisung zur Singkunst*, Leipzig, 1804.
CORRI, Domenico, *The Singers Perceptor*, London, 1810.
LICHTENTHAL, Pietro, *Dizionario e Bibliografia della Musica*, Milano, 1826.
GARCIA, Manuel, *Traité complet de l'art du chant*, Paris, 1847.

tells the singer quite frankly just where and why he begins to feel apprehensive. To help the singer understand his own and the conductor's tempo
problems, I shall try to present them as simply and concisely as I can.

Harmless tempo changes

Operatic composers have always tried to achieve musical variety and
dramatic credibility in their works. To accomplish this, they have
often created a change of tempo. Unfortunately for performers, these
changes can sometimes be very tricky. Tempo changes are difficult and
dangerous only if they involve changes in beat frequency. During many
tempo changes, the speed of the beat remains the same and such tempo
changes do not present any problems. In the example from Verdi's *Falstaff*
(Example 6–29), the beat continues unchanged. What is changed is the

Example 6–29. FALSTAFF, I, SC. 2

note value of the beat. In the first two measures the conductor indicates
six beats (one for each eighth note); in the allegro measure he gives four
beats (one for each quarter), but the important thing is that all the beats
are of the same speed and are very easy to hear, feel, and follow.

Another type of harmless tempo change occurs when the new beat
bears such a close relationship to the old one that, for all practical purposes, they are one and the same. What happens is that the new beat is
either twice or half as fast as the preceding one and can be clearly felt
while the first one is still going on. This trick of feeling the new beat
ahead of time is the most important feature of all smooth tempo changes
and is, in fact, the only thing that the singer must understand in order
to help the conductor.

Observe the seemingly startling tempo change which occurs in the
opening scene of *Aida*. Here Verdi introduces the theme associated with
Princess Amneris' jealous suspicions. Slowly and suggestively, the princess
has just asked Radames about his desires and hopes. Afraid to betray his

secret love for Aida, Radames shrinks away. His guilty look inflames Amneris' wild suspicions, which are musically portrayed in the next measure. This measure is very fast and must be played quite softly, yet with great precision. It is marked "allegro agitato e presto." Since this passage must be attacked immediately after Radames' short exclamations, Verdi arranges it so that the tenor's very first word (although it is still sung in the last measure of the slow tempo) anticipates the beat of the next allegro (Example 6–30). If the tenor sings his *i-o* strictly in time, it clearly indicates the frequency of 132 beats per minute (which is the speed of the allegro), makes things comfortable for everybody, and enables the conductor to indicate ahead of time two full measures of the new tempo, just as if the last half of the final slow measure were notated as in Example 6–31. Although my notation differs from Verdi's, it shows that the two speeds co-exist, and this co-existence of the slow and fast tempos permits the smooth transition from one to the other. It is essential for the tenor to sing his unaccompanied words in strict time. I would suggest that the conductor not only ask him to do so, but also explain to him the reasons for this request, since unaccompanied exclamations of this sort ordinarily imply a great deal of rhythmic freedom. It is even possible that Verdi went to the trouble of notating the Italian word *io* with two separate notes—*i-o* instead of the usual *io*—because he considered it important for the vowel "o" to be placed so as to indicate the new tempo precisely.

Example 6–30. AIDA, I, sc. 1

Example 6–31

The next three examples demonstrate Mozart's realistic approach to ensemble problems in opera. When a plot called for the interruption of the existing action by the unexpected arrival of new characters, Mozart naturally wanted their music to be surprising and more agitated. A new tempo was obviously desirable here, but since the new arrivals had to sing as soon as they entered, Mozart could not give them much time to become adjusted to the change of speed. Furthermore, as an experienced theatrical craftsman, he knew that the very act of walking when entering the stage makes it even more difficult to keep exact time. Mozart saw to it, therefore, that the new tempo could be felt quite clearly and precisely while the old one was still in progress. Antonio's entrance in the second act of *The Marriage of Figaro* (Example 6–32) is one instance of how

Example 6–32. THE MARRIAGE OF FIGARO, II, Finale no. 15

Mozart introduces a new tempo. While Antonio stands outside the door waiting to knock and make his entrance, he listens to the music of the four singers on stage, and as they reach their last words he can super-impose a subtext based on their music but notated in the tempo of his music, which then continues with the orchestra and leads him directly to his vocal line (Example 6–33).

The change of tempo that accompanies Donna Elvira's entrance in the last scene of *Don Giovanni* seems particularly violent because here an *alla breve* (duple meter) is interrupted and supplanted by new music which is in 3/4 time. Since the underlying beat remains the same, the soprano has only to superimpose a subtext in triplets on the last two measures of the preceding music (Example 6–34). The half note of the preceding tempo is equal to the dotted half of the new one. It does not matter whether the conductor beats two half-note beats per measure at one second per beat (♩ = 60) or four quarter-note beats at half a second

* Since the metronome did not exist in Mozart's time, the metronome marks in these examples are obviously not his. They happen to be the ones taken in the performance of my company and are quoted here in order to give the reader an idea of the approximate speeds of music in these examples.

each (♩ = 120), as long as Elvira, who is waiting to enter, listens only
to the slower (one per second) beat and mentally divides it into triplets.
The subtext ("Surely it's time now to *enter* the stage and sing") provides
her with four preparatory measures in the new tempo and also tells
her exactly when to make her entrance.

Example 6–33

Example 6–34. DON GIOVANNI, II, Finale no. 24

Our final example of a Mozartian tempo change is particularly fascinating because it features the rare phenomenon of a new speed which is three times as fast as the preceding one, and even though the effect of this tempo change is quite startling, Mozart provided a musical co-existence that makes it relatively simple to handle (Example 6–35). It occurs at the point in the last act of *The Marriage of Figaro* where Susanna enters disguised as the Countess and prevents Figaro from rushing into the pavilion to avenge his honor. The first tempo is a larghetto in 3/4 time which moves at a speed slightly slower than one quarter note per second. The intermediate notes in the accompaniment are triplets of eighth notes played by violins at the corresponding speed of about 160 per minute. The new tempo is an allegro molto which remains in 3/4 time, but it is so much faster than the preceding larghetto that three of the new quarter beats equal one of the old ones: ♩. = ♩ = 54. The new beat of 160 quarter notes per minute coincides exactly with the preceding speed of the eighth notes in the violins. By listening to these triplets (which Mozart entrusted to all the violins to make them unmistakable) and by converting these triplets into a subtext of quarters, Susanna can comfortably anticipate the new tempo and enter the stage in complete confidence.

Example 6–35. THE MARRIAGE OF FIGARO, IV, Finale no. 28

In all the examples of tempo changes quoted so far there was some unifying, constant beat which made it possible to feel the basic identity of two succeeding tempos and to arrange for a co-existence. In the *Aida* and the first *Marriage of Figaro* examples the speed of the eighth notes in the andante was equal to that of the half notes in the allegro; in *Don Giovanni* the half note became a dotted half; and in the second *Marriage of Figaro* example we had two correspondences: the earlier quarters equalled the later dotted halves and the triplet eighth notes were the same as the later quarters.

There is still another type of common denominator which can help singers predict a completely new tempo with certainty even when the speed of the beat does not remain constant. This happens when the meter signature changes while the speed of the intermediate notes remains constant. Consider Example 6–36. If the speed of the eighth notes remains the same, it will by necessity result in a change in the speed of the beat.

Example 6-36

Example 6-37

If the dotted quarter-note beat in the 6/8 measure is equal to one second, then the quarter-note beat in the 2/4 measure will be only two-thirds of a second. It does not matter whether or not the notation of intermediate notes remains the same. If in Example 6–37, the quarters of the second measure equal the preceding eighth notes, the relationship between the dotted quarter-note beats in the 6/8 measure and the half-note beat in the 4/4 measure will be the same as in the earlier example. Tempo changes of this type are very common in the operas of Richard Strauss and other twentieth-century composers, and they help to give these works their great rhythmic fluidity. Mozart, who anticipated many procedures generally associated with much later musical styles, employed this method of changing speeds when he wanted to underline some particularly startling and sudden dramatic development. In the last scene of *The Marriage of Figaro*, when the Count collars Figaro in the belief that he has caught his wife's lover, we can observe (in Example 6–38) the changes in tempo, meter, and beat frequency described in our last example (6–37). One would imagine that so drastic a tempo change would create a problem in synchronization, but the evenness of the intermediate eighth notes and quarters gives this jolting sequence a surprising rhythmic stability and ease of execution. The subtext helps to pinpoint both the change in the tempo and the exact moment when the Count catches Figaro.

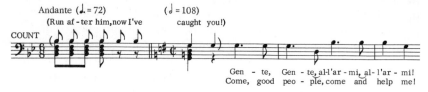

Example 6-38. THE MARRIAGE OF FIGARO, IV, Finale no. 28

Tempo changes which require adjustments

We have seen that tempo changes are fairly simple when a common denominator and a co-existence of beat speeds enables performers to feel a new tempo ahead of time. A difficult tempo change is one where these conditions are not present and where singers must participate in a new tempo before they have a chance to become fully familiar with it. In these cases, where common denominators are not automatically present, the thing to do is create them artificially. The most obvious way to do this is to adjust the first tempo so as to bring it into an easy relationship with the second one. When I say that this method is obvious, I mean that it is the one most often used by the composers themselves. Many composers—Gluck, Mozart, Weber, Rossini, Verdi, and Wagner, among others —were practicing opera conductors and were very familiar with conducting headaches. They probably did not think in terms of common denominators and co-existences, but their scores demonstrate quite clearly that they knew how to anticipate a new tempo and how to adjust an existing one in order to match it up with a new one. How did they adjust to these tempo changes without common denominators? Either by slowing down or speeding up the existing tempo to anticipate the new one. Sometimes these adjustments are indicated by the words *rallentando* or *accelerando*; sometimes, however, the adjustments are only implied, and these implied notations can be quite ambiguous. Even so, it is usually possible to figure out just what the composer had in mind.

In tempo changes requiring accelerandos or rallentandos, a performer might imagine that all he has to do is to accelerate or decelerate the first tempo until it reaches the next one. But there is another way to accomplish this. When a gradual change from a moderate tempo of 80 to a fast tempo of 120 is desired, there are two possibilities: the moderate tempo can be speeded up directly or it can be slowed down to 60 and then doubled.* The second possibility is often more effective since it produces more of a contrast. From the point of view of difficulty, these two ways of adjusting tempo are about the same. The following two examples will illustrate some of the methods for handling these adjustments.

A passage from the final scene of *Falstaff* (Example 6–39) shows a speed-up combined with a change in the note value of the beat. By means of doubling the speed of the beat, this acceleration takes us to the fastest existing tempo: prestissimo. The singer performing Bardolfo is

---

In Carmen's Card Scene (page 194) we encountered an example of the reverse of this, i.e. an acceleration followed by a halving of the speed. This procedure is rather uncommon, however.

waiting offstage and must listen very carefully to the four measures leading to the prestissimo. There are three things to listen for: the rate of the acceleration, the number of beats until the new tempo sets in, and the exact moment when he is to enter the stage. A subtext such as the one given here will help him solve all three problems at once. Keeping track of a few sentences is much easier than counting sixteen beats. The word "go" tells him exactly when to start moving onstage, and synchronizing his words (or thoughts) with the orchestra helps him to arrive at the exact speed of the new tempo, since the last "Who is there?" of the subtext is identical in speed with the one he sings immediately afterwards.

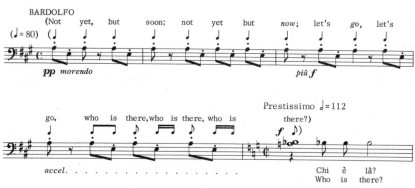

Example 6–39. FALSTAFF, III, sc. 2

The following example (6–40) involves a group of vocalists who must all be synchronized with each other as well as with the orchestra. In the second scene of the first act of *Rigoletto*, at the very moment of a tempo change, a large group of tenors and basses have to attack a whispered staccatissimo passage accompanied by the orchestra and requiring the greatest possible precision. This is one of those situations that are really difficult and call for considerable alertness on the part of the singers. The first tempo is "andante assai mosso" with a metronome marking of ♩ = 88. At the very first measure of the new tempo (allegro marked ♩ = 144) the chorus must make its vocal attack. Since in performance both tempos are taken at speeds somewhat faster than those indicated by the composer, the actual translation goes from ♩ = 100 to ♩ = 160. There is a ritardando notated in the final three measures of the andante. If the singers listen carefully to the sixteenth notes in the cellos which serve as the all-important intermediate signals of the ritardando, they will be able to follow the gradual slowing-down from the original ♩ = 100 all the way to ♩ = 80, which is reached in the last measure of the andante. Here the repeated staccato eighth notes of the cellos, sounding for all the world like a metronome ticking at a speed of 160, enable the singers to prepare themselves with an easy subtext (Example 6–41). With eight preparatory beats in the new tempo (seven of which are doubled in the orchestra) our choristers should be completely oriented and ready for a perfect attack and a crisp and assured execution.

Example 6-40. RIGOLETTO, I, no. 7

Example 6-41

Such terms as "ritardando" are not the only signs that have been used to indicate a slowing-down. Composers of the eighteenth and early nineteenth centuries were fond of a method which has gone out of favor in the last hundred years: they used fermatas. Nowadays fermatas are used only to elongate individual notes, chords, or rests; but in former centuries they served other purposes. In Rossini's operas, for instance, a fermata seems to have the general meaning of "Stop and reorganize!" Before practically every change of tempo in *The Barber of Seville,* we find this stop sign which solves the problem of a smooth transition between different tempos by simply ignoring the whole issue. Instead of worrying about the change between two musical sections of different speeds, Rossini simply ended one with a fermata and started the next from scratch. To avoid difficulties with singers, he did not introduce the vocal lines until he was certain that the beat was clearly established by the orchestra.

Mozart had a different and much more subtle attitude towards fermatas: he used them not only for smooth transitions between tempos, but also to create rhythmic effects which modern composers achieve by means of different meter signatures. The second-act Dorabella-Guglielmo duet in *Così fan tutte* features five fermatas in the first sixteen measures.

This music, which Mozart notates in 3/8 time, would probably be notated today in the form of eight measures, of which the second, fourth, and last would be in 6/8 time and all the rest in 7/8. Such metric signatures were unheard of in Mozart's day, so he was forced to use available symbols to achieve the desired effect. This insight into Mozart's special use of fermatas helps us to understand his intentions in many places that otherwise appear to be rather puzzling. One such place is the transition to the famous canon in the final scene of *Così fan tutte* (Example 6–42). The tempo changes here from "andante alla breve" to "larghetto" in 3/4 time, moving from approximately ♩ = 96 to ♩ = 50. The last measure of the andante section contains two fermatas, one over the dotted eighth note sung by the four singers and one over an eighth-note rest. I feel quite certain that Mozart, by means of this notation, meant to convey the idea of a gradual slow-down and used the fermatas to anticipate the meter and the mood of the coming larghetto. For the benefit of the singers, I find it useful to convert Mozart's ambiguous notation into its more accurate modern equivalent, which permits singers to feel all the intermediate beats with perfect clarity (Example 6–43).

Example 6–42. COSÌ FAN TUTTE, II, Finale no. 31

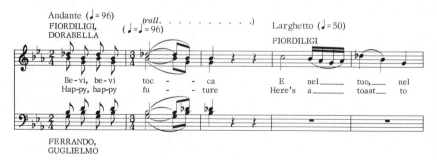

Example 6–43

In our last examples the adjustments preceding a new tempo were clearly indicated either by such words as *accelerando* and *ritardando* or

by fermatas. There are, however, a great number of places involving similar tempo changes where all such notations are missing. Composers probably thought that in these places the internal logic of their music would
automatically dictate a slight slowing down or speeding up. As a matter
of fact, it does. For example, who has ever heard a bass-baritone singing
the role of Monterone in *Rigoletto* who did not slow down at the end
of his solo in the first scene, in spite of the fact that there is no ritardando
marked there? His automatic slowing down serves as the necessary adjustment to prepare for the next allegro. Monterone begins his solo in an andante sostenuto marked ♩ = 80. Then in his final sentence the declamatory force of his vocal climax slows him down to ♩ = 60, which is also
♪ = 120 and therefore co-existent with the ♩ = 120 of the next
allegro. The first few measures of the next allegro, consisting of short,
successive ejaculations by the Duke, Rigoletto, and the three solo
courtiers, are an open invitation to musical trouble. To make matters
worse, at the very point the allegro begins, the orchestral accompaniment in the strings is so soft as to be barely audible. It is therefore
particularly important that the Duke, who sets up the sequence of
vocal cues, be rhythmically precise. All problems are solved the moment
the Duke realizes that Monterone's last four notes indicate exactly the
tempo of the coming allegro. By converting the last measure of the andante into the notation of the new tempo, we can ask the Duke to practice a subtext that connects directly with his exclamatory lines (Example
6-44).

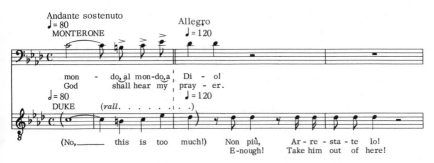

Example 6-44. RIGOLETTO, I, no. 2

Difficult tempo changes

Before going on to discuss particularly thorny problems of synchronization, it may be helpful to look into the general questions of operatic
ensemble. From the examples we have studied, it is clear that by paying
close attention to the orchestra and the other performers on stage, a singer

can adjust his own timing. As every singer knows, this is much easier when he himself is not singing, since producing vocal tones often sets up a considerable vibration in the singer's head and interferes with his listening. This interference explains why a singer with a relatively small voice is sometimes found to be a "better musician" than his booming colleagues. The light-voiced singer naturally synchronizes better because it is easier for him to hear others when he is singing. Since the vocal process so often interferes with listening, it is when a singer is silent that he can best adjust his timing to that of the rest of the ensemble.

To understand still better the mechanics of synchronization, we can borrow the term "feed-back" from the modern science of communication. The orchestra and the singers "feed" signals to each other, and this alternating feeding leads to constant adjustments on both sides. If orchestral signals come in a little sooner than a singer expects, he attacks his line a shade sooner or sings it a shade faster; if the singer sings a little faster or slower than the orchestra is playing, then the orchestra—guided by its collective ear, the conductor—adjusts accordingly. From the singer's point of view, subtexts are valuable in this adjustment process: they help him, when he is not singing, to check the accuracy of the synchronization between his imaginary timing and the actual timing of the orchestra. These adjustments go on constantly, but with fine performers they are so minute as to be unnoticeable. As long as the singer can hear the orchestra and the conductor can hear the singer, and as long as the music provides a sufficient number of signals, all is well. In a steady, well-established tempo, the beats continue to be felt for quite a while so that an occasional lack of signals is not critical. It is when the beat changes and the signals are scarce (or non-existent) that the ensemble is likely to become shaky. It is here that the conductor and the singer must put their heads together and reach a good understanding.

The reader, familiar with standard operatic practices, has undoubtedly been wondering for quite a while why I have not said that the easiest way to avoid mistakes and to ensure good ensemble is for the singer to watch the conductor's beat. One would think that the more complicated the problems of entrance and tempo changes, the more obvious the need to have the singer turn to the conductor's baton.

There are several good reasons why this method, so generally practiced and accepted, should be used as sparingly as possible. The most important objection is that it diverts the singer's attention from the action at hand and thereby seriously disturbs his dramatic performance. Singers who stare at the conductor have made opera the laughingstock of the theatrical world. It is true that the ridiculous aspects of open staring are greatly lessened if the singer learns to use peripheral vision, and it is undeniable that many fine performers have succeeded in doing this very skillfully and discreetly. But today, when both performers and audiences are increasingly interested in the visual aspect of opera, the singer who can handle tricky musical moments without the slightest sacrifice of dramatic intensity will definitely enhance the effect of his performance. Furthermore, by considering solutions to his own problems from the point of view of improving his musicianship, the singer gains confidence and helps create mutual respect between himself and the conductor. When all is said and done, the conductor has no special desire to have the singer watch him. What the conductor does desire is to be blessed with singers who are dependable and accurate artists. Perhaps there are ensemble problems that cannot be solved without watching the conductor. I have never encountered such problems, and I believe that after experimenting with a few of these seemingly insoluble moments, singers will agree that they can always keep their eyes from the pit and yet remain completely secure, provided they have the cooperation of the conductor. Most conductors are only too willing to cooperate with intelligent artists, and should the singer discover that here and there he still has to catch a glimpse of the baton, he will nevertheless be ahead of the game, having gained some very valuable insights into the machinery of music.

The cooperation of the conductor consists in his willingness to watch the singer in certain difficult moments so that he can occasionally take a cue from *him*. The idea of having singers give cues to conductors may seem sheer madness, but to me it is perfectly logical. Without doubt there are times when auditory cues are not sufficient and one must rely on visual communication. Since having singers watch the conductor has obvious disadvantages, why not have the conductor watch the singer, a process which has no disadvantages? We must remember that these cues have been set up and well rehearsed by the conductor, so that singers do precisely what he wants. I have never known an opera to contain more than a dozen such critical spots, and it really takes no more than ten minutes for a singer and a conductor to set up and rehearse a code that will ensure complete musical synchronization in one of these troublesome moments. After all, conductors have followed singers since the beginning of operatic time, and adjusting to a singer's breathing is something that is done by all experienced conductors. I believe that many conductors of the old school object to the idea of taking a cue from the singer simply because they do not trust the singer to be dependable musically, and they do not always share our overwhelming desire to make opera more convincing theatrically. I feel certain that the world of unmusical singers and unbelievable opera is the world of yesterday, and I hope that the following examples will demonstrate how a simple understanding between the singer and the conductor can enhance some of opera's most memorable moments.

In the middle of Aida's "Ritorna vincitor," there is a very tricky vocal entrance which occurs right after a transition from an andante to an allegro. In the last measure of the andante, just as the rallentando sets in, the orchestra plays only two long notes, one on the first and the other on the third beat of the measure (Example 6–45). The absence of intermediate signals makes it difficult for the singer and the conductor to reach the beginning of the allegro at precisely the same time. In such situations the orchestra normally plays on the downbeat of the new tempo, but in this case we have only silence. During this silence, the conductor starts beating the faster tempo of the allegro, and immediately after his second beat (still before the orchestra) the soprano begins to sing (Example 6–46). To solve this difficulty, the soprano usually starts watching the conductor in the last measure of the andante so that she can observe both the last four beats of the slowing-down and the first two beats of the allegro. Admittedly, this is a "razor-blade" moment which can never become automatic, but the audience must not be aware of it. By learning a subtext, the soprano can solve it in a way which keeps its razor edge hidden, which is preferable dramatically, and which is absolutely safe musically (Example 6–47). In rehearsals the conductor listens to her sing this passage and helps her adjust her rallentando so that it is identical with the way he conducts it. It is useful if the conductor counts aloud the beats of this passage so that the singer can learn to match her subtext to his counting (Example 6–48). Having achieved a perfect accord with the conductor, the soprano then adds a clearly visible stage movement to coincide with the downbeat of the allegro. She can do this by changing her posture or by making a suitable gesture, but whatever it is, it permits the conductor to give his downbeat at precisely the same time. All this sounds complicated when described on paper, but it takes very little rehearsal time and rewards both participants with results that are both dramatically and musically satisfying.

Example 6–45

Example 6–46

Example 6–47

Example 6–48

Another famous moment in opera that permits an effective dramatic solution to a tricky musical problem is the beginning of Tosca's "Vissi d'arte." The opening phrase must be attacked with perfect exactness by the soprano and the orchestra after a long rallentando which culminates in a sustained chord lasting four measures. During this time the beat continues to slow down inaudibly, and this is followed by an equally ill-defined new tempo. Even so, it is possible to devise a fairly simple coordination system which, without so much as a glance at the conductor, will assure the accuracy of both the attack and the new tempo. During the seven beats that follow Scarpia's "vita," Tosca can walk down left to the couch, thinking a subtext (Example 6–49). The clarinets start their rallentando while she thinks the second "how dreadful" of her subtext, thus permitting her to check whether or not she is slowing down at a rate identical with the conductor's. By the time the clarinets reach their long sustained note, Tosca has arrived above the couch and is leaning on it while facing stage left. She continues thinking her final "oh, how dreadful" while continuing to slow down at approximately the same rate as in the preceding measure. With her last "-ful," Tosca turns slightly counterclockwise (so as to stand with her back to the conductor and the audience) and passes her left hand behind her, using it to lean on the couch in back of her. She attacks the first note of her aria at the moment her left hand touches the couch. This gesture also serves as the conductor's cue. The gradual slowing-down has brought Tosca to the speed of eighty quarter-note beats per minute

($\quad$ =80), which is identical to the eighth notes of the aria ($\quad$ = 80). The length of the last word in the subtext is the same as the first note of the aria. She can then begin her famous "Vissi d'arte" exactly on time, standing with her back to the audience in a pose of eloquent despair, and seemingly oblivious to all musical problems. By converting the measures preceding the aria into a different notation, we can clarify the process still further (Example 6–50).

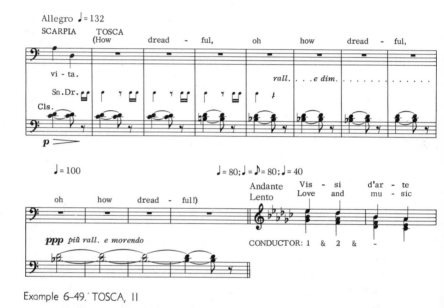

Example 6–49. TOSCA, II

Example 6–50

The reader may think that this solution is too difficult and could be used by only the most gifted and experienced singing actress. But this is not true: any normally talented singer can perform it. Like the following two examples, this is not just a theoretical solution, but one that has been successfully used in my company in scores of performances involving dozens of different singers.

I am quite aware that some directors and singers may not approve of this dramatic interpretation for the staging of "Vissi d'arte." But my point here is that these particular techniques can ensure accurate musical execution no matter what stage solution is desired.

Those of us who are devoted to dramatic credibility are especially baffled by the problem of how the singer and the orchestra can attack a new tempo simultaneously after a long silence. Such a critical situation occurs in the last act of Mozart's *The Marriage of Figaro* at the moment when Count Almaviva realizes to his enormous embarrassment that he has been caught red-handed and has made a fool of himself, and that the only thing left for him to do is to offer his humblest and most abject apologies. He finally does so (Example 6–51), but not before a long silence where he, hardly believing his eyes, looks from Susanna (who is on stage left) to his wife (who has just emerged from the pavilion on stage right).

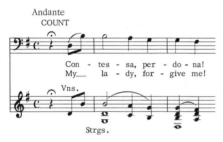

Example 6–51. THE MARRIAGE OF FIGARO, IV, Finale no. 28

The problem is that the violins have to sing this phrase with the baritone, and while the tempo here is easy enough to remember, the moment of the attack has to be timed very precisely. From the dramatic point of view, it is absolutely essential that the Count's eyes be glued to his wife, so that his apologies are addressed to her and not to anyone else, especially not the conductor. The solution to this problem is so simple that it almost seems a shame to give it away. What happens is this. After the silence has lasted long enough, the Count starts walking towards his wife and, by agreement with the conductor, starts singing at the exact moment he takes his third step. With the Count's first step, the conductor is alerted; with his second step, he gives the upbeat to the violins; and on the third step there is a beautifully synchronized attack which leaves all the other conductors in the audience trying to figure out just how this miracle was accomplished.

Our final example (6–52) concerns a musical synchronization that I personally find just about as difficult as any I have ever encountered. It takes place in the second act of *La Traviata* when Violetta is completely shattered by Father Germont's demand that she abandon Alfredo for all time. After Violetta's exclamation, "No, mai!" (No, never!), Verdi not only puts a fermata over the rest, but adds another full measure containing another fermata as well as the words "pausa lunga." He obviously wanted this to be a very long silence.

Example 6–52. LA TRAVIATA, II, sc. 5

One might think that the long pause would make it easy for all concerned to prepare for the new tempo, but this is not so. It is what comes after the silence that is very tricky. To begin with, it is uncomfortably fast.* Besides notating it "vivacissimo," Verdi added an "agitato" which I find quite unnecessary, since both the singer and the conductor are sufficiently agitated as it is. What makes this place really difficult, however, is not only the fast tempo but the type of orchestral passage that must be executed by the strings at this speed (Example 6–53). Since there is no attack on the downbeat, the preparation for it is particularly important. The conductor has to give a very clear upbeat of the same length as the following beats, and in order to do this he must know exactly when the soprano will begin her phrase. What one really needs here is one full preliminary measure in the new tempo, and here the singer can be of enormous help. She can turn at this point, making her turn in two steps which are timed to indicate the beats of the extra measure. She then sings her "Non sapete . . ." (Example 6–54) immediately after the second step, and the tempo is safely under way. Because of the long skirts worn by women in the *Traviata* period, one cannot be sure of seeing these two steps, so they must be supplemented by other stage movements or gestures in order to clarify the beat. All this has to be done without a hint that anything mechanical or technical is being executed.

---

* Verdi's metronome mark here— ♩. = 108—is one of those indications that no one—not even Toscanini, whose *Traviata* is probably the fastest ever conducted by anyone—can possibly reach. In my performances, it has usually been timed at ♩. = 92, and even this is faster than the tempo taken by most conductors.

Example 6–53

Example 6–54

If the razor-blade sharpness of this moment cannot be completely hidden from the audience, one might as well look directly at the conductor.

As we mentioned earlier, most of these methods for avoiding mistakes in entrances, pitches, and synchronizations depend upon the singer's ability to hear the music played by the orchestra. In soft passages, instrumentalists generally play in a discreet and transparent manner so as not to drown out the voices. This is ideal from the audience's point of view, but it often prevents the sound of the orchestra from reaching the stage. What is obviously wanted is some magic trick to keep the orchestral sound soft enough for the listeners and loud enough for the singer.

This magic trick exists. It is quite inexpensive, as well as very easy to obtain and install. It consists of one microphone in the pit and two small speakers placed behind the proscenium arch and facing upstage. With this device even the softest music can be picked up and transmitted to every area of the stage at all times. The "live" sound of the instruments in the pit makes it impossible for the audience to hear the sound coming from the loudspeakers. This system should be in operation in all stage rehearsals as well as performances. It serves as an excellent preventive medicine for such common ills of opera as off-pitch singing and faulty synchronization of beats between the pit and the stage. Because this system is the best remedy for musical headaches ever invented, it does wonders for the nerves of singers and conductors.

Unfortunately, many organizations still shy away from using this system, perhaps because of the fear that it will be heard by the audience or because it does not always work immediately. But it should not be discarded for this reason. By pointing the loudspeakers away from the pit and by adjusting their volume, this system can always be made to function smoothly.

Since, for one reason or another, many opera companies are reluctant to use mechanical aids, singers will often find themselves in situations where communication by ear is insufficient, if not impossible. In such cases they must rely on visual cues. When this is necessary, it is of course much better not to stare at the conductor, but to catch sight of his baton by looking over his head or by using peripheral vision.

The realities of an operatic career

As we come to the end of our discussions devoted specifically to young singers, I would like to offer them a few final words of advice. Many years ago, when I had just graduated from the Piano Master Class at the Academy of Music in Budapest, my three colleagues and I were told to report for one last instruction period which would be given to us by our teacher, Ernest Dohnànyi, at his country home. Having been subjected to a whole series of grueling tests in the form of solo recitals, appearances with the orchestra, and extremely nerve-racking examinations before a panel of the entire piano faculty, the four of us were rather puzzled by the idea that our illustrious mentor had any further words of musical wisdom to dispense to us. When we arrived, we were ushered into a large bedroom where Dohnànyi was waiting for us with a welcoming smile. "My dear young friends," he said, "during the last two years we have had many discussions dealing with musical and pianistic matters, but now I want to show you something that may prove even more valuable in your careers as concert artists." He then took a full-dress suit from his clothes closet and taught each of us in turn how to fold it in such a way that when we arrived in a city for a concert engagement, it could be taken out of the suitcase and worn to the auditorium without needing to be pressed. I have been folding my full-dress suits according to Dohnànyi's formula ever since, always thinking with gratitude of my beloved master. I will not attempt to teach singers how to fold and pack their theatrical costumes. I only want to help them reach the point where they will be engaged to wear them.

Many a young singer who has won a contest in his home town or starred with his local opera group, fails to see his own achievements in their proper perspective. Having received nothing but praise in his own town, he feels sure that when he goes to the Big City all the agents and impresarios will vie for the privilege of making him a star. What he does not realize is that the professionals have been dealing for years with everyone in the operatic field, including international stars, and that in this context a beginner can expect no verdict more encouraging than "very promising." In this day and age, no singer, however talented, is swooped into immediate stardom. Beginning an operatic career is extremely difficult, and I hope that the following remarks will help gifted singers to go about it in a more sensible manner.

Every year scores of aspiring young vocalists come to New York City hoping to find operatic employment. After singing countless auditions and not landing a single job, many of them become discouraged and begin to wonder if they have what it takes for a career in opera. It would help them if they could see how their hectic activity looks from the vantage point of the impresario who is interrupting his regular tasks in order to hear them.

Like many of my colleagues, I make it a habit to set aside a day every month or so when I listen to fifteen or twenty singers who have approached me in the general hope of singing with my company. I look at their resumes, hear them sing at least two arias, and keep a record of their names along with some notations which, for privacy's sake, I scribble down in Russian. A notation may read "might make a pretty good Susanna" or "middle voice not bad." It can consist of a horrified "good Lord!" or of the single word "no!" Whatever it is, in a week or so I am sorry to say that I remember very little about these singers except the fact that I did not hire them.

There are other times, however, when I need a certain type of performer for an opera I am about to produce. Perhaps the tenor I have engaged for the role of Don Ottavio in *Don Giovanni* is suddenly unavailable. Listening to singers now becomes a very different matter. I am no longer a civic-minded member of the musical community who is generously giving his time so that deserving young singers can be heard. I am now a producer who has agreed to perform *Don Giovanni* within a certain number of weeks and who needs a Don Ottavio. I start telephoning other producers, agents, managers, voice teachers, and regular members of my company, letting it be known far and wide: Goldovsky is looking for a Don Ottavio! The tenors who audition for me now are no longer facing a man "who has generously consented to hear them." Instead, they are singing for an impresario who must engage one of them. The same tenor who only two weeks ago was a deserving young singer I did not hire, can now easily turn out to be exactly the man I am looking for. This is the only kind of audition in which a singer should be interested; others are likely to be discouraging. One always thinks of the many poor youngsters searching for jobs in the field, but for a moment it might be valuable to consider the poor impresario who listens to hundreds of singers as a matter of duty, knowing that he cannot use them and that he simply cannot listen to so many with the attention and interest they may deserve. I sometimes wonder if I do not unconsciously develop a negative attitude towards a singer's name simply because he once sang for me at a time when I did not need him. All that remains in my memory is the fact that I did not engage him, and perhaps this tends to create the suspicion that he wasn't good enough.

Admittedly, it is not easy for a singer, especially a newcomer, to discover which impresario is in need of his particular brand of vocal and artistic goods. But by keeping his ears open, by consulting his musical friends and colleagues and, if necessary, by employing an agent whose business it is to unearth this information, the ambitious singer can usually increase his chances for success and avoid the frustrating effects of indiscriminate auditioning.

In order to make a good impression in auditions, a singer should avoid two other pitfalls: he should shun obscure arias and he should refrain from acting out the pieces he has chosen to perform. When I listen to an aria from a standard opera, I am able to form an immediate and very precise opinion of the singer's vocal equipment and musical talent. On the other hand, when I am confronted with an unfamiliar selection, my attention is apt to focus on the composition rather than the performer. Not knowing, furthermore, how well this particular music can be interpreted by an accomplished artist, I cannot be certain that the singer I am hearing is doing it full justice. It is equally unwise to attempt to act out an aria in audition. Normally singers are heard in halls which are completely bare of all theatrical trappings (scenery, costumes, props, or partners). Under these conditions, a display of stage movement and gestures almost invariably produces an unpleasant or even ridiculous impression. It is enough if a singer succeeds in convincing his listeners that he thoroughly understands the character of his role and the meaning of the words he is singing. This can be done with a minimum of theatrical attitudes.

Sooner or later every reasonably gifted singer has a successful audition and is given a chance to prove himself. An engagement, however, means relatively little in itself; it is the re-engagement that counts. Many young artists imagine that if their debut is applauded by audience and critics, they have nothing more to worry about. But audience acclaim has only a minor influence on producers. Such commonplace virtues as punctuality, dependability, and courtesy are an indispensable part of a performer's professional equipment. Besides doing his job well, the young singer should devote his energies to being quick, useful, cooperative, and pleasant; in short, to being someone people enjoy having around. These observations may seem picayune, but I can remember several occasions when I did not re-engage a man with a serviceable voice simply because he was more trouble than he was worth. It is the singer who combines artistic ability with a disciplined professionalism and an even-tempered disposition who is considered valuable and often indispensable. And once he achieves this kind of reputation, an impresario is only too happy to recommend him to other producers when he cannot use him himself. These recommendations are the true building stones of a lasting career. Like many of my colleagues, I am reluctant to engage an unknown quantity, and a solid recommendation from a fellow producer means more to me than scrapbooks of reviews.

True, there are certain very successful singers who are reputed to be very disagreeable. But these belong to the handful of internationally famous names known in managerial parlance, as "box-office attractions." Becoming one of these stars is a matter of luck as well as talent and personality, and the dedicated beginner should not depend on lucky breaks. Too often young performers are fascinated by the trappings of success and the glamorous facade of our profession. They grow up in the belief that their ultimate goals are fame and wealth. This is a very common delusion. Many years of observing the world of music have convinced me that the two enduring satisfactions in an artistic career are: (a) using your talents regularly for a high artistic purpose, and (b) being respected by those members of the profession whom you happen to admire. Comfort and security are also desirable, of course, but they are much less fundamental to an artist's well-being.

This is just another way of saying that an artist finds his most profound and lasting pleasures in partnership with greatness.

～7

Operatic stage direction

CONSIDER the intricate nature of opera. Audiences listen and look; they hear words which are sung and music which is played by the orchestra; they behold a variety of sights, such as scenery, properties, costumes, lighting; and, above all, they see the singers—their appearance, facial expressions, gestures, and movements on the stage. The impressions that reach the audience have many meanings in terms of words, music, and sights, and of the overall mood and level of excitement. The beholder responds to all these impressions intellectually, emotionally, and aesthetically. A clear understanding of opera and, particularly, a sensible discussion of its problems is naturally enormously complicated by this great number of components and the endless subtleties of their interaction. To make things even more difficult, several of these components, such as the theatrical impact of instrumental music and the details of bodily movement, do not lend themselves to a description in words. This is undoubtedly the main reason that there are so few books dealing with the technique of operatic acting and staging.

In the process of working with singers, the stage director does of course use words and explanations, but there are three other important ways in which he can awaken the sensitivity of the performers and communicate his ideas and desires to them: (*a*) he can sing and act out fragments of the role, thus demonstrating the relevant musical-dramatic connections; (*b*) he can have portions of the score played on the piano for them; and (*c*) he can manipulate the singers bodily and save himself a great deal of time and cumbersome verbal description. The four main methods of live instruction are therefore: explanation, demonstration, music-making, and manipulation. Since only explanations are possible here, perhaps the most effective way of dealing with this subject is to present an example and analyze it in detail. Before doing so, however, it will be useful to make a few general observations about the task of actors, singers, and stage directors as they relate to a play, a libretto, and an opera.

A play is a story which is acted out while it is recited; an opera is a story which is acted out while it is sung with an orchestra. Both the actor and the singer deal with an existing text, with words which have to be brought to life in a theatrical setting, but the problems confronting them are by no means identical. In at least one important respect, their tasks are diametrically opposed. While the singer's vocal lines are already in existence, the actor has to compose his own. The actor may not think of himself as a composer, but by necessity he has to perform many of the composer's duties. For purposes of stage presentation, the words provided by the playwright are hardly more than a framework. Each sentence of the actor's script can be read in dozens of different ways, depending upon emphasis, intonation, intensity, spacing, timbre, mood, and tempo. This is equally true of the length of the pauses and the timing of all theatrical business, so that practically all the nuances of the execution are left to the discretion of the actor and the stage director. Even when the playwright has very definite and precise ideas regarding the method of delivery, he has no adequate notation for indicating his intentions to the performer. In this respect, the opera composer is in a much more favorable position. He pre-sets the melodic contour, the accents, and the length of each syllable in each work; he indicates the loudness and softness and all the fluctuations of swelling and decreasing tone; he gives directions for the tempo and all its gradations; he spaces not only the words in each sentence, but also the rests between the sentences and he pre-sets as well, the overall duration and timing of the theatrical actions.

The actor in the spoken play starts out with a verbal blueprint and only gradually develops the details of his delivery from his understanding of the role and its motivations. The operatic vocal score, on the other hand, furnishes most of these details and the singer's task is not to invent inflections and timings, but to realize the composer's expressed wishes in the most convincing manner. A trained singer encounters no special difficulties in following the composer's interpretation of the verbal text. If needed, the voice teacher, the vocal coach, and the conductor are available to see that this task is performed to the limit of the singer's ability.

But words, whether sung or spoken, are only a part of the activities of actors and singers. Of at least equal importance is the appearance and behavior of the performer. This includes posture, facial expressions, gestures, placement within the scenic picture, changes of position, movement in relation to the scenery, props, other characters, lighting, and so on. In theory these elements of the production are subject to the stage directions given by the playwrights and the librettists, but in reality they differ from performance to performance, depending upon the scenic background and upon the imagination and talent of stage directors and the actors themselves.

Here again music provides much more specific guidance than the sketchy stage directions found in the script or libretto. Through the details of the vocal line, and particularly through the orchestral music, the composer is in a position to control the timing, the mood, and quite often, the dramatic significance of the action.

The theatrical message implicit in the orchestral part of the score is particularly important in the strictly instrumental sections, and it is at this point that the singer needs help from the director most urgently. While the singer delivers his vocal line, he is seldom in doubt regarding the type of behavior which is appropriate, but without the text to guide him, he is apt to stand around helplessly waiting for his next cue. A sensible interpretation of these instrumental sections in opera requires a full mastery of the language of music, as well as a thorough knowledge of the theater. A stage director who is equal to the task can guide the singer to an impersonation of the role which completely blends with both the words and the music. The staging and the acting must reflect, justify, reinforce, and complete every detail of the verbal and musical text.

The role of the stage director

When helping singers to develop suitable stage behavior, the beginning director will find it useful to distinguish between general and specific activities. General activities fit all roles and all situations. No matter whom they impersonate, all singers enter and leave the stage from time to time; all of them walk from one spot to another, sit down, get up, gesture, and address other singers. Of course, these actions are important and must be executed with great skill, but the director who bases his entire mise-en-scène solely on this type of behavior will hardly win the respect of his company or the admiration of his audiences. To give substance and zest to a performance, actors must depend on other, more specific activities.

General and specific activities can be compared to the ingredients in a soup. General activities are like the water in the soup and specific ones like the solid elements and the condiments. To prepare soup, water is indispensable, but without certain amounts of meat, fish, vegetables, spices, and wines, all soups would taste pretty much alike. Similarly, if a singing actor limits himself to walking right and left and making an occasional gesture while wearing different costumes, he will be serving up the same watery broth for all his roles in slightly different soup tureens.

It may be argued that the primary responsibility for devising specific actions rests not with the stage director, but with the librettist. Operatic characters are engaged in drinking, dancing, writing letters, strumming guitars, hiding in dark corners, fighting, being wounded, and dying. These activities are thoroughly characteristic and specific, and they are part and parcel of the actions indicated by the librettist in the score. And one could add that operatic plots abound in actions of even more individual flavor, actions so exceptional that the mere mention of them identifies the personage, the situation, and the opera. To pick at random, what could be more specific and unique than displaying a volume containing the names of hundreds of women seduced by one's master? Or stabbing one's beloved in front of a bullfighting arena? Or committing hara-kiri in the presence of one's child? Or presenting a silver rose to a lovely young girl? No opera lover can fail to identify these actions, which are quite definitely the fruit of the librettist's and not the stage director's imagination. It would be truly ungrateful to minimize the importance of characteristic actions invented by the authors of the texts. But no matter how imaginative and diligent a librettist may be, he cannot possibly indicate more than a fraction of the specific elements needed in an adequately staged operatic production.

The conscientious director is apt to wonder whether or not his staging ideas coincide with those which the creators themselves had in mind. Doubts of this kind had beset me regularly until a lucky accident succeeded in reassuring me for all time.

In the summer of 1959, in connection with my duties as head of the opera school of the Berkshire Music Center in Tanglewood, I was preparing the premiere of Jan Meyerowitz's one-act opera *Port Town*. In one of the early scenes of this charming work there is an argument between a policeman and a group of boisterous sailors. The Cop (as he is called in the opera) tries to clear the square in front of the dock by urging the sailors to go into the corner saloon. At first they pretend to obey him, but when he turns his back, they startle him with one last thunderous outburst. Immediately after this unexpected vocal fortissimo, the orchestra adds one more measure of truly monumental explosion where trumpets and trombones, reinforced by a snare drum, join the winds and the strings in an earsplitting guffaw which then quickly subsides into a fairly long postlude, during which the sailors exit. The plot of the opera calls for an empty barrel which later serves as a hiding place for a young girl. Since I was using this barrel in the sailors' chorus, I decided to take advantage of it for the noisy orchestral passage, and I made the sailors roll it at the Cop. This idea served several purposes: it moved the barrel to its proper playing position for later events, it dispersed the sailors and thereby made their retreat to the saloon more gradual, but most important of all, it provided a wonderful visual counterpart to that rampaging orchestral measure. The rolling of the barrel, the Cop jumping to protect his toes, the sailors moving like a tidal wave behind the barrel, all fitted the energy and timing values of the music perfectly. Unfortunately, neither the libretto nor the score gave any stage directions at this point and although I was very pleased with the effect of my staging, I was a little afraid that the composer's theatrical ideas might not coincide with mine.

About a week before the premiere, Jan Meyerowitz came to Tanglewood and was naturally asked to help us put the final touches on the production. As soon as he saw the episode with the rolling barrel, he gave loud expression to his delight.

"What a wonderful idea!" he said. I was greatly flattered, of course, but also curious.

"What staging did you have in mind here?" I asked him.

"I had nothing special in mind," he answered. "Why should I? I am not a stage director."

"But you composed this extraordinary orchestral passage," I retorted in some amazement. "You must have had *something* in mind here."

"Of course I did," he said. "This passage shows the sailors' state of mind, their boisterousness and rowdiness. I am a composer. I put the inner life of my characters into my music. You are the stage director. It is your business, not mine, to exteriorize this inner life, to make it visible."

Meyerowitz's words were a revelation to me, and the more I thought of them, the more clearly I realized that he expressed the true relationship between the composer and the stage director more accurately than I could ever have done. I feel sure that most opera composers of the past identified with the characters of the play as Meyerowitz does. They relived their thoughts, feelings, moods and cravings. They entrusted to the voices and to the orchestra what Meyerowitz so aptly termed the "interior" meaning of the drama. To bring out the full theatrical value of these interior meanings, one must make them *exterior*, make them visible and fully comprehensible to the beholder. While it is essential that the singers think and feel in character, this alone has no theatrical value. Their thoughts and emotions must be projected to an audience forcefully and with the utmost clarity. In this sense one might say that the composers create the ideas of the work and that the performers, guided by the stage director, give these ideas their external shape, their actual life and power.

We know that at one time there were no stage directors and that the composers themselves were held responsible for the behavior of the singing actors. How did they interpret the theatrical values of their vocal lines and their orchestral interludes? Not too much is known on this subject, but even if we could learn more about it, I doubt if it would substantially influence our attitudes in this respect. Performance procedures change and develop; they depend on the state of theatrical technology and also on the whims of fashion. It is not likely, for instance, that Mozart could have staged the Countess' cavatina in *The Marriage of Figaro* along the lines I choose to do it. For one thing, the Countess could hardly have begun to sing as far upstage as she does in my staging. The lack of adequate illumination in the theaters of the eighteenth century would have made such a position sadly ineffective. Many other procedures which today's singers take for granted would have been similarly unacceptable in Mozart's time. Consider the increased fluidity of movement in our stagings, or such generally accepted modern practices as turning one's back on the audience or singing while showing one's profile and walking. But while the details of operatic execution vary from generation to generation, the essential attitudes of musicians remain surprisingly stable. One needs only to read Mozart's letters to his father on the subject of *The Abduction from the Seraglio*, or study Wagner's minute instructions for the acting out of the aria of the *Flying Dutchman*, to become aware to what extent their approach is identical with ours.

How a stage composition is developed

When studying the example in this chapter, the reader may get the impression that the staging has been developed by cold logical computation. In reality this is not so. Although it is true that there are a great number of elements involved, the stage director does not deal with them as separate entities. He thinks simultaneously with his intellect and his musical ear; he evaluates the stage picture as a painter, an architect, a psychologist, and with a dancer's understanding of distance, movement, and muscular effort. Obviously, no one can possess all these qualities in the same degree, and depending upon an individual stage director's background, the relative importance given to these facets may vary greatly. In one way or another, the various verbal, musical, pictorial, and muscular ideas coalesce, and the staging composition emerges as a completely satisfactory answer to all the various requirements.

To find this completely satisfactory answer, the best way to begin is to study the libretto. This acquaints the stage director with the story line, the characters and their interaction, and helps him in general to visualize the work in terms of what happens. A careful analysis of the music will stimulate his ideas in regard to how things happen. In addition to these basic sources of information, many valuable hints can be obtained from the plays, novels, and short stories on which the plots of the operas are based. The staging of the opening of the second act of *The Marriage of Figaro*, which concludes this chapter, contains many details derived from the two Beaumarchais plays dealing with the characters found in Mozart's opera. Such a basic fact as the Countess' age, for instance, is not given in the libretto. The embroidery screen, which is one of the key props in my staging of this act, has also been suggested by an incident in one of the Beaumarchais comedies. In an earlier chapter, the Santuzza and Filippo pantomimes provided still other examples of the use of background texts.

Thirty years ago, when I was beginning my operatic activities, many of the plays and novels on which the operas are based were practically unobtainable, but this situation has changed, and it is much less difficult today for a young stage director to find and consult these texts. A short bibliography at the end of this volume will facilitate this task still further.

There are a few operas composed to completely original texts (such as *Così fan tutte, Aida,* and *Der Rosenkavalier*), for which no additional information can be found. The obscurities and inconsistencies in these works can be cleared up only by inventing one's own explanations. In the Appendix, the reader will find an example of such an explanatory essay; to unravel some of the mysteries in *Aida,* I invented a fictional letter written by Radames to his uncle. The ambitious young stage director may want to contribute to this fascinating form of operatic research by providing a comparable explanation for Mozart's *Così fan tutte.* Such a background text could tell us much about Fiordiligi and Dorabella (why do they live alone? where are their parents? what is their social position? how do they happen to know Don Alfonso?). It might throw a more realistic light on Despina's astonishing virtuosity as a quick-change artist and perhaps give us a better insight into the personalities of Ferrando and Guglielmo. If nothing else, such exercises in fleshing out operatic librettos are excellent means for strengthening one's powers of imagination and stimulating one's original thinking.

To be sure, the mechanism governing originality and creativity is quite mysterious. When questioned, stage directors who possess it usually assert that brilliant solutions reach them in a flash. But there are obviously many for whom it is not so easy. After questioning a number of people in the field, I found that while less gifted practitioners have to work their way through a great number of potential solutions, their more creative colleagues, shielded from more pedestrian notions by a sort of "protective filter," consider only very few alternatives. These men are rarely confronted by more than two or three valid possibilities, and since one of these is usually clearly superior to the others, their final choice is rapid and seems to appear as though in a flash. Looking more closely into the concept of the "filter," I have found that the less gifted contingent also uses a screening process. They do not, after all, consider any possibility that comes their way, but only those that make, let us say, dramatic sense. To the more gifted stage directors these dramatically sensible ideas are often quite "obviously" not worthy of consideration because they do not make sufficient musical, spatial, or timing sense. It thus seems apparent that the more brilliant stage directors use a number of filters simultaneously, while the others rely on a single criterion or use different filters separately, thus greatly impairing their ability to arrive at completely valid results. Clearly, it is necessary for operatic stage directors to develop all their filters to the maximum of their abilities and to learn to use them simultaneously. This can be done only by increasing one's knowledge and understanding of all the components which make up the operatic theater. The staging composition presented here seems to satisfy all the requirements, but I am well aware that there are any number of other solutions which would strike other directors with equal force.

THE MARRIAGE OF FIGARO, ACT II: The Countess' cavatina

Mozart's *The Marriage of Figaro* offers most instructive opportunities for the study of operatic stage direction. Not only is Da Ponte's text a skillful adaptation of Beaumarchais' justly famed comedy, but the analysis of the plot is further facilitated by the additional information found in *The Barber of Seville*, Beaumarchais' earlier play dealing with the same characters. The Countess' cavatina which opens the second act of the opera is particularly well suited to our purposes. Since the words of its text offer no hint of any theatrical action, the director has to rely entirely on the message contained in Mozart's score. Needless to say, the Countess' stage behavior should not only do justice to the immediate situation and the music, but it must be integrated with a prescribed scenic setting and coordinated with the larger aspects of the story.

The setting

The libretto calls for a very elegant room with an alcove, three doors, and a window. One of these doors serves as the main entrance, and the other two lead respectively to Susanna's quarters and to a small dressing room. Beaumarchais' scenic directions mention in addition a large bed in the alcove and a raised platform in front of it. The instructions in the play and in the score concerning the relative positions of the window and the doors are quite specific. I prefer a different arrangement, one which gives greater prominence to the dressing room which plays such a vital role in the action of this act. But—since at this point we are primarily interested in the Countess' cavatina and how to do theatrical justice to her mental and emotional state—a discussion of later events of the plot would lead us too far afield. The scenic background is only of minor importance in this context, except that it is, of course, impossible to arrange a mise-en-scène of any portion of a play without knowing the exact placement of the scenery and the props. Diagram 7–1 gives us the basic information we need.

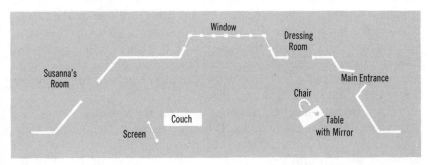

Diagram 7–1

The couch and the dressing table are normal furnishings of a lady's boudoir, and they are of invaluable assistance in the grouping and regrouping of the nine characters who take part in the startling events of this act. The embroidery screen, however, is an invention of mine and requires an explanation. It is introduced here principally because it gives the Countess a quiet and suitable occupation for the opening tableau of this act, an occupation, furthermore, that can be justified by other evidence. We know from *The Barber of Seville* (Act 2, Scene II), that the Countess used to embroider when she was a girl in her guardian's house, and it is not illogical to assume that she would occasionally indulge in this pastime after her marriage, especially at times when her husband leaves her to her own devices. In my staging of the opera, this large embroidery screen has still another raison d'être, inasmuch as it is used later in the act as a protective shield behind which Susanna can hide during the C-Major trio. However, this need not concern us now.

The story

"Three years make a marriage so respectable!" These words, spoken by the Count in the fifth act of Beaumarchais' play, inform us that the Almavivas have been married a relatively short time. In *The Barber of Seville* Rosina could not wed Count Almaviva without the consent of her guardian, and it is evident that she is still a very young woman, at the most in her early twenties.

This is the Countess' first appearance in the opera. She is alone and voices her unhappiness by addressing a touching prayer to the god of love. It is a *lamento*, a musical complaint of the type that was considered indispensable in the operas of the seventeenth and eighteenth centuries. We cannot blame the Countess for feeling dejected. It became apparent to us in the first act of the opera that the Count was chasing after girls. There was a mention of the gardener's daughter, Barbarina, and of course we ourselves saw him making advances to his wife's chambermaid, Susanna, and promising her a dowry if she would submit to his desires. Susanna has no intention of gratifying the Count's wishes, and at some point between the first and the second acts, she confides the whole story to her mistress. The opening sentences of the conversation which follows the opening aria make it clear that the Countess had been fully informed before the curtain opened on the second act.

Beaumarchais' play has no monologue for the Countess—his second act opens with the conversation between the mistress and the maid. Later in the act, however, during her altercation with her husband, the Countess voices a sentiment which is closely akin to the mood of the aria: "I am no longer the Rosina whom you pursued so ardently," she says. "I am the poor Countess Almaviva, the sad, forsaken wife whom you no longer love!" This feeling of being "la pauvre femme délaissée" (the sad forsaken wife) is the essence of the emotional content of the aria which opens the second act.

> Porgi amor qualche ristoro
> Al mio duolo, a miei sospir:
> O mi rendi il mio tesoro,
> O mi lasci almen morir.
>
> Grant me, Love, a ray of comfort,
> See my suffering, hear me sigh.
> If you can't restore my treasure,
> Then, I beg you, let me die!

Were these lines spoken in a play, the actress could easily introduce a number of stage activities. She could wring her hands, shed an occasional tear, pace up and down, or invent some other theatrical business to be performed before, after, or during these lines. On the other hand, she could also recite this quatrain without a single gesture or change of position while either standing or sitting down in any part of her room. There is, after all, only one single thought expressed here: "I want to regain the love of my husband." In other words, the performer could consider many possibilities and choose the one best suited to her taste and talent. In the opera, on the other hand, the emotional state of the Countess has been detailed for us in Mozart's music, and this music carries an important and, in many respects, quite specific message.

The vocal line and its orchestral accompaniment

A glance at the vocal line shows that Mozart arranges for two pauses between the lines and sets their duration at two and a half measures for the first interlude and at one and a half measures for the second one. Furthermore, Da Ponte's original quatrain is expanded to eleven and a half lines in the sung text:

1. Grant me, Love, a ray of comfort,
2. See my suffering, hear me sigh.

First Pause—Orchestral Interlude No. 1

3. If you can't restore my treasure,

Second Pause—Orchestral Interlude No. 2

4. Then, I beg you, let me die,
5. Then, I beg you, let me die!
6. Grant me, Love, a ray of comfort,
7. See my suffering, hear me sigh.
8. If you can't restore my treasure,
9. Then, I beg you, let me die,
   yes, let me die!
10. If you can't restore my treasure,
11. Then, I beg you, let me die!

We have here a repetition of complete lines as well as parts of lines. The "let me die!" idea is emphasized not only by the recurrence of the thought in the fifth, ninth, and eleventh lines, but also by the vocal progression to the high A-flat, by adding the wind instruments and a crescendo at this point, and finally, by the extra length of the high note. (See measures 34 and 35, through the fermata in measure 36.) When the opening sentence returns in the sixth and seventh lines, the dissonant harmony entrusted to the bassoon gives a strong added poignancy to the word "sigh" (see measure 38).

It is standard operatic procedure to emphasize certain ideas of the text by repeating them and by melodically and harmonically highlighting them, although it is true that no composer has ever employed these devices with more skill and subtlety than Mozart. One of the purposes of this chapter is to demonstrate how the stage director can help the singer to reflect such textual and musical masterstrokes by means of movement and action.

What many singers fail to understand is that the theatrical impact of their performance must be continuous, and the impression they are making must not fade into nothingness the moment they stop singing.

Many fine vocalists seem to function in a sporadic, intermittent manner—
the characters they portray seem alive only while they sing. It then becomes the duty of the stage director to help them fill out the role when
they are silent. In watching first-rate operatic impersonations, one is
not aware of any noticeable change in the total theatrical impact between
the vocal and the purely instrumental sections.

The instrumental prelude

Mozart prefaces the Countess' opening utterance with an important
orchestral prelude entrusted to strings, clarinets, bassoons, and French
horns. The seventeen measures of this introduction fall into five distinct
episodes:

1. (measures 1 and 2) A short preliminary section to accompany the
   raising of the curtain.
2. (measures 3–6) The main theme introducing the Countess, played
   by softly singing strings.
3. (measures 7–10) A sudden interruption of the quiet mood by an
   exclamatory motive in the winds. Strong conflict of emotions
   evident in the alternation of forte and piano sections.
4. (measure 12 and first half of 13) Hesitation and worried uncertainty (syncopated strings) lead to a feeling of dejection (deceptive cadence), followed by (second half of measure 13 and measure
   14) a sudden energetic decision to act.
5. (measures 15–17) Breakdown of energy. A descending soft arpeggio
   of French horns leads to a mood of resignation.

This attempt to describe the orchestral introduction to the cavatina
illustrates the difficulty, one might almost say the futility, of using words
in connection with musical phenomena. Musicians are justly annoyed by
the vagueness and arbitrariness of such terms as "worried uncertainty,"
"energetic decision," or "mood of resignation" when referring to unique,
vivid, and organically interrelated musical phrases. Non-musicians are
only led astray by such circumlocutions. The only purpose of the preceding section was to point out that instrumental music is composed of
episodes of various lengths, each of them representing a complex of
meanings which have a close (though not easily definable) kinship with
thoughts, moods, and bodily movements. Having made this point, I shall
proceed directly to the staging itself, hoping in this way to demonstrate
how musical and theatrical concepts can be combined into a meaningful
and consistent entity. Once a singer or a stage director has become fully
aware of the relationship between musical and dramatic events, he begins
to experience vocal and instrumental music in human and theatrical terms

and to connect it with the psychology of the characters, with the story, the setting, the props, and with all the other theatrical elements which, along with the music, make up the totality we call opera.

The staging of the cavatina

Measures 1 and 2. The curtain rises. The Countess, sitting near the right corner of the couch, is busy embroidering flowers on a large screen which is standing to her right.

Measures 3, 4, 5, and 6. Although she pretends to be calm, the Countess is quite upset. Susanna has told her of the Count's attempt to bribe her into submitting to his amorous desires, and the Countess does not know how to deal with this shocking revelation. She is a little afraid of her dominating and imperious husband and does not dare to bring the matter into the open by asking for an explanation. It is early afternoon, and the Countess is aware that her husband is planning to go hunting, but she half expects that he will come to see her and kiss her good-bye before he leaves. She is slightly indisposed and is wearing a negligee. She hopes that the emotional shock she has suffered has not affected her appearance. Under the circumstances it is important that she look her best. She finally decides to pretend to be her usual calm self, to work on her embroidery, and to wait for her husband. The Count does not arrive, however.

Measure 7. Unable to pretend any longer, the Countess turns toward the main entrance. She is visibly upset. ("I wonder if he is still in the castle and if he will come to see me, after all!"*)

Measure 8. The Countess resumes work on her embroidery. ("I must take hold of myself and must not make a mountain out of a molehill!")

Measure 9. The Countess becomes even more concerned and turns toward the window. ("Has he really gone away without bothering to inquire whether I feel better!")

Measure 10. The Countess turns to face downstage. ("What shall I do? I can't just sit here and pretend that all is well!") She gets up, fighting to keep back her tears.

Measure 11. Trying to reach a decision, the Countess stands at the couch.

Measure 12 and first half of 13. The Countess picks up the screen, intending to carry it to its normal resting place in the right corner of the room. She stops, however, after a step or two and puts down the screen. A new thought strikes her—the idea of death makes its first appearance here, as the descending scale runs into a deceptive cadence. She shakes

---

* It must be clearly understood that the lines in parentheses do not appear in either Beaumarchais or Da Ponte, but are my own personal deductions of what the Countess is thinking.

her head sadly. ("If that's what life has in store for me, I would rather be dead!") This interpretation of the meaning of the deceptive cadence is confirmed later, in measure 43, when the same musical sequence is verbalized in the vocal line.

Second half of measure 13 and measure 14. The Countess shakes off her despondency and makes a courageous decision. ("I will find him and present him with an ultimatum!") She turns toward the main door and goes left, crossing above the couch. The music has an almost military mood. ("I will repeat to him what Susanna told me, and let come what may!")

Measure 15. By the time the Countess gets near the door, the weakness of her position becomes apparent to her. ("He will deny it, and then what can I say? He was so looking forward to this hunting trip . . . he is probably gone by now . . .")

Measure 16. The Countess turns and goes to the window, hoping to catch a glimpse of her husband riding away, but the Count is nowhere to be seen. The Countess' thoughts become filled with a strong yearning for the love of her husband. ("I must win him back through the power of my love!")

Measure 17. The Countess turns away from the window and faces downstage.

Measures 18 through the first half of 25. The Countess sings, addressing her lament to the god of love. She faces toward downstage left and imagines the deity high in the air beyond the walls of the auditorium. Considering the loveliness of the melody and the subdued character of the string accompaniment, any additional emphasis in the form of gesturing or bodily movement is unnecessary and disturbing at this point. A pleading tone of voice, coupled with expressive phrasing and clear enunciation, will take care of all the musical and theatrical values of this episode.

Second half of measure 25 and measure 26. The clarinets introduce the instrumental interlude with the phrase which was first enunciated in the seventh measure of the prelude by the violins. The energetic quality of the earlier passage is now softened and spiritualized by the tenderness of the Countess' amorous pleading. Thinking of her husband, she moves toward the main entrance (crossing above the dressing table to up left of it). ("If he could see me now, I am sure I could persuade him that I am still his own lovely Rosina!")

Measure 27. The Countess notices the hand mirror which is lying on her dressing table, and this changes the trend of her thoughts. ("But am I still the lovely Rosina whom he courted three years ago? Or has my beauty faded, and is this perhaps the reason that he is attracted to younger and prettier girls?") She turns and goes down right to the left side of the dressing table.

Measure 28. She picks up the hand mirror with her right hand and then turns her head to address the god of love over her left shoulder.

Measure 29. As she sings, she passes the mirror into her left hand.

Measure 30. The Countess extends her left arm so that she can look at the reflection of her face in the mirror.

Measure 31. The sight of her pale, suffering face makes her feel sorry for herself. She replaces the mirror on the table and backs up slightly, to up left of the chair.

Measures 32 and 33. The Countess is now facing down right. This is the first mention of death, and the thought affects her strongly enough to repeat the phrase on a higher level of emotional and physical energy.

Measure 34 through the fermata in measure 36. These two measures, culminating in the fermata, represent the vocal climax of the cavatina. Until here the singing line was accompanied only by softly playing strings, but now the clarinets and horns (joined later by the bassoons) support the crescendo of the vocal progression, as well as the sustained forte of the Countess' high A-flat. Carried by the force of this emotion, she crosses above the chair and goes right to up right of the table.

Measure 36 (after the fermata). Compared with the effusion of the preceding phrase, the music assumes a much quieter tone. The softness of the string accompaniment should not deceive us, however. The decided nervousness of the vocal line (a syllable to each sixteenth note) makes it clear that the preceding episode has not dissipated all the energy of the Countess' emotion.

Measure 37. Feeling her tears welling, she takes a small handkerchief from the left sleeve of her negligee and lifts it to her left cheek.

Measure 38. A hot tear falls on the Countess' left cheek (G-flat of the bassoon), and she wipes it off lightly, holding the handkerchief in her right hand.

Measures 39 and 40. The Countess looks over her left shoulder, in the same direction where she earlier imagined the god of love.

Measure 41. The Countess looks toward down right and goes to the left corner of the couch. (While it is possible for her to stand still at this point, I feel that the emotional urge of the ascending scale calls for a certain amount of bodily expression.)

Measure 42 and the first half of measure 43. The thought of "not wanting to live," which made its first appearance in the instrumental prelude (measures 12 and 13), now finds its complete verbal and emotional expression. ("When I thought of it earlier, I was angry, but now I see that I really meant it.")

Second half of measure 43 and measure 44. The chords in the wind instruments give this quiet vocal phrase a certain solemn dignity. ("I am not going to weep . . . I am just going to die!") The Countess wipes the tears from her right cheek and puts the handkerchief back into her left sleeve.

Measure 45 through the first half of measure 49. She turns to face down left and backs up a step or two. Her final sentence sums up her determination. The vocal line must sound almost like an ultimatum to the god of love: *"Either* restore my treasure *or* let me die!"

Last half of measure 49 to the end. This is the postlude. The Countess has decided that her husband's love shall be restored to her, no matter what the cost. She does not know how she will go about the task of regaining it, but she is ready to take the necessary steps, whatever they may be. She goes left to the dressing table and sits down in order to repair the damage done to her lovely face by her sorrow and her tears.

I am often asked where the stage director gets his ideas for blocking the overall pattern of a scene and for motivating its stage movement in a situation, such as the one that was just discussed, where the words do not suggest any associative connections between the thoughts of the characters and different stage locations. What, for instance, does the Countess think about in this cavatina? About her husband, obviously, but also about the god of love and about death. This much we know from the plot and from the words she is singing. Furthermore, it is very likely that the Countess wonders why her husband is neglecting her for other women and whether or not she is still attractive enough to compete with her rivals.

Let us now try to establish connections between these thoughts and the scenic picture. Where is the Count? He is either in his own apartments (outside the main door of the Countess' boudoir), or in the park of the castle (and this suggests the window). What about the locations of such abstract ideas as "the god of love" and "death"? Here we must create more artificial connections. Since the main entrance is upstage left and the window is upstage center, we will choose two other, different locations—down left for the god of love and down right for death. But that is not all. A woman concerned about her looks wants to consult her mirror, and that points to the dressing table. Finally, the music in the beginning of the introduction seems to call for a quiet tableau, and that brings us to the one location which has not been utilized so far, namely, the couch.

The grand plan of the staging demands that the different sections of the music each have its own, separate acting areas. Once the necessary connections between thoughts and locations have been established, the general blocking falls into place almost automatically. The introduction plays near the couch; the main theme of the vocal line, by the window; from here to the dressing table for the middle section, and to the center for the final episode. The wish to see her husband motivates the Countess' walk from the couch to the door and thence to the window; the desire to consult the mirror takes her to the dressing table; and finally, the thought of death makes her move to the right, toward the center of the stage.

It is essential that such a skeleton framework of the action be completely established before the director starts working out the details of the scene. When this foundation is securely built, the rest becomes a matter of musical perception and of acting technique. If one is fortunate enough to have a gifted and well-trained cast, it is surprising how much of this elaboration can be left to the talent and imagination of the singers themselves.

~ 8

Vocal ensembles and choral scenes

IN CONTRAST to the spoken drama, where words are generally delivered by only one person at a time, the vocal lines in opera are often uttered simultaneously, resulting in an orderly and harmonious ensemble.

The problems of staging vocal ensembles often mystify directors who come to opera from the legitimate theater. To excuse their perplexity, some of them take refuge behind the fiction that in these portions of opera "drama stands still and music takes over." Nothing could be more erroneous. With the sole exception of the dialogues that are spoken between musical numbers in certain lighter types of opera, operatic music and drama are not separable entities. One might as well say about a human being that there are occasions when "his blood stops circulating and his breathing takes over."

Vocal ensembles may present a theatrical riddle, but they also offer their own very special staging opportunities. As soon as one becomes aware of the clues contained in the distribution of vocal lines, the mystery is dispelled. The grouping of the voices provides a perfectly simple and logical set of additional stage directions. To give these vocal groupings a visual counterpart on the stage, one follows two main rules:

1. Characters whose vocal lines *belong together* should be kept in physical rapport with each other.
2. Any distinctive or unusual musical feature of the vocal ensemble must be dramatically motivated and staged.

The arrangement of groups of singers, as well as their re-formation into new ones can often be read directly from the pages of the score. In the example (8–1) from the second-act quintet of *Carmen* it is clear that what was at first a closely knit cluster of five singers suddenly dissolves into a solo and a quartet. If Frasquita moves away from the others, her physical person becomes as isolated and highlighted as her vocal utterance.

Example 8–1. CARMEN, II, no. 14

To make this move dramatically believable, the director must give Fras-quita a special reason to separate herself from her companions and go to another part of the tavern.

Another "picture" of a stage grouping is taken from the second-act finale of *The Marriage of Figaro* (Example 8–2). It is quite obvious that the seven characters are divided into three groups: a quartet, a duet, and a solo. In the fourteenth measure of this passage, the Countess joins Figaro and Susanna; we are then faced with only a quartet and a trio.

The vocal groupings in a score are not always as clear, in terms of visual representation, as in the two preceding examples. In the following excerpt from the sextet in *Don Giovanni* (Example 8–3) it is not im-mediately apparent that we are dealing with what I call a "shuttle" ar-rangement. The two duet groups—Anna-Ottavio on one side of the stage and Zerlina-Masetto on the other—take turns addressing Elvira, and she, by adding her voice, transforms each duet into a trio. The stage grouping I recommend here is

OTT ANN   ELV   ZER MAS

so that Elvira can shuttle back and forth between the singers on her right and those on her left.

Example 8–2. THE MARRIAGE OF FIGARO, II, Finale no. 15

Different types of ensembles

The application of the first rule pertaining to vocal and stage group-ings can be studied with excerpts from the final fugue of *Falstaff*. The second rule will be illustrated by a number of passages from such diverse operas as *The Marriage of Figaro, Così fan tutte, Don Giovanni, Hansel and Gretel, The Bartered Bride,* and *Faust.*

The famous final fugue from the epilogue of *Falstaff* provides the best possible illustration of how groupings of vocal lines can be matched with stage groupings of the individuals who sing them. It demonstrates that a purely theatrical technique of stage movement can be applied to

* In most published scores the vocal lines of Susanna and the Countess are re-versed, but I believe the distribution given here is more logical.

Example 8–2 (continued)

a musical composition and made more interesting to the eye, much clearer for the ear, and infinitely easier to learn and perform.

Applying the technique of fluid groupings and regroupings to this epilogue may seem especially surprising because, when it is sung, the play as such is finished. The ten principal characters of the drama and the chorus have become almost dehumanized voices, presenting only the moral of the fable:

All in the world is folly,
Man is born to be jolly!
All are deceivers, nothing is sacred under the sun.
But there's no harm in laughter that is meant just for fun!

As these sentences pass from character to character, each vocal line seems to consist of a chaotic collection of contrapuntal fragments. When

Example 8–3. DON GIOVANNI, II, Sextet no. 19

the pieces are set side by side and fitted together, this frighteningly complicated web is suddenly transformed into simple melodies that are astonishingly easy to comprehend and to learn. Between measures 42 and 46, for instance, we can fit together no less than four duet groupings (Examples 8–4 through 8–7).

Example 8–4. FALSTAFF, III, sc. 2

Example 8–5

Example 8–6

Example 8–7

If, at this point in the ensemble, the various duet groups are kept in direct and close rapport, the entire "composition" comes into focus and the participants can not only sing comfortably, but can also act to each other. The grouping I like to achieve by measure 42 of this fugue is:

PIS FOR BAR   CAJ FEN   QUI   MEG   ALI NAN
                                          FAL

Looking at it from stage left to stage right: Nanetta and Alice curtsey to each other, Meg and Quickly circle (Cclw) around Falstaff and point at his fat belly, Fenton and Cajus bow to each other, and Ford addresses first one and then the other of his neighbors. Falstaff, who does not sing for four measures, can stand with his back to the audience. As Meg and Quickly walk around him, he also rotates in a Cclw direction. Just before measure 46, after a full circle and a half of this rotation, they end up as:

MEG FAL QUI

and Falstaff can comfortably address Quickly, who now stands to his left.

If all this is so simple, the reader may ask, why couldn't these characters be placed in this line-up from the very beginning of the fugue? This would be impossible, because in earlier sections the vocal lines are arranged in groupings that are totally different from the one shown for measure 42. Between measures 25 and 29, for instance, Nanetta, Meg, and Cajus are entrusted with a closely knit and most important trio passage where they sing identical words and rhythms (Example 8–8).

Example 8–8

When the performers stand near each other, this type of ensemble phrase offers no difficulties whatsoever. Were Nanetta, Meg, and Cajus grouped in measure 25 as they appear in measure 42, they would not hear each other clearly and the coordination of their rhythms and pitches would suffer accordingly. In my staging of the fugue, the line-up in the beginning of measure 25 is:

CAJ

FEN QUI ALI   MEG   NAN

This arrangement permits the trio on stage left to function as a single unit and to address the group located to their right. It also enables Quickly to cross the non-singing Alice in order to answer the trio singers, while Fenton addresses himself to Alice. This maneuver can then be repeated in measure 27, with Alice and Quickly changing places.

These transitions from one grouping to the next are accomplished by three quite elementary procedures:

1. Characters having several measures of rests can go to their next destinations by crossing above their singing partners.
2. Characters who have to change their grouping while singing must cross below non-singing partners.
3. To make room for the newcomers in the group, the other singers must adjust themselves by means of the accordion technique discussed on pages 61 and 62.

Naturally, all this must be carefully planned well ahead of time by the stage director.

Opera lovers who are used to a permanent and motionless grouping during ensemble sections of this type may object that having singers act and move around might make them lose track of the music. Quite the opposite is true. As a matter of fact, it was my experience with the rigid line-up that led me to the development of this system of fluid groupings.

My first encounter with *Falstaff* took place in the fall of 1934, when I was assisting Fritz Reiner with the productions he was conducting in the Philadelphia Orchestra's season of operas. The singers were excellent musicians and had been drilled for many weeks. Yet when it came to the final number of this opera, some member of the ensemble would invariably miss an entrance. The difficulty of this fugue became a subject of endless discussions and admonitions. The tension grew to such a point that, in the intermission before the last act of every single performance, all the singers were asked to assemble in one of the rehearsal rooms and the entire fugue was sung over two or three times. When actually performing it, the singers stood motionless, counting the beats and measures of their rests and desperately looking for entrance cues, which were thrown to them not only by Reiner, but also by the prompter and by two musical assistants placed in the wings.

Matching stage groupings with those of vocal lines helps to banish this nightmarish fear of committing an inaccuracy. With this method singers are cued and prompted in the most natural and musical manner by the lines their own partners sing in the immediate vicinity.

I have produced Falstaff many times, both with professionals and students, and have never had the slightest problem with this final fugue. On one occasion—at the end of a performance held in 1947 in the old Boston opera house—I decided to prove the point and had the entire fugue sung and acted without conducting it at all. It went very smoothly. When staged according to vocal groupings, this piece turns out to be remarkably simple.

Among distinctive and unusual features of vocal ensembles, I would list canonic and other contrapuntal imitations, sudden changes in dynamics, and unexpected and prolonged rests.

The term *canon*, or *canonic imitation*, refers to a form of voice leading where, in the words of Grove's dictionary: ". . . one voice begins a melody which is imitated precisely . . . by some other voice, either at the same or a different pitch, beginning a few beats later and thus, as it were, running after the leader." The final words of this definition hint at possibilities for the visual interpretation of these canons. The stage character entrusted with the voice that is "running after the leader" can imitate whatever actions the leader is performing. In translating these canons into stage movement, the director must make certain that the singers understand both the choreographic intent of their actions and the dramatic reasons behind them. Here are a few examples chosen from the operas of Mozart, who was particularly fond of this device.

In Duet No. 5 from *The Marriage of Figaro* (Example 8–9), Marcellina and Susanna have just come face to face at the main entrance to the room. Each refuses to be the first to leave. To show their determination they walk away from the door. Marcellina leads and Susanna follows. Four measures later Susanna, who does not wish to be outdone by her rival, assumes the leadership and Marcellina becomes the follower.

In Duet No. 20 between Fiordiligi and Dorabella in *Così fan tutte*,* the canon found expression in a dance movement that was motivated by sheer vitality. Dorabella led the action both times and then waited for Fiordiligi to follow her.

Whenever possible, the second character's "delay" should be justified by the dramatic situation. In the canons just discussed, for instance, Marcellina and Dorabella initiated all previous activities, and the canon sequences helped to reinforce this relationship between them and their followers.

In the preceding two examples the imitating voices sang the same pitches as their leaders, but canonic imitations also occur at different melodic distances and can produce a variety of unusual musical effects,

* See pp. 121–125, for a detailed discussion.

Example 8–9. THE MARRIAGE OF FIGARO, I, Duettino no. 5

all of which should be faithfully reflected in the stage action. Example
8–10 shows a canon sung at a distance of a whole tone by Donna Anna
and Zerlina in the sextet from *Don Giovanni*. I find these dissonances
extremely suggestive. It is as if something or someone were being painfully
sawed in two. I have Anna and Zerlina sing this canon standing in a
threatening posture over the kneeling Leporello, who holds his hands
over his ears as if terrorized by both the sounds and the menacing gestures
of the two women.

Example 8–10. DON GIOVANNI, II, Sextet no. 19

Not all imitative passages turn out to be true canons, incidentally. Quite often the follower starts out with the same notes as the leader, but later pursues a different melodic path. The important thing to remember is that all delayed imitations lend themselves particularly well to dramatic paraphrases. There is a moment in the second act of *The Marriage of Figaro*, for instance, where Susanna and Cherubino discover that they are locked in the Countess' room (Example 8–11). Since there are two doors in this setting, Susanna can try one and Cherubino the other. I have them go to their respective doors in the preceding measure, but I place them so that Susanna is much closer to her door. While she is turning the knob, Cherubino is still running toward the door on the opposite side. Obviously he cannot sing his lines until he discovers that his door is also locked.

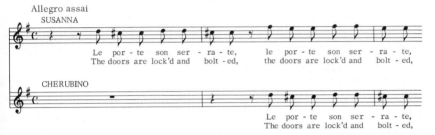

Example 8–11. THE MARRIAGE OF FIGARO, II, Duettino no. 14

Sometimes a delay can be justified by some unusual condition in the mental or physical make-up of the person who follows the leader. In the example (8–12) from the sextet of *The Marriage of Figaro* the delaying voice belongs to a man who stutters. In my staging of this moment Curzio tries to begin his phrase at the same time as the Count, but his preliminary stuttering gets in his way and creates a very amusing effect that is completely in character.

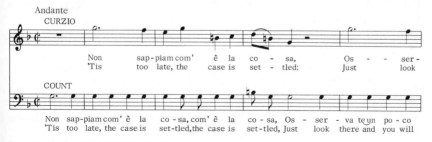

Example 8–12. THE MARRIAGE OF FIGARO, III, Sextet no. 18

An example (8–13) from *Hansel and Gretel* shows how even very minor vocal events can be converted into appropriate visual equivalents. The passage in question occurs in the Forest Scene, at the point when the children kneel down and fold their hands in prayer. During the first eight measures they sing together, mezza voce, with an accompaniment of pianissimo strings. After Hansel finishes his phrase in the eighth measure, he stops and does not rejoin Gretel until the tenth measure. Here the orchestra embarks on a poco crescendo which gets still louder in the twelfth measure, but then retreats quite unexpectedly into a whispered pianissimo subito. I feel that this sequence of events is worthy of special attention. In my staging of this passage, Hansel stops singing because he falls asleep. Noticing this, Gretel nudges her brother with her elbow. Hansel wakes up with a slight start and then resumes praying with such fervor that his sister has to calm him down by putting her finger to her lips, thus bringing about the sudden pianissimo. When timed correctly and performed with the required delicacy, this little byplay produces the most enchanting effect.

In the last musical illustration, the two crescendos were notated only in the orchestral portions of the score. The absence of these indications in the music allotted to Gretel and Hansel is neither a mistake nor an accident. Symbols referring to degrees of softness and loudness are frequently omitted from vocal lines. It is generally taken for granted that, whenever it is felt to be necessary, orchestral dynamics may be automatically interpreted as being applicable to the lines sung on stage.

The opera singer's basic approach to vocal loudness and softness was discussed earlier. (See p. 173) In ensemble scenes it is often desirable to give these nuances additional dramatic significance. The total effect of a sudden forte or piano can be greatly enhanced by carefully coordinating the behavior of the singers.

Two examples from the first act of *Così fan tutte* demonstrate the type of concerted action that I have in mind. At the end of the opening scene of this opera we find a series of phrases where sotto-voce singing alternates with a full-throated forte (Example 8–14). During the orchestral introduction preceding the first sotto-voce passage I feel that the two officers and their friend, Don Alfonso, should pick up glasses filled with champagne. Their forte sentence can then be highlighted by having all three of them raise their arms in a salute to the god of love. Before the next two soft phrases they can clink their glasses and get into a conspiratorial huddle. With the successive forte sentences they again raise their glasses, thus illustrating the *brindis replicati*, the repeated toasts that the winners of the bet propose to drink in the future to celebrate their victory.

Example 8–13. HANSEL AND GRETEL, II, sc. 2

Example 8–14. COSÌ FAN TUTTE, I, no. 1

In the first garden scene of this opera, an effective bit of ensemble action accompanying a suddenly subdued vocal passage can be added to the "tears-and-laughter" quintet. In my staging of this episode the second piano subito (Example 8–15) is emphasized by a correspondingly sudden, emotionally motivated gesture of the two couples. After gazing rapturously at their fiancés, Fiordiligi and Dorabella turn away from them and sink into each other's arms as if unable to endure any longer the sight of the lovers from whom they will so soon be separated. The loss of vocal energy is thus reflected in the emotional and physical collapse of the two sisters. Ferrando and Guglielmo's gentle whispers are translated into solicitous embraces, designed to console the grieving young women. Incidentally, this visible acting-out of the second soft passage helps to motivate Don Alfonso's reaction. Amused by these exaggeratedly emotional farewells, he guffaws and tiptoes to the opposite corner of the garden, where he can give vent to his fit of suppressed laughter.

The activities of non-singing partners have been discussed at some length in preceding chapters. Techniques mentioned earlier have included the art of listening and reacting, as well as the knack of devising special occupations and distractions. In ensemble scenes, this problem acquires a new dimension, and it is occasionally necessary to have a singer leave the scene temporarily or permanently.

Removing a character permanently from the scene of action is something that, under normal circumstances, is planned and arranged by the playwright. Sometimes, however, opera librettists and composers become so engrossed in the activities of the singers that they do not provide any motivations for the exits of an important silent character and, in fact,

Example 8–15. COSÌ FAN TUTTE, I, no. 9

seem to forget about his very existence. These oversights, which must be rectified by the stage director, are fortunately rare.

The need to remove a character from the scene temporarily arises much more frequently. This procedure is indicated when one of the members of the ensemble is silent for a long period of time and it is less awkward to take him from the stage than to keep him there.

The sextet from the last act of *The Bartered Bride* presents an unusual situation that involves removing one character permanently and another temporarily. During the scene that precedes the sextet Mařenka receives seemingly incontrovertible proof of Jeník's unworthiness. Her position becomes even more difficult when young Vašek identifies her as the girl who flirted with him earlier. He is delighted to discover that she is the one who has been chosen to be his future wife. Observing the eagerness of the formerly reluctant groom, the marriage broker, Kecal, urges Mařenka to sign the document pledging her consent to the match, but the unhappy girl asks to be left alone for a few moments of solitary meditation. Seeing the tears in her eyes, her parents, the marriage broker, and her future in-laws feel that they should grant her this favor. Before leaving the stage, however, they join in consoling the crying girl by assuring her that marrying Vašek is really in her own best interests.

As for Vašek, neither the score nor the libretto gives any clue to his actions. Since he does not participate in the sextet, he should not be present. Looking for a suitable motivation for Vašek's exit, I noticed the prolonged rests in the vocal lines of his parents. During the opening seventeen measures of the sextet his father, Míha, is completely silent and his mother, Háta, sings only intermittently. Taking advantage of these periods of silence, I imagined the following sequence of events: when Mařenka begins to cry. Vašek feels so sorry for her that, although he does not know why she is miserable, he also begins to snivel; Kecal, who does not want Vašek to make a poor impression at this point, signals to Háta that it would be wise to get the boy out of the way; she leads her son to Míha and, while the orchestra plays the introduction, both father and son leave the stage; Háta accompanies them part of the way and then returns to join the others. After her first sentence she turns to look for her husband; after her second sentence she goes to fetch him and beckons him to come back, so that by the eighteenth measure of the sextet they are both in position to address Mařenka. Thus we see that the distribution of vocal lines in this ensemble suggested and helped motivate three forms of activity: Vašek's permanent exit, Míha's temporary exit, and Háta's division of attention between those who remained on stage and those who had left it.

In staging ensemble scenes it is useful to distinguish between similar and contrasting situations. In most of the examples cited so far the characters on stage expressed nearly identical sentiments. As a result, both the vocal and orchestral music was always applicable to everyone present on stage, whether or not he happened to be singing. For instance, even if Miha had remained on stage during the opening seventeen measures of *The Bartered Bride* sextet, the music sung by the others and played by the instruments would not have been incompatible with his feelings and silent thoughts.

In situations involving contradictory moods expressed by different characters, the problem becomes more complicated. Here singers and stage directors must adjust to the inevitable discrepancies between the music and the divergent actions. Such a conflict can be observed in the quartet that closes the third act of *La Bohème*, where a spirited quarrel and a tender love scene must be acted out at the same time. Fortunately, the pace at which this episode moves is so rapid that, in places where the music highlights the behavior of one couple, the other pair can easily fill in with unobtrusive background actions. In operas where contrasting sections are elaborated at length, the authors themselves usually arrange for a temporary absence of the non-participating characters.

A series of such departures and re-entries can be studied in the quartet from the Garden Scene of *Faust*. It consists of a succession of alternating courtship duets, one tender and the other cynical. Marguerite and Faust depart first, leaving Marthe and Mephisto alone. After a while the situation is reversed, and it becomes Marthe's and Mephisto's turn to relinquish the stage to the returning couple. Both of these temporary absences are ostensibly prompted by the participants' desire to take a walk in the garden that surrounds Marguerite's cottage. One must bear in mind, however, that unless the underlying motives of the characters are clearly communicated to the audience, the various exits and entries can all too easily turn into rather contrived and mechanical staging devices.

The mise-en-scène must make it clear that Marguerite and Marthe expect to remain together and that it is Mephisto who detains and befuddles the older woman in order to keep her from interfering with the growing romance of the young couple. During Marthe's chatter Mephisto must keep an eye on the offstage activities of Faust and Marguerite, and it is only when he notices that they are ready to return that he steers Marthe into the wings. In staging this sequence of events the director must see to it that the author's intentions are made sufficiently believable and presented with proper clarity. When arranging, on the other hand, for an exit not contemplated by the librettist, he must proceed very circumspectly and weigh with great care all arguments for and against it.

At the beginning of this very same quartet scene I consider it highly desirable to delay Marguerite's confrontation with Faust. We know that the girl's thoughts have been filled with the handsome stranger ever since her return from church. When Faust appears so suddenly and without warning, we would expect her to have a very strong emotional response to him. But the music Gounod provides for the entrance of the two men concerns itself exclusively with Mephisto and Marthe. The feelings of Marguerite and Faust are completely ignored by the orchestra, and the two protagonists usually stand around most awkwardly, waiting for their turn to sing. Since at this crucial moment neither of them is, musically speaking, aware of the other, I consider it much better if they do not see each other until later. This can be easily arranged if Marguerite leaves the stage before the entrance of Faust and Mephisto. Taking back the spinning wheel which she carried in earlier provides a simple and logical reason for her to return to her house. Now that her neighbor has come to visit her, spinning and similar chores cannot be continued until later, and everything outside and inside the cottage must be put in perfect order.

When first pondering the advisability of making this change in the conventional mise-en-scène, I found several excellent arguments in favor of it, but also ran into one major difficulty that had to be resolved before taking Marguerite from the stage could be seriously contemplated. On the positive side was the fact that her first words after the arrival of the men give the impression that she has not heard Mephisto's announcement of the death of Marthe's husband. If she hears Marthe's startled exclamation while she is still inside the cottage, or just as she opens the door to re-enter the garden, her own worried "Qu'est-ce donc?" (What is wrong?) becomes much more logical. As she runs to Marthe's assistance, Marguerite, who is still wearing the jewels, suddenly finds herself face to face with Faust! Now the tremolando in the strings, the crescendo in the trombones, trumpets, and kettledrums, and the poignant A-flat that alters the innocent C-Major harmony all fit her surprise, shock, and embarrassment to perfection.*

But what about Mephisto's earlier aside to Faust, pointing out that the jewels had been "well received"? If Marguerite is not on stage at that moment, this remark has to be justified in some manner not envisaged by the librettists. I solved this problem by having Marthe not only admire the jewels, but by having her actually try on a necklace. When Mephisto enters, he catches the older woman in this act and makes her feel guilty. After her short and somewhat embarrassed question, "Qui m'apppelle?" (Who is calling me?), she hurriedly removes the necklace, replaces it in the casket, and walks away adjusting her clothing, all the while trying to recapture her customary aplomb. This entire by-play helps to "protect" Mephisto's aside, which under the circumstances assumes a much more humorous character.

Naturally it is debatable whether or not the advantages of this new arrangement outweigh its drawbacks, and I realize that other stage

---

* Someday I hope to find a Marguerite who can emulate Eleonora Duse's fabled ability to blush at will. What a splendid opportunity this musical and dramatic moment would give her to display her rare gift!

directors could quite legitimately disagree with me on this point. All changes in the music, the text, or the dramatic meaning of an opera are in the final analysis subject to individual evaluation. The aspiring stage director will find the technique of removing characters from the stage extremely useful, but he must keep in mind that it lends itself to abuses. I must particularly warn against the practice of removing non-singing partners for the purpose of turning operatic scenes into solo arias. Whether it is done in order to simplify or to flatter the ego of a singer, it always results in a serious violation of both the letter and the spirit of the operatic theater.

Scenes with soloists and a chorus

The duet with chorus (No. 5) from *Don Giovanni* and the "Morceau d'Ensemble" from the third act of *Carmen* will demonstrate that the method of staging according to the distribution of vocal lines is applicable to scenes involving choruses as well as to ensembles of solo singers.

In the scene from *Don Giovanni*, a number of peasants join gaily in the wedding festivities of two of their companions, Zerlina and Masetto. The bride and groom look forward to the joys of married life and advise their friends to follow their example and find themselves loving mates. Even though Zerlina and Masetto playfully call each other "sposa" and "sposo" (bride and groom), their wedding has not yet taken place, a fact that offers much amusement to their friends. The men find a vicarious pleasure in alternately encouraging and restraining the groom; the women make it their business to protect the bride from any untoward and premature slip. This gives rise to much playful teasing, during which Zerlina and Masetto are first kept apart and then allowed to join each other.

This duet with chorus consists of an orchestral introduction and three stanzas of a lilting, G-Major, allegro theme in 6/8 time. The seventeen-measure orchestral introduction, which accompanies the entrance of the wedding party, is made up of five sections of alternating loud and soft phrases. These sections are arranged in unusual lengths of three, four, three, two, and five measures, respectively. The unexpected forte entrances in the seventh and thirteenth measures produce an additional effect of irregularity.

In the first stanza, Zerlina presents the theme in her sixteen-measure solo and takes it toward a new ending in the key of the dominant; in a seven-measure chorus the girls second Zerlina's sentiments and reinforce her D-Major conclusions.

The second stanza begins with Masetto's seventeen-measure solo, in

which he sings a slighly different version of the music, first in the dominant and then returning to the tonic. The fellows repeat Masetto's tonic
ending with enthusiasm.

In the third stanza, Zerlina and Masetto sing a twelve-measure duet,
voicing a new and somewhat shortened variation of the theme in which
all attempts to escape into other tonalities are abandoned. Eight measures
of mixed chorus and an orchestral postlude of three measures celebrate
a similarly unchallenged G-Major contentment.

In spite of the great difference in the lengths of the individual
phrases, the basic structure of this piece is extremely simple and can be
described in four words: entrance, women, men, everyone. To give dramatic meaning to this sequence of events, I start the staging with a mock
quarrel between the fellows and the girls. As a result, the women decide
to go off by themselves and pretend to exchange secrets. When the fellows try to eavesdrop, they are shooed away unceremoniously. Next the
men decide to play the same game, and it is the girls' turn to become
curious. After everyone has had his fun, Zerlina and Masetto have a reconciliation while their friends make certain that the couple do not
offend propriety and keep at a respectable distance from each other.

The scenic setting is the same as in Elvira's and Leporello's scenes.*
During the orchestral introduction, all the peasants enter through the
gate on the right. Masetto and the fellows enter first and form an aisle
with the men divided equally on each side. Masetto hides behind the first
two peasants on the right.

Subtext (measures 1 through 3):

MEN: "Let us follow that lucky Masetto, that lucky Masetto."

Zerlina enters, followed by the girls (Diagram 8–1).

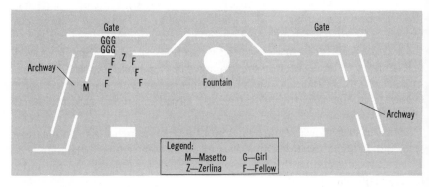

Diagram 8–1. Position at the end of measure 3

* See pages 166 and 225.

Subtext (measures 4 through 7):

GIRLS: "This is truly a wonderful day, a wonderful day, a wonderful day!"
MASETTO: "You are mine!"

Zerlina is looking for Masetto and expects him to be among the men on the left. Not finding him there, she turns to her right (with the second "a wonderful") and again to her left to see if he has gone toward the left bench. As soon as she turns away, Masetto comes out of hiding and embraces her from behind with "you are mine" (Diagram 8–2).

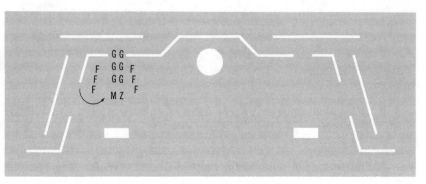

Diagram 8–2. Position at the end of measure 7

The girls run toward Zerlina and help her break loose from Masetto.

Subtext (measures 8 through 10):

MASETTO: "Now I've caught you, you won't get away!"
GIRLS: "Just leave her, we say! Just leave her, we say!"

While the girls admonish the fellows, Zerlina goes down left toward the left bench. With the second "just leave her" the girls go left to Zerlina (Diagram 8–3).

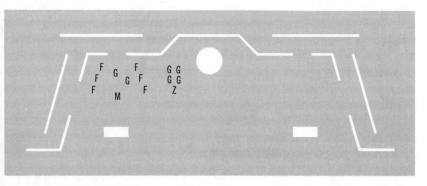

Diagram 8–3. Position at the end of measure 10

In measures 11 and 12 Zerlina turns (her subtext: "Go away, go away!") and motions Masetto and the fellows to go and leave the girls to themselves (Diagram 8–4).

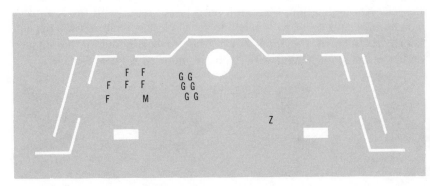

Diagram 8–4. Position at the end of measure 12

Zerlina turns and goes to up right of the left bench. The girls energetically repeat Zerlina's admonitions and then turn and go to surround her. The fellows slink away and group themselves to the right of Masetto (Diagram 8–5).

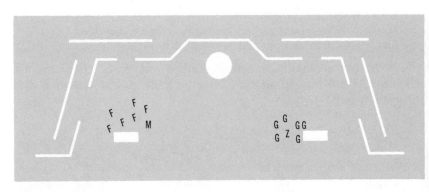

Diagram 8–5. Position at the end of measure 17

Subtext (measures 13 through 17):

GIRLS: "Don't you dare to come near her, go away! Here we come, here we come, but speak softly, we pray!"

At the beginning of the first stanza, Zerlina and the girls form a tight semicircle. In the fourth measure of this stanza, Masetto and the men start tiptoeing toward the left, trying to overhear what Zerlina is saying.

She notices them in the beginning of the seventh measure and waves them away. They pretend to obey her, but start coming back again in the tenth measure. Zerlina and the girls shoo them away more energetically (she does it in the twelfth and thirteenth measures, the girls do it in the first and second measures of their own singing). The men retreat to the right bench, where they surround Masetto. The girls use the last four measures of their chorus to return to Zerlina's left. They want her to continue to talk to them, but Zerlina is stopped when she hears Masetto's voice at the beginning of the second stanza.

In the fifth measure of this stanza, Zerlina starts moving toward the men, beckoning the girls to follow her (notice the cajoling violin octaves). At the beginning of the seventh measure, Masetto and a few of the fellows wave the girls away. They retreat and act offended, but nevertheless they eye the men coyly over their shoulders. In the thirteenth measure, Masetto turns to Zerlina and stretches out his arms, inviting her to come to him. She does so and, while the men sing, the bride and groom dance, circling to center, where they are surrounded by a semicircle of couples who come running to each other from both sides (Diagram 8–6).

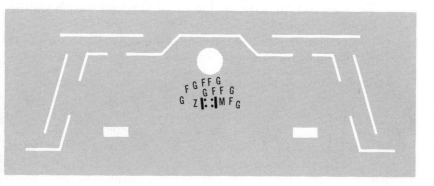

Diagram 8–6

Zerlina and Masetto arrive in the center holding hands, but, as they begin their duet in the third stanza the girls pull the bride away and the men do likewise to the groom. The lovers are thus forced to separate slightly, but in the eighth and ninth measures of their singing they turn to their companions and motion them to step back. In the last two measures of their duet Zerlina and Masetto embrace, upon which their friends start circling around them, singing. In the fourth measure of the final chorus the entire group of peasants dances off to the right. During the orchestral postlude they notice Don Giovanni, who came in a little earlier through the left gate. The girls curtsey deeply and the men bow with much respect.

The "Morceau d'Ensemble" from the third act of *Carmen* is essentially a gay song of praise addressed to Frasquita, Mercedes, and Carmen, whose special talents are needed to help their friends, Dancairo and Remendado, out of an annoying predicament. During the spoken dialogue* that precedes this ensemble it became apparent that the gypsies' project of smuggling British merchandise into Seville is endangered by an unexpected change of customs guards. Learning the names of the new sentries, Frasquita, Mercedes, and Carmen burst into laughter and tell the others not to be concerned. It appears that the gay charmers know these guards only too well and will be delighted to sidetrack them in order to remove all danger of interference. When Don José angrily shows signs of jealousy, Dancairo orders him to remain behind, proceed to a nearby rocky height, and act as a lookout.

While studying the mise-en-scène of this ensemble, the reader should keep these points in mind:

1. Dancairo is the chief of the gypsy band; Remendado is its lighthearted buffoon. These two men are not given any individual singing lines in this ensemble; they sing along with the tenors of the chorus.
2. Frasquita and Mercedes are the sweethearts of Dancairo and Remendado, respectively.
3. For the sake of brevity, Frasquita, Mercedes, and Carmen will be referred to as the "trio."

Looking at the grouping of the vocal lines in this ensemble, we find four distinct arrangements: trio alone (A); trio with the chorus of women (B); trio with everyone (C); and trio with the chorus of men (D). The sequence and duration of these sections can be represented by the simple scheme A B C D A B C—A (8 measures), B (8 measures), C (8 measures), D (8 measures), A (8 measures), B (6 measures), and C (14 measures). The purely orchestral sections are restricted to a two-measure introduction and a twenty-nine-measure postlude, during which all the gypsies march off toward Seville.

Having identified the four basic groupings, we must allot to each a separate location on stage. In my own staging of the preceding events of this act, I reserve the upstage left area for the bales of merchandise that were brought in by the smugglers; most of the campfires where the women were cooking food are distributed along the right side of the stage, and a special chest used for the fortune-telling business is placed in LB2. Before allocating the various areas, we must decide how best to occupy Dancairo, Remendado and the chorus members when they are not singing. Since the gypsies are now about to depart for Seville, a few obvious

---

* The spoken lines in the original version of the opera are, dramatically speaking, much more informative than the sung recitatives added by Ernest Guiraud after Bizet's death.

preparatory chores immediately suggest themselves. The men, under the guidance of Dancairo and Remendado, can busy themselves with the merchandise and decide which of the bales are to go to Seville and which, for the time being, should remain behind. The women can pack away the cooking and eating utensils and extinguish the campfires. This places the men upstage left, the women on stage right, leaves the chest area for the trio, and still keeps the center of the stage for the sections when everyone sings together.

Now ready to go ahead with the blocking of the mise-en-scène, we can start to fill in a few details. During the orchestral introduction the trio groups itself around the chest while the rest of the gypsies proceed to their allotted areas and get ready for the departure. In the last two measures of the A section the trio singers move to stage right, where they are soon surrounded by the women of the chorus. The men, in the meantime, continue to sort out the bales. Near the end of the B section the entire band of gypsies moves toward the center of the stage and gets ready for the next episode. The staging of this portion of the piece must reflect its special vocal effects: the three explosive ensemble shouts, each answered by a solo line sung by a member of the trio, with a final solo sentence of Mercedes added at the end.

Here I make use of Remendado, who, as the comedian of the outfit, cannot resist the temptation to play the fool. In the first tutti measure, he dances with his own girl friend, Mercedes, who rewards him with a pat on the cheek. Next he kneels before Carmen, who laughs at him and walks away. Finally, with the third choral shout, Remendado waltzes with Frasquita, who takes advantage of her answering line to slap him on the wrist. Now Mercedes makes believe that she is jealous and, with her final solo sentence, takes possession of Remendado while Dancairo joins in the fun and pretends to scold Frasquita for being a flirt. This playful interlude leads to Section D, during which the women of the chorus return to their chores around the campfires while the girls of the trio and all the men form three separate groups strung out in the upper part of the stage between the left wing and the center. While Carmen sings with the basses, the tenors split up into two groups: the first joins Dancairo and Frasquita as the second crowds around Remendado and Mercedes. In the remaining portion of this vocal ensemble the basic A B C pattern of the three opening sections is repeated: down left (around the chest), then to the right (by the campfires), and finally to the center. Variations in the distribution of vocal lines are again mirrored in the stage movements and groupings. During their one moment of respite (the fourth measure of the second B section) Frasquita and Mercedes run to fetch their sweethearts, while Carmen remains with the altos of the chorus. Toward the end of the second C section the men return to the bales, lift them on their shoulders, and, with their last vocal measure, get ready to march offstage.

Large choral scenes

At the end of the section dealing with the technique of the proscenium stage (page 57) I indicated several methods to make groups of singers look more natural and attractive. When staging massive choral scenes, however, the director is faced with new problems since he is dealing now with clusters of singers rather than single characters. Before considering the best manner of placing the participants and bringing them to life, he must decide on the best arrangement of the vocal parts, and this decision hinges not only on the dramatic context, but on the purely musical aspects of each choral situation as well.

From the musical point of view, we must distinguish between the homophonic style of choral writing, where all the voices sound together in harmonic blocks, and polyphony, in which the several parts move independently or in imitation of each other.

In homophonic choruses it is usually desirable to have the women mingle with the men, and in general to distribute the voices in such a manner that each group of singers has a fair representation of all vocal parts. People expressing the same sentiments normally tend to assemble in "close-friendship" or "family" gatherings. Arrangements of this type not only look more atttractive and convincing from the theatrical point of view, but also help to insure a truer intonation in singing and a smoother blending of the voices. The chorus of peasants and domestic servants in the first act of *The Marriage of Figaro* (Example 8–16) is a typical example of a homophonic chorus that looks and sounds better if the choristers mingle in such a seemingly random fashion.

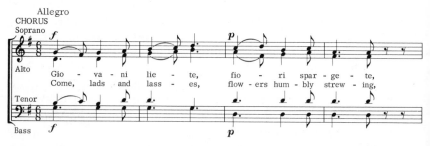

Example 8–16. THE MARRIAGE OF FIGARO, I, Chorus no. 8

Polyphonic choruses, on the other hand, gain in clarity if the various musical lines are kept in correspondingly separate stage groupings. In these choruses we must distinguish between those where several voice parts move in imitation of each other, and those where the entire chorus is fragmented into independent dramatic groupings that first function separately and then are combined and musically superimposed on one another.

When dealing with imitative polyphony—which seldom occurs in standard operas—the director should endeavor to give a clear visual equivalent to the entrances and progression of the vocal lines. The March of the Priests near the beginning of the Triumphal Scene from *Aida* provides a fine example of such polyphonic imitation. The four groups intoning the theme enter at intervals of three measures (Example 8–17), and end with a so-called *stretta,* where the voices follow each other in close succession (Example 8–18).

Fragmentation of the choral masses into dramatically independent units is much more common and is found in operas of all types and styles. A completely satisfactory and effective handling of such choruses must be based on a careful analysis of their musical, verbal, and dramatic content.

Normally, each of the heterogeneous groups is given its own distinctive words and musical phrases. If, however, several groups participate in a related form of activity, they will, without necessarily uttering the same words, often share the same musical theme. A typical example of such treatment is found in the opening number of the "Kermesse" scene in *Faust* (Act I, sc. 2). Although the chorus here is divided into six clearly differentiated vocal units, the music features only four thematic ideas. The three groups that are presented first—the student drinkers (baritones), the soldiers (basses), and the older burghers (first tenors)—are each given their own characteristic phrases; the next three groups—the young girls (sopranos), the cavaliers (second tenors), and the older matrons (altos)— share the same music (Example 8–19) and act out three variations of a similar dramatic theme. These can be described as aggressive flirtation, reluctant flirtation, and competitive flirtation. After the six groups make their separate musical and dramatic entrances, the young girls and matrons start a quarrel that is observed and commented upon by all the men except the baritones, whose devotion to drinking makes them impervious to any distractions.

When planning the mise-en-scène of intricate choruses which are fragmented into several characteristic units, it is wise to begin by considering which stage locations the various groups should occupy during the climactic passages, when all the participants are present and singing simultaneously. In this instance it is obvious that in the final fifty-nine ensemble measures the most important and vigorous action is performed by the quarreling sopranos and altos. The women, therefore, should be given the use of the central portion of the stage.

Example 8–17. AIDA, II, sc. 2

Example 8–18

Example 8–19. FAUST, II, no. 3

Having made this basic decision, the director must next arrange positions for the three groups of men who observe the fighters and for the baritones who ignore them. A simple way to segregate these groups is to divide them among the down-right, up-right, down-left, and up-left stage areas and to provide some platforms or other elevations from where the upstage observers can watch the squabbling ladies.

The façade of the tavern, which is used later for Mephisto's wine trick, is usually placed on stage left. Let us give this tavern area an upstage terrace and allocate this elevation to the older burghers, since at this juncture they sing not only of their nagging wives, but also of the wine which they they are sipping. The down-left section of the stage area adjoining the tavern entrance is obviously the habitat of those single-minded drinkers, the baritone students. To make their disregard of the other participants more believable, we should arrange to have a low wall or fence separating the outdoor portion of the tavern from the square proper.

The situation on stage right should not offer any great difficulties. Since the quarreling women constantly refer to the young cavaliers, these second tenors can quite logically occupy the down-right portion of the square, which happens to be the most convenient focal area for the glances and gestures of the fair contestants.

Finally, the soldier basses, whose remarks about women have a more general character, can fill the up-right platform, which will later be occupied by the musicians playing—or rather pretending to play—the waltz.

During the final section of this choral scene, therefore, the stage with its two elevated areas, would be apportioned as in Diagram 8–7. Once these locations have been chosen, the director should decide how to move these various groups to their final destination in a manner that is consistent not only with their words, but also with the character and duration of their music.

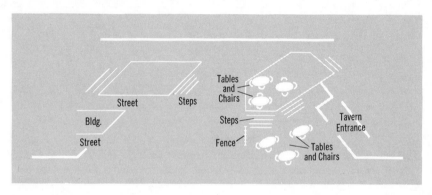

Diagram 8–7

Disregarding for the moment the twenty-six measures of the orchestral introduction, let us proceed directly to the opening F-Major vocal portion sung by the baritone students and their ringleader, Wagner. This choral contingent is obviously on its way to some serious and dedicated drinking. Some of them are already seated at the outdoor tables of the tavern and urge the others, who can be scattered in the center, to join them. At the end of this initial section most of the students can go inside the tavern where, predictably, they will order additional libations.

Next comes the B-flat-Major section featuring the bass soldiers. Since their singing is preceded and followed by an eight-measure military march, complete with snare drum and trumpet, it is wise to start them from offstage and give them plenty of space for their entrance and exit. I have them come in from up left, above the tavern terrace, and leave the stage through the street that leads into the down-right wing. The sound of the military music attracts the attention of the older men, who assemble on the up-right platform. The "parade" should also be watched by a few women who emerge from the two streets on stage-right as well as by others who ascend to the tavern terrace by way of an upstage stairway. As the soldiers march off, these women also drift away, leaving the stage to the tenors who are now located on the elevation and ready to embark on their portion of the choral sequence.

Having listened to the basses brag of conquering fortresses and feminine hearts, our senior citizens return to the main key of F Major and declare that they do not mind being armchair generals and gladly leave all real war-making to their younger colleagues. Daydreaming of a pleasant holiday on the banks of a quiet river, they become thirsty and wend their way toward the tavern, where they eventually secure glasses of wine and take possession of the terrace overlooking the square.

It is at this point that the modulation into D Major brings us to the middle section of this choral number with its three variations on the theme of flirtation. There is a four-measure introduction during which the young sopranos enter from the right. Noticing that they are being followed by the cavaliers, the girls slow down to give the young men a chance to catch up with them. Filling the area adjoining the tavern wall, they throw inviting glances toward the second tenors. These fellows have indeed followed the eager young women both physically and musically, but—as they tell us in their G-Major paraphrase of the music—they are being careful to "hold on to their hearts." As a result of the young men's defensive tactics there is an open space left between the sopranos, who huddle to left of center, and the cavaliers, who remain in the down-right area of the square. This space is now usurped by the altos, who enter from upstage left and brazenly intone a C-Major version of the flirting theme, claiming to be at least as desirable as their young rivals.

During the singing of this sixth and last isolated group, the baritones emerge from the tavern and the basses re-enter the stage from up right to ascend to the elevated position on the right platform. Since the first tenors secured their places on the tavern terrace somewhat earlier, we have now not only arrived at the exact distribution of groups indicated in Diagram 8–8, but have also clarified the relative placement of the sopranos and altos.

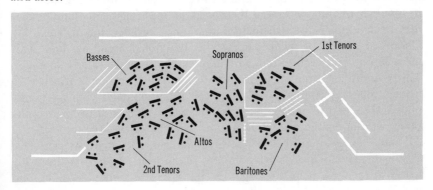

Diagram 8–8

To add variety and energetic movement to this grouping, the director can take advantage of the two occasions when the women stop singing for four measures. As they face each other, the two battling contingents can first rotate in a wheel formation, exchanging their right-left positions, and can later use similar maneuvers to return to their original locations. During the orchestral postlude the intervention of the cavaliers and soldiers helps to separate the ladies and to prevent their verbal brawl from deteriorating into a hair-pulling contest. The outraged women either flee of their own accord or are led away by the men so that, as the choral number ends, the attention of the audience can be drawn to Valentine, who begins his solo on the platform which has by now been vacated by the soldiers.

Having arranged for the essential placement and movements of all the singing groups, the director should have no difficulty organizing the stage activities for the orchestral introduction to this chorus. If he wishes to present a picture of festive hustle and bustle, all he has to do is have the various choristers mingle with each other, promenading in such a fashion that they end up in the correct locations for their eventual entrances as self-contained groups. A number of soldiers, for instance, can start out from the down-right area of the square and walk up left to join their companions for their later military march entrance. A few of the sopranos and second tenors can move in the opposite direction. Some of the baritones can proceed downstage from the right platform and meet a couple of the older burghers who have entered from the tavern and are on their way to the right wing.

Countless details of positioning, movement, and expression can be added in rehearsals. It is essential, however, for the director to arrive at his first staging session with a complete and precise plan of entire mise-en-scène. Unless he learns to analyze not only the verbal implications, but also the musical structure of a complicated ensemble or choral number, he will waste endless rehearsal hours and hardly ever achieve a satisfactory solution.

Homophonic and polyphonic types of choral writing do not always maintain their distinct forms. Quite often a choral number will start out in simple harmonic blocks and then break up into fragmented groups that may or may not feature thematic imitations. Consider, for instance, the Chorus of the People, which opens the Triumphal Scene of *Aida*. This piece begins in a regular four-part homophonic fashion (Example 8–20). Thirty measures later there is a sixteen-measure section entrusted to women alone (Example 8–21). This episode begins and ends in homophonic three-part harmony, but it features a few phrases of two-part imitational writing on the words "Danziam, fanciulle egizie" (Example 8–22). All these purely musical developments, changes, and contrasts can serve as valuable clues which, when added to the information derived from the words of the text, help the stage director to create a sensible, fluid, and varied movement in his choral groups.

Example 8–20. AIDA, II, sc. 2

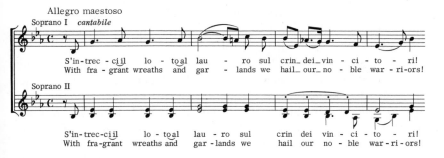

Example 8–21

Example 8–22

The text makes it quite clear that the opening four-part chorus of the Triumphal Scene is directed to the procession exalting the King of Egypt and various nobles of the realm. Once this chorus is over, the men of this particular choral group remain silent for quite a while, so I send them upstage to be on the lookout for the returning soldiers. The words of the women's chorus that follows are less specific in terms of possible stage activities. They do, however, mention the crowning of the returning heroes with wreaths made of lotus flowers and laurel leaves, which enables us to combine several of the scene's dramatic and musical ideas.

Having sent away the male singers, I emphasize the feminine character of the coming episode by seeing to it that the next procession consists exclusively of women. Princess Amneris comes first, then Aida, followed by two girls holding the laurel crown that will later be placed on Radames' brow, and finally by a bevy of female slaves, some of whom carry fans and exotic musical instruments. The women of the chorus, clutching bouquets of lotus blossoms, join the procession and surrender their flowers to various female attendants of Amneris. As their music reaches the two-part polyphony, the singing girls divide themselves accordingly and return with gentle dancing movements to their original positions.

The activities of the strictly polyphonic chorus of priests who enter next were discussed earlier on page 317. At the end of this episode the men of the people's chorus return to their places among the women, and all the singers, including the priests, unite in the final homophonic chorus in praise of heaven and the gods of Egypt.

To demonstrate that the ideas presented here regarding the staging of choruses are neither new nor radical, and that the results achieved by these methods have been greatly appreciated by those who are sensitive to both dramatic and musical values in opera, I should like to quote a few excerpts from an article written more than seventy years ago by George Bernard Shaw, one of the most ardent devotees and astute critics of opera. Reporting on the first Bayreuth production of *Lohengrin* in the summer of 1894, Shaw wrote:

What I feel bound to record concerning the Bayreuth *Lohengrin* . . . is that its stage framework is immensely more entertaining, convincing, and natural than it has ever seemed before. This is mainly because the stage management is so good, especially with regard to the chorus. In *Lohengrin* there are only two comparatively short scenes in which the chorus is not present and in constant action. The opera therefore suffers fearfully on ordinary occasions from the surprising power of the average Italian chorister to destroy all stage illusion the moment he shambles on the scene with his blue jaws, his reach-me-down costume, his foolish single gesture, his embarrassed eye on the prompter, and his general air of being in an opera chorus because he is fit for nothing better. . . . Now I am not going to pretend that at Bayreuth the choristers produce an overwhelming impression of beauty and chivalry, or even to conceal the fact that economic, social and personal conditions which make the Covent Garden chorus what it is in spite of the earnest desire of everybody concerned that it should be something quite different, dominate Frau Wagner just as they dominate Sir Augustus Harris, and compel her to allot to Elsa a bevy of maidens, and to Henry the Fowler a band of warriors, about whose charms and prowess a good deal of make-believe is necessary. The stouter build of the men, the prevalence of a Teutonic cast among them, and their reinforcement by a physically and artistically superior class of singers who regard it as an honor to sing at Bayreuth, even in the chorus, certainly help the illusion as far as the Saxon and Brabantine warriors in *Lohengrin* are concerned; but this difference in raw material is as nothing compared with the difference made by the intelligent activity of the stage manager.

One example of this will suffice. Those who know the score of *Lohengrin* are aware that in the finale to the first act there is a section, usually omitted in performance,* in which the whole movement is somewhat unexpectedly repeated in a strongly contrasted key, the modulation being unaccountable from the point of view of the absolute musician, as it is not at all needed as a relief to the principal key. At Bayreuth its purpose is made clear. After the combat with Telramund and the solo for Elsa which serves musically as the exposition of the theme of the finale, the men, greatly excited and enthusiastic over the victory of the strange knight, range themselves in a sort of wheel formation, of which Lohengrin is the center, and march round him as they take up the finale from Elsa in the principal key. When the modulation comes, the women in the white robes break into this triumphal circle, displace the men, and march round Elsa in the same way, the striking change of key being thus accompanied by a correspondingly striking change on the stage, one of the incidents of which is a particularly remarkable kaleidoscoping of the scheme of color produced by the dresses.

Here you have a piece of stage management of the true Wagnerian kind, combining into one stroke a dramatic effect, a scenic effect, and a musical effect, the total result being a popular effect the value of which was proved by the road of excitement which burst forth as the curtains closed in.†

---

* This is no longer true today.

† Shaw, George Bernard, "Bayreuth, 1 August 1894," in Eric Bentley, ed., *Shaw on Music* (Garden City, N. Y.: Doubleday, 1955), pp. 122–124.

～9

Various problems of staging opera

THE STAGING of any operatic scene involves five steps: (*a*) The director familiarizes himself with the plot, the music, and the scenic setting of the entire opera. (*b*) He analyzes the scene in question and ties up whatever loose ends may have been left over by the libbrettist. (*c*) He tries to penetrate into the inner life of his characters and to read their minds, paying special attention to their silent thoughts which take place during orchestral introductions, interludes, and postludes. (*d*) He converts all their thoughts, whether spoken or silent, into action impulses. (*e*) He sees to it that the action he selects for his mise-en-scène matches as closely as possible the mood, energy, timing, and form of the existing music.

Whenever my examples were chosen from standard operas, I have taken it for granted that the reader was familiar with their stories and the main features of their music. Following the same procedure in this chapter, I shall begin my discussion with the second of these five steps.

Much of the director's preliminary work of analysis is accomplished by asking such questions as: What is this place? Who are the various characters? Where were they before they came here? What brings them here? Searching for the answers, one usually discovers that the librettist has left certain things unexplained. The background text on which the opera is based will, as a rule, either clear up the difficulty, or at least offer a clue that will help to tidy up the operatic continuity. When such missing links in the continuity of the action cannot be filled in by consulting a background text, it is up to the director to invent a logical sequence of events that will complete and justify the story in every detail.

This basic framework, once established, leads to the next phase of the staging process. Identifying himself with each character in turn, the director now seeks to discover their dominant thoughts. This form of mind reading is not as difficult as it may sound. Like all people who are in the throes of powerful emotions, operatic heroes and heroines tend toward monomania. Their minds are usually possessed by one or two persistent ideas which are verbalized when they sing and which occupy their thoughts when they are silent.

Applying the various steps of the director's thinking process to specific examples, let us turn first to the staging of short orchestral introductions and move only gradually to more complicated problems.

Orchestral introductions

In the third act of *Faust*, Marguerite's solo scene (No. 9) begins with a fifteen-measure orchestral introduction that accompanies her entrance. One wonders why Marguerite arrives in her garden so much later than Siebel, Mephisto, and Faust, in spite of the fact that she left the preceding scene of action well ahead of these three men. Taking a hint from Goethe,* we can suggest to our Marguerite that on her way home from church she changed her mind and decided to visit Marthe Schwerlein. Finding that her neighbor was not in, Marguerite left her a note and continued on her way. Having thus dealt with the girl's hidden life, the director is ready to stage the orchestral introduction that precedes her singing.

As Marguerite enters her garden, her thoughts are quite obviously filled with the handsome stranger who accosted her on her way home from church. The first words she sings express her wish to learn his name and social standing. Later, she tries to concentrate on her work, but her mind keeps returning to her recent encounter with the dashing young man who she feels must surely be a noble lord. Thus the two persistent ideas in Marguerite's mind are: "I cannot forget him!" and "I must work!"

Having spelled out Marguerite's dominant concerns, the director now has to help her communicate them to the audience. As we know, the actor must be able to make his thoughts visible as well as audible. Applying the technique of motogenic ideas† to Marguerite's thoughts, we ask: "Where is the handsome stranger?" "Where is work?"

Although Marguerite does not actually know Faust's whereabouts at this moment, she remembers that she saw him last at the Kermesse square which lies outside her garden gate in the direction from which she came. Identifying Faust with the road leading to the garden gate should be reinforced and can be accomplished with a hint from the orchestral accompaniment to her entrance. The bassoons and clarinets play a soft

* Near the end of the seventh scene of Goethe's play, when Faust is anxious to inspect Gretchen's dwelling, Mephisto cautions him that this will have to wait until the girl goes out to visit her neighbor.

† See Chapter 3, p. 109.

phrase that comes to a sudden stop; then there is a silence. A repetition of the first phrase, with the clarinets playing their part a third higher, leads to another silence. The music moves, hesitates, and stops; it moves again, hesitates, and stops again. Should Marguerite's actions reflect these moves, hesitations, and silences? We know very well who occupies her thoughts. Perhaps she is listening for him, or thinks he is following her. He did, after all, accost her boldly in front of all those people. And he may have remained outside Marthe's house while she waited in vain for the return of her neighbor.

When the bassoon and clarinet music appears for the third time, it is doubled by the strings and continues for four measures without stopping. At this point, we hear a new musical thought, which I like to associate with Marguerite's realization that instead of dreaming about noble strangers she should be finishing the domestic task which was interrupted when she went to church.

This brings us to the second motogenic question: "Where is work?" The libretto indicates that during the Song of the King of Thule, Marguerite sits behind her spinning wheel, which is seen standing in the garden. As I identify myself with Marguerite, I find this idea completely incompatible with my habits. An innocent German girl who (according to Goethe's Mephistopheles) goes to confession without having anything to confess, who gives a protective sacred medal to her brother, who curtly rejects the arm of a handsome stranger; a girl whose room is so tidy that (again in Goethe's play) Faust is moved by its "Quiet orderliness, and contentment" (even the devil admits that "not every girl is so neat"): this girl does not leave her spinning wheel outside when she goes to church! Domestic work may be taken to the garden, but it is kept inside the house.

As the music becomes more business-like, Marguerite enters the house, finds the room stuffy, opens the window, takes off her coat and hat, drops them on a chair, picks up her apron, and, tying it around her, returns to the open window. During her short recitative on the theme of the "noble lord" she can unpin her hair and let down her braids. This action, as well as the notion of the "stuffy room" and the opening of the window, are ideas that have been borrowed from Goethe. The two-and-a-half-measure postlude that follows is an obvious echo of the opening phrase of the introduction. It blends with the words Marguerite has just sung and does not require any special elucidation. A deep sigh coupled with a smiling gaze into the distance is all that is needed at this point. The spell of Marguerite's meditation is soon broken by the orchestral strains prefacing the Song of the King of Thule. Marguerite acts out this vigorous, "enough-of-this-nonsense" music by picking up her carding utensils and her batch of wool and carrying them to the garden, where she sits down on a bench and proceeds to work. Before the second verse of the song, she can return to the house and fetch her spinning wheel.

There is no harm in her being seen sitting behind it, putting the wool around the distaff and attaching a thread to the spindle, provided that she respects the injunction against turning wheels that was spelled out earlier (see page 86).

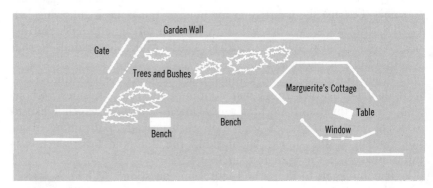

Diagram 9–1. The setting for Marguerite's actions

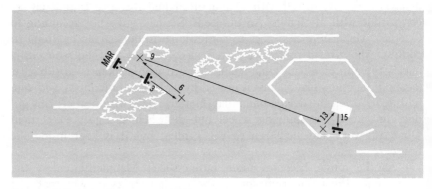

Diagram 9–2. Andantino, measures 1–23

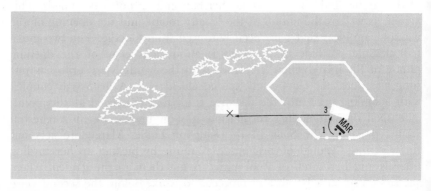

Diagram 9–3. Moderato maestoso, measures 1–5

There are two performers, Susanna and Figaro, involved in the gay orchestral introduction that begins the first act of *The Marriage of Figaro*. This introduction contains two separate sections. The words that later accompany the opening vocal phrases make it abundantly clear that the first half of this introduction belongs to Figaro and depicts his efforts ˋ to find the best place for the newlyweds' marital bed. The second theme, which appears in the middle of the ninth measure, is just as obviously associated with Susanna, who is ensconced behind a little table sewing orange blossoms on her small bridal wreath.

This is Figaro's and Susanna's wedding day, and the plot of the opera deals largely with their attempts to defeat the various intrigues designed to prevent their marriage from taking place. As a result, the bride and groom soon become involved in so many counterplots that they have neither the time nor the opportunity for amorous dallying. The opera has nothing resembling a formal love duet and it is not until the end of the third-act sextet, when the major threat to their happiness has been miraculously removed, that the two central characters manage to exchange a few words of tenderness. Even then their amorous dialogue is accompanied by the glances and observations of four other members of the cast, not all of whom are in sympathy with the rapture of the young lovers. Consequently, it is only in the opening scene, when they are alone and undisturbed, that the atmosphere is relaxed enough to permit a display of the normal bride-and-groom relationship. It is therefore all the more important that the stage director make a special effort in this direction while the situation still allows it.

The words of the text do not contain any allusions to love-making, but in the instrumental accompaniment to Susanna's theme there is a curious passage which strongly suggests "making a pass at a girl" (Example 9–1). This short passage makes me think of all sorts of caresses:

Allegro

sfp

Example 9–1. THE MARRIAGE OF FIGARO, I, no. 1

a quick embrace, an attempt to steal a kiss, a pat on the cheek, or a chuck under the chin. The duration and the accentual contour of this phrase lend themselves equally well to gentle self-defense tactics. Put in terms of subtexts, I hear it either as Figaro's "Oh, you're adorable!" or as Susanna's "We're not married yet!" While it is true that the words of Da Ponte's text do not suggest any amorous activity, some of Beaumarchais' dialogue in the parallel scene of the play is remarkably appropriate. At the end of Susanna's talk with Figaro, just before she leaves the room, we read:

FIGARO: . . . give a little kiss!

SUSANNA: To a lover today? No sir! What would my husband say tomorrow? (*Figaro kisses her.*) Now, now!

FIGARO: You don't know how much I love you.

SUSANNA (*adjusting her dress*): When will you learn not to bore me with it from morning till night?

FIGARO (*as if telling a secret*): Why, when I can prove it to you from night till morning. (*The bell rings again.*)

SUSANNA (*blowing him a kiss from the door*): There's your kiss, sir. I have nothing else of yours to return.

I see no reason why this playful skirmish should not be introduced earlier and woven into the action of the opera. Here, as so often, music provides the initial clue, and the seemingly insignificant accompaniment figure can serve as a spur to the stage director's imagination. Four separate trains of thought eventually coalesced in my mind when I first staged this duet:

1. At first there was only a mild puzzlement regarding the purpose of a musical passage which did not seem to fit with the words that were being sung at the time. The knack of "muscular listening" identified this phrase as "gesture music" with certain specific characteristics of energy and duration.

2. On a different level, there emerged the question: "What is this duet all about? What is the main action of this scene?" The answer was not hard to find. Marital beds and wedding wreaths point in certain obvious directions. The immediate male and female preoccupations are clearly outlined. For him: "Where will I make love to her?" For her: "How can I look my best?" But with the groom and bride alone on stage, why was there no direct reference made to their feelings and appetites? Why, specifically, was Figaro so reticent?

3. Here Beaumarchais came to my rescue and offered a valid explanation. He endows Figaro with his full share of impatient virility, but his Susanna is not only wise in the ways of the world, she is also innately virtuous. She means to preserve both her reputation and her self-respect. As Beaumarchais's Figaro so aptly describes her, she is "A ravishing girl! Always gay, laughing, full of life, wit, love, joy—and how well-behaved!"

4. Another look at the musical passage that sparked this entire train of thought showed that it recurs no less than eight times throughout the duet. Perhaps it would be a good idea to associate it every time it occurs with an interplay of caresses and gentle de-

fenses? Having restrained Figaro's initial attempts at love-making, Susanna might later feel inclined to undertake some modest endearment of her own just to reassure her fiancé that, when the time is ripe, she will be a responsive mate.

Such a close association of music and action serves two purposes here. It helps to establish the "morning-of-the-wedding" atmosphere and it organizes the action by giving the singers a clear-cut scheme of behavior which is synchronized with the words and the music. Figaro's assignments are measuring the floor, attempting to make love to Susanna, and admiring her headdress. Susanna's actions include trying on the wreath, looking at it in the mirror and modeling it for Figaro, defending herself against his impetuousness, and occasionally rewarding him for his good behavior with a gentle caress of her own. All this can be foreshadowed in the orchestral introduction.

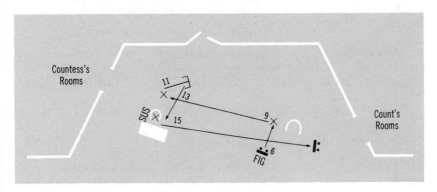

Diagram 9–4

The sprightly opening of Così fan tutte involves three singers. This eight-measure allegro, which features an accentual peak in the sixth measure, calls for a matching action of comparable vigor. In the absence of a background text, all the fleshing-out of particulars affecting the scenic setting, additional personnel, and characteristic action must by necessity be imagined and developed by the stage director.

Since the scene is set in a public establishment, it is desirable to justify the absence of other guests. As the curtain opens, it reveals the inside of a coffee house. Through a large window (in the left portion of the center wall) we can see by the dim light of a street lamp two young men in uniform and an elderly gentleman in civilian clothes. The café itself is well illuminated, but it is empty and, judging by the chairs which are piled up on top of some of the tables, it is about to be closed for the night.

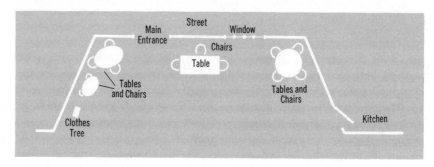

Diagram 9–5

The three friends have spent the evening together (perhaps attending a theatrical performance) and are now on their way home. Just before the curtain opens, we can imagine the following conversation:

DON ALFONSO: I repeat: all women are fickle!

FERRANDO: What an outrageous statement! My Dorabella . . .

GUGLIELMO: Gentlemen, I am ravenous! Do you mind if we continue our argument inside this cafè?

DON ALFONSO (*peering through the window*): It looks closed for the night.

GUGLIELMO: I'll go and see.   [*Curtain*]

Guglielmo (followed by Alfonso and Ferrando) goes to the main entrance located in the right section of the center wall. He enters, looks around for the waiter, notices him standing offstage in the left wing, and continues going down stage to center. He signals toward the open kitchen door (in LA1) to attract the waiter's attention, makes a questioning gesture ("Are you still open for business?"), gets an affirmative answer, turns (Clw) to face Alfonso (who has stopped inside the entrance door), beckons him to enter, and goes right to RA1 where he hangs his hat on the clothes tree and begins to take off his overcoat. As soon as Guglielmo invites him to enter, Don Alfonso goes down left to center. Ferrando follows him, but remains up right of him. At about the same time, the waiter enters from down left. Alfonso indicates to him that they will need a table for three. The waiter nods and goes up right to above Alfonso, where he removes the chairs from the top of the table and busies himself wiping the furniture. As Ferrando begins to sing, Alfonso turns (Clw) to listen to him.

To make all this work out in exactly the right way from the opening of the curtain, when Guglielmo leaves his friends at the window, until he hangs his hat on the clothes tree, the singer must learn to contour his actions very precisely with the music of this introduction. I re-

commend, therefore, that Guglielmo memorize the following subtext*
which can be made to coincide with the outline of the melody played by
the first violins:

I|go, and I|go, and I|enter the|room. Is someone inside? "Hey there, good
fellow! Still open? That's good." (*Addressing Alfonso*) "It's open!" Go to
the|right. Off with the|hat and hang it|up!

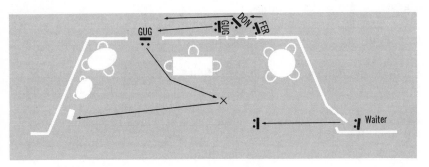

Diagram 9–6

Achieving variety in actions, groupings, and stage positions

For many years, operatic acting was not only stilted, but also very
static. The traditional pattern of staging was to assign characters certain
locations—the Germans called them *Standorte*, standing places—which
were theirs as long as they remained on stage. Kings and high priests
belonged on stage right; the common people congregated on the left.
Much importance was attached to entrances and exits, but there was little
other movement and practically no changes in grouping and stage positioning.

There is no doubt, of course, that a great deal of fine acting can
be done with the voice, the words, and the general bearing and appearance of a character. Constant running around and regrouping is no
substitute for expressive acting. Yet, obviously, if an operatic production
is to have any visual variety (or believability and clarity, for that matter),
meaningful changes of position and grouping are indispensable.

The degree of variety in facial expression, gesturing, and arrangement
of props must always remain in keeping with the character of a role.
Older and more sedate personalities will naturally not need as many
diversified actions as youngsters and busybodies. Variety in grouping and
stage locations must reflect the dramatic ideas of the text and be carefully coordinated with the score. Making the changes in stage position

* This subtext is to be thought (or recited) in the rhythm of the opening theme.
The lines between the words indicate the position of the barlines.

conform to the structure of the music is an essential part of a good operatic mise-en-scène. It not only prevents monotony, but adds a graphic orderliness to the unfolding of musical and dramatic events.

These principles can be safely applied to all operatic styles. We can isolate a number of useful methods for achieving variety by examining the Frugola-Giorgetta scene from *The Cloak (Il Tabarro)*, which is a typical example of Puccini's devotion to everyday realism, enlivened by a generous use of hand props.

Musically, this scene* is divided into two main parts: (*a*) a brief, preparatory allegretto in 2/4 time, and (*b*) a fairly long allegro energico in 3/8 time.

The allegro consists of four sections, which can be graphically represented by the pattern A, B, A', A'', where the A's stand for variations of the same musical idea and B is a contrasting passage. We have therefore, a total of five sections of music, each of which has its own story to tell and each of which should have its own characteristic arrangement of actions, groupings, and stage locations.

In this scene, a scavenging rag-woman named Frugola ("prowler") comes on the deck of Michele's barge looking for her husband, the longshoreman Talpa. Left alone with Michele's wife Giorgetta, Frugola shows the young woman some of the loot she has collected during the day.

First section, Allegretto in 2/4 time. Frugola greets Giorgetta and Michele from the embankment and then goes up the gangplank to the barge. After Michele leaves, Frugola tells of curing her husband's backache by massaging him with an application of rum. She then offers Giorgetta a comb decorated with rhinestones, describing it as the best thing she has found in many a day. Giorgetta accepts the gift and praises Frugola's prowling talents.

Second section, Allegro energico in 3/8 time, Section A. After a vigorous orchestral interlude lasting eight measures, Frugola shows Giorgetta some strange items from the collection in her bag, such as a tuft of feathers and pieces of lace, velveteen, and silk.

Third section, Allegro energico, Section B. Frugola displays a packet of letters tied with ribbons and observes that they represent joys and torments of the rich and poor alike. Giorgetta asks about the contents of a small carton, which Frugola put aside earlier, and is told that it is a beef heart to be eaten by Frugola's Maltese cat, Caporale. Giorgetta says the cat is lucky to get such a choice tidbit. "He deserves it," says Frugola, guffawing loudly. An energetic interlude of seven measures leads to:

Fourth section, Section A'. Frugola praises her pet as a faithful companion with whom she has had a long-standing love affair "without ceremonies or jealousies." She asks Giorgetta if she wants to hear the cat's philosophy and proceeds to relate it in:

---

* The scene begins with the *a tempo* two measures before 30 with Frugola's "eterni innamorati, buona sera."

Fifth section, Section A″. Amidst much purring, Frugola recites Caporale's two main gems of wisdom: "It is better to be master in a humble hut than a slave in a palace," and "It is better to feed on some slices of a beef heart than to eat out one's own heart in hopeless love!" During the sixteen measures of the orchestral postlude Frugola repacks her bag of scavenged loot.

Beginning to stage this scene, I am immediately attracted to the idea that Frugola can illustrate how she massaged Talpa by kneeling down and using the bag to represent his back. I am pleased to have imagined this specific gesture, one I have never used in any other opera. I force myself, however, to defer thinking about such acting details and remind myself "not to start with interior decorations before the house is built!" I must first find five different stage locations to correspond to the five-part structure of the music.

I can easily imagine the first two locations: the allegretto place where Frugola talks about her husband and gives Giorgetta the comb, and the "unpacking" place for the first section of the allegro. But how can I later induce Frugola to move away from her bag? Can Giorgetta perhaps be helpful here? She has just received a present, a comb . . . Suddenly Giorgetta's thoughts begin to flash in my mind. "Comb . . . pretty . . . shall I put it in my hair? No, not clean enough. Frugola found it in some refuse, no doubt! Must clean comb . . . wash it . . . find water." I remember that earlier, in staging the beginning of the opera, I was looking for some quiet, domestic occupation for Giorgetta. Why not have her water some geranium plants set up along the upper railing of the barge? "I will go and fetch a pail of water which I left there. And then I will sit on the deck of the barge and listen to Frugola while I clean the comb. When I finish washing it, I must return the pail to its proper place!" At this point Frugola, who is no longer involved with the contents of her bag, will want to follow Giorgetta and tell her more details about her cat.

Notice that "as Giorgetta" I am concerned about cleaning the comb; as stage director, however, my main interest is in providing Frugola with a strong motive for changing her stage location, and I am particularly anxious to lure her upstage, from where she can easily continue in almost any direction. To achieve variety in staging, it is essential to arrange for changes not only in the lateral right and left locations, but also in respect to the upper and lower portions of the stage.

Now I have four well-motivated locations:

1. *Allegretto.* In the center of the barge. Frugola gives the comb to Giorgetta.
2. *Allegro, section A.* During the orchestral introduction Frugola goes left to a box, where she sits down to unpack her bag. At the same time Giorgetta fetches the pail and returns to sit on the floor of the deck to listen to Frugola.

3. *Allegro, section* A'. The orchestral interlude leading up to this section has two separate energetic passages. This is very convenient. During the first one Giorgetta returns the pail to its original place; during the second, Frugola follows Giorgetta.
4. *Allegro, section* A''. Giorgetta walks away toward down right. There are several possible motivations here, and at this point I don't even try to decide on the best one. During the "cat's philosophy" section Frugola follows Giorgetta; she can do it in two stages, perhaps, one for each of the cat's "gems of wisdom." During the orchestral postlude, Frugola goes left to repack her bag while Giorgetta remains down right.

At this point I again feel a great temptation to start working out details of the actions, but I remember that I have not provided a change of location or grouping for the B section of the allegro. I decide to have Giorgetta turn away from Frugola to admire how the clean rhinestones sparkle in the rays of the sunset. Frugola (who has just put down the carton with the cat's food) wants to show the love letters to Giorgetta, so she gets up and crosses over to the right. The young woman soon turns away (motivation to be decided later) and asks about the package lying on the box. Frugola returns to the box, picks up the package, and hands it to Giorgetta, who opens it and looks inside while Frugola puts down the love letters. While remarking about the cat's luck, Giorgetta returns the package to Frugola, places the comb in her hair, and is now ready to walk upstage with the pail.

Having decided how to handle section B, I must now consider how best to motivate Giorgetta's movements after Frugola joins her upstage and how to justify her turning away from Frugola in the middle of section B. I notice that in each case Frugola has just spoken of love: first about love letters and then about her love affair with her cat. Since Giorgetta is in the throes of a dangerous, illicit passion, any mention of love should make her nervous. Knowing the sharp, prowling eyes of the older woman, she is afraid she might give herself away. This makes her turn away and change the conversation in section B. To justify walking away later, Giorgetta might pretend to be looking for a mirror. She will find one and use it to admire herself with her new comb while the orchestra is playing the postlude.

It is only now that I feel I can safely turn to my first thought of "massaging" the bag and "interior decorating" the rest of the stage actions. Once the basic positions are established, these details are easy enough to invent. Giorgetta can hug the kneeling Frugola to thank her for the comb, and later she can refuse the offer of the tuft of feathers. Frugola can use her arm to represent a cat and "scratch its head" when she pantomimes its purring. She can even try to illustrate the meowing which is so cleverly imitated by the orchestra at the end of section B. The problem with details of action in Puccini's operas is not what to do, but rather how not to overdo!

In this scene we have observed the use of two basic and most important methods of staging: (*a*) moving the supporting actor, and (*b*) "exploiting" props.

When music and drama seem mismatched

The development of musical phrases generally relies on a considerable amount of repetition. This is why operatic stories deal so frequently with situations that lend themselves particularly well to repetitive treatment. We know that strong emotions are very persistent and can be spun out almost indefinitely. It is not surprising, therefore, that the pleasures and torments of love have proven to be favorite subjects for lyrical expansion. The laments, farewells, jealousies, quarrels, and reconciliations of lovers are ideally suited for musical repetition and rank high on the list of topics chosen by opera composers. Other, less emotionally laden, activities that lend themselves to considerable prolongation are work-songs, serenades, lullabies, prayers, processions, dances, and card games.

Unfortunately, there are certain actions that do not tolerate expansion or repetition, and the resulting conflict between musical and real time has led to many complaints and sarcastic comments by those who enjoy scoffing at opera. Deeds that call for prompt execution in real life are often delayed in the musical theater for what may seem to be an unreasonably long time. Typical examples of such apparent mismatching of operatic and everyday time are the so-called "andiam" or "let us hurry and leave!" chorus scenes, where the participants express an urgent need to depart, but cannot leave the stage until their singing lines are over. Battle scenes featuring combatants who sing of mayhem yet never come to blows and ensembles where everyone is frozen in prolonged statuesque immobility have contributed to the criticism that opera is "irrational entertainment."

The fault, however, lies not so much with opera as with performers and directors who are willing to treat an operatic work as if it were a concert rather than a continuous dramatic experience. To bring opera to life we must accept and impersonate its characters as people who think, feel, and behave as the rest of us do. Complete passivity in acting is comparable to total lack of expressiveness in a musical performance. Musicians will sometimes disagree about the relative importance or the proper "dosage" of certain nuances. One conductor, for instance, may prefer more swelling and tapering than another. But a total absence of musical inflections is not really endurable for more than a short span of time, and the constant flow of the meaningful sounds we call operatic music surely deserves to find its logical counterpart in thoroughly lifelike presentations of the drama.

One must never forget that even the most solemn and seemingly actionless operatic situations are set to music that is apportioned into clearly defined sections, where phrases of varied importance develop melodic highlights that pass from the instruments to the voices, and from character to character. To the extent that these vocal and orchestral events exist and are audible, they can and should be reflected in the grouping and behavior of the singers who act out the music.

A stage director whose ears have become attuned to the subtle messages of these multiform musical clues will learn to convert into gently unfolding theatrical actions even such seemingly static operatic tableaux as the quartet from *Fidelio* and the quintet from *Die Meistersinger*, where the solemnity of the mood did not prevent the composers from providing an expressive and fluid musical texture, and where neither the words nor the vocal lines justify the rigor mortis that one so often sees implanted on the faces and in the limbs of the singers.

In operatic scenes where an urgent forward drive of the drama is combined with lengthy and repetitive music, the stage director must step in and develop or invent additional details to justify the delay in the execution of the action.

In *Rigoletto*, for example, there are two very tense and urgent moments where the action all too often grinds to a dead stop, presumably in order to permit the unfolding of musical ideas. The first episode occurs at the end of the second scene, during the almost sixty measures of the "Zitti, zitti" chorus; the second takes place near the end where Sparafucile's stabbing of Gilda is delayed by the fairly extended trio sung by the victim, the killer, and the killer's sister, Maddalena.

Without going into every detail of the execution, here is an outline of some suitable staging that permits the singers to do justice to the music and at the same time prepare convincingly for their criminal acts.

The lanterns brought in at the end of the second scene were extinguished as soon as the courtiers became aware of Rigoletto's approach. By the time the "Zitti, zitti" chorus begins, however, the jester has been safely blindfolded and a few of the courtiers can busy themselves relighting the lanterns. The abductors are aware that the gate to Rigoletto's garden cannot be opened from outside without using the key that is in the jester's pocket. The latch can, however, be unbolted from inside. A young pageboy, brought along for this very purpose, is made to climb a ladder and jump down into the garden. It is quite dark on the garden side of the wall, and it takes the boy a little while to find his bearings. He eventually manages to unlatch the gate and the kidnapers enter, one by one. A few of the gentlemen of the court remain outside in the street, ostensibly to help Rigoletto hold the ladder, but in reality to make certain that the jester does not spoil their fun by removing his mask too soon. Still other courtiers enter the house cautiously in order to locate Gilda's bedroom; in a few moments, two of them emerge and indicate by gesturing that they have found the girl and need help. In due time Gilda is carried out and, after a few of the abductors surround her to make certain that she has been properly gagged, all the men file out of the garden and leave, as they came in, through the street on stage left. The relighting of the lanterns, the encouraging of the pageboy (who is at first reluctant to climb the ladder), the entering of the garden and the house, and all the rest of the elaborate staging provide suitable action for the duration of the chorus. They motivate all the events, and do full justice to the drama as well as to the whispers, crescendos, and quickly suppressed accents of the music.

The example from the final scene of *Rigoletto* illustrates with even greater clarity the special difficulties that often arise out of the necessity to reconcile the musical and dramatic exigencies of opera.

This trio elaborates two main musical ideas, one of which is connected with wind and thunder, and the other with lightning and rain. The "wind" sections are based upon a chromatic theme hummed by the offstage male chorus (Example 9–2). These sections carry the dramatic

Example 9–2. RIGOLETTO, III, no. 13

ideas of the plot in an almost recitative-like parlando that moves with great momentum. The "lightning" portions of this scene, on the other hand, are intended to be uttered with considerable vocal intensity and belong to the type of music that requires much reiteration and development (Example 9–3).

Example 9–3

The first of these "lightning and rain" sections poses no unusual acting and staging problems. All the characters are in highly emotional states: Gilda is torn between the fear of death and the desire to save her lover; Maddalena keeps imploring her brother to spare the life of their handsome visitor; Sparafucile is irritated almost beyond endurance by his sister's tears and is trying to make her aware of the extravagance of her request. All these ideas lend themselves quite readily to considerable repetition, so that the words and the music manage to co-exist without any serious conflict. It is the second stanza of the "lightning" music that imposes the real strain on dramatic credibility. The imminent approach of midnight was one of the main topics of Maddalena's and Sparafucile's dispute, and the situation is one of great urgency. Since the sack containing the body of the victim must be delivered to Rigoletto in less than half an hour, the Duke's fate seems to be sealed. Now, almost miraculously, a guest seeking shelter knocks at the door of the tavern. Chance has played into Maddalena's hands, and all that remains to be done is for Sparafucile to grasp a convenient weapon and accomplish the deed, which, according to his own boast in the second scene of the opera, he has trained himself to perform with effortless dispatch. Instead of this obvious and logical continuation, the second stanza of the "lightning" music claims its rights, and we are presented with an unexpected and awkward delay. In order to satisfy the laws of musical development and balance, the singers must first enunciate the theme in well-sung, four-measure phrases:

> MADDALENA: Oh hurry, I tell you, for time passes quickly;
> His life must be saved, and there's danger in store!
> SPARAFUCILE: I frankly confess that I did not expect it—
> At night, in this weather, a knock at our door!
> GILDA: Believe me, oh father, although you will suffer,
> I'm happy to die for the man I adore!

An even greater strain on dramatic credibility is imposed by the thirty-measure ensemble that follows, where each participant keeps repeating his lines with some minor variations. Here, for instance, are Maddalena's words:

MADDALENA: Oh hurry, I tell you, for time passes quickly;
His life must be saved, and there's danger in store!
Be quick, I tell you! Be quick, I tell you!
Be quick, I tell you! Be quick, I tell you!
His life must be saved, and there's danger in store!
His life must be saved, and there's danger in store!
His life must be saved, and there's danger in store!

To directors who try to present opera as a string of convincing and logical events, procrastinations of this type can be most aggravating. But, starting with the premise that operatic plots and situations are always inherently sensible, I tried to discover a good reason for deferring the action. In this instance, I assumed that there must be something amiss with Sparafucile's dagger. Putting myself in his shoes, I find the weapon in an old trunk and discover that it is shockingly rusty and dull. This takes place during Maddalena's initial solo phrase. Now I have to think quickly! The situation is urgent. The killing of the stranger must be performed rapidly and silently so as not to wake the man who is sleeping upstairs. If my dagger is to penetrate the rain-drenched clothing of the new victim, its edges have to be razor-keen and its point properly sharpened. This thought leads to the next one: a whetstone must be found! I remember seeing one in the fireplace on the opposite side of the room. I go there (during Gilda's solo) and start making a search. On my way there I take the lamp that Maddalena was holding, but now I beckon her to come closer to hold the light so that I can use both my hands to sift through the ashes. Once the stone is found, Maddalena and I proceed to the table, where I take time to sharpen the dagger and test its blade.

Moving Sparafucile and Maddalena from the entrance door to the trunk, then to the fireplace and the table; having them handle the lamp, search for the stone, sharpen the edges and point of the dagger, then test it: all this gives the singers a great number of sensible and time-consuming actions that help them fill the forty-two measures of this ensemble with musically and dramatically credible behavior.

Dance sequences

The staging of operatic ballets presents very special problems. A stage director who is not a trained dancer or choreographer naturally needs to be assisted by experts in this field. He should, nevertheless, always insist that the dancing be integrated into the dramatic continuity of the opera. If a ballet is intended for the amusement of important characters in the drama, the director must be sure to place these personages so that the entertainment can, at least to some extent, be "addressed" to them.

Dance sequences in such operas as *Aida* ought not to be treated as extraneous inserts. Dancing slaves certainly should not have to turn their backs on Princess Amneris or the King of Egypt, for whose benefit their exertions are presumably intended.

Dancers as well as singers should be made aware of the reasons behind their activities. In the ritual scenes of such operas as *Orfeo*, *Samson and Delilah*, and *Aida*, the religious import of the ceremonies should be explained to the performers so that they in turn can make it clearly understandable to the audience.

When dances are accompanied by singing, the director should make certain that the words of the vocal text and the movements of the dancers relate to the same subject matter. In the second act of *La Traviata*, Gastone and the male choristers tell of the Andalusian maiden who refuses to give her hand in marriage to the handsome Piquillo until that worthy matador subdues five bulls in a single *corrida*. All too often the Spanish ballet danced at this point has not the remotest connection with this gallant tale of proud Iberian courtship.

Dances accompanied by words are often intended to be symbolic representations of the opera's main action. When this relationship exists the director should try to emphasize it by showing the effect of the entertainment on the principal characters, whose inner conflicts are mirrored by the ballet. The Pastorale that is sung and danced in the second act of *The Queen of Spades* is an example of such an allegory. Its portrayal of the contrast between "gold" and "love" carries a special and different meaning for Lisa and Gherman. By highlighting their reactions to this play within a play, the director can add a great deal of meaning to what can otherwise be a completely extraneous interlude.

When a dancing sequence serves to develop the plot, the dramatic idea behind the dance must not be obscured by too much concentration on graceful movement or other purely choreographic considerations. In many librettos, dances are introduced as preliminary moves in amorous plays of temptation or seduction. In staging these episodes, a director must take into account well ahead of time the underlying motivation leading to a particular modus operandi. The logic of the drama always takes precedence over plasticity of execution in such instances.

A short discussion of three operatic scenes in which dancing is initiated for such "ulterior motives" will demonstrate how dramatic and musical elements can influence both the mise-en-scène and the choreography.

The minuet sequence in the opening scene of *Rigoletto* is clearly part of the Duke's campaign to seduce Countess Ceprano, and it should also make the audience aware of her husband's strenuous efforts to prevent this seduction from taking place. In my staging of this episode the Duke gives the signal for the music to begin and tells Borsa to convey to the Countess his invitation to dance. The other courtiers are aware of what is afoot and, being anxious to cooperate with their master, move or dance discreetly away. The husband's efforts to eavesdrop on his wife's conversation with the Duke are frustrated by Rigoletto. As the Duke becomes more and more passionate, he gives up all pretense of dancing. The Countess, keeping an eye on her husband, does her best to uphold the proprieties. She tries to calm the Duke's impetuous advances, making it obvious at the same time that his attentions are far from unwelcome.

The governing principle behind this dancing episode is the Duke's desire for privacy. The direction of the dance, therefore, is away from the husband. It can start in the center of the stage, but it must gradually drift to one of the corners where the Duke and the Countess can vanish from sight just as suddenly as the minuet disappears from the score.

The habanera, sung and danced in the first act of *Carmen*, is a typical example of feminine exhibitionism, intended to attract the attention and arouse the desires of a stubbornly indifferent beholder. Carmen, used to being admired by every man who crosses her path, is piqued at Don José's total lack of interest in her. The habanera, which starts in the spirit of fun, soon becomes a test of strength and a matter of prestige. Carmen soon feels she must prove to her friends that she can make this handsome corporal fall in love with her. The cigarette girls, cavaliers, and dragoons who crowd the square cannot help but become involved in this fascinating duel between the town's most renowned siren and the young soldier who seems completely impervious to her charms.

The music contains two contrasting ideas. The first follows the outline of a slithering, descending chromatic scale (Example 9–4). The second is built on a zigzagging diatonic motive (Example 9–5). When Carmen discovers that the voluptuously sinuous chromatics of the first theme do not achieve the desired result, she decides to try the more

Example 9-4. CARMEN, I, Habanera no. 4

Example 9–5

direct approach of the second subject, which incorporates an explosive "shock-treatment" device for which Carmen needs the cooperation of the entire chorus (Example 9–6). I like to highlight the dramatic effect of this moment by transplanting onto the stage the tambourine that is normally played by a member of the percussion section in the orchestra pit. I give this tambourine to a blind beggar, whom I place in the opposite corner of the stage from Don José. During the choral repetition of the chromatic theme, I route Carmen's dancing steps in the direction of the beggar, so that just before the onset of the diatonic theme, she can pick up the tambourine. Holding it behind her back, she now retraces her steps, arriving in the vicinity of Don José immediately before the first explosive "Beware of love," the rhythm of which (just as it is indicated in the score) she then duplicates on the tambourine.

Example 9–6

The basic idea behind the episode of the three simultaneous dances in the first-act finale of *Don Giovanni* is spelled out by the Don himself in the aria he sings in the preceding scene of the opera. He plans to take advantage of the general confusion engendered by his guests' disorderly dancing activities to add to his list of conquests not only Zerlina, but several other victims as well.

The *Carmen* example demonstrated to what extent dramatic and musical clues can help in the choreographing of a dancing sequence. In the *Don Giovanni* scene, we find that the reverse can also be true. Here such purely choreographic devices as the stamping of feet and the clapping of hands serve to clarify not only the plot, but also the unusually complicated configurations of the music.

Before the episode of the three dances begins, there is a four-bar introduction in 4/4 time, during which Don Giovanni orders the orchestra for the minuet to begin playing and tells Leporello to help his guests find dancing partners.

The minuet consists of sixty-two bars in 3/4 time, played by strings, oboes, and horns. It contains two alternating musical ideas: phrase A, which starts in the tonic and ends in the dominant (Example 9–7), and phrase B, which starts in the dominant and ends in the tonic (Example 9–8). These phrases alternate in a succession of eight stanzas. Each stanza has eight bars except the last one, which, because it is interrupted by Zerlina's shouts for help, has only six bars.

The unique feature of this episode is that first a country dance in 2/4 time (Example 9–9) and then a waltz in 3/8 time (Example 9–10) are superimposed on the minuet (Example 9–11). The country dance and the waltz are performed by two separate groups of string players, whose preliminary tuning-up adds still another witty touch to this musical extravaganza (Examples 9–12 and 9–13).

A satisfactory presentation of this episode poses a number of problems, by far the most serious being that of musical clarity. Mozart's daring joke of combining three dances with different meters looks fine on paper, but as a rule produces little or no effect. The ear of the average listener cannot successfully cope with the simultaneous occurrence of three unrelated tunes, only one of which is closely familiar. It would be different if Mozart had given the country dance and the waltz a better chance to impress themselves on the attention of the audience. As things stand, only a fragment of the country dance—played offstage, without its opening measures—was heard in the preceding scene. Otherwise, this dance appears only in counterpoint with the minuet. The waltz has even less of an opportunity to catch the ear of the listener, since it is never heard at all except in conjunction with the other two dance tunes. Under these circumstances, it is hardly surprising that very few opera lovers can identify the melodies of either the country dance or the waltz. On the other hand, four stanzas of the minuet were heard offstage in the preceding scene, and it continues to receive preferential treatment in this finale, where four more of its stanzas are played before either of the two tunes is added to it. When all three orchestras play simultaneously, it is no wonder that the country dance and the waltz pass by without attracting much notice.

Yet these two dances are intimately associated with important dramatic activities that cannot be presented with sufficient clarity unless these tunes are rescued from their relative obscurity. The almost hypnotic effect of the downbeats of the minuet must be overcome by giving the rhythm of the other dances some vigorous additional stress. To do full justice to this episode, one must isolate and highlight the salient points of both the music and the action. The logical way to do this is to bring the musicians in closer touch with their respective groups of dancers. This in turn brings up the question of the scenic arrangement for this particular section of the finale.

Example 9–7. DON GIOVANNI, I, Finale no. 13. Phrase A.

Example 9–8. Phrase B.

Example 9–9

Example 9–10

Example 9–11

Example 9–12

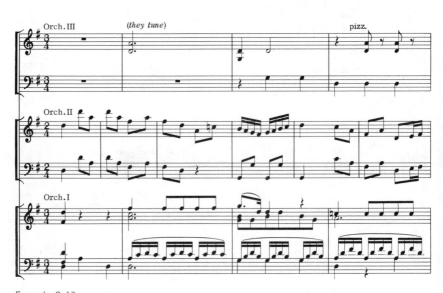

Example 9–13

Long ago I came to the conclusion that, for the sake of musical and dramatic clarity, this scene should not be played in a ballroom, but in a setting that would permit me to separate the noble and rustic elements of both the music and the plot. A view of the façade of Don Giovanni's palace, with a terrace projecting into the gardens, serves this purpose best. The peasants feel more comfortable outside the palace; the minuet orchestra is seated inside so that it is only partially visible through the windows; the masked members of the nobility dance on the terrace, from where they can readily observe the Don's preliminary tactics with Zerlina and Leporello's efforts to distract Masetto.

Under these conditions the music of the country dance and the waltz can be entrusted to a few ambulating musicians* who should be summoned from opposite wings by the Don and Leporello. These players, who enter through arbored arches on the garden level, can now be placed in the very thick of the action. The tuning-up, which as a rule passes completely unnoticed, is now done with a flourish, under the fascinated eyes of the peasants and in full view of the audience.

During the first four stanzas of the minuet, Don Ottavio divides his attentions between his two partners, first dancing with Anna and then with Elvira. The peasant fellows, not being familiar with the minuet, refuse to attempt this dance of the upper classes. Their girls are more venturesome. Zerlina accepts Don Giovanni's invitation to dance; Gianotta and Sandrina, the two pretty peasant girls with whom Leporello was flirting earlier in the scene, seem quite willing to learn the minuet steps from the Don's servant. The choreography of all the dances should be arranged so that the singers who must exchange confidential remarks find themselves—as if by chance—standing quite near each other.

Having called in the musicians, the Don takes Zerlina to the area reserved for the country dance on stage left. The leading violinist of this group should be placed in a prominent spot and encouraged to use his bowing arm and his tapping foot to exaggerate the rhythm of his tune. The contrast between the minuet and the country dance should be further emphasized by the peasant couples who clap their hands lustily on each downbeat of the 2/4 measure.

On stage right Leporello does his best to distract Zerlina's fiancé. In his efforts to make Masetto dance, he enlists the help of some of the girls who belong to the peasant group occupying the right side of the stage. The summoning of the orchestra players and the tuning-up proceed very much as they did earlier on stage left. Since the peasants do not feel the same awe for Leporello as for his master, a few of the couples begin to dance as soon as they hear the lilting strains. The others beat their palms on every second bar of the waltz, so that the clapping of hands on the two sides of the stage falls on alternating beats. This is the only way I know to segregate the waltz from its companions and give it a distinct and individual rhythmic character.

---

* For the best results I recommend three violinists and two bass players for each of the orchestras, although one violinist and bass player on each side is actually quite sufficient.

Asides and mistaken identities

People who converse together want to be near each other. Actors who desire to address their partners move closer to them. This urge for proximity can also take the form of wanting to be face to face with the other person. A singer who walks away from his partner thus induces him to follow, and one who turns away can stimulate the partner to change his stage location so that the two of them will again be facing other. The technical name for these actions is *luring*. The supporting actor who walks upstage lures his partner into following him there; by turning away from his partner, who is on his left, he lures him to cross above him and go to his right.

Turning away is also used for the opposite reason: the desire for privacy. When a character wants to hide his thoughts, words, or actions, he naturally walks away from his partner. Anything that he must say or perform in secret will induce him to move away from other performers. It is advisable to apply this principle to the execution of asides, which are private thoughts made audible for the benefit of the audience. Singers and directors should take pains to protect these asides; the singer can do it by turning away and using a subdued tone of voice, the director by helping the silent partner find some reason to move in the opposite direction. If a character becomes aware that his partner wishes to be alone, he will move away either because he is asked to do so, or out of a feeling of delicacy.

Movements serving to connect and disconnect performers are among the most important devices for arranging changes in stage location and grouping. One should keep in mind, however, that these actions will not be completely believable unless they are clearly motivated. The singer must know why he walks or turns, and he must make certain that his motivations are readily understandable and credible. Special care must be taken to justify all movements that lead away from one's singing partners.

Many scenes (particularly in eighteenth-century operas) present situations where one character is unaware of the presence of another or is mistaken regarding his identity. By imposing great restrictions on the movements of the actors, these scenes help both the performers and the director to pinpoint the few acceptable positions and groupings. A drastic reduction in the number of possibilities always serves to simplify the task of staging a scene.

Donna Elvira's first appearance in *Don Giovanni* (Act I, No. 3) provides an instructive example of a situation which is so restricted that it virtually stages itself with an almost mechanical necessity. This scene plays on a square near Don Giovanni's palace. The setting features two gates, three arches, two benches, and a fountain that can be used as a hiding place (Diagram 9–7).

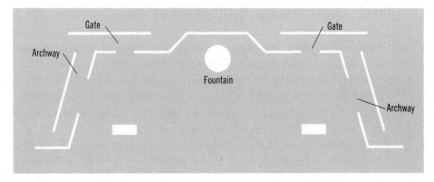

Gate

Gate

Archway

Fountain

Archway

Diagram 9–7

A conversation between Don Giovanni and Leporello is interrupted when the Don senses the approach of a woman and suggests to his servant that they both hide and do a bit of reconnoitering. Donna Elvira, a noble-looking lady wearing traveling clothes, enters in great agitation. Although we do not at first realize that she is one of the Don's recent victims, we gather from her words that she is searching for a man whom she loved and who abandoned her. She vows to find him and to "tear out his heart!" Don Giovanni and Leporello remain in the background and observe the young woman closely. The Don announces his intention to console her, and Leporello reminds us that some eighteen hundred others have been similarly "consoled" by his master.

It is not easy to make the interplay of these three characters believable. Great care must be taken to help the audience accept the fact that Elvira is not aware of the presence of the two men. Even though she is silent when they sing, she does not hear their remarks. The mise-en-scène must also make it credible that the Don, who watches Elvira with great interest, does not recognize her.

Leporello's participation in this scene permits more than one interpretation. It is generally taken for granted that what applies to the master holds good also for the servant. I prefer a different approach. In my opinion the scene gains in dramatic interest if Leporello recognizes Elvira right from the very beginning. He is greatly amused by this unexpected turn of events, decides to keep his mouth shut, and looks forward with glee to the moment when his master will face, instead of a prospective seductee, one of his discarded "wives."

The situation imposes severe restrictions, and the director must see to it that:

1. Elvira's agitation, which is so clearly expressed in her singing, continues to be evident throughout the entire scene; she must convince us that she is so distracted by her unhappy thoughts as to be blind and deaf to everything else.
2. The men always remain outside Elvira's line of vision, well upstage of her.
3. When the men sing they stand as far as possible from Elvira, and their voices have the right tone of secrecy.
4. The Don never has an opportunity to see Elvira's face; her back must be turned to him whenever he watches her and, when she moves in his general direction, he must be provided with some appropriate distractions of his own.
5. The Don's delay in approaching and addressing his prospective victim must be justified by some preparatory actions or by some other means.

A great deal of the music that Mozart allotted to Elvira in this opera exhibits an almost hysterical agitation. At her first appearance on stage, this quality is immediately evident in the unsettled orchestral dynamics and in the angry octave jumps of the violins, which give Elvira's complaints a pathetically desperate character. These octaves are also prominent in Elvira's D-Major aria, No. 8, which she sings later in the first act.

The orchestral passages that accompany the remarks of the men are much more subdued. Guided by this slackening of energy, as well as by the Don's compassionate tone of voice and his wish to console the lady, we can guess that when Elvira is not fulminating against the "barbaro" who broke his faith, she is either on her way to one of the benches or sits on it crying and drying her tears.

The musical form of this aria, with its two subjects and assorted codettas, is reminiscent of a sonatina. The pattern is symmetrical and strongly suggests a stage action divided between stage right and stage left. The 108 measures are distributed as follows:

Orchestral introduction (11 measures)

Exposition: 1st subject (10 measures)
                2nd subject and codettas (36
                    measures)
                (B-flat)

Recapitulation: 1st subject (10 measures)
                2nd subject and codettas (24
                    measures)
                (E-flat)

Coda (17 measures)

Letting ourselves be guided by the various musical and dramatic clues, we have no difficulty in determining the principal locations. Because of the need for secrecy and distance in the portions of the aria when the men sing and Elvira sits crying on one of the benches, there are only two possible arrangements for these sections. Since the musical form is symmetrical and the situation occurs twice (in the dominant and in the tonic), it seems logical to use both of these arrangements. If we allot the B-flat-Major sequence to the left bench and the E-flat repetition of it to the right one, then Diagram 9–8 will apply to measures 53 through 57 and Diagram 9–9 to measures 88 through 91.

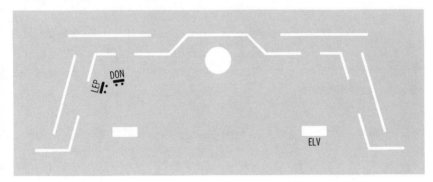

Diagram 9–8. Measures 53 to 57

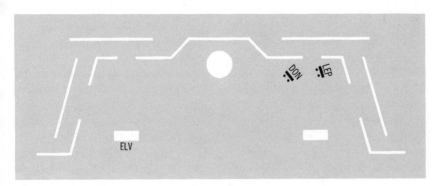

Diagram 9–9. Measures 88 to 91

In measures 41, 48, and 83, Don Giovanni's remarks are interrupted by vigorous outbursts from Elvira. It is not likely that she would utter these while sitting down, nor would we want her to get up from the bench merely in order to sing them. It seems more fitting if she walks toward the bench just before singing these sentences, and since at this point she must not be aware of the Don's presence, it is preferable to have her move away from him. As a result of these considerations we can add three more groupings for Elvira and the two men (Diagrams 9–10, 9–11, and 9–12).

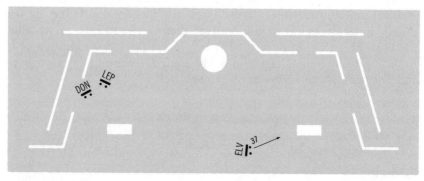

Diagram 9–10. Measures 32 to 36

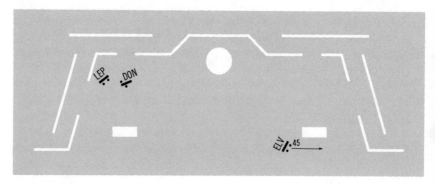

Diagram 9–11. Measures 41 to 44

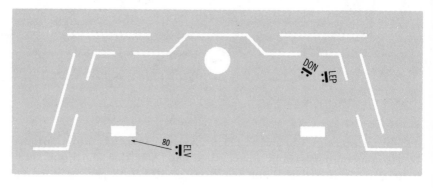

Diagram 9–12. Measures 76 to 79

Having established five basic positions for Elvira (Diagrams 9–8 to 9–12), it only remains to fill in the connecting links. The rest of the mise-en-scène then becomes, as the chess manuals would say, "merely a matter of technique." First we must decide by which route Elvira should reach the position indicated in Diagram 9–10 and also how she should get from her location in Diagram 9–8 to that in Diagram 9–12. Since for the second of these transits we know not only the destination, but also the point of departure, it may be simpler to consider it first.

The vigorous beginning of the recapitulation section (measure 57) is obviously the place where Elvira gets up from the left bench and moves a bit closer to the center. She need not leave this location while she restates the first subject of the aria. The opening measures of the second subject, with their explosive orchestral interludes, are made to order for excited stage walks.

In deciding which route Elvira should take from here to the area of the right bench, we may recall that in Chapter 2 we warned against the over-use of lateral walks of the "pendulum" type. Since we will probably want to have recourse to these in the final section of the aria, it is best not to anticipate them here, especially because the first orchestral interlude (measure 68) gives Elvira an excellent opportunity to retake the stage by walking up right. She can then take advantage of the second interlude (measure 72) to change her direction and go down right, crossing above the right bench to RA1. If she is to reach her position in Diagram 9–12 in time to turn and walk back to the bench while the Don sings his lines, she must turn and go left not later than measure 75.

Having arranged Elvira's locations and transits from measure 36 through 92, it is time to consider where she should enter the stage at the beginning of her aria and how she can best get to her position in Diagram 9–10.

The discussion in Chapter 2 acquainted us with the advantages of using diagonal lines while proceeding toward the downstage area. This method of approach is particularly desirable in situations in which a character's inner agitation must be acted out in a fairly long pantomime. During the orchestral introduction to the aria Elvira can use as much stage space as is available, so we unhesitatingly choose the right gate for her entrance.

During the eleven measures of the orchestral introduction she can stop for a while down right of the fountain and then move toward the left bench, a location that she can maintain for the duration of her opening vocal phrase. During the first of the orchestral interludes that initiate the second subject (measure 22) she can walk down left, crossing above the left bench to LA1, and during the second interlude (measure 26) and her subsequent vocal phrase she can traverse the distance from there to her position in Diagram 9–10.

Diagrams 9–13 and 9–14 give a complete sequence of all locations occupied by Elvira until the Coda which begins in measure 92.

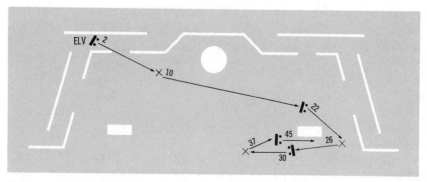

Diagram 9–13. Measures 1 to 56

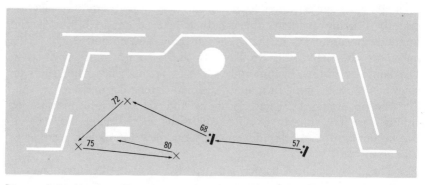

Diagram 9–14. Measures 57 to 91

Elvira's activities during the final section of the aria (measures 92 to 108) do not offer any special problems. Vocal climaxes of this kind do not leave us with many alternatives; they gravitate quite naturally to the downstage center area. It is best, however, if Elvira's back is turned to Don Giovanni during the short postlude so that she does not recognize him until the very last moment. A pendulum walk, first to the left and then to the right (after she gets up from the bench in measure 92), accomplishes this in the simplest possible fashion.

Although Don Giovanni's and Leporello's actions during this aria are governed by very different considerations, they are so closely related that they need not be discussed separately.

With the last words of his recitative, the Don playfully twirls Leporello around and runs outside the left gate to scan the surroundings for any unwelcome passer-by who might disturb his forthcoming flirtation. He is so proud of his "nose" for pretty women that he does not even bother to glance in the direction from which his latest victim is approaching. Leporello, on the other hand, decides to take a look and tiptoes over to the right gate. His curiosity is rewarded when with the very first E-flat-Major chord of the orchestra—he recognizes Donna Elvira. His immediate reaction is to urge his master to take to his heels in order to avoid the inevitable recriminations of his former inamorata. But first Leporello himself must run for cover, so he dashes into the center archway, flattening himself against the upstage wall. After standing there for a few seconds, he decides that it might be more fun to say nothing to his master and to let matters take their course. Since the success of his joke will depend on his not being seen and recognized by Elvira, he does not move until she turns in the other direction. His chance to slip away comes with the second set of octave jumps in the violins (measure 7) when Elvira turns to the right, wringing her hands. The moment she turns her back on him, Leporello runs to join his master outside the left gate where both of them remain hidden (or just barely visible) until the second subject of the aria. At this point (measure 22) the Don re-enters through the left gate and observes Elvira's back as she walks down left to LA1. He notices the elegance of her clothing and feels that, before accosting her, he must have Leporello inspect and adjust the neatness of his own attire. Turning clockwise (so that his back is turned to Elvira), the Don beckons Leporello to join him and then proceeds to the right archway. Leporello follows the Don and, after his master turns clockwise to face him, busies himself smoothing the front of his collar and coat.

Consequently, during measures 26 to 32, while Elvira is facing and walking toward the right, the Don is either on his way to the right archway or is facing Leporello, who has joined him and is standing up left of him (Diagram 9–15). Once Elvira has turned away to face down left

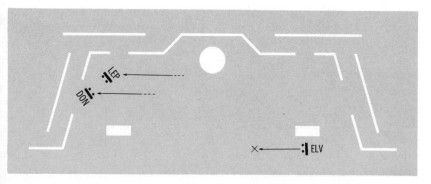

Diagram 9–15. Grouping during measures 30 to 33

and there is no longer any danger of the Don's catching a glimpse of her face, he goes slightly left, crossing Leporello. While allowing his servant to inspect the back of his costume, the Don is in position to admire Elvira's figure and to listen to her complaints (Diagram 9–16).

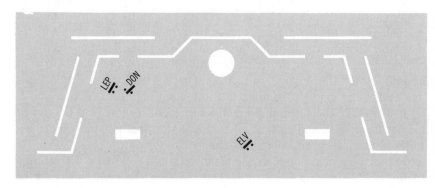

Diagram 9–16. Grouping during measures 34 to 37

Don Giovanni's remarks in measures 37 to 41 should be sung softly and casually over his right shoulder to Leporello. At the end of this sentence, he takes a few steps toward Elvira, so that his first "what a pity" is sung in her direction; the second one is addressed to Leporello. At this point the Don notices that his lace cuffs could stand a bit of fluffing up. He returns to his servant and holds out his left arm; a little later he turns counterclockwise and stretches out his right arm. It is in this position that he sings of his yearning to console the young woman. As he comes to the end of this sentence, he finally seems satisfied with his appearance and goes left, intending to cross above the bench to address the crying lady from up left. Leporello begins his sarcastic observations from his position near the right archway, but with his last words (measure 56) he edges closer to the fountain. This is the moment for which he has been waiting, and he does not want to miss any part of the fireworks that are certain to explode when Elvira suddenly finds herself face to face with the man whom she has been seeking so persistently.

At the precise moment the orchestra plays the opening chord of the recapitulation section (measure 57) and Don Giovanni is passing above the left bench, Elvira gets up and takes a couple of steps to the right. Leporello barely has time to take refuge behind the fountain while Don Giovanni, hat in hand, finds himself facing an empty bench. Having wasted an elegant bow, the Don turns and goes into the left archway. It takes him a little while to recover from this unexpected setback. Facing up left, away from the audience, he adjusts the brim of his hat and takes his time replacing it on his head. In performing these actions he must look and act the part of the frustrated wooer, but everything he does must be performed as background action without in any way distracting the audience's attention from Elvira's vocal and emotional agitation. By the time the second subject of the aria reappears (measure 68) and Elvira starts her walk toward up right, the Don has recovered his equanimity and goes right in an effort to intercept his prey before she eludes him through the right gate. When Elvira stops down right of the fountain, Don Giovanni notices that his boots need a bit of polishing. In measure 72, at the same time that Elvira goes down right, the Don motions Leporello to come out of his hiding place behind the fountain. In measure 76, he bends slightly to show Leporello a particularly offensive spot on his right boot. Leporello kneels down right of his master and busies himself wiping the boot with his sleeve. With the second "what a pity" the Don extends his left leg, ordering Leporello to change his position to shine the other boot. The "consolation" lines are therefore sung while Leporello is positioned down left of the Don (Diagram 9–17). At the end of this sentence (measures 90 and 91) we have a mirror image repetition of the actions in the corresponding place in measures 55 and 56. Don Giovanni goes right to address Elvira. Leporello gets up, but remains in the same location near the left archway. As the Coda begins and Elvira goes left, the Don again finds himself facing an empty bench.

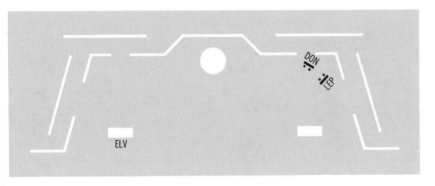

Diagram 9–17. Measures 86 to 89

The staging of the final section of the aria (measure 92 to the end) is merely an elaboration of familiar motives. With the first of Elvira's high B-flats the Don goes left, intending again to address her face to face. With the repetition of her vocal phrase (measure 95) she turns away from him to face toward the right. He stands helpless for two measures and with her second high B-flat he turns to Leporello, who runs forward to meet his master up right of the left bench.

After the last speck of dust is removed and Elvira has reached the final note of her aria, Don Giovanni makes his final and successful approach to his slippery victim. He removes his hat, makes an elaborately deep bow, and finds himself faced with an upsetting misadventure!

Leporello, who has run to the left bench, can hardly keep himself from exploding with laughter.

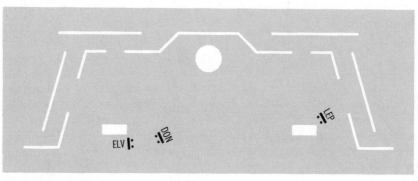

Diagram 9–18. Grouping at the end of the scene.

~ 10

Imaginative staging

WHETHER THE OPERATIC stage director wants it or not, whether he is equal to the task or not, it is his lot to complete and fill out much of the dramatic action that, theoretically at least, should have been invented by the librettist and the composer.

Most opera-goers think that the stage director functions mainly as the intermediary between the librettist and the actors, in the same sense that the conductor acts as the middleman between the composer and the instrumentalists. Up to a point this analogy is true. The composer creates the music; the conductor interprets the composer's intentions and transmits them to the actual players. The division of responsibilities is perfectly clean-cut. The composer does not have to be a competent conductor, nor does the conductor have to complete an unfinished score.

The situation is quite different with the stage director. Unlike the noncomposing conductor, he is more or less forced to ply the trade of a dramatic author. Even the most cursory perusal of operatic librettos and scores reveals that very few of them contain a sufficient number of acting instructions, while most of them contain pitifully few or none at all. It is possible that the audiences of the past did not expect opera singers to act, or perhaps they were satisfied with very little when it came to dramatic values. Today, however, a more serious approach to operatic acting and staging is taken for granted, and the problem of applying additional dramatic values has fallen into the lap of the stage director. The results are not always happy, for there is a great difference between being able to transmit someone else's dramatic ideas and being able to invent one's own. Each of these tasks calls for highly specialized talents, all of which are not necessarily granted to one and the same person. I have had occasion to observe the work of gifted men who could obtain excellent results when imparting existing staging ideas to singers, but who could not devise interesting stagings of their own. I have also known remarkably inventive directors who lacked communicative powers to such an extent that they elicited nothing but antagonism from the singers who worked with them.

Experience shows that it is easier to teach techniques than to stimulate original thinking, and I am fully aware that products of superior creativity are not likely to result from methods described in a book. The need for more imaginative dramatic procedures in opera is so great, however, that I want to offer three somewhat unorthodox approaches that have proven useful to me and to a number of my students.

For want of better terms, I shall call these methods *elaborations*, *transpositions*, and *extensions*. All of them are intended to clarify the relationship between operatic characters and to strengthen the various elements of the plot.

Elaborations

Dramatic ideas

The quarrel between Rigoletto and Count Ceprano, which is such an important link in the chain of dramatic events in Verdi's opera, offers several opportunities for elaboration and can be used to draw the audience's attention early in the opera to Rigoletto's malicious pleasure in abetting the Duke's amorous pursuits and to the sadistic delight the jester takes in hurting the feelings of the courtiers.

In my staging of the opening moments of the opera, I have Rigoletto appear carrying, and occasionally rolling, a large hoop which he then uses to encircle one of the page boys who is welcoming the arriving guests. All this proceeds with playful good humor until Rigoletto notices the approach of the Count and Countess Ceprano. While the Countess, escorted by a young man, goes ahead and crosses the stage to greet a group of her friends, Rigoletto hides and lies in wait for her grotesquely fat* husband, who follows with a lumbering gait. As Ceprano crosses in front of him, the jester trips him by catching one of the Count's legs in his hoop. The fat courtier's clumsy efforts to free himself elicit the laughter of the guests and the mortified glances of his wife. All this happens before the entrance of the Duke, by which time the fuming and furious Ceprano has joined his wife and Rigoletto has run off in the opposite direction to look for other opportunities to indulge his malicious jokes.

Later, when the Duke dances the minuet with Countess Ceprano,

* In Victor Hugo's play, De Cossé (the opera's Ceprano) is described as one of the four fattest men in France.

the jealous husband wishes to eavesdrop on their conversation. Here again the jester makes himself obnoxious, dancing between the Count and the couple and annoying Count Ceprano in various ways to prevent him from hearing the Duke's passionate remarks. By the time Rigoletto addresses his opening mocking lines to the Count, the animosity between the two men has already reached an advanced stage. Rigoletto's later suggestions to the Duke that he abduct the Countess and that he behead her interfering and stupid husband become simply additional thrusts in a well-advanced campaign of hostilities.

A similar opportunity to elaborate an important relationship occurs in the opening scene of *La Traviata*.

Of course it is understood that in the beginning of the opera Violetta Valery is a kept woman, but this fact is not spelled out clearly in the text or in the stage directions of the score. In order not to offend the sensibilities of their contemporaries, Verdi and his librettist obviously had to soft-pedal all references to Violetta's unsavory status. The modern theater has long since outgrown such Victorian prudery. Audiences are no longer shocked by revelations of immorality, and since we know that Baron Douphol is the lover of the moment, his position as host and "Mr. Moneybags" should be strengthened and developed. I try to accomplish this by introducing a jeweler who enters with a small box ordered for delivery that evening. The Baron pays the jeweler from a well-filled wallet, taking care, however, not to be seen by Violetta, who at that moment is busy talking to Dr. Grenville. All this takes place during the twenty-nine bars of orchestral music that follow the prelude and precede the entrance of Flora and the guests who come in with her. Later the Baron opens the box and takes out a gleaming diamond bracelet. After showing it to Flora and the Marquis, Douphol presents it with a grand gesture to Violetta, who graciously lets him place it on her wrist. This bit of added business identifies the Baron as the current "protector" of Violetta. It also helps to contrast Douphol's vulgar ostentation with the delicate attentions of Alfredo, who, as Gastone informs us, came daily during Violetta's illness to inquire about her. During the rest of this scene, I continue to stress the Baron's intimacy with Violetta. When the guests get ready to leave the party at the approach of dawn, Douphol stands next to Violetta, bidding his friends good-bye and acting as if he fully expects to spend the rest of the night with his mistress. This makes Violetta uncomfortable. She runs to Flora and, in a discreet pantomime, asks her to explain to the Baron that his continued presence will be unwelcome on this occasion. When later, during her aria, Violetta hears Alfredo singing outside, she slips the Baron's bracelet off her arm and throws it on a table, thus symbolically discarding the golden fetters that chain her to a life that is rapidly becoming repulsive to her.

It is essential, of course, that all these new dramatic "elaborations" be compatible with the existing vocal and orchestral events. In this instance, the integration of musical and theatrical ideas does not offer the slightest problem. Near the beginning of the act, when Violetta invites her guests to partake of the food and wine, the chorus sings two gay sentences separated by a sixteen-measure instrumental passage. It is during this interlude that the Baron makes his presentation of the bracelet, and the second vocal outburst of the assembled company ("E al convito che s'apre ogni cor") becomes a fitting expression of the admiration and envy of Violetta's male and female friends. The brilliant scale played by the violins near the end of the farewell chorus becomes a perfect illustration of Violetta's run to Flora, and her emotional, broken sentences during Alfredo's first offstage singing seem made to order for the final business with the bracelet.

These two examples demonstrate how one elaborates existing dramatic ideas. In *Rigoletto*, it was the long, drawn-out quarrel between a courtier and the court jester; in *La Traviata*, the loveless liaison between a wealthy "protector" and his demimondaine mistress. Elaborations are often stimulated simply by the presence of secondary characters and can also be applied to existing props and costumes.

The elaboration of existing props is a most fruitful means of stimulating one's dramatic imagination. The first hint I had of this simple and effective method came from Richard Wagner, to whose extraordinary mind we owe so many basic musical and dramatic procedures. When Felix Mottl prepared his edition of Wagner's *Ring of the Nibelung* for the C. F. Peters publishing house, he included in it verbal remarks made by the composer during the musical and stage rehearsals that took place in Bayreuth in 1876. In the final scene of *Das Rheingold*, near the end of Wotan's solemn greeting to Valhalla, a fortissimo trumpet intones the motif of the sword. Wagner's printed direction for Wotan at this point says: "To be sung very decisively, as if moved by a mighty thought." Mottl adds here the following remark made by Wagner to the singer Betz, who was portraying Wotan: "Before Fafner leaves the stage, he contemptuously discards an insignificant-looking sword that belongs to the hoard of gold. Now Wotan sees it and, as a symbol of his 'mighty thought,' lifts it up toward the fortress." Translating this into our terminology, we can say that Wagner wanted to externalize Wotan's concept of Valhalla as a defense against Alberich's forces and thus hit upon the idea of reusing a prop in a manner not originally planned by him. This is precisely what we mean by the term *elaboration*.

In earlier chapters, the reader has already encountered several examples of prop elaborations. Donna Elvira's inquisitive leafing through Leporello's catalog (page 165) and Donna Anna's discovery of her murdered father's sword (page 69) are both typical applications of this highly useful technique.

Even a minimal elaboration of a prop can often help clarify things and make a later development more believable. Consider, for instance, Father Germont's sudden appearance at Flora's mansion, near the end of the second act of *La Traviata*. How, one wonders, does the old gentleman —who is certainly a total stranger to the Paris demimonde—manage to discover his son's whereabouts? It is most unlikely that he would get this information from Alfredo. Fortunately, this difficulty can be overcome very simply. Near the beginning of the preceding scene, we saw Violetta read a letter from Flora, inviting her to attend a party that very same evening. It is the accidental discovery of this invitation that informs the distraught and vengeful Alfredo just where he will be able to find his mistress. According to the stage direction in the score, Alfredo "rushes off, followed by his father." This is precisely what makes the sequence of events so unconvincing. I stage the ending of this scene so that, before rushing off, Alfredo throws Flora's letter on the table. Anxious to understand the reason for his son's wild behavior, the elder Germont picks up the letter and thus becomes aware of Flora's existence and of the festivities planned for that evening. Realizing the urgency of the situation, and hoping to prevent his son from committing some rash and unworthy act, the old gentleman feels compelled to take direct action. As we know, he arrives at Flora's too late to accomplish his mission.

Imaginative exploitations of existing props can also be very helpful in providing unobtrusive background activities for non-singing personages at times when they are not directly involved in the leading action.

In the scene preceding the second-act finale of *The Marriage of Figaro*, the Count enters with a crowbar which he intends to use to pry open the locked door of his wife's dressing room. As soon as the Countess confesses that Cherubino is hidden there, the Count puts down the crowbar. Now that his wife no longer has any justification for withholding the key to the closet, the Count has no further need for the crowbar, and in most productions it becomes a "dead prop" at this point. I feel, however, that its dramatic usefulness is by no means exhausted. In a later section of this finale, when Figaro tries to persuade the Count that it was he who hid in the closet and later jumped from the window, I have Antonio find the crowbar. Recognizing it as one of his own tools and being completely puzzled by its presence in the bedroom of the Countess, the tipsy gardener picks it up and shows it to his niece, Susanna, and to her mistress, the Countess. Annoyed by her uncle's meddling in matters that are none of his business, Susanna leads Antonio back to his broken flower pot. They arrive there just in time to take part in their respective supporting and leading actions: Susanna's running to massage Figaro's presumably sprained ankle and Antonio's displaying the papers that were dropped near the flower bed by the escaping page boy. When Antonio finally leaves the Countess's room, he carries the crowbar, along with the flower pot, offstage with him.

Dramatic inventiveness of this type is by no means restricted to operas that furnish—like those of Mozart—only a minimum of printed stage directions. Even Puccini, whose devotion to minute, everyday realities earned him the nickname "the poet of the little things," by no means exhausted the possibilities inherent in an imaginative employment and reuse of existing props. To add to our earlier example from *Il Tabarro* (page 336), I should like to describe another opportunity for prop elaboration that presents itself in the last act of *Tosca*.

During the lovely haunting passage for divided cellos that precedes his aria "E lucevan le stelle," Cavaradossi has enough time to write down several sentences of his farewell message to his beloved. I see no reason why he cannot go on with his writing after the aria. The orchestral interlude that accompanies the entrance of Spoletta, the Sergeant, and finally Tosca, is quite long, and its opening measures can certainly be employed to continue the action that was interrupted for the emotional reliving of Cavaradossi's memories. Whether or not Cavaradossi keeps on writing after he finishes his aria is relatively unimportant, however. What matters is that at least part of the letter is written, that it lies on the table, and that an ideal opportunity for exploiting its presence is provided later by the dramatic situation, the music, and the text.

I arrange the mise-en-scène in such a way that Tosca moves toward the table during the section where she describes how she and her lover will embark on a sailboat at Civitavecchia. At the end of her phrases describing how all nature awaits the sunrise, she sees the letter, picks it up, and starts reading it. The lines that Cavaradossi sings at this point—they are marked "dolcissimo" and "with the most tender emotion"—begin with the words:

> Amaro sol per te m'era il morire
> Da te la vita prende ogni splendore.

For singing purposes I render these lines as:

> How painful was the thought that I would leave you!
> To part from you made death itself more frightful.

In either language, this sentence is the most direct imaginable reference to Cavaradossi's sentiments when he was penning the letter. Reading her lover's farewell at the very moment she is so certain of his deliverance from death gives Tosca a chance to react to his passionate words with a depth of feeling quite different from the generalized expression of tenderness we usually witness here. After reading it, Tosca folds the letter and hides it in her bosom. She does it in a way that makes us certain that she plans to treasure it and reread it the rest of her life.

Costumes

Elaborations of costumes lend themselves particularly well to scenes involving mistaken identities and disguises. It is often advantageous to clarify these disguises by having them executed in full view of the audience. For instance, when Elvira, Anna, and Ottavio enter the stage to plot the undoing of Don Giovanni toward the end of the first act of the opera, they do not yet need to wear their dominos and masks. These can be carried by servants, and each character's domino can be put on while his partner is singing. This helps both to liven up a rather static scene and to relieve the audience of any doubt regarding the identity of the disguised ladies. The facial masks, furthermore, need not come into play until the offstage strains of the minuet warn the conspirators that they are about to be observed by Leporello and the Don.

Elaborations of costume disguises can often be prompted by very fundamental dramatic considerations. I am thinking particularly of the last act of *The Marriage of Figaro*, where the Countess and Susanna assume each other's appearance in order to punish their respective husbands. How and when should this exchange of costumes take place? According to the score, the mistress and the maid are already disguised when they enter the stage, but I have always felt that this is quite illogical. Susanna, who has been forewarned by Marcellina, knows that the jealous and suspicious Figaro is hiding nearby. In order to teach him a lesson, she proceeds to sing a recitative specifically designed to convey the impression that she, Susanna, is rapturously awaiting the embraces of the Count. It is obvious that if Figaro can hear her every word (and if he cannot, then neither Susanna's recitative and aria nor Figaro's subsequent remarks make any logical sense), he can most probably also catch a glimpse of her. Susanna is clever enough to realize that if Figaro saw his bride dressed up as the Countess, her entire elaborately planned scheme would be given away immediately. In my opinion, this scene is meaningful only if Figaro's bride is still recognizable as herself at this point.

A real problem arises after Susanna's aria, when in a matter of seconds the Countess must be able to assume the appearance of her servant. I solve this difficulty by having both women wear a very similar basic dress so that when changing their appearance they need concern themselves only with such minor, but characteristic, accessories as the maid's dust cap and apron and the mistress's fan and shawl. These can be very quickly and visibly exchanged in the corner of the stage opposite the one where Figaro is hiding. In the meantime the night has been advancing, and the stage has become quite a bit darker during Susanna's aria. By the time Cherubino enters and mistakes the Countess for her maid ("By the headdress I know it is Susanna!"), a change in silhouette is quite sufficient to explain the boy's misunderstanding.

The dramatic possibilities inherent in costume elaborations are quite extensive. Two more examples will serve to show their variety and scope.

Fiordiligi's and Dorabella's exaggerated lamentations over the departure of their fiancés in *Così fan tutte* can be given an amusing twist by a continuous change in costuming from the third scene on. When the sisters return to the stage after the arrival of the mock Albanians, their desperate sense of loss can be pointed up by giving their attires a touch of mourning in the form of black shawls and handkerchiefs. In the following scene they can continue with this metamorphosis and appear outfitted in a complete ensemble of widow's weeds. To reflect their later change of heart, their costumes in the second act can go through an opposite series of transformations, culminating in the wedding gowns that they parade in the final scene of the opera.

Finally, the amusing "tigress-in-lamb's-clothing" sequence in *Don Pasquale*, which is the main feature of the second act, can be greatly enhanced if, at the appropriate moment, Norina removes her overgarment and is revealed wearing a brilliantly colored dress with a daring decolletage that provides the most shocking contrast to her initial appearance as a prim and modest convent-bred maiden!

Characters

Elaborations of characters offer a wide scope for the exercise of a director's dramatic ingenuity. Playwrights and librettists are usually so preoccupied with presenting the main events of their plots that they tend to neglect characters who are not directly involved in the main action.

In the third act of *The Marriage of Figaro*, for instance, we meet the slow-witted judge, Don Curzio, who stutters his way amusingly through the sextet scene and, having served his purpose, disappears never to be mentioned again. I feel it is a pity not to profit from the existence of such a colorful theatrical personage. In my staging of the festivities that close the act, I have Don Curzio lead the wedding procession, prepare the documents for the civil marriage ceremony, assist the Count and the two couples in the signing of the papers, and even add his tenor twang to the final chorus. Such an elaboration of a character after he has been officially dismissed from the action I call "exploiting." If I find that I can use a character before his first scheduled appearance, I refer to it as "planting" him.

In the second act of *Rigoletto*, for example, the main action cannot progress until the jester becomes aware that his daughter is concealed in the palace and that the Duke is with her. The librettist accomplishes this by introducing a page who is prevented from delivering a message because the Duke, in the courtiers' words, "may not be disturbed" at the moment. This is the pageboy's first and only appearance in the score, but I arrange it so that the audience becomes acquainted with him at the very beginning of the act when he, along with another page, helps the Duke get out of his student outfit. This bit of "planting" not only smoothes out the continuity of the plot (see page 202), but also gives validity to the page's words when he assures the courtiers that he had seen his master earlier that morning.

Character elaborations are especially helpful in large ensemble scenes where the non-singing personnel—even when they are leading characters— are apt to be neglected by the librettist and left to their own devices for long stretches of time. The standard rule for these non-singers is to listen to what the other characters say and react in an appropriate manner. This is a good rule and it often suffices, but many elaborations in the form of characteristic actions can always be invented. Here again it is up to the stage director to complete the task that was left unfinished by the author of the text.

Even in the operas of Wagner, who was not only his own librettist, but also a brilliant theatrical craftsman fully aware of the need to provide accurate and detailed acting instructions for singers, there are sections in which the non-singing characters are given no directions for many pages of the score, and it is necessary for the stage director to elaborate their roles. A scene from *Lohengrin* provides an especially good illustration of this problem.

Near the beginning of the third scene of the second act we encounter four Nobles who, unlike the rest of the Brabantian knights, are not enthusiastic over the prospect of embarking on warlike adventures under the leadership of King Henry and Lohengrin. These dissident Nobles draw together and in furtive tones cast doubts on the advisability of the impending expedition. Telramund joins them and informs them of his intention to accuse Lohengrin of sorcery. The Nobles are in sympathy with the banished knight, but seeing that the bridal procession is about to begin, they hasten to hide him from the wrath of the populace.

These four Nobles appear again in the next act. They are the ones who accompany Telramund during his ill-starred intrusion into Elsa's wedding chamber, and it is they who later carry Telramund's corpse from the scene of the slaying to the banks of the river Scheldt. What is significant here is that after these Nobles help Telramund hide, they seem to disappear from the activities of the second act. Wagner does not give them any singing lines nor does he mention them in any of the acting directions. They are treated as totally unimportant characters who, once they have served their limited purpose, can either fend for themselves or leave the stage. I much prefer to keep these Nobles on hand and provide them with suitable actions to strengthen the anti-Lohengrin sentiment in the coming dispute.

Even more significant is Wagner's treatment of Ortrud, who is of course anything but a minor character. Ortrud's behavior in this scene is described with great care long before she begins to sing, and for a while she is the recipient of the author's most minute attention. She is first seen marching in the wedding procession, which winds its way from the women's quarters on stage right to the cathedral steps on the left. Wagner describes her appearance and position in the marching order. He also provides for the preliminary highlighting: "Among those who follow Elsa near the end of the procession is Ortrud, attired in rich clothing; the women next to her hold themselves aloof in thinly disguised disdain, so that she appears as if isolated from the others; her face bespeaks a rising anger." During the procession she marches silently without participating in the choral ensemble, but at the end of this musical section we read that "as Elsa is about to ascend the cathedral steps, Ortrud hastily comes forward and, placing herself on the first step, compels Elsa to back away from her."

This action initiates the important episode in which Ortrud claims precedence over Elsa and gloats over the young woman's ignorance of her future husband's name. The ensuing spirited altercation between the two principal women is presented with great musical and dramatic vigor, and the reactions of the knights, waiting ladies, and page boys are annotated in ample detail. This lengthy episode is interrupted by the arrival of King Henry and Lohengrin with their retinue of knights. Elsa rushes to her bridegroom to complain of Ortrud's malicious behavior, whereupon Lohengrin confronts Ortrud and orders her to stay away from his bride. According to Wagner's stage direction at this point, Lohengrin "fixes his eyes upon Ortrud, who freezes into helpless immobility before his commanding glance." Up to this point the author's acting instructions for Ortrud have been elaborate and precise, but now, as Lohengrin turns to console his bride, Wagner seems to lose all interest in Ortrud. The next stage direction for her does not occur until just before curtain comes down on the act. During the intervening six important dramatic episodes, containing some 440 measures of music, Ortrud is completely ignored. It is true that she participates in the solemn musical ensemble inspired by Elsa's inability to repress the doubts sown in her by Ortrud and Telramund. But even subtracting the seventy-nine measures of this ensemble, we are still left with more than 350 measures during which Ortrud's behavior is not described in any way by Wagner even though she remains fully visible to the audience.

I am sure that it is not in the nature of this ambitious and imperious woman to remain a passive observer of the events that are so essential to her very existence. It seems to me that she would continue to plot against Lohengrin and to dominate her credulous and dull-witted husband. I think it is she who should bring Telramund out of hiding and induce him to make his impassioned speech accusing Lohengrin of sorcery. Wagner makes it amply clear that in the Telramund household it is the wife who is in charge. Therefore, it seems only logical that the husband look for support and guidance from his trusted helpmate during his violent outburst. I am thinking chiefly of Telramund's rather malicious innuendo that Lohengrin surely cannot consider King Henry unworthy of his confidence. This subtle maneuver is much too sophisticated to have been invented by the brawny warrior. It seems much more likely to have been thought up by his wife and then suggested to him by an appropriate look or gesture. Later on it should be Ortrud again who leads her husband to Elsa and urges him to approach her with the unholy proposal of wounding her husband in order to force him to reveal his identity. After Telramund's painful confrontation with Lohengrin, Ortrud should seek out the four Nobles who have shown their sympathy for Telramund and take them to her husband for a whispered conference, thus preparing their subsequent joint attack on Lohengrin. Her triumphant gesture of shaking her fist at Elsa at the end of the act will have more zest if she can feel that she and her husband have acquired these valuable friends and allies.

This example from *Lohengrin* demonstrates how a stage director can give theatrical life to characters the author has neglected by involving them directly in the activities of other characters. Elaborations of this sort always bring about a substantial gain in credibility and variety, but care must be taken that the added business does not detract from the proper highlighting of the main action.

Transpositions

This method is closely related to the method of elaborations, except that the ideas, props, costumes, and characters used in transpositions originally appear in other portions of the opera, where they serve different purposes.

Props

The props used in transpositions are usually symbolic of the dramatic ideas to which they are attached, so that when a prop is transplanted, the idea goes with it quite automatically. Here are a few fairly typical examples.

Leporello's catalog in *Don Giovanni* is the visible symbol for the idea of keeping an up-to-date list of the Don's feminine conquests. Da Ponte and Mozart use it only in the first act, but I find that an excellent opportunity for transposition presents itself in the Graveyard Scene of the second act, during the following conversational exchange:

DON GIOVANNI: A few of the adventures that have happened to me since we parted I will save until later. But the best one you must hear right away.

LEPORELLO: Another woman?

DON GIOVANNI: What else!

(Leporello holds up his hand, asking his master to wait a moment, and then takes out the catalog, kneels behind a gravestone, and gets ready to write down the name of the latest victim.)

DON GIOVANNI: During the evening I encountered a young and very beautiful lady. First I approached her, then took her by the hand. She acted timid, and when I reassured her, she mistook me—can you guess for whom?

LEPORELLO: I've no idea. *(His hand is poised for writing, but he is bored to death by all these irrelevant details.)*

DON GIOVANNI: For Leporello!

LEPORELLO: For me? *(He can hardly believe his ears.)*

DON GIOVANNI: For you!

LEPORELLO: How flattering! *(He gets up, as if in a daze, and puts away the catalog.)*

Asking his servant to inscribe the name of his own girl friend in the catalog is a bit of meanness that obviously gives the Don a very special sadistic pleasure. It also happens to be a dramatic tidbit much enjoyed by performers and audiences.

In the last scene of *Carmen*, there is mention of a ring that Don José once gave to his fiery friend. This ring, however, has not been previously mentioned or shown in any other scene of the opera. What could be more natural than to have Don José put this ring on Carmen's finger at the end of the second act, when he finally decides to throw in his lot with the gypsy smugglers? This is a sensible idea that lends itself well to dramatic action, but what makes it truly valid is that it fits so perfectly, from the point of view of both mood and timing, with the loud and jubilant C-Major strains with which Bizet closes this particular act.

Transpositions of props can also be used with excellent effect in comic situations, especially if the device serves to strengthen some important feature of the plot.

A charming opportunity to transpose a whole roomful of props offers itself in *Don Pasquale*. The main action of the opera centers around a joke played on an old bachelor in order to cure him of his foolish desire to take a young wife. In the text, this educational process begins immediately after the mock marriage ceremony of the second act, when the 'bride" starts criticizing and changing all the established household arrangements in her new home. This idea can be elaborated in a very amusing manner in the beginning of the next act by having Don Pasquale's solid and old-fashioned furniture carried out of his library—which was the setting of the opening scene of the opera—and replaced by Norina's frilly and feminine furnishings, which the audience also saw during an earlier scene. The entire, rather frantic, removal-and-transposition can take place while the dispossessed master of the house, who vainly pretends to be reading a book, is seen perched on top of his library ladder. The incongruous final appearance of this room—especially Norina's delicate pink couch surrounded by the gnarled oaken walls of the library— symbolizes the absurdity of this union, while the hustle and bustle of the furniture movers fits the music of the opening chorus to absolute perfection.

Susanna's wedding veil in *The Marriage of Figaro* is a symbolic prop; obtaining the Count's blessing for the marriage is the dramatic idea. In the text of the opera, this veil is mentioned only in the first and third acts, but it can be very profitably transposed into the second act. During the great finale of this act there are two analogous quartet situations during which the Count is cornered and almost forced to give his consent to the marriage of Figaro and Susanna. On each of these occasions I have Susanna kneel down in front of the Count while the Countess hands him the veil. All of this serves to highlight the suspense of these two moments when the luck of the battle seems to have deserted the Count. The veil is already in his hands when, each time, he is rescued by a knock on the door and by the entrance of new characters (Antonio first, and later Marcellina, Basilio, and Bartolo) whose arrival furnishes new excuses for the Count's delaying tactics.

Dramatic ideas

Dramatic ideas as such do not lend themselves particularly well to transposition, but when combined with props this method is surprisingly effective. I strongly recommend that young stage directors make complete lists of props and scan them systematically with the idea of locating useful transpositions.

It is occasionally possible to transpose even a dramatic idea if it has a sufficiently strong association with a musical phrase played by the orchestra. Making full use of such associations not only enriches the stage action, but also helps to clarify when a singer should carry the leading action (when an orchestral passage refers to him) and when he should retreat to the shadows of relative passivity (when a passage clearly relates to another character). The value of using and transposing instrumental associations can be seen in an episode from the second act of *Lohengrin,* where several independent actions succeed each other in such a way that a clear and effective staging must be coordinated very precisely with the information provided by the orchestra.

By accusing Lohengrin of sorcery, Telramund has succeeded in planting the seed of doubt in Elsa's mind. Taking advantage of the fact that Lohengrin is temporarily distracted by Saxon and Brabantian knights, who gather around him to assure him of their loyalty, Telramund attempts to persuade Elsa to let him unmask Lohengrin. Here is the wording of this scene as it appears in Wagner's libretto:

> *(While Lohengrin—surrounded by the knights and shaking each man's hand in turn—remains in the background, Telramund, unnoticed by the others, manages to creep closer to Elsa, who, filled with embarrassment, shame, and confusion, and not daring to glance at Lohengrin, is standing in the foreground struggling with herself.)*
>
> TELRAMUND *(secretly)*: Trust me! Let me show you a way to obtain certainty!
>
> ELSA *(frightened, but without raising her voice)*: Stay away from me!
>
> TELRAMUND: If I could wound him—and were it only the tip of his finger —I swear to you that his secret would be clearly revealed to you, and that he would then remain your own forever!
>
> ELSA: No, never!
>
> TELRAMUND: I shall be near you at night. Call me and the deed will be done, without harming him.
>
> LOHENGRIN *(stepping quickly into the foreground)*: Elsa, with whom are you consorting?
>
> *(Elsa, turning away from Telramund with an expression of heart-rending doubt, sinks down, greatly disturbed, at Lohengrin's feet.)*
>
> LOHENGRIN *(addressing Telramund and Ortrud with a terrifying voice)*: Depart from her, you cursed people! And never let my eyes light upon you again!
>
> *(Telramund makes a gesture of tortured rage.)*
>
> LOHENGRIN: Arise, Elsa! The course of our happiness is in your hands and in your faith. Does the anguish of doubt rob you of your peace? Do you wish to question me?
>
> ELSA *(in a turmoil of shame and confusion)*: You rescued me! You brought me salvation! etc.

This scene, involving the leading personages of the opera, can be said to consist of three separate duet situations, entrusted first to Telramund and Elsa, then to Lohengrin and Telramund, and finally to Lohengrin and Elsa. Wagner's orchestra informs us not only of the frame of mind and details of behavior of the characters who carry the leading action, but also at which precise moment the third member of the group embarks on the transitional steps that bring him into the limelight or, conversely, retire him to the shadows of background action.

During Elsa and Telramund's first confrontation, the orchestra elaborates on the sinister phrase referring to evil and doubt. Its threefold development is entrusted to the lower woodwinds (bass clarinet, bassoon, and English horn), and it grows in intensity with each repetition. When Elsa sings "never," the entrance of the tremolando violins makes it clear that, in her perturbation, she has reached the point of visible trembling. Since all this time Lohengrin's background action has not been represented in any way in the orchestra, he must, while shaking the hands of the nobles who gather around him, remain practically invisible. The short, accented chord with which the woodwinds and horns punctuate Telramund's third sentence indicates the exact moment when Lohengrin glances in Elsa's direction and notices that she is conversing with someone. At the end of Telramund's sentence, Lohengrin comes closer to Elsa and becomes fully aware of the evil forces that are trying to influence her. After asking "with whom are you consorting?" Lohengrin goes all the way to Elsa. Notice how clearly this music (with its "descending" passage in the lower strings) helps to illustrate Elsa's turning away from Telramund and sinking down at Lohengrin's feet. It is also during this music that Ortrud—who has been watching her husband and Elsa from a distance—joins Telramund so that Lohengrin can address his "terrifying" sentence to her as well as to her husband.

Lohengrin puts his hand to his sword with the descending scale played by the entire complement of strings. The continuous use of this string figure in the first-act battle between Telramund and Lohengrin has associated it with the idea of the sword. I find it very effective to transpose this association here. When, with the weakened repetition of this very same scale, Telramund tries to draw his own sword, he realizes to his inexpressible anguish that the weapon had been taken away from him after his ignominious defeat. Becoming fully aware of his degradation, he acts out the following three measures by wringing his hands in a gesture of tortured rage, turning away from Lohengrin and Elsa, and then staggering away from the area of the leading action. It is in the third measure of this phrase that Lohengrin bends down to address his bride. The girl, who in the preceding section was motionless and withdrawn from the action, is now brought back into the limelight. She is, however, too upset at first to obey Lohengrin's request to arise. After waiting for a moment (notice the fermata over the rest), he reminds Elsa that their future happiness lies completely in her hands.

The two short woodwind passages that are played here and two measures later do not have any special associations in this opera. They do, however, bear an uncanny resemblance to the motive in Wagner's *Tristan and Isolde* that refers to the look the ailing knight gave the Irish princess, a look that has haunted her ever since. This interpretation seems to fit quite naturally into the immediate situation involving Elsa and Lohengrin, and since it derives quite clearly from Wagner's highly personal musical vocabulary, I feel no reluctance in borrowing its associative meaning from *Tristan* and transposing it here.

In my staging of this scene, I have Elsa get up with this music and direct a soul-searching glance at Lohengrin. With the somewhat heightened repetition of this motive, she turns to observe Ortrud and Telramund, as if comparing that haughty couple with the man she loves. The third passage, which is carried by the solo oboe, has a very different quality. It seems to me that the two preceding "looks" have helped to dispel Elsa's doubts. During this passage she glances to heaven as if thanking it for its assistance and, when she is finally able to answer her bridegroom, her voice and bearing are filled with confidence and trust.

Characters

The transposition of characters presents certain problems. When important dramatic personages appear on stage, the audience naturally expects them to have something to say. New vocal lines cannot be added to an existing operatic scene, so a transposition of major characters is seldom feasible.

In one of the leading European opera houses, many years ago, the Countess was brought in for the choral-ensemble scene of the first act of *The Marriage of Figaro*. The wordless actions she performed on this occasion were neither necessary nor convincing, and the whole thing was so embarrassing that it cured me once and for all of any desire to experiment with the transposition of major roles. With minor characters, on the other hand, this method works remarkably well. In the same scene where the Countess made such an unfortunate impression, an unscheduled appearance of little Barbarina can be recommended without any qualms. She can enter with the rest of the peasants, bring in Susanna's wedding veil, help her cousin to attach it to a wreath of orange blossoms, send sidelong glances to the Count, flirt discreetly with Cherubino, and sing along with the chorus. All this adds variety and life to the proceedings and serves to acquaint the audience with a secondary, yet important, character whom they would not otherwise meet until the middle of the opera's third act.

As long as a minor personage can perform sensible, in-character activities that relate meaningfully to the main action, one should feel no hesitation in transposing him. In the opening scene of *La Traviata*, Annina can be called in by Flora to assist her mistress during the sudden attack of Violetta's illness; Dr. Bartolo's servants, Berta and Ambrogio, can be kept busy in the final scene of *The Barber of Seville*; and the page-boy, whose activities in the second act of *Rigoletto* were discussed earlier, can make himself useful in the first act.

Extensions

This method offers the most promising way to develop vital and imaginative staging ideas. Extensions, as the term implies, are achieved by following up, or extending, dramatic ingredients in such a way as to introduce completely new theatrical elements. To qualify as a genuine extension, a staging idea must have a close connection with the main action of the opera and must be expandable in its own right; that is, it must be applicable on more than one occasion and in more than one way. Furthermore, it should never appear to be intentional and dragged in for a special purpose. The ultimate reason for introducing a new prop, for instance, should always be camouflaged by using it in some casual way that makes it seem a natural part of the play's dramatic landscape.

Although it is not possible to provide a foolproof method of evolving valid and original extensions, a comparison of two staging interpretations of a musical passage from the first finale of *Così fan tutte* may serve to illustrate the difference between an idea that is merely a theatrical gimmick and one that becomes a catalyst stimulating a whole set of elaborations and transpositions.

The finale is set in the garden where, soon after the curtain opens, the two sisters are heard lamenting the departure of their two fiancés. If a stage director is musically sensitive, his attention will immediately be drawn to this prominent episode played by two flutes in the orchestral introduction (Example 10–1). With its upward-surging scales and liquid descending arpeggios, this passage is a typical case of "gesture music" that clamors for some form of dramatic action.

Example 10–1. COSÌ FAN TUTTE, I, Finale no. 18

In a production I saw at the Vienna Staatsoper in the spring of 1966, Dorabella was seated at this point beside a little pond, holding a fishing pole. Acting out the first of the flute scales, she pulled up the rod and ran downstage rejoicing at the sight of a little goldfish that was dangling at the end of her line. With the repetition of this music two measures later she removed the fish from the hook and ran back to her original place at the pond. All this was done with exquisite grace and was timed and contoured with great skill. It soon became apparent, however, that in spite of its charming execution, this novel bit of action was essentially unproductive. It had no organic relationship with the plot; it could not be repeated or developed. As a matter of fact, when this entire musical idea returned twenty-two bars later, it was not utilized for this or any other stage action.

I interpret the message of this musical phrase in a somewhat similar fashion, but instead of relating it to fishing, I prefer to connect it to the idea of watering flowers. I give each sister an elegant watering can and allot to each her own music where she lifts the can and then gently lets drops of water fall on the blossoms. This activity is less flamboyant than the business with the fishing pole, but since it is less obviously contrived, it can be safely repeated with the return of the music. Although these flowers originally came to mind merely as a means of complementing a musical passage, they can be given a much more intimate connection with the story and used to carry a far-reaching extension. They can become symbols of the crucial fidelity-infidelity aspect of the plot. Transposing them backward to the earlier garden scene, I convert them into floral offerings that the departing officers present to their broken-hearted fiancées. This presentation takes place during the first of the two soldiers' choruses, where one needs some fairly protracted, sensible occupation for the two loving couples. The watering of flowers in the first-act finale now becomes indicative of the tenderness that the sisters still feel for their fiancés. In the second act, when these passions begin to cool off, the flowers are allowed to wither. During the later serenade of the Albanians, they are used again for another staging idea, a reverse of the earlier one. At this point, Despina directs the girls of the chorus to remove and discard the wilted bouquets and to replace them with the far more colorful and exotic floral gifts brought in by the generous and impetuous new admirers.

As this example indicates, theatrical inventions—in opera, at least—are often mothered by necessity. The search for this extension began, as usual, with a whole series of dissatisfactions. Wanting a visual equivalent for a musical phrase and needing some suitable theatrical business to liven up two different choral scenes, I hit upon the idea of using flowers, which —first given as gifts, later watered, and finally discarded—filled all these needs.

Extensions are usually discovered in just this manner. Once one learns to articulate one's dissatisfactions, the correct solutions are not hard to find, and with luck a single idea may suffice for all requirements.

When I first approached the task of producing *Tosca*, I found myself confronted, in Act I, with three seemingly unrelated problems: (*a*) how to create a greater variety of groupings in the long and stormy scene between Floria and Mario; (*b*) how to make the Sacristan's asides in his scene with Mario more believable; and (c) how to strengthen, coordinate, and clarify everything connected with Mario's activities as a painter.

The problem of variety in the grouping of the principal singers concerned me most of all. Their long duet scene consists of more than a dozen clearly defined musical sections, each of which deserves its own location and grouping. It would be extremely helpful, I felt, if the lovers could occasionally sit down. Unfortunately, a church transept seems to offer no logical place for this. I had seen many productions where Mario and Floria reclined on the risers that lead to the scaffolding in front of the painting. This, however, was a most unlikely spot for the elegantly dressed Tosca, and the whole arrangement always looked so uncomfortable and clumsy that I wanted no part of it. What I needed was something as flexible and versatile as a free-standing bench, but I could not imagine how to inject such a piece of furniture into these surroundings without making it look hopelessly artificial and contrived.

In the meantime I remembered that in Sardou's play, on which the opera is based. Cavaradossi enters carrying a piece of material, which he later uses as a model for painting the folds of Mary Magdalen's cloak. Why not include this characteristic idea in the action of the opera in order to help make Cavaradossi more convincing as a painter? A piece of suitable material was easy enough to procure, but where was it going to be suspended? In addition to a bench-like piece of furniture, I now needed still another, taller prop on which to hang the drape, and I began to wonder if perhaps some object that belonged to a painter's normal equipment could serve both purposes. What about an artist's tool chest? When suspended over its open lid, the drape could be arranged in natural folds to serve as a model for the cloak in the painting; with its lid closed and the drape thrown over it, a large tool box should make a perfectly acceptable seat for the most fastidious of prima donnas. This was it! But it was only the beginning, for a genuine extension invariably yields unexpected dividends.

It is established right at the start that the Sacristan cleans Cavaradossi's paint brushes. Why couldn't some other chore of this type occupy him while Mario soliloquizes about the different aspects of feminine pulchritude? It was not long until the newly-invented tool chest housed a mortar and a pestle. Cavaradossi handed these to the Sacristan, along with a piece of blue pigment, which the worthy cleric dutifully crushed into powder while he sat in an opposite corner muttering imprecations against unbelievers who used visiting females as models for saintly Mary Magdalens. But what could the Sacristan sit on? The extension mechanism that had started humming with Sardou's drape now came forth with a footstool that the Sacristan brought with him when he first entered the chapel. Camouflaging its more essential later function as a seat, he first climbed on it to replace a candle in one of the chapel's large iron candelabras.

Now that Cavaradossi had the drape, the blue paint, and the clean brushes, it would hardly be believable if he suddenly decided not to use all this equipment. Mario simply *had* to be made into a proficient painter of murals. This miracle was accomplished by a trick of theater magic so simple that I almost hate to reveal it. The painting of Mary Magdalen's blue cloak was as carefully finished as her lovely blonde head with its enormous blue eyes. Before each performance, however, the cloak was covered with a white chalk that made this entire section of the painting look like ordinary greyish-white stucco with just a faintly sketched-in outline of the cloak. Dipping his brush into a water container concealed in his palette, Mario "painted" over the prepared portion of the picture, and dissolving the chalk, revealed the underpainted blue folds to the admiring eyes of the audience, members of which often congratulated me later on having found such an unusually talented and versatile singer.

The elaborations, transpositions, and extensions described in this chapter originally suggested themselves as answers to a variety of needs. Once a need was clearly articulated, it goaded a search that eventually led to the desired solution.

In the *Così fan tutte* example, the spark was ignited by the need to find a suitable action for a prominent musical phrase. The *Tosca* search was stimulated by the need for a greater variety in the grouping of the principal singers. In these instances, as in many others, we have observed the almost magical way a lucky invention kept branching out and assisting in the solution of other dramatic problems.

The French have a word for such a lucky inspiration. They call it *une trouvaille*—literally, "a find," but with a much more exciting connotation than its English equivalent. I like to compare these *trouvailles* with truffles, those savory growths so prized by connoisseurs of fine cooking. Just as it takes a specially trained pig to sniff out one of these pungent underground roots, so must the stage director develop a "nose" for its dramatic counterpart and learn to recognize its special "flavor." The first symptom of its presence is a feeling of restlessness and dissatisfaction. One senses that something is missing, or not quite logical, or out of place. One must learn to recognize this condition, for here is the moment and the spot where the director has to start "digging."

In discussing this entire process with aspiring stage directors, I have observed that while the concept of the need is quite obvious to them, the technique of "sniffing out truffles" is apt to remain rather mysterious. When pressed to explain his bafflement, the student is apt to formulate it as: "Why should I start digging here rather than in some other place?"

The best advice I can give is: Begin your quest by identifying with each character in the opera; study carefully all the stage directions and all the words of the other participants that refer to this character. In doing this, a director must not only scrutinize the words and actions of a character when he is audible and visible, but also fill in his hidden life before and between his appearances on stage, along the lines indicated in the discussion of Rosina's aria in Chapter 5. This approach, of course, does not always lead to imaginative and novel insights, but it is surprising how often it rewards the director with useful ideas that might otherwise have escaped his attention.

Here, for instance, are two results of this filling-in method. One is fairly obvious, while the other concerns an important detail so well concealed that it seems to have remained unnoticed by anyone for more than a century and a half. The first has to do with Colline's appearance in the second act of *La Bohème*. Since we know that Colline visits a barbershop during the first meeting of Mimi and Rodolfo, his freshly shaved and neatly trimmed countenance in the Café Momus scene should contrast quite noticeably with the unkempt and shaggy "bear" that the audience sees in the first act.

A much more surprising and valuable dramatic truffle is hidden among the busy comings and goings in the third act of *The Marriage of Figaro*. Susanna's entrance in the middle of the sextet is not only puzzling, but completely inexplicable. She comes in brandishing a purse to pay off Marcellina in order to prevent her from marrying Figaro. In the sequence of events of the opera, there is no way for Susanna to learn that the Count has decided Figaro must either marry or pay Marcellina, and consequently no way to account for the girl's sudden decision to sacrifice her dowry.

This startling break in the motivational continuity of an otherwise carefully constructed plot has escaped the attention of the countless Mozart experts who have dealt with the intricacies of *The Marriage of Figaro*. I wish that I could claim the honor of having discovered this glaring dramatic non sequitur. The truth is that I did not notice it until it was brought to my attention by a very young singer who was about to perform the role of Susanna for the first time in her life and to whom I had given the assignment of filling out her character's hidden offstage life and reconstructing the reasons for her entrances and exits in all four acts of the opera. The young lady accomplished this task quite readily in the first two acts, but when it came to her re-entrance in the third act, she apologized for being unable to understand how she could know of the need for the money. "When I leave the stage after my duet scene with the Count," she said, "I am absolutely certain of his good will. So much so, that when I run into Figaro as I exit, I whisper to him that he won't need a lawyer because his case against Marcellina has already been won. Convinced as I am that the Count will rule in Figaro's favor, I wouldn't dream of giving any money to that old woman."

At first, frankly, I thought that she had overlooked something, but the more I analyzed the situation the clearer it became that as far as the existing operatic continuity was concerned, my Susanna's reasoning was sound. Consulting Beaumarchais' play, I found a very different situation. There, Susanna's uncle, the gardener Antonio, is present at the judgment scene and, after hearing the Count's unfavorable verdict, leaves the stage with the words: "I'm off to tell my niece all about it." It is not surprising, therefore, to have Susanna rush in a few minutes later with a purse in her hand, exclaiming, "My lord, stop everything! Do not marry them: I've come to pay this lady with the dowry Madam has given me."

Once one is aware of this unusual oversight by Da Ponte and Mozart,* it becomes necessary to find some means of rectifying it. Adding Antonio to the sextet and rewriting the recitative to include his sentence about informing Susanna should, of course, be avoided if at all possible. I solve the problem by having Susanna re-enter the stage immediately after the Count's aria, along with the other litigants. She is very sure of herself, encourages Figaro to make his appeal to the bench, and throws sidelong, flirtatious glances at the Count. She knows perfectly well that Almaviva is the supreme judge of Andalusia and that Don Curzio is a mere underling, and she looks forward to the moment when the Count will reverse the judicial decision of his stuttering and feeble-minded subordinate. The Count in the meantime is savoring his revenge. As he renders his verdict condemning Figaro "to pay Marcellina or marry her," he smiles sadistically and watches the effect his words produce on the double-crossing chambermaid. At first Susanna is completely dumbfounded. Then, realizing that only the most heroic measures can save her tottering marriage plans, she hurries offstage to fetch the dowry money.

In his search for such truffles it is necessary for the director to restrict himself to the essential core of the plot and to try to avoid the irrelevant. The ability to separate productive thoughts from irrelevant ones is to some extent a matter of innate talent, but it can be fostered and developed. It is my fervent hope that the many examples presented in this volume will stimulate the student to embark on some original digging of his own. As a final illustration of a quest for dramatic truffles, I shall describe the thought processes that led me to a number of juicy finds in a scene abounding in particularly severe dramatic problems.

The first-act finale of *The Barber of Seville* is a very long scene consisting of a great many repetitions, asides, and extended ensemble sections. The action centers on Count Almaviva's strenuous efforts to gain a foothold in Dr. Bartolo's house, and on Bartolo's equally vigorous attempts

---

* It is possible that the authors were unable to follow Beaumarchais' procedure because, in the Viennese premiere of the opera, the roles of Dr. Bartolo and Antonio were sung by the same performer, the company's basso and stage manager, Antonio Bussani. Since Bartolo's presence is essential in the sextet, Antonio had to be sacrificed.

to dislodge the unwelcome intruder. It is a continuous struggle that involves every member of the household and eventually attracts the police and the neighbors.

When, some fifteen years ago, I was first confronted with the task of staging this finale, I recognized a number of difficulties, among which were one major problem and a variety of minor needs and puzzlements. The major problem concerned finding suitable action for the vivace section that ends this scene. Here the stage director is confronted with some 420 bars of vigorous music* during which the assembled characters express their growing bewilderment. From the opening sentence—"My poor head has been immersed in some dreadful iron cauldron where the noise of mighty hammers makes me deaf and numbs my mind"—to the very end, the text is devoid of anything even remotely suggesting appropriate stage activity.

In all the performances of this scene that I had witnessed, the principals and the chorus were lined up in two straight rows and sang the entire vivace in concert style with just a few descriptive gestures. Ensemble sections where everyone is shocked into a motionless tableau are perfectly acceptable dramatic devices, but only if the music also has a comparable frozen quality. In this particular finale such an ensemble is found in the A-flat-Major andante, where all the principal singers assure us of being "cold and immobile like a statue" and their condition is confirmed by the orchestra. The music of the final vivace, however, is anything but frozen, and I felt it required an equivalent excitement on stage. There is nothing either in the text or the situation to indicate what the characters are doing here, so I decided to see if the last exciting dramatic action could be elaborated and exploited at this point.

This took me back to the arrival of the policemen. The Sergeant and his men enter fully determined to put a stop to the noisy quarrel and to arrest the culprit. Following a riotous ensemble, where each of the characters accuses someone else, the Sergeant orders the arrest of the intruding soldier. This logical culmination of the scene dissolves when the intruder identifies himself confidentially to the Sergeant as a personage who not only may not be arrested, but who must be treated with the greatest possible deference. It is this "lion-into-lamb" transformation of the Sergeant and his men that motivates both the "statue" and the "cauldron" ensembles that follow.

What about the feelings of the arresting officer? Having made such an inexcusable faux pas, he would certainly want to redeem himself in the eyes of the Count and prove his subservience and investigative efficiency. Since someone else was obviously at fault, he would naturally try to put the blame on one of the Count's enemies. Don Basilio and Dr.

* In most performances this section is shortened to almost half its original length; this curtails the problem, but does not solve it.

Bartolo suggest themselves as likely victims. After both these gentlemen have repulsed the Sergeant, he could try to get instructions from Figaro and the Count, or he could write down the words of the chattering women as if they were depositions of important eye witnesses. The idea that the Sergeant would listen to these far-fetched observations and write them down as if they were statements of crucial significance appealed to me also for another reason. His actions would naturally be copied by his subordinates, and this would go a long way toward justifying the singing lines of the soldiers when, a while later, they repeat over and over the words sung by Bartolo and Basilio. There was no doubt that this "accusation and investigation" sequence offered excellent possibilities, but it had the weakness of not leading to an appropriate climax. The scene needed a snappy and unexpected ending, such as the arrest of an innocent bystander. Waiting for the additional truffle to materialize, I turned to other aspects of my assignment.

A while ago, when describing the difficulties I first encountered in the staging of this finale, I spoke of puzzlements. I give this name to those fairly rare occurrences when the librettist introduces some words or actions that seem out of character, illogical, or just puzzling. A conscientious director always tries to get to the root of these matters and, in so doing, occasionally hits upon a useful extension. One of these puzzling events occurs in the midst of this finale, when Don Basilio enters the stage singing solfeggio: "sol, sol, sol; sol; sol, sol, sol; do; re; mi; fa, re, sol, mi, la, fa, si, sol; do." It is only after this that he notices the presence of the tipsy soldier and begins to realize that something out of the ordinary is afoot.

Why is Basilio engaged in these vocal exercises at this point? He has been described by Figaro in the first scene of the opera as a hypocrite and penniless marriage broker, who is also Rosina's music teacher. When we meet Basilio in the flesh, the first part of Figaro's description is fully confirmed: Basilio clearly reveals himself as a hypocritical and greedy meddler in other people's matrimonial affairs. There is not a single word, however, on the subject of music. Basilio's only concern during his first appearance in the opera is to persuade Dr. Bartolo that the best way to run Count Almaviva out of town is to slander him. This culminates in Basilio's famous aria, following which Bartolo observes quite sensibly that there is no time for such roundabout procedures. The aged doctor announces that, as the best defense against unwelcome admirers, he himself will become Rosina's husband without any further delay. Consequently, the next thing to do is draw up the marriage contract, and it is for this purpose that the two men withdraw to Bartolo's quarters.

To give the subsequent events of this act their most logical continuation, I assume that, while working on the marriage contract, they run out of paper. Remembering the six pieces of stationery he always keeps in the living room, Bartolo goes next door to fetch them, but when he takes them out of the drawer he discovers that one is missing. All this, by way of Bartolo's scene with Rosina, leads to the events of the finale.

In the meantime, Don Basilio remains all by himself in Dr. Bartolo's office. We are not told what he does there, but whatever it is, it should somehow result in his singing "sol, sol, sol, sol" when he re-enters the stage. I thought perhaps some clue could be found in something Basilio said or did later in the opera. Pursuing this quest, I discovered, somewhat to my amazement, that throughout the rest of the score Basilio's role did not contain a single word or action relating him directly to music. There is no doubt about his being a musician, of course. When the Count appears, disguised as a cleric, he announces himself as "a professor of music and a pupil of Don Basilio," pretending to have been sent as a substitute for his ailing teacher to give Rosina a music lesson. The opera is filled with musical activities: Rosina sings her lesson song accompanied on the piano by the Count; Bartolo defends his preference for a more conservative type of music by parading an old-fashioned arietta; Figaro dances and plays the guitar. They all speak of music and make music. Only Don Basilio, who is ostensibly the one professional among them, never mentions or practices his art, with the single exception, of course, of that moment of solfeggio-singing in the middle of the finale, where it appears without any apparent rhyme or reason. One could shrug it off and ignore it, but I felt that this bit of solfeggio had to be justified. The only way I saw to accomplish it was to extend Basilio's musical personality and then to plant, transpose, exploit, and elaborate this extension throughout his entire role.

I finally decided to have Basilio compose a wedding cantata that he must finish in time to be performed at the nuptials of his pupil and her guardian. Bartolo's sudden decision to hurry up the wedding arrangements means that the cantata has to be completed without delay. Thus it is perfectly natural for the anxious composer, when left alone in Bartolo's study, to use this free moment to write out some of the missing choral parts. His solfeggio-singing in the finale now turns into the commonplace task of checking the accuracy of the freshly notated passages (and the cantata explains the score's stage direction "Basilio enters with papers in his hand"); it can also be used for the actual business of writing down, or correcting, some of these notes. I decided, therefore, that Basilio should always be seen with a large briefcase containing the music of his cantata.

But how could I acquaint the audience with this new facet of Basilio's musical personality? The simplest way was to make a slight alteration in the opening lines of his first encounter with Bartolo. After Bartolo announces his intention to marry Rosina "not later than tomor-

row" ("dentro domani sposar la mia Rosina. Avete inteso?"), I added the
following insert:

BASILIO *(opening his briefcase and displaying some music manuscripts):*
But the cantata for the wedding is not yet finished!
BARTOLO: A man of your talents should make short shrift of that!
BASILIO: Never mind the cantata . . .

After this, the recitative continues as before with Basilio's words:
"Did you know that Almaviva has arrived in Seville?" ("E giunto il conte
d'Almaviva?")

Naturally, changing the music of an established and respected opera
is a liberty that one takes with only the greatest reluctance. As we have
seen repeatedly, the meaning of novel staging ideas can usually be made
clear without altering the existing text. Occasionally, however, pantomimes and props alone do not suffice, and one is forced to find recourse
in new words.

Many musicians have an almost superstitious fear of adding notes,
changing them, or indulging in anything that could be described as interfering with the composer's intentions. Proper regard for an author's wishes
must not, however, be allowed to deteriorate into an unthinking and
uncritical acceptance of the printed page. Most music publishers continue
to re-issue standard scores without the slightest attempt to rectify even
the most glaring errors, and one sees misprints and inaccuracies of every
imaginable sort preserved and performed with an almost religious zeal.
"It must make sense!" is a far better motto than "The score says so!"
When textual changes seem necessary, arguments for and against them
must always be weighed with great care and, as I am the first to agree,
excessive respect is preferable to unbridled license.

In the case of my suggested *Barber* insert, the decision was made
easier by the fact that even the most rabid musical purists cannot perform
the recitative in question as it stands. Since the "slander" aria is notated
in D Major and is always sung a whole tone lower, a corresponding adjustment in the preceding music must be made whether one wants to or not.
This, incidentally, is a good example of a discrepancy between the printed
page and common practice. In every edition of the orchestral and piano-
vocal score of *The Barber of Seville* that I have ever seen, the Calunnia
aria is in the key of D Major, just as it was set down in Rossini's own
handwriting in the Bologna autograph of the score. Every Don Basilio
in the world, on the other hand, performs the aria in the lower key of C
Major, thus making a change in the preceding recitative a foregone conclusion. We do not know why Rossini wrote the aria in the higher key,
but anyone who has ever tried to perform it in D Major has soon given
up the attempt. Considering everything, therefore, it seems fair to say
that the harm of adding three recitative sentences is negligible, while the

gain in terms of dramatic potential is very real. Making Basilio a real composer not only helped me to solve the puzzling solfeggio sequence, but it also suggested some useful dramatic details for the "cauldron" ensemble. In his search for a piece of writing paper on which to notate the "depositions," the Sergeant could now pick up a sheet of Basilio's cantata. The frantic composer would retrieve his precious manuscript and exchange it for a few sheets of Bartolo's stationery. The Sergeant would take one of these and the rest would eventually find their way into the hands of the soldiers and be used for writing down Basilio's and Bartolo's words. Furthermore, the wedding cantata made it possible to add a new and very funny touch to the final number of the opera. Exploiting this extension, I assumed that having worked on his composition most of the afternoon—which, incidentally, was the reason that he arrived so late to give Rosina her music lesson—Basilio managed to finish it in time to have it sung at the sudden marriage of Rosina and the Count. In the final scene, after the servants hand out the music to the newly arrived neighbors and soldiers, Basilio himself climbs on a chair and conducts the assembled company—including the instrumentalists in the pit—thus ending the opera with an unexpected and exciting tableau.

Another detail that puzzled me in the first-act finale had to do with the sleight-of-hand trick that Rosina plays on Dr. Bartolo when she hands him a laundry list instead of the Count's letter. This entire sequence is an invention of Rossini's librettist, Cesare Sterbini. In Beaumarchais' play Rosina substitutes for the Count's *billet doux*, a letter that she had received quite legitimately from one of her cousins. I find the version used in the opera much funnier, but, in a way, less convincing. Why should Rosina have a laundry list on her person when she enters the stage in this scene? It smacks of premeditation, and while one expects Rosina to be vivacious and quick-witted, too much slyness is not attractive in a girl of her age. I have seen Rosinas who displayed so much virtuosity in the arts of lying and deception that one began to question the Count's wisdom in wanting to marry her. It is better, therefore, if the substitution of the laundry list can be made to look like a completely unplanned and lucky accident.

How could I arrange this? Digging a little deeper, I came to the conclusion that a laundry list really belonged with the housekeeper, Berta, and that its rightful place was inside a laundry basket along with the soiled clothes. Berta, however, is not on stage during the substitution scene. And why would she leave the basket in the middle of the living-room floor? But Berta went to open the front door when she heard the Count knocking, and the Count, entering as a drunken soldier, alarmed Berta to such an extent that, forgetting to pick up her laundry basket, she ran directly to Dr. Bartolo to inform him of the rowdy visitor's arrival.

I felt confident that my newly invented prop could be converted into a genuine extension. Transposing it to an earlier scene and planting it there was easy enough. At her very first appearance in the opera, Berta could readily introduce both the basket and the list. She could count the laundry, make entries on a strip of paper, and easily combine these activities with the continuous sneezing that is her main acting assignment. As for the finale, I hoped that the basket would come in handy not only in the substitution episode, but also in connection with the still unsolved climax of the vivace section and with handling of many nasty timing problems.

It was the familiar story of "too much music." Just as in the *Rigoletto* examples (pages 340–343), it was necessary to invent some plausible reasons for the fact that various characters did not notice things sooner, sing their lines sooner, and react sooner to some fairly potent provocations. But whereas in *Rigoletto* I could elaborate on the ladder, the lantern, the dagger, and other existing props, the *Barber* finale did not offer any obvious help from available materials.

Before attempting to locate an additional extension, I decided to list my most urgent needs. My list took the form of a questionnaire:

1. (measures 18–25) Why doesn't the Count notice Bartolo's presence sooner?
2. (measures 23–25) Why doesn't Bartolo address the Count sooner?
3. (measures 76–87) Why isn't Rosina's presence noticed sooner by the two men?
4. (measures 87–91) Why is Bartolo so slow to notice the conversation between the Count and Rosina?

I realized that clever performers could solve some of these problems without my help. Skillful timing of one's reactions is, after all, one of the essentials of good acting. I felt, nevertheless, that it was neither fair nor realistic to expect singers to resolve all these difficulties unassisted and that it was my duty to facilitate their task by providing them with some appropriate theatrical business. I thought of the laundry basket that had been left behind by Berta, and I decided it could be used to answer the second of my questions. Bartolo, on his way to address the Count, could bump into the basket, then pick it up and put it aside. Berta could easily leave this prop in just the right spot to make Bartolo's action believable, and then he could move the basket to the place where it would be handiest for Rosina's substitution trick.

All this made good, in-character sense and contributed an additional facet to the basket extension, but it took care of only one, and actually the least urgent, of my staging needs. Something else had to be invented, something that could logically occupy and distract both the Count and Bartolo. Where could I find it? In what place and in what direction should I start digging for this elusive truffle?

Looking back on what I had accomplished so far, I saw that in trying to find a suitable activity for the final vivace section, I had managed to borrow an idea from the earlier "investigation and arrest" sequence; the wedding cantata had suggested itself as an answer to the solfeggio passage; and the basket was a logical elaboration of the laundry list. In the opening pages of the finale, I was confronted with something new: a situation that seemed barren of any immediate staging clues. I decided that I would try to connect whatever I did as closely as possible with what I earlier called the essential core of the plot. This, quite obviously, was the Count's attempt to get lodging in Bartolo's house. A truffle, if there was one, would have to grow out of this housing idea, and here is where I started digging.

What would be my course of action, I asked myself, if I were a soldier assigned to a certain house expecting to find lodging there? I would surely bring all my belongings along with me. This idea seemed to have merit. A couple of large valises, perhaps, or a trunk, could prove very useful in this situation. Bartolo would obviously insist on getting this luggage out of his house, while the Count would be just as determined to bring it back. It would be still better if all this carting around were handled by a servant. My first thought was that Fiorello, the Count's valet who was seen in the opening scene, could perhaps be drafted for this purpose, but then I decided he was too utterly dull for such an assignment.

Fortunately, another servant was available: none other than the yawning Ambrogio, whom Figaro had drugged with a sleeping potion at the same time he administered the sneezing powder to Berta. Rossini and his librettist treated this Ambrogio rather shabbily and included him in only one short scene of the opera; most producers dispense with him altogether. I, however, was only too pleased to resuscitate him, for he was clearly the ideal luggage carrier. Awakened by the Count's pounding on the door, he could enter the stage in the opening measures of the finale, stumble out to fetch the ferocious visitor's belongings, and then, no matter where his actions took him, he could lean on the trunk and fall asleep instantly. No director could wish for better characteristics in a role restricted to supporting and background actions.

It soon became apparent that in the trunk-hauling Ambrogio I had hit on a most versatile extension. It not only filled the "occupation and distraction" needs of the opening portion of the finale, but it also provided me with the heretofore missing climactic denouement of the first act.

When, after the motionless "statue" ensemble, the principals and the chorus begin to ready themselves for the hectic activities of the vivace section, Ambrogio gets hold of the laundry basket, and, spreading a large bed sheet over the trunk, lies down to sleep right in the center of the stage. Undisturbed by the growing crescendo of the music and the tramping of the soldiers who swarm all around him, he seems a tranquil island in the midst of a raging storm. During the coda he wakes up and, carrying the basket in his arms, makes his way downstage to turn his sleepy countenance on the wildly arguing and gesticulating assemblage of singers. The Sergeant, who has been frantically searching for a likely victim on whom to vent his growing frustration, turns a baleful eye on this defenseless candidate for arrest and trial. Obeying the commanding gesture of their chief, the policemen surround Ambrogio, push him into the laundry basket, and, as the curtain begins to descend, carry them both offstage.

~~~ Appendix A

Opera in English

WHEREVER OPERA LOVERS gather the question of opera in English is certain to be raised. Those who dislike opera in English insist that the operatic vocal line loses its authentic sound unless it is sung in the original language. The proponents of English counter this by saying that the popularity of opera depends upon the audience's ability to understand the words. At this point the champions of authenticity argue that the poor enunciation of opera singers makes it impossible to understand their words in any language, that all operatic texts are silly, and that English is unsuitable for singing opera (an extraordinary claim!). There is no harm in these operatic controversies, and their very intensity reflects the passionate feelings that are inspired by the subject. Even so, all this is becoming quite tiresome.

To begin with, the very term "opera in English" is a misnomer. It is applied without discrimination to two completely different types of works: English operas (operas composed to an original English libretto) and translated opera. I wonder how many devotees of imported, foreign operas know what has been happening in the field of original English opera in the last fifteen years. The latest handbook of opera production, published several years ago, lists a total of 259 operas, standard and otherwise, which are described as "material of permanent value." The selection which was made by the author, Quaintance Eaton, together with an advisory board, is supposed to represent operas of the most immediate interest to American opera producers. It is a surprise to discover that about ninety English operas have appeared between the years 1950 and 1961. Thirty-seven composers, almost all of whom reside in the United States, completed sixty English operas and saw them produced here within these ten or eleven years. In addition, the very same handbook gives a supplementary list of another 260 operas, most of which happen to be original English operas of recent vintage. Although the term "explosion" is badly overworked these days, it is the only word to describe this sudden and spectacular flowering of operatic creativity.

Having perused a great many of these new operas in English and having produced twelve of them, I find their quality to be very uneven, but I do believe that a substantial number of them will withstand the ravages of operatic attrition and will remain in the repertoire for quite a few years. The lover of traditional, standard operas may dislike modern musical idioms and he may doubt the worth or the permanence of these new operas, but he must certainly be impressed with the startling vitality of this original opera-in-English movement, and if he is truly devoted to the lyric theater, he cannot fail to rejoice in it.

It is true, of course, that operas written to original English texts are not the ones that arouse the wrath of the operatic traditionalist. He may despise them and refuse to listen to them, but he does not deny the propriety of producing them in English. It is translated opera that is the center of the controversy. And here again I suspect that most of the trouble arises from a confusion of issues. The warring sides fail to notice that what separates them is not so much their attitude to language as their basic disagreement concerning what constitutes acceptable opera. The term *opera* is applied to several types of musical-theatrical offerings, each having its own special appeal. If the composer's aim is limited to simple entertainment, if he chooses a musical style which can be enjoyed effortlessly upon first hearing, then his works most likely belong to the class of musical comedies, or to give them their European name, operettas. Works which are written in a more ambitious and distinguished musical idiom are called operas, but here again one differentiates between the more spectacular and the more intimate operas. This distinction is reflected in the Italian terms of *opera seria* and *opera buffa*, the French *grand opéra* and *opéra comique*, and the German *Grosse Oper* and *Singspiel*. The spectacular type of opera has a specific name in English—we call it grand opera, but the more intimate variety lacks a generally accepted label, although it is becoming more and more widely known as the opera theater. Each of these categories of opera has its own large and enthusiastic following. The devotees of grand opera expect it to be a thrilling spectacle with lavish settings, masses of participants, and an orchestra of symphonic dimensions. They are not satisfied unless they hear glorious voices bearing famous names and see their favorite stars attired in magnificent costumes, performing in vast opera houses to crowds of festively dressed spectators. The lovers of the opera theater much prefer a smaller auditorium and a discreet orchestra, surroundings which enable the audience to catch fine points of ensemble acting and singing, and to appreciate the more subtle nuances of meaning and musical expression. The high spots of grand opera come in the arias where the singers more often than not sing almost concert style, hardly moving and facing the audience from downstage center. The leading singers of grand opera are generally less mobile than their opera-theater colleagues, most of whom have a considerably wider range of expressiveness in such theatrical skills as mimetics, gestures, and body movement. Grand opera produces its most potent effects through vocal intensity, the opera theater through believable musical-dramatic behavior. Clearly, the emphasis is on different facets of the operatic totality, and each aspect of opera has its strengths and weaknesses. The language preferences of the two schools are, quite logically, extensions of their other attitudes.

It is not surprising that grand-opera addicts prefer performances in foreign languages. Vocal and orchestral splendor is not dependent upon words. As we have seen earlier, clarity of enunciation may occasionally interfere with vocal intensity. The lover of grand opera is not concerned with the exact verbal meaning of the vocal line; a general knowledge of the situation is quite sufficient for him. From his point of view, the foreign language does offer many advantages. Most important, the theatrical weaknesses of the performance are much less noticeable. When the words are incomprehensible, a paucity of meaningful action is not too disturbing. It is surely preferable for singers accustomed only to grand-opera behavior to perform long stretches of music concert style in costume against a picturesque background than to attempt a performance in English. With this static presentation, a clear understanding of every word is a definite disadvantage. The English text, heard unclearly through the sound of an oversized orchestra, distracts the audience; it dilutes the impact of vocal and orchestral splendor; it throws a spotlight on the lack of theatrical believability; and it manages to create all these negative effects without offering any of the compensations of the opera theater.

As for those who enjoy the theatrical side of opera, they will continue to clamor for opera in the vernacular. They have discovered that the full meaning of opera can only be derived from singers who have an intimate and immediate understanding of the text and who sing for an audience that can enjoy and evaluate not just the high points, but everything they see and hear. Of course, singing in English does not automatically guarantee good opera. Opera can be just as stilted, vague, and meaningless in English as in any other language. All too many singers treat English as a vocal exercise, as a succession of vowels interspersed with consonants. But opera sung in English makes good theater a real possibility; performances given in a language which neither the singer nor the audience understands lead inevitably to a neglect of theatrical values. For this reason, the opera theater style loses most of its effectiveness when a foreign language is sung by American singers for American audiences. But a word of warning is needed. Even though opera in English offers great opportunities, it is also replete with great dangers. When it is done poorly, it is a sorry spectacle: defects inherent in a performance suddenly become intensely noticeable. It is this which probably accounts for most of the antagonism to opera in English. Therefore, unless a producer can suceed in organizing a fine performance, he will be much wiser to stick to opera in a foreign language. Many unattractive details of his production will remain hidden behind the merciful veil of incomprehensibility. It is also true that foreign singers should not be encouraged to sing in English unless they have mastered the intricacies of its meaning and pronunciation. Were one to follow this train of thought to its logical conclusion, one would have to recommend a division of the operatic world into two separate communities. Some organizations would specialize in grand opera and produce only works of foreign origin in the original language; others would dedicate themselves to operas sung in English. This suggestion has definite merits, but it does not satisfy the true lover of opera, who is repelled at the idea of acknowledging and stabilizing a division predicated upon supposedly ineradicable weaknesses. The optimistic opera enthusiast hopes to find ways to correct the theatrical shortcomings of grand opera and to inject more vocal and orchestral splendor into the opera-theater style. I would like to suggest therefore that a moratorium be declared on all bickering over opera in English, and that opera lovers concentrate their attention on ways of improving the faults of both camps.

The shortcomings of operatic productions everywhere can be traced to two primary causes—a lack of money and a lack of talent. The art of music and the art of the theater are both taxing and complicated. Each art is very difficult and very expensive. When combined, as they are in opera, they become extremely difficult and prohibitively expensive. Opera, incidentally, is probably more expensive in the United States than anywhere else. Mass production and automation, while they have permitted this country to cut costs in so many other fields, do not seem to be applicable to opera. Whether it is grand opera or opera-theater, the only aspect of the production that is always certain to be spectacular and grandiose is the deficit. The financial plight of operatic organizations in the United States is nothing short of catastrophic. I do not know of a single one which is not on the verge of bankruptcy. The traditional American form of subsidy—support by wealthy individuals—is no longer sufficient. Too few individuals have the necessary wherewithal, and those who have it are seldom interested in the performing arts. Fortunately, there are indications that industry, the great foundations, and the government (municipal, state, and federal) may soon be ready to coordinate their efforts with individual patrons in an effort to salvage opera, as well as other musical and theatrical enterprises. Right now, however, we are still in the midst of our lean and desperate years.

The lack of money is a most serious handicap, but at least it is one that is generally recognized and deplored. The lack of talent is a more insidious deficiency because on the surface there appears an abundance, even an overabundance, of every kind of operatic talent. Hundreds of promising singers compete for prizes, scholarships, and for available professional vacancies. Droves of youngsters and older enthusiasts clamor for opportunities to conduct, stage direct, design, translate, organize, and produce operas. There is hardly a college, university, or conservatory that does not boast of an opera school. Summer and winter opera workshops are the rage. The opera-production handbook, which I mentioned earlier, speaks of more than seven hundred organizations that produce opera in one form or another in our country. All this is perfectly true and truly wonderful. But quantity is not everything, and it is frightening how difficult it is to perform opera acceptably, with reasonable justice to its vocal, musical, histrionic, and scenic requirements. We still have too many narrow specialists, and fine opera depends on people with versatile gifts. In some respects this situation is improving. The number of fine singers who are also competent musicians and actors is growing annually. Even grand opera is gradually losing its unmusical and ungainly stars. It is in the field of leadership, however, where the greatest lack is still felt. We still have conductors who are contemptuous and ignorant of theatrical values, stage directors who are blissfully unaware of the theatrical implications of instrumental music, translators who are unversed in musical grammar and syntax, and producers who are interested mainly in box-office values and in peddling name artists, many of whom arrive at the last minute just in time for a hasty musical run-through. As long as opera is afflicted with these lopsided personalities, it will remain unattractive to many serious and conscientious music and theater connoisseurs. Opera has been a butt for cartoonists and gag men for too long. It must reorganize its forces and mend its weaknesses. Grand opera and the opera-theater each have an important place. We want to hear the great foreign singers in their own language; we also want to give an opportunity to the fine singing actors and actresses of all countries. To quote from *The Barber of Seville*, let us offer a bilingual toast—"*pace e gioia*—peace and joy"—to all good opera and to all eager and sincere opera lovers.

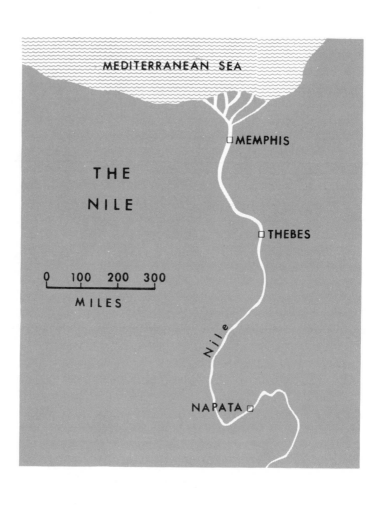

Appendix B

Reconstructing an operatic plot: an essay in dramatic research

ALTHOUGH THERE WAS a time when opera lovers were interested almost exclusively in the musical side of opera, stage directors and producers, as well as singers and audiences, are today becoming more and more fascinated with the details of operatic stories and with the psychological subtleties of operatic characters. Most of the operas in the French and Italian repertoire are based upon existing stories, novels, or well-known plays, and when one is looking for dramatic details that are not contained in the actual scores, a study of these background texts is invaluable. There are a few operas which are not based on previously existing material and for which the study of the historical period has no particular value. The most outstanding example is *Aida*. For our conceptions of the various characters in Verdi's masterpiece we must rely solely on the text of the opera, which leaves many motivations and important facts unexplained. How, for example, can Radames declare that his honor has remained unsullied when he was willing to desert his post and escape to Ethiopia? Why does Aida fail to confide to Radames, whom she loves so desperately, that she is the daughter of the Ethiopian king Amonasro? Why do all Egyptians believe so readily Amonasro's statement that the king of Ethiopia was killed in battle? How can we reconcile the incidents of the plot with the huge geographic distances between the three scenes of action—Memphis, Thebes, and Napata? When authentic information is lacking, the only thing to do is to invent it, and for this reason I have imagined a letter written by Radames to his uncle, the contents of which, I believe, fit all the facts given in the opera and explain those that have been left unexplained in the work as we know it.

Dear Uncle:

By now, you must surely have heard that the son of your sister has been officially proclaimed a traitor. Traitor! The priests have thrown this word at me so often that now it seems to stare at me from every wall of my cell. And yet, I know that I am not a traitor. I have acted honorably, according to the

precepts which you have instilled in me since childhood. I have never forgotten what you told me when I was a little boy: "A real man always knows
the meaning of justice, truth, and honor. No matter what the rules of the
world say, he looks into his heart; for justice, honor, and truth are in a man's
heart, and he can always find them there." When I look into my heart, I see
the image of a girl. I tried to deal with her justly and honorably, and I love
her more than life.

I will die soon, Uncle, and as the events of my past keep running through
my mind in crazy procession, I sometimes feel that perhaps I am a traitor.
Not in the way that *they* thought, but in the way that you might think, in
the sense that I betrayed the truth, justice, and honor that you taught me so
long ago. I am taking a look into my heart, a long and careful look. I want to
retrace the road that brought me to this cell, and I want you to walk this road
with me. (The guard who brings me food has served under my command,
and has promised to deliver my message to you.) If you decide that I betrayed your teaching, so be it.

You remember the Ethiopian campaign of five years ago in which I participated as lieutenant to your old friend, the supreme commander. This was
a happy time for me. I liked the country with its fragrant forests and cool
valleys, and I was lucky in my military adventures. The old chief used to say
that I was the only Egyptian who really understood the thinking and the
fighting ways of the Ethiopians. The one thing that spoiled it for me was the
senseless brutality of war, the looting of the cities, the inhuman mistreatment
of the civilians, and the outrages perpetrated on the children and women. I
mentioned my feelings of revulsion to the chief, who, as you know, was well
disposed toward me (more for your sake, I imagine, than my own), and he
told me that he also regretted the excessive cruelty, although not on senti-
mental grounds, for he was too old and too hardened in the ways of war. He
regretted most the resentment of the native population that fostered a desire
for revenge. It was this desire for revenge, he maintained, that was mostly
responsible for the eternal recurrence of the Ethiopian and other frontier
uprisings.

"How was it then," I asked the chief, "that we were able to stop our
men from desecrating and looting the Ethiopian temples?"

"That is different," he answered. "Our men are afraid of the Ethiopian
gods, just as the Ethiopians are afraid of ours. Looting Ethiopian temples
would be unwise in any event," he said. "We have important temples of our
own near the Ethiopian borders—the great shrines of Isis and Phtah on the
upper Nile in the immediate vicinity of Jebel Barkal and Napata. These
temples will be safe only as long as we can insure the inviolability of the
enemy places of worship. Respect for temples is thoroughly instilled in our
soldiers, and if you can imbue them with the same reverence for pretty Ethiopian women," he added with a smirk, "you are a better man than I am."

That ended the conversation, but somehow his words made me want to
try to mitigate these conditions. An opportunity soon presented itself. A
group of young Ethiopian girls had been rounded up by one of our detach-
ments, and the men were just in the process of dividing up the girls when I
arrived on the scene. The sight of these children—none of them looked older

than twelve or thirteen—moved me to action. I announced that this group of prisoners was destined for special service as slaves in the royal palace. It was generally known that Moorish girls were used for domestic work in Memphis, but my reputation as the chief's favorite was well enough established, and the men accepted my word without demur. They grumbled a bit, but obeyed, and the girls, about twenty of them, were set aside under special guard to await transportation down the Nile, first to Thebes and thence to Memphis. Among these girls there was one who attracted my attention not only by her exceptional beauty, but also by the reverence with which she was treated by her companions. I tried to interrogate a few of the captives, but they were so terrified by their recent experiences that I could elicit no information other than that the girl was the daughter of an important government official and that her name was Aida.

When I reported my actions to the chief, he told me that questioning Ethiopian prisoners was an utter waste of time since all Ethiopians were trained from earliest childhood to withhold all information, no matter how trivial. Threats and torture were useless with this race, the chief said. One could kill them, or capture them, or even release them, but one never bothered asking them any questions. At any rate, the girls were eventually shipped to Memphis, and I completely forgot this little episode. The soldiers whom I deprived of their girls soon found others to replace them, and, realizing that depredation and plunder were an unavoidable part of all wars, I became somewhat disillusioned with the prospect of continuing my career in this kind of military adventure.

I was not too displeased, therefore, when shortly after the campaign I was appointed captain of the guards in the royal palace in Memphis, a position much coveted in the service for its opportunities to marry into families of wealthy courtiers.

I welcomed this assignment mainly because it put me in close touch with the High Priest, Ramphis, to whom I was warmly recommended by the chief. Ramphis was the real power behind the throne and was able to dispense favors of all imaginable kinds. Life in the palace was pleasant enough. One of my duties was the safekeeping of the crown jewels, including the more valuable necklaces and priceless tiaras belonging to the young princess Amneris. I had to be present when the gems were released for use in the various ceremonies and festivals, and again when they were returnd to the vaults. Imagine my surprise when I discovered that the attendant entrusted with the fetching and returning of the princess' special jewels was none other than Aida, the Ethiopian child whom I had rescued two or three years before. She was now a thousand times more beautiful than when I had first seen her in her native land. How can I describe her to you, Uncle? She was so lovely that my whole body ached when I looked at her. She immediately recognized me as the man who saved her from the dreadful attentions of the invaders, and we became close friends. I learned much from Aida about the daily life in the forbidden wings of the palace, but whenever I brought up anything that had to do with her native country, she would become silent. When I tried to pursue the subject, she blushed and started crying so bitterly that I gave up any attempt to learn about her family and her childhood. Otherwise, she was gay and chattered like a little bird. It seems that Ethiopian slaves had a reputation of being unmanageable and untrustworthy, and when my contingent of prisoners arrived in Memphis, no one wanted to bother with them. But Aida's looks and gentleness set her apart from the others, and it was the princess herself who insisted on keeping her as one of her attendants. Just about that time, you may remember, the king's other daughter died in an accident, and Princess Amneris remained as the dynasty's only surviving heir. Amneris had always been the king's favorite, and now she became the terror of the household, ruling all officials and servants with an iron hand. Fortunately, she seemed to be genuinely fond of Aida, treated her like a sister and showed her every kind of favor. Aida was free to come and go pretty much as she chose, and since she was the only one whom Amneris trusted with her jewels, her duty took her almost daily into the area of my jurisdiction. Suffice it to say, Uncle, that fairly soon we became lovers and I lived in a haze of indescribable happiness which I realized even then could not last very long.

Two things happened about that time to alert us to the dangers of our situation. One day, the High Priest interrogated me, putting me through quite an ordeal. Besides the obvious questions relating to my military career, he also seemed to be strangely curious about my private life and amorous involvements. I managed to reassure him that I was not involved in any of the usual intrigues with the ladies of the court, affairs which were considered normal for members of my class. I did not know at the time that the high priest's inquiries were prompted by Princess Amneris, who had taken it into her head to have me as her husband. Otherwise I should have told Aida of the princess' unfortunate infatuation and warned her to be doubly careful not to betray our love. Alas, I had no inkling of the princess' feelings! I saw her regularly at the various ceremonies which we both had to attend, but my whole being was so filled with thoughts of Aida that I never paid any attention to any other woman's looks or behavior.

The other event that happened at the time was much more obviously dangerous and filled both Aida and me with apprehension. One of the Moorish dancing girls in Amneris' retinue was caught having a love affair with one of the palace guards. Amneris' rage upon discovering this was frightening to behold. The soldier was put in jail, and it was officially announced that the girl had been sent away to one of the Lybian settlements, but, according to the palace rumor, she had been put to death. Amneris' serving maidens were expected to remain virgins. Any deviation was considered to be a personal affront to the princess and was punished as such. The thought of what might happen should Amneris hear of our meetings in the jewelry vaults filled us both with mortal dread.

Something had to be done, and soon. I was desperately in love with the girl and wanted to marry her more than anything in the world, but as long as she remained a slave, this was of course unthinkable. It was imperative to set Aida free, and since she was still technically a prisoner of war, I hit upon a scheme that had a fair chance of success, although it depended upon quite a succession of lucky circumstances. A new war with the Ethiopians was certain to break out before long. These things recurred about twice in each decade and the time was ripe for the next one. If I could manage things, I would be named supreme commander of the Egyptian troops, and if I returned victorious (an outcome of which I had no doubt), I would be in a position to ask the king to appoint me governor of Ethiopia. Successful military commanders were often chosen for such tasks, and although past attempts to establish a provincial government in that land had not proven feasible, I could persuade the priests and the king that were I to take an Ethiopian wife (so as to give the natives a ruler of their own race) I could bring permanent peace to this troublesome country. I would first have to insist that all Ethiopian prisoners of war be set free, but in the flush of victory such a favor could be obtained without too much trouble. The first step was to find out whether I had a chance of being appointed commander of the Ethiopian campaign. And so I went to visit the old chief, who, as you know, had suffered a stroke, but whose influence in these matters was still formidable. The old man was a pitiful sight, but he greeted me with much warmth. "Well, well," he said when I hinted of my military ambitions, "I thought that you had lost interest in provincial campaigning. However, this is quite a coincidence, for that old fox Ramphis was asking about your qualifications just the other day, and I told him that while I would hesitate to pit you against the Persians or the Lybians, you were the perfect man against the Ethiopians. If they were looking for a fellow who could vanquish, tame, and maybe even govern those savages, you were my choice. Ramphis said, naturally, that it was all up to the decision of Isis, but you and I know who decides these things for the goddess!"

Needless to say, I was elated, and events progressed more rapidly than I had any right to expect or hope. Soon we heard rumors that the Ethiopians had invaded Egypt and had started on their usual long march toward Thebes. Ramphis, whom I met while he was on his way to see the king, stopped long enough to tell me that the goddess had already chosen the supreme commander—"young and valiant" he called him. Was my dream really coming true? Oh, to return victorious, to say to Aida "For your sake, I have fought, for your sake, I have vanquished!" To take her back to her native land, to set her up as a queen, as the queen of my heart on a throne close to heaven! While I was thus daydreaming, I was accosted by Princess Amneris, who started teasing me about a possible romantic attachment in Memphis. For a moment I imagined that she had read my mind, and when at this very moment I saw Aida approaching, all bathed in tears, I had the chilling thought that the princess had somehow discovered or guessed our secret. My alarm was increased when Amneris, apparently noticing my confusion, turned to Aida to inquire about the reason for her tears. It turned out that it was then she first began to suspect that there was a secret understanding between her favorite attendant and the captain of the palace guards. But suspicion is not proof, and at the time I was not too seriously concerned about Amneris' prying. Little did I know that the deadly venom of jealousy was gnawing at the heart of the princess, and that this jealousy would later inspire her to lay a subtle trap for Aida and make her reveal her love for me.

The anxiety caused by this chance encounter with the princess was swept away almost immediately by the arrival of the court, and by the official announcement that the goddess had indeed selected me to be the supreme commander of the Egyptian troops. I will not deny, dear uncle, that for a while I was quite swollen with pride at being elevated to such an exalted post. The acclaim of the populace, the solemn ceremonies in the temple of Phtah, the pomp of sacred banners, swords, and processions had an intoxicating effect upon me. But once I was in the field far away from the false glamour of crowds, palaces, and temples, I realized again that all the noise and vanity of glory was foreign and repulsive to my better self. The beloved image of Aida was my guiding star, and my only ambition was to perfect a scheme whereby I could deliver her from bondage and claim her as my own.

The Ethiopians were no match for our men, and the campaign was less arduous than I had expected. We gathered enough trophies to impress the court and a good number of prisoners, among whom there was a very impressive looking warrior who was obviously one of the tribal chiefs, although it later turned out that I had been completely fooled by him. It was he who presided over the long and solemn funeral ceremony for the Ethiopian king Amonasro. Of course, today we all know that all this was an extraordinary bit of trickery imagined by Amonasro's fiendishly fertile mind. Since none of us had ever seen Amonasro, we had no reason to suspect that the slain warrior who was buried with such lavish pomp was someone else, and that the man who conducted the ceremony was in fact the king himself. The purpose of this fantastic fraud was to lull us Egyptians into a feeling of false security and to induce us to withdraw our garrisons from Thebes and the other southern fortresses. Considering future events, it seems strange to say that Amonasro's death appeared at the time to be a lucky omen for my own plans. A country bereft of its natural head would be less antagonistic to an outsider, especially if he brought a native consort with him. I permitted the Ethiopians to complete the funeral rites to show them that I respected their religion. This interlude delayed our return to Egypt, but this too fitted well into my plans. As the campaign was nearing its end, I sent word to Memphis suggesting that the victory celebrations be held in Thebes. It had been many years since the king, the chief priests, and the leading ministers had visited the capital city of the south. It would raise the morale of the Thebans and have a salutary effect on all neighboring lands. This was my official recommendation. My real reason was that I wished to remain closer to Ethiopia, which I hoped would become the seat of my government in the very near future. Knowing of Princess Amneris' passion for celebrations, I had no doubt that she would also brave the long journey from Memphis and bring her entire household with her. The desire to be reunited with Aida at the earliest possible moment was perhaps the strongest motive for my trying to launch hundreds of boats and barges on the two-week trip up the river from Memphis to Thebes.

The reaction of the court was favorable. The king had planned to visit Thebes for quite some time, I was told, and a military triumph was the best possible justification for such an extended voyage. That was the message from Ramphis. Along with it came a personal scroll from the king, praising me in extravagant terms and promising to reward me in a manner befitting my exploits. "Ask me anything your heart desires, be it half of my kingdom," the message ran, "and I swear by the sacred gods, by the splendor of my crown, that I will grant your request." Looking at it in retrospect, I realize that this was a thinly veiled hint encouraging me to ask for the hand of Princess Amneris. All it meant to me at the time was that I could obtain Aida's freedom by the simple act of requesting the liberation of all Ethiopian prisoners of war. My sin, Uncle, if there was one, consisted in trying both to serve my country and at the same time to assure the happiness of the woman I loved. If I had not been so anxious about Aida, I would have noticed other suspicious circumstances that escaped my attention during that campaign. Our military successes were much too easy, the Ethiopians asked for peace and surrendered much too readily, the prisoners we took were much too willing to be caught, and the pick of the Ethiopian warriors were obviously not in the field, but were held back for some nefarious purpose. I have since come to the conclusion that Amonasro had purposely let us catch him and take him to Egypt. He had two aims—the rescue of Aida and the destruction of our armies. Taking advantage of my love for his daughter, he very nearly succeeded in having his way. I cannot help but admire the man who master-minded this plan and who, right in the midst of our triumphal celebration, was already plotting and directing a brilliant strategy of revenge.

Oh, that triumphal celebration! You were there, Uncle. You made that tiring boat trip along with other counsellors. You did not have to attend the ceremony, but you wanted to witness the triumph of your nephew, didn't you? That bitter triumph! The shattering of all my dreams! And I was so sure of myself. What could go wrong when I had the king's sacred promise? It almost makes me laugh when I think of the shock it must have been to the king and to Ramphis when, instead of requesting Amneris' hand, I asked for the release of the prisoners! And why could he not set them free? Amonasro being dead (and remember that we all believed it was so), a handful of liberated Ethiopians could not really be considered dangerous. I often wonder why Ramphis suggested that Aida and her father remain among us. Did he suspect that Amonasro was more important than he claimed to be? Was it priestly second sight? Or was it just pure spite—the desire to show all of us that a high priest's word carried more weight than a king's solemn promise?

It was at this point, you will remember, that the king took things into his own hands and, instead of granting my request in its totality (which it was his sworn duty to do), presented me with the hand of his daughter and the prospect of succeeding him on the throne of Egypt. This was the last thing I expected, and, I swear to you, it was the last thing I wanted. I wonder what crossed your mind when you saw your sister's son glorified as the king's son-in-law and as the future ruler of our country. You must have thought I was overwhelmed with joy at this unheard-of honor. It was true that I was stunned, but it was horror, not joy, that paralyzed me. How could I refuse this honor right there in front of all the people and the court? How could I insult the princess, the king, and the gods of Egypt? All I saw was the face of my beloved bathed in tears, and I knew that the throne of Egypt was not worth Aida's love. After the ceremony I felt helpless and shattered for I could see no way out of my predicament. One thing was certain in my mind: under no circumstances would they force me to marry Amneris, that coquettish, cruel, and spoiled darling of the court. I begged the king to release me from the command of the troops, but he would not hear of it. "The war is far from over," he asserted. "Our spies report that the Ethiopians are even now plotting a counter move of vast proportions. The only way to forestall their attack is by means of a preventive invasion, but it has to be done in greatest secrecy, as a complete surprise to the enemy." In the past we had always allowed the foe to take the initiative, but now we were going to strike them at a time when they least expected it.

It was Ramphis who conceived the details of a strategem which for sheer malice and ingenuity was worthy of our opponent, Amonasro. Large numbers of Egyptians would move south to the border for the ostensible purpose of taking part in the wedding celebration of the commander-in-chief and the princess. The great temples of Isis and Phtah were chosen as the main arenas for the rituals. The ceremonies would be given the greatest possible publicity and then on the very day officially selected for the wedding, the troops would stream through one of the numerous mountain passes. They would then surround and destroy the unsuspecting enemy camps in one mighty blow. I was to stay out of the preparations and act like an expectant bridegroom. Then, at the last moment, I would join the troops and direct the campaign. No one, not even the princess herself, would be told of the deception. My participation in the final stages of the invasion was considered absolutely essential, not only because of my reputation with the men, but even more because of my intimate knowledge of the terrain. In spite of myself, I was impressed by the magnitude and the boldness of this plan. I was also more than pleased at the idea of not being present on the day of my wedding to the princess. Was there not, however, something the plotters had overlooked? "What will Princess Amneris say," I asked the king, "when she finds herself without a groom on the day of her wedding?"

"My daughter is a true Egyptian," the king retorted. "Ramphis will be with her continually, and when the situation is fully explained to her, she will be the first to rejoice at the cleverness of our strategy. Besides, Amneris would much rather be married in the great temple of Memphis than in that wilderness on the upper Nile." So the wedding was deferred until we all returned to Memphis after the new war was finished. That, at least, gave me two or maybe three months to come up with a solution to my problem. If only I could see Aida and assure her of my fidelity and undying love! But I was no longer the captain of the guards in the royal palace. I was the chosen groom of the princess, and was barred from approaching my betrothed until the wedding ceremony. The forbidden wing of the palace was doubly forbidden for me, and the lack of even a single word from Aida was heartbreaking as well as most puzzling. As the favorite slave of the princess, she should have been able to get in touch with me.

For a long time I heard nothing. Then one evening, as I was returning to my quarters alone, I heard a whisper from a shadowy veiled figure huddling in a doorway. "Do not look," the voice said, "but listen in silence. This is a message from your friend: I am guarded and watched night and day. The lady of the house knows everything. She told me you were dead and then admitted that she had lied. In my grief, my confusion, and then in my joy I gave myself away. All is lost. Farewell forever." I stood there petrified with grief, and when I finally turned around hoping to find out more, the messenger was gone. And so Amneris knew the truth. My poor darling! She was still alive, but I was horrified at what was in store for her. That cruel woman could have killed Aida a thousand times had she wanted to do so. But she was obviously planning to torture my beloved by keeping her in the palace as the humblest of slaves so that after our wedding she could gloat daily and hourly over my darling's broken heart. I had to see Aida, I had to tell her that I would never consent to that marriage in spite of all the kings and all the gods of Egypt.

Arranging to see Aida proved to be an assignment of almost insuperable difficulty. Also, I spent sleepless nights trying to find ways to persuade the king to revoke his decision about my marriage to Amneris. A new and more decisive victory over the Ethiopians might give me another opportunity to request a favor, but deep within me I felt hopeless. Ramphis' plan in the meantime had been worked out to the last detail. To avoid any impression of secrecy, he allowed everyone, even Aida's father, to attend the festivities arranged in preparation for the wedding. A whole new city of magnificent tents was erected near the temple of Phtah while the disguised soldiers were quietly smuggled into the secret camps along the Ethiopian border. All my attempts to communicate with Aida while the court was in Thebes proved futile. Only Ramphis had access to the apartments of the royal bride, and he was hardly the man in whom I could confide. I decided finally to wait until the eve of the so-called wedding day, the day of the invasion. In accordance with tradition, Amneris was to pass that night in prayer in the temple of Isis. It was expected that the usual palace regulations would be suspended, or at least relaxed, in the improvised royal mansions near the banks of the upper Nile. Luckily, the pilot of the boat assigned to the princess and her retinue was an old schoolmate of mine, and he consented to transmit a message to Aida. It was short and simple: "Your friend will meet you by the shore of the river as soon as the lady of the house begins her vigil in the temple."

During that day I rejoined my men in the secret camp. The exact invasion route was decided upon by me alone that very afternoon and was known only to my two trusted lieutenants. We would use the gorge of Napata, but to avoid giving away our plans to spies or possible lookouts of the enemy, the surroundings of that route were to be left completely deserted until the hour of the attack, which was set at noon of the next day, the very hour when the wedding procession was to begin.

When dusk was falling I left the camp, telling my lieutenants not to worry about me, and I cautiously made my way to the temple of Isis. There she was, my Aida, my own, my life, my endlessly loved one. She was waiting for me, and as I saw her, Uncle, I knew that, come what may, I would set her free from the terrible bondage to which I myself had condemned her and from the torture which she was enduring because of me, of me who loved her so desperately and yet so hopelessly. At first I tried to cheer her up by telling her about the new war and how I would throw myself at the feet of the king and win his permission to spend the rest of my days with her, my own beloved. But women are so much more clear-sighted than we are, Uncle, and she knew right away that it was but a foolish dream. And suddenly I realized that she was a woman who was sentenced to certain death. Not maybe, or at some time in the uncertain future, but the very next day. The fury of Amneris would require a victim, and the axe of the executioner would fall on Aida no matter what I did or said. That girl had only a few hours left to live! And then she herself suggested the way to save her—escape to Ethiopia.

I do not expect you, Uncle, to condone desertion from duty. But please understand that I did not do it for the sake of a love affair, so that I might enjoy myself in some far away oasis with the girl I loved. I *had* to save this girl's life, I *had* to do it, I tell you. Running away was the only possible solution. I was going to run away, and I would do it again. If that is dishonorable, then the word honor has no meaning for me.

They also accuse me of betraying a military secret to the enemy. But that is pure childishness. When I mentioned to Aida the name of our escape route, and when her father came out of hiding and announced that he was Amonasro and would arrange to have our men ambushed in the gorge of Napata, I lost my head for a moment. It all seemed like a nightmare of treason and dishonor, but I soon came to my senses. Even if we had not been stopped by Ramphis and the guards, our troops would still be safe. Without me, our men would not have gone on with the invasion plans.

The charge of desertion is understandable, and from the point of view of the priests, it is quite justified. I did not defend myself against their accusation, but to you, Uncle, I say: "I did not ask to be the heir to the Egyptian throne and I did not ask for the Princess' hand. They were asking me to choose between standing by helplessly while they murdered my loved one or leaving my past behind me forever." I made my choice, and I still say: "My intentions were pure and my honor remains unsullied." That is what I told Princess Amneris when she offered to intercede for me with her father, if I were willing to forget Aida. I am mentioning that distasteful conversation with the princess only because she told me (and I could see that she was speaking the truth) that Aida had escaped safely. This gives me great happiness and a feeling of having accomplished my mission.

Tomorrow they are going to bury me alive in a subterranean vault of the temple of Phtah, the same temple chosen for that ephemeral wedding ceremony. I would die still happier if I would know that you had forgiven me for the disgrace I brought to you, but this I shall never know.

Your nephew,

Radames

Appendix C

Operas and background texts

NO ONE IS CERTAIN how many operas have been composed since 1600, although some authorities estimate them to be about 40,000. The *Dictionnaire des Opéras*, by Clément and Larousse, describes more than 15,000 operas written before 1904, and Loewenberg's *Annals* catalogs nearly 4,000. From such a vast literature it is impossible to agree on the hundred or so most important works. I shall evade the issue by listing here only the operas with which I have been associated as producer, teacher, lecturer, or radio commentator. This accounts for my inclusion of such operas as Gluck's *Iphigénie en Aulide* and Janáček's *Katia Kabanova*, while omitting these composers' *Armide* and *Jenufa*.

To be of maximum practical use, a list of operatic background texts should give quick and complete answers to such questions as:

1. Does a background text exist?
2. If it is a foreign text, does it exist in an English translation?
3. Is it readily available, out of print, or a rarity?
4. Is it available in an inexpensive paperback edition?

To provide the answers, I have divided the information into two separate sections. In the first there is an alphabetical and chronological list of composers and their operas. The numbers after the titles of the operas refer to the numbers by which the pertinent literary sources are listed in the succeeding bibliography. When there is no number after an opera's title (as with such famous examples as *Così fan tutte*, *Aida*, *Pagliacci*, and *Der Rosenkavalier*), this means that the opera was composed to an original libretto for which there are no background texts.

The second section, the bibliography, is arranged alphabetically by authors and divided into four subsections:

1. English background texts
2. Background texts available in English translations
3. Texts available only in the original languages
4. Biblical and anonymous (mythological and legendary) texts.

In this second section the reader will find names of translators, publishers, dates of publication, and other relevant information, such as the accessibility of each book and whether it is available in an inexpensive paperback edition or only in hardcover. In the case of the Bible and the works of Shakespeare, any edition will suffice. In a few instances it seemed advisable to warn the student not to expect much relevant information from the listed background text. The reference to Gianni Schicchi in Dante's *Inferno*, for example, is too fleeting to be of any use when working on Puccini's opera. Some texts are only distantly connected with the librettos treated by the composers. Thus, although *Lulu oder die Zauberflöte* is generally considered to be the basis of Mozart's *Magic Flute*, Liebeskind's fairy tale is related only to the opening episode of the opera. Beginning with the second scene, the two stories pursue completely different paths. Similarly, while it is true that *Le Mariage de Loti* started the train of thought that led to Delibes' *Lakmé*, the resemblance between these works is very remote. Then again, there are plays—Maeterlinck's *Pélléas*, or Gold's *La Houppelande* (*Il Tabarro*)—that are almost identical with the librettos of the operas and therefore virtually devoid of any new material. Without wanting to deprive the student of the pleasure of hunting down and reading these books, I will designate as "unprofitable" those texts in which he should not expect to find additional characteristic touches helpful in acting or staging the operas in question.

After each volume listed in the bibliography, the name of the composer to whom it applies is given in brackets. The title of the opera will be listed there only if it is different from that of the literary source.

Although this catalog is intended primarily for singers and stage directors, it should also be brought to the attention of librarians and linguists. I urge all university librarians to acquire the readily available basic texts. The purchase of the thirty or forty paperbacks listed in the bibliography should present no financial problems.

I hope that the list of texts which at present exist only in the original languages will encourage scholars to embark on translations. It is quite shocking that the Spanish plays which form the basis of such well-known operas as Verdi's *Il Trovatore*, *La Forza del Destino*, and *Simon Boccanegra* cannot at this point be read in English. Furthermore, I was startled to discover that even the original Spanish text of García Gutiérrez' *Simon Boccanegra* could not be purchased in either New York or Madrid. I had to be satisfied with a photographic reproduction of the copy in the rare-book division of the Boston Public Library.

The situation with most out-of-print volumes is equally distressing. At the time this book went to press I could not locate a single copy of the English version of Murger's *Vie de Bohème*. After calling some thirty book dealers in New York, Boston, and London, and advertising (without success) in a magazine serving the antiquarian fraternity, I finally had to borrow a copy from an English friend who happened to own it. This whole problem affecting foreign-language books and those that are out of print is highlighted much more clearly, I hope, by the arrangement of the background texts into four subdivisions.

In spite of all difficulties, I can assure the reader that all the volumes listed here *can* be obtained and that in fact every one of them, even if in facsimile form, graces the shelves of my own library.

Operas: alphabetical listing

BEETHOVEN (1770–1827) — *Fidelio*, 73

BELLINI (1801–1835) — *Norma*, 89

BERG (1885–1935) — *Wozzeck*, 20

BERLIOZ (1803–1869) — *Les Troyens*, 69, 93, 94, 95

BIZET (1838–1875) — *Carmen*, 47

BORODIN (1833–1887) — *Prince Igor*, 92

BRITTEN (1913–) — *Albert Herring*, 46; *Billy Budd*, 10; *Midsummernight's Dream*, 13; *Peter Grimes*, 4; *The Turn of the Screw*, 7

CHARPENTIER (1860–1956) — *Louise*

CIMAROSA (1749–1801) — *Il Matrimonio Segreto*, 3

DEBUSSY (1862–1918) — *Pélléas et Mélisande*, 45

DELIBES (1836–1891) — *Lakmé*, 83

DONIZETTI (1797–1848) — *Don Pasquale*, 8; *Lucia di Lammermoor*, 12

GERSHWIN (1898–1937) — *Porgy and Bess*, 5

GLUCK (1714–1787) — *Alceste*, 25, 93, 94, 95; *Iphigénie en Aulide*, 58, 93, 94, 95; *Iphigénie en Tauride*, 26, 93, 94, 95; *Orfeo ed Euridice*, 93, 94, 95

GOUNOD (1818–1893) — *Faust*, 30; *Roméo et Juliette*, 13

HUMPERDINCK (1884–1921) — *Hänsel und Gretel*, 33

IBERT (1890–1962) — *Angélique*

JANÁČEK (1854–1928) — *Katia Kabanova*, 51

LEONCAVALLO (1858–1919) — *Pagliacci*

MASCAGNI (1863–1945) — *Cavalleria Rusticana*, 68

MASSENET (1842–1912) — *Le Jongleur de Nôtre Dame*, 28; *Manon*, 53; *Thais*, 27; *Werther*, 29

MENOTTI (1911–) — *Amelia al Ballo*; *The Consul*; *The Medium*; *The Old Maid and the Thief*; *The Telephone*

MEYEROWITZ (1913–) — *The Barrier*, 6; *Esther*, 85, 90

MONTEVERDI (1567–1643) — *L'Incoronazione di Poppea*, 64

MOUSSORGSKY (1839–1881) — *Boris Godunov*, 57

MOZART (1756–1791) — *Così fan tutte*; *Don Giovanni*, 48, 65; *Die Entführung aus dem Serail*, 74; *Idomeneo*, 75; *Le Nozze di Figaro*, 19; *Die Zauberflöte*, 82

Operas: chronological listing by composers' date of birth

MONTEVERDI (1567–1643)   *L'Incoronazione di Poppea*, 64
PURCELL (1659–1695)   *Dido and Aeneas*, 69, 93, 94, 95
PERGOLESI (1710–1736)   *La Serva Padrona*
GLUCK (1714–1787)   *Orfeo ed Euridice*, 93, 94, 95; *Iphigénie en Aulide*, 58, 93, 94, 95; *Iphigénie en Tauride*, 26, 93, 94, 95; *Alceste*, 25, 93, 94, 95

CIMAROSA (1749–1801)   *Il Matrimonio Segreto*, 3
MOZART (1756–1791)   *Idomeneo*, 75; *Die Entführung aus dem Serail*, 74; *Le Nozze di Figaro*, 19; *Don Giovanni*, 48, 65; *Così fan tutte*; *Die Zauberflöte*, 82

BEETHOVEN (1770–1827)   *Fidelio*, 73
WEBER (1786–1826)   *Der Freischütz*, 16
ROSSINI (1792–1868)   *Il Barbiere di Siviglia*, 18; *La Cenerentola*, 52; *Le Comte Ory*

DONIZETTI (1797–1848)   *Lucia di Lammermoor*, 12; *Don Pasquale*, 8

BELLINI (1801–1835)   *Norma*, 89
BERLIOZ (1803–1869)   *Les Troyens*, 69, 93, 94, 95
NICOLAI (1810–1849)   *Die Lustigen Weiber von Windsor*, 13
THOMAS (1811–1896)   *Mignon*, 31
WAGNER (1813–1883)   *Der Fliegende Holländer*, 34; *Tannhäuser*, 35, 81; *Lohengrin*, 24; *Tristan und Isolde*, 63, 93; *Die Meistersinger*, 39; *Der Ring des Nibelungen*, 91; *Parsifal*, 24, 67, 93

VERDI (1813–1901)   *Nabucco*, 90; *Ernani*, 43; *Macbeth*, 13; *Luisa Miller*, 60; *Rigoletto*, 42; *Il Trovatore*, 78; *La Traviata*, 22, 23; *Simon Boccanegra*, 79; *Un Ballo in Maschera*, 88; *La Forza del Destino*, 86; *Don Carlo*, 59; *Aida*; *Otello*, 13; *Falstaff*, 13

GOUNOD (1818–1893)   *Faust*, 30; *Romeo et Juliette*, 13
OFFENBACH (1819–1880)   *Les Contes d'Hoffmann*, 36, 37, 38, 71
SMETANA (1824–1884)   *The Bartered Bride*
J. STRAUSS (1825–1889)   *Die Fledermaus*, 84
BORODIN (1833–1887)   *Prince Igor*, 92
PONCHIELLI (1834–1886)   *La Gioconda*, 41
SAINT-SAENS (1835–1921)   *Samson et Dalila*, 90
DELIBES (1836–1891)   *Lakmé*, 83
BIZET (1838–1875)   *Carmen*, 47
MOUSSORGSKY (1839–1881)   *Boris Godunov*, 57
TCHAIKOVSKY (1840–1893)   *Eugene Onegin*, 54; *The Queen of Spades*, 56

MASSENET (1842–1912)	*Manon*, 53; *Thais*, 27; *Werther*, 29; *Le Jongleur de Nôtre Dame*, 28
RIMSKY-KORSAKOFF (1844–1908)	*The Golden Cockerel*, 55
JANAČEK (1854–1928)	*Katia Kabanova*, 51
LEONCAVALLO (1858–1919)	*Pagliacci*
PUCCINI (1858–1924)	*Manon Lescaut*, 53; *La Bohème*, 50; *Tosca*, 87; *Madama Butterfly*, 1, 9; *Suor Angelica*; *Il Tabarro*, 76; *Gianni Schicchi*, 21; *La Fanciulla del West*, 2; *Turandot*, 32, 61
CHARPENTIER (1860–1956)	*Louise*
DEBUSSY (1862–1918)	*Pélléas et Mélisande*, 45
MASCAGNI (1863–1945)	*Cavalleria Rusticana*, 68
R. STRAUSS (1864–1949)	*Salome*, 70, 90; *Elektra*, 40, 62; *Der Rosenkavalier*; *Ariadne auf Naxos*, 49; *Arabella*; *Die Frau ohne Schatten*; *Capriccio*; *Die Schweigsame Frau*, 8
VAUGHAN WILLIAMS (1872–1958)	*The Riders to the Sea*, 15
RAVEL (1875–1937)	*L'Heure Espagnole*
STRAVINSKY (1882–)	*The Rake's Progress*
HUMPERDINCK (1884–1921)	*Hänsel und Gretel*, 33
BERG (1885–1935)	*Wozzeck*, 20
IBERT (1890–1962)	*Angélique*
PROKOFIEFF (1891–1953)	*The Love for Three Oranges*, 77; *The Duenna*, 14; *War and Peace*, 66
GERSHWIN (1898–1937)	*Porgy and Bess*, 5
POULENC (1899–1963)	*Les Mamelles de Tirésias*, 17; *Dialogues des Carmélites*, 72, 80
SHOSTAKOVICH (1906–)	*Katerina Ismailova*, 44
MENOTTI (1911–)	*Amelia al Ballo*; *The Old Maid and the Thief*; *The Medium*; *The Telephone*; *The Consul*
MEYEROWITZ (1913–)	*The Barrier*, 6; *Esther*, 85, 90
BRITTEN (1913–)	*Peter Grimes*, 4; *Albert Herring*, 46; *The Turn of the Screw*, 7; *Midsummernight's Dream*, 13; *Billy Budd*, 10
WARD (1917–)	*The Crucible*, 11

Bibliography of background texts

English background texts

1. BELASCO, David, "Madame Butterfly," in *Six Plays by David Belasco* (Boston: Little, Brown, 1928). Hardcover; out of print. [Puccini]
2. BELASCO, David, *The Girl of the Golden West* (New York: French, 1915). Paperback. [Puccini]

3. COLMAN, George, and GARRICK, David, "The Clandestine Marriage," in *The Beggar's Opera and Other Eighteenth Century Plays* (New York: Dutton, 1928). Paperback. [Cimarosa, *Il Matrimonio Segreto*]

4. CRABBE, George, "Peter Grimes," in *The Penguin Book of Narrative Verse* (Baltimore: Penguin, 1960). Paperback. [Britten]

5. HEYWARD, DuBose, and Dorothy, *Porgy* (New York: Dell, 1959). Paperback. [Gershwin, *Porgy and Bess*]

6. HUGHES, Langston, *Mulatto* (Bloomington; Indiana University Press, 1963). Hardcover. [Meyerowitz, *The Barrier*]

7. JAMES, Henry, *The Turn of the Screw* (New York: New American Library, 1962). Paperback (Signet Classic). [Britten]

8. JONSON, Ben, *Epicoene, or The Silent Woman* (Lincoln: University of Nebraska Press, 1966). Paperback. [Donizetti, *Don Pasquale*; R. Strauss, *Die Schweigsame Frau*]

9. LONG, John Luther, *Madame Butterfly* (London: Methuen, 1905). Hardcover; out of print. [Puccini]

10. MELVILLE, Herman, *Billy Budd, Foretopman* (New York: Bantam, 1965). Paperback. [Ward]

11. MILLER, Arthur, *The Crucible* (New York: Bantam, 1959). Paperback. [Ward]

12. SCOTT, Sir Walter, *The Bride of Lammermoor* (New York: Dutton, 1955). Hardcover (Everyman's Library). [Donizetti, *Lucia di Lammermoor*]

13. SHAKESPEARE, William, *Henry the IV* (*Part I*), *The Merry Wives of Windsor, Macbeth, A Midsummernight's Dream, Othello, Romeo and Juliet*. [Nicolai; Verdi; Gounod; Britten]

14. SHERIDAN, Richard B., *The Duenna* (New York: Hill & Wang, 1957). Paperback (Mermaid Drama Book). [Prokofieff]

15. SYNGE, John Millington, "Riders to the Sea" in *Chief Contemporary Dramatists* (Cambridge, Mass.: Houghton Mifflin, 1915). Hardcover. [Vaughan Williams]

Background texts in English translation

16. APEL, Johann August, "The Fatal Marksman," in *The Collected Writings of Thomas De Quincey*, Vol. XII, trans. by Thomas De Quincey (Edinburgh: A & C. Black, 1890). Hardcover; out of print. [Weber, *Der Freischütz*]

17. APOLLINAIRE, Guillaume, "The Breasts of Tirésias," in *Modern French Theatre*, trans. by Louis Simpson (New York: Dutton, 1966). Paperback. [Poulenc, *Les Mamelles de Tirésias*]

18. BEAUMARCHAIS, Pierre Caron de, "The Barber of Seville," in *The Genius of the French Theater*, trans. by Albert Bermel (New York: New American Library, 1961). Paperback (Mentor Book). [Rossini]

19. BEAUMARCHAIS, Pierre Caron de, "Figaro's Marriage," in *The Classic Theatre*, Vol. IV, English version by Jacques Barzun (Garden City, N.Y.: Doubleday, 1961). Paperback (Anchor Book). [Mozart]

20. BUECHNER, Georg, *Woyzek*, trans. by C. S. Mueller (New York: Hill & Wang, 1963). Paperback (Mermaid Drama Book). [Berg]

21. DANTE ALIGHIERI, *Inferno* (Canto XXX and Notes, p. 352), trans. by Henry W. Longfellow (New York: Collier, 1962). Paperback. Unprofitable. [Puccini, *Gianni Schicchi*]

22. DUMAS, Alexandre (fils), *Camille* (play), English version by E. Reynolds and N. Playfair (New York: Hill & Wang, 1957). Paperback (Mermaid Drama Book). [Verdi, *La Traviata*]

23. DUMAS, Alexandre (fils), *Camille* (novel) (New York: Random House, n.d.). Hardcover (Modern Library). [Verdi, *La Traviata*]

24. ESCHENBACH, Wolfram von, *Parzival*, trans. by H. M. Mustard and C. E. Passage (New York: Knopf, 1961). Paperback. [Wagner, *Parsifal, Lohengrin*, (pp. 429 & 430)]

25. EURIPIDES, *Alcestis*, trans. by Philip Vellacott (Baltimore: Penguin, 1953). Paperback. [Gluck]

26. EURIPIDES, *Iphigenia in Tauris*, trans. by Philip Vellacott (Baltimore: Penguin, 1953). Paperback. [Gluck]

27. FRANCE, Anatole, *Thais*, trans. by Ernest Tristan (Greenwich, Conn.: Fawcett, 1961). Hardcover. [Massenet]

28. FRANCE, Anatole, "Our Lady's Juggler," in *Mother of Pearl*, trans. by Frederic Chapman (New York: Dodd, Mead, 1925). Hardcover; out of print. [Massenet, *Le Jongleur de Nôtre Dame*]

29. GOETHE, Johann Wolfgang von, "The Sorrows of Young Werther," in *Great German Short Novels*, trans. by William Rose (New York: Random House, 1952). Hardcover (Modern Library). [Massenet]

30. GOETHE, Johann Wolfgang von, *Faust*, trans. by Bayard Taylor (New York: Random House, 1950). Hardcover (Modern Library). [Gounod]

31. GOETHE, Johann Wolfgang von, *Wilhelm Meister's Apprenticeship*, trans. by Thomas Carlyle (New York: Collier, 1962). Paperback [Thomas, *Mignon*]

32. GOZZI, Carlo, "Turandot," in *The Genius of the Italian Theater*, English version by Jonathan Levy (New York: New American Library, 1964). Paperback (Mentor Book). [Puccini]

33. GRIMM, Jacob, and Wilhelm, "Hansel and Gretel" in *Grimm's Fairy Tales*, trans. by Margaret Hunt (New York: Pantheon, 1944). Hardcover. [Humperdinck]

34. HEINE, Heinrich, "The Memoirs of Herr von Schnabelewopski," in *Heine: Prose and Poetry*, trans. by Havelock Ellis (New York: Dutton, 1961). Hardcover (Everyman's Library). Unprofitable. [Wagner, *Der Fliegende Holländer*]

35. HEINE, Heinrich, "Tannhäuser" (poem), in *Heine: Prose and Poetry*, trans. by Margraet Armour (New York: Dutton, 1961). Hardcover (Everyman's Library). Unprofitable. [Wagner]

36. HOFFMAN, E. T. A., "The Sandman," in *The Tales of Hoffman*, trans. by Michael Bullock (New York: Ungar, 1963). Paperback. [Offenbach, *Les Contes d'Hoffmann*]

37. HOFFMANN, E. T. A., "Adventures of a New Year's Night," in *Tales of Hoffmann*, trans. by James Kirkup (London: Blackie, 1966). Hardcover. [Offenbach, *Les Contes d'Hoffmann*]

38. HOFFMAN, E. T. A., "The Cremona Violin," in *Great German Short Novels and Stories*, trans. by J. T. Beally (New York: Random House, 1952). Hardcover, (Modern Library. [Offenbach, *Les Contes d'Hoffmann*]

39. HOFFMAN, E. T. A., "Master Martin the Cooper," in *Weird Tales*, trans. by J. T. Beally (New York: Scribner, 1923). Hardcover. Unprofitable. [Wagner, *Die Meistersinger*]

40. HOFMANNSTHAL, Hugo von, "Electra" (play) in *Three Plays*, trans. by Alfred Schwartz (Detroit: Wayne State University Press, 1966). Hardcover. [R. Strauss, *Elektra*]

41. HUGO, Victor, "Angelo, Tyrant of Padua," in *The Works of Victor Hugo: Dramas*, Vol. II, trans. by Burnham Ives (Boston: Little, Brown, 1909). Hardcover; out of print. [Ponchielli, *La Gioconda*]

42. HUGO, Victor, "The King Amuses Himself," in *Three Plays by Victor Hugo*, trans. by Frederick L. Slous (New York: Washington Square, 1964). Paperback. [Verdi, *Rigoletto*]

43. HUGO, Victor, "Hernani," in *Three Plays of Victor Hugo*, trans. by Camilla Crosland (New York: Washington Square, 1964). Paperback. [Verdi, *Ernani*]

44. LESKOV, Nikolai, "Lady Macbeth of the Mtsensk District," in *Selected Tales*, trans. by David Magarshack (New York: Noonday, 1961). Paperback. [Shostakovich, *Katerina Ismailova*]

45. MAETERLINCK, Maurice, "Pelleas and Melisande," in *Chief Contemporary Dramatists*, trans. by Richard Hovey (Boston: Houghton Mifflin, 1915). Hardcover. Unprofitable. [Debussy]

46. MAUPASSANT, Guy de, "Madame Husson's Rose-King," in *Guy de Maupassant's Short Stories*, trans. by Marjorie Laurie (New York: Dutton, 1934). Hardcover (Everyman's Library). Unprofitable. [Britten, *Albert Herring*]

47. MERIMÉE, Prosper, *Carmen*, trans. by Edward Marielle (Baltimore: Penguin, 1965). Paperback. [Bizet]

48. MOLIÉRE, Jean Baptiste, "Don Juan or The Statue at the Feast," in *The Miser and Other Plays*, trans. by John Wood (Baltimore: Penguin, 1962). Paperback. [Mozart, *Don Giovanni*]

50. MOLIERE, Jean Baptiste, "The Would-be Gentleman," in *The Miser and Other Plays*, trans. by John Wood (Baltimore: Penguin, 1962). Paperback. Unprofitable. [R. Strauss, *Ariadne auf Naxos*]

50. MURGER, Henry, *Vie de Bohème*, trans. by Norman Cameron (London: Hamish Hamilton, 1949; also, London: The Folio Society, 1960). Hardcover; out of print. [Puccini, *La Bohème*]

51. OSTROVSKY, Alexander, "The Thunderstorm," in *Nineteenth Century Russian Drama*, trans. by Andrew MacAndrew (New York: Bantam, 1963). Paperback. [Janacek, *Katia Kabanova*]

52. PERRAULT, Charles, "Cinderella," in *The Arthur Rackham Fairy Book* (Philadelphia: Lippincott, Hardcover. [Rossini, *La Cenerentola*]

53. PRÉVOST, Antoine Françoise, *Manon Lescaut*, trans. by D. C. Moylan (Garden City, N. Y.: Doubleday, 1960). Paperback (Dolphin Book). [Massenet; Puccini]

54. PUSHKIN, Aleksandr, *Eugene Onegin*, trans. by Vladimir Nabokov, Bollingen Series LXXII (New York: Pantheon, 1964). Hardcover. [Tchaikovsky]

55. PUSHKIN, Alexander, *The Tale of the Golden Cockerel*, trans. by Babette Deutsch (New York: Random House, 1936). Hardcover (Modern Library). [Rimsky-Korsakoff]

56. PUSHKIN, Alexander *The Queen of Spades*, trans. by T. Keane (New York: Random House, 1936). Hardcover (Modern Library). [Tchaikovsky]

57. PUSHKIN, Alexander, *Boris Godunov*, trans. by Alfred Hayes (New York: Random House, 1936). Hardcover (Modern Library). [Moussorgsky]

58. RACINE, Jean, "Iphigenia," in *Phaedra and Other Plays*, trans. by John Cairncross (Baltimore: Penguin, 1963). Paperback. [Gluck, *Iphigénie en Aulide*]

59. SCHILLER, Friedrich von, *Don Carlos*, trans. by Charles Passage (New York: Ungar, 1959). Paperback. [Verdi]

60. SCHILLER, Friedrich von, *Love and Intrigue*, English version by Frederick Rolf (Great Neck, N. Y.: Barron, 1959). Paperback (Barron's Educational Series). [Verdi, *Luisa Miller*]

61. SCHILLER, Friedrich von, *Turandot, The Chinese Sphinx*, freely translated by Sabilla Novello (London: French, 1872). Hardcover; out of print. [Puccini]

62. SOPHOCLES, *Electra*, trans. by H. D. F. Kitto (New York: Oxford, 1964). Paperback. [R. Strauss]

63. STRASSBURG, Gotfried von, "Tristan and Isolt," in *Medieval Romances*, trans. by Jessie L. Weston (New York: Random House, 1957). Hardcover (Modern Library). [Wagner, *Tristan und Isolde*]

64. TACITUS, *The Annals of Imperial Rome*, trans. by Michael Grant (Baltimore: Penguin, 1956). Paperback. [Monteverdi, *L'Incoronazione de Poppea*]

65. TIRSO DE MOLINA, "The Trickster of Seville," in *The Classic Theatre*, Vol. III, trans. by Roy Campbell (Garden City, N.Y.: Doubleday, 1961). Paperback (Anchor Book). [Mozart, *Don Giovanni*]

66. TOLSTOY, Leo, *War and Peace*, trans. by Rosemary Edmonds, 2 vols. (Baltimore: Penguin, 1961). Paperback. [Prokofieff]

67. TROYES, Chrétien de, "Perceval, or the Story of the Grail," in *Medieval Romances*, trans. by R. S. Loomis (New York: Random House, 1957). Hardcover (Modern Library). [Wagner, *Parsifal*]

68. VERGA, Giovanni, "Cavalleria Rusticana" (play), in *The Modern Theatre*, English version by Eric Bentley (Garden City, N.Y.: Doubleday, 1955). Paperback (Anchor Book). [Mascagni]

69. VIRGIL, *The Aeneid*, a new verse translation by C. Day Lewis (Garden City, N.Y.: Doubleday, 1952). Paperback (Anchor Book). [Purcell, *Dido and Aeneas*; Berlioz, *Les Troyens*]

70. WILDE, Oscar, "Salome," in *Plays*, trans. from the original French by Lord Alfred Douglas (Baltimore: Penguin, 1954). Paperback. [R. Strauss]

Background texts available only in the original languages

71. BARBIER, Jules, and CARRÉ, Michel, *Les Contes D'Hoffmann* (French) Paris: Calman-Lévy, 1881). Out of print. [Offenbach]
72. BERNANOS, George, *Dialogues des Carmélites* (French, play) (Paris: Editions du Seuil, 1956). Paperback. [Poulenc]
73. BOUILLY, Jean Nicolas, *Léonore ou l'Amour Conjugal* (French, libretto for Pierre Gaveaux) (Paris: J. N. Barba, 1799). Rare facsimile. Unprofitable. [Beethoven, *Fidelio*]
74. BRETZNER, Christoph Friedrich, *Belmont und Constanze oder Die Entführung aus dem Serail* (German, libretto for Johann André) (Leipzig: Schneider, 1781). Rare facsimile. Unprofitable. [Mozart, *Die Entführung*]
75. CRÉBILLON, Prosper, Jolyot de, "Idoménée" (French) in Oeuvres de *Crébillon* Tome I (Paris: Lefevre, 1828). Hardcover; out of print. [Mozart]
76. GOLD, Didier, *La Houppelande* (French). Typescript. Rare facsimile. [Puccini, *Il Tabarro*]
77. GOZZI, Carlo. *L'Amore delle Tre Melarance* (Italian) (Milano: Sonzogno, n.d.). [Prokofieff, *Love for Three Oranges*]
78. GARCIA GUTIÉRREZ, Don Antonio, "El Trovador" (Spanish), in *Tres Dramas Románticos*, (Garden City, N.Y.: Doubleday, 1962). Paperback (Collección Hispánica). [Verdi, *Il Trovatore*]
79. GARCIA GUTIÉRREZ, Don Antonio, *Simon Bocanegra* (Spanish) (Madrid: La Imprenta de Yenes, 1843). Hardcover; rare. [Verdi]
80. LE FORT, Gertrud von, "Die Letze am Schaffott" (German), in *Die Erzählungen* (Weisbaden: Insel Verlag, 1966).* Hardcover. [Poulenc, *Dialogues des Carmélites*]
81. HOFFMAN, E. T. A. "Der Kampf der Sänger" (German), in *Die Serapionsbrüder*, Vol. II (Salzburg: Das Bergland-Buch, n.d.). Hardcover. [Wagner, *Tannhäuser*]
82. LIEBESKIND, August Jacob, "Lulu oder die Zauberflöte" (German), in *Dschinnistan*, Vol. III, Wieland's Collection of Fairy Tales (Winterthur, 1810). Hardcover: rare facsimile. Unprofitable. [Mozart, *Die Zauberflöte*]
83. LOTI, Pierre, *Le Mariage de Loti* (French) (Paris: Calmann-Lévy, 1886). Hardcover. Unprofitable. [Delibes, *Lakmé*]
84. MEILHAC, Henri, and HALÉVY, Ludovic, "*Le Réveillon*" (French), *Théatre de Meilhac et Halévy*, Vol. V (Paris: Calmann-Lévy, n.d.). Hardcover; out of print. [J. Strauss, *Die Fledermaus*]
85. RACINE, Jean, *Esther* (French) (Paris: H. Nicolle, 1818). [Meyerowitz]
86. RIVAS, Duque de, "Don Alvaro o la Fuerza del Sino" (Spanish), in *Tres Dramas Románticos*. (Garden City, N.Y.: Doubleday, 1962). Paperback (Collección Hispánica). [Verdi, *La Forza del Destino*]
87. SARDOU, Victorien, "La Tosca" (French), in *Théatre Complet*, Vol. I (Paris: Albin Michel, 1934). [Puccini]

* While the book was in press it came to my attention that a translation of Gertrud von Le Fort's story does exist: "The Song at the Scaffold," trans. by Olga Marx (New York: Sheed and Ward, 1933).

88. Scribe, Eugene, "Gustave III ou le Bal Masqué" (French), in *Théatre Complet*, Vol. XIV Libretto for Auber. (Paris: Aimé André, 1835). Hardcover; out of print. [Verdi, *Un Ballo in Maschera*]
89. Soumet, Alexandre (with Jules Lefevre), *Norma* (French) (Paris: J. N. Barba, 1831.) Rare facsimile. [Bellini]

Biblical and Mythological Background Texts

90. *The Bible*, Old Testament: Judges 16: 4–31 (Saint-Saens, *Samson et Dalila*); Esther (Meyerowitz); Daniel 4: 31–37 (Verdi, *Nabucco*); New Testament: Matthew: 14: 1–12; Mark 6: 14-29 [R. Strauss, *Salome*]
91. *The Nibelungenlied: A Heroic Epic by an anonymous poet*, trans. by A. T. Hatto. (Baltimore: Penguin, 1966). Paperback. [Wagner]
92. *The Song of Igor's Campaign*, trans. by Vladimis Nabokov (New York: Knopf, 1960). Paperback (Vintage Books). [Borodin, *Prince Igor*]
93. *Bulfinch's Mythology* (London: Spring Books, 1962). Hardcover. [Purcell; Gluck; Berlioz; Wagner, *Tristan und Isolde* and *Parisfal*]
94. Graves, Robert, *The Greek Myths*, 2 vols. (Baltimore: Penguin, 1955). Paperback. [Purcell; Gluck; Berlioz]
95. Hamilton, Edith. *Mythology* (New York. New American Library, 1940). Paperback (Mentor Book). [Purcell; Gluck; Berlioz]

Index of operas

In Appendix C—Operas and Background texts, pages 409–420—all titles, except those of Russian and Czech works, are listed under their original names. Russian and Czech titles are given their English equivalents. Thus *The Golden Cockerel*, *The Queen of Spades*, and *The Bartered Bride*, rather than *Le Coq d'Or*, *Pique Dame*, or *Prodaná Nevěsta*. In the body of the book, several other well-known operas are similarly identified by their English titles: *Le Nozze di Figaro* appears as *The Marriage of Figaro*, *Il Barbiere di Siviglia* as *The Barber of Seville*, *Die Zauberflöte* as *The Magic Flute*.

421

Bringing Opera to Life

Boris Goldovsky

Based upon Dr. Goldovsky's many years of professional directing and teaching, *Bringing Opera to Life* is designed primarily for persons planning operatic careers either as singers or as directors of operatic productions. It stresses the interdependence of drama and music and discusses opera from the viewpoints of the singer, the stage director, and the intelligent listener.

As the author points out: "The skills analyzed in *Bringing Opera to Life* are more than practical. What composers and playwrights actually create is not the work of art itself, but only a symbolic blueprint, a recipe for bringing it to life. The creations of painters and sculptors stand alone; no one else is needed to complete them. But librettists and composers need conductors, instrumentalists, and scenic designers. And most of all they need singing actors and stage directors. In a very real sense these performing artists become the author's actual partners. It is this feeling of artistic collaboration that gives the professions of the operatic singer and the stage director their intoxicating aura."

Included in the work are detailed discussions of scenes from many of the major operas, reflecting the particular responsibilities of the stage director in working with opera, and the singer's role in presenting a convincingly dramatic as well as musical production. There are over 100 diagrams to illustrate the placement and movement of singers in specific operatic scenes, and over 150 musical examples to further clarify the problems of bringing opera to life.